UNCORRECTED

M000249407

Title:	**CORPORATE GOVERNANCE:** *Promises Kept, Promises Broken*
Author:	Jonathan R. Macey
US Publication Date:	November 2008
ISBN:	978-0-691-12999-0 Cloth $35S
Pages:	344 pages, 1 line illus. 5 tables. 6 x 9

For additional information or questions, please contact:

Andrew DeSio, Publicity Manager
Tel 609-258-5165
Fax 609-258-1335
andrew_desio@press.princeton.edu

PRINCETON UNIVERSITY PRESS
41 William Street, Princeton, NJ 08540
(609) 258-3897 Phone, (609) 258-1335 FAX

In Europe contact:
Caroline Priday, Publicity and Marketing Manager
cpriday@pupress.co.uk
Princeton University Press
6 Oxford Street
Woodstock, England
OX20 1TW
Tel +44 (0) 1993 814503
Fax+44 (0) 1993 814504

CORPORATE GOVERNANCE
Promises Kept, Promises Broken

Jonathan R. Macey

In the wake of the Enron meltdown and other corporate scandals, the United States has increasingly relied on Securities and Exchange Commission oversight and the Sarbanes-Oxley Act—which set tougher rules for boards, management, and public accounting firms—to protect the interests of shareholders. Such reliance is badly misplaced. In *CORPORATE GOVERNANCE*, Jonathan Macey argues that less government regulation—not more—is what's needed to ensure that managers of public companies keep their promises to investors.

Macey tells how heightened government oversight has put a stranglehold on what is the best protection against malfeasance by self-serving management: the market itself. Corporate governance, he shows, is about keeping promises to shareholders; failure to do so results in diminished investor confidence, which leads to capital flight and other dire economic consequences. Macey explains the relationship between corporate governance and the various market and nonmarket institutions and mechanisms used to control public corporations; he discusses how nonmarket corporate governance devices such as boards and whistle-blowers are highly susceptible to being co-opted by management and are generally guided more by self-interest and personal greed than by investor interests. In contrast, market-driven mechanisms such as trading and takeovers represent more reliable solutions to the problem of corporate governance. Inefficient regulations are increasingly hampering these important and truly effective corporate controls. Macey examines a variety of possible means of corporate governance, including shareholder voting, hedge funds, and private equity funds.

CORPORATE GOVERNANCE reveals why the market is the best guardian of shareholder interests.

Jonathan R. Macey is the Sam Harris Professor of Corporate Law, Corporate Finance, and Securities Law at Yale Law School. His books include *An Introduction to Modern Financial Theory*; *Insider Trading: Economics, Politics, and Policy*; and *Macey on Corporation Laws*.

NOVEMBER
978-0-691-12999-0 Cloth $35.00S
344 pages. 1 line illus. 5 tables. 6 x 9.
BUSINESS ζ LAW

CORPORATE
GOVERNANCE

CORPORATE GOVERNANCE

PROMISES KEPT, PROMISES BROKEN

JONATHAN R. MACEY

PRINCETON UNIVERSITY PRESS

PRINCETON AND OXFORD

Library of Congress Cataloging-in-Publication Data

Macey, Jonathan R.
Corporate governance : promises kept, promises broken /
Jonathan R. Macey.
p.   cm.
Includes bibliographical references and index.
ISBN 978-0-691-12999-0 (hbk. : alk. paper)
1. Corporate governance. I. Title.
HD2741.M223 2008
658.4′2—dc22
2008016531

British Library Cataloging-in-Publication Data is available

This book has been composed in Sabon

Printed on acid-free paper. ∞

press.princeton.edu

Printed in the United States of America

1   3   5   7   9   10   8   6   4   2

CONTENTS

PREFACE

This book presents my views about what corporate governance is all about and what sorts of corporate governance institutions and mechanisms work best. Corporate governance consists of a farrago of legal and economic devices that induce the people in charge of companies with publicly owned and traded stock to keep the promises they make to investors. I develop three original insights about corporate governance, which can be summarized succinctly:

1. Corporate Governance is about promises. I believe that it is more accurate to characterize corporate governance as being about promises than it is to characterize corporate governance as being about contracts. One reason I believe this is because the relationship between public shareholders and corporations is so attenuated than it is misleading to characterize their relationship with the corporation as contractual in nature, rather than promissory. Shareholders have almost no contractual rights and virtually no contractual rights to corporate cash flows. Shareholders' investments are based on trust. This trust, in turn, is based on the belief that the managers who run corporations will keep the promises that they make to investors. Another reason why I believe that corporate governance is about promise is because the idea of promise captures the primordial fact that *trust* rather than reliance on the prospect of enforcement is the focal point of a successful system of corporate governance.

2. Since corporate governance is about promise, then it stands to reason that the various institutions and mechanisms of corporate governance can be evaluated on the basis of how well they facilitate the keeping of promises by corporate managers. The bulk of this book analyzes various devices and mechanisms of corporate governance for the purpose of determining which ones work well and which do not work so well.

3. Having analyzed which corporate governance devices work well, it is then possible to analyze these corporate governance devices *politically*. Regulation can impede, discourage, and even ban the operation of particular corporate governance devices. Likewise, regulation also can facilitate, encourage, and even require corporate governance devices to operate—or to operate in a particular way. One of the principal contributions of this book is to point out that many of the most effective corporate governance devices, such as certain kinds of trading and activities in the take-

over market, are either heavily regulated or banned outright. On the other hand, the mechanisms and institutions that I regard as the *least* effective, corporate boards of directors and credit rating agencies, for example, are facilitated, encouraged, and even directly or indirectly required by regulation. Chapter 3 develops this point and presents the results of my analysis in chart form.

This is the book in a nutshell. If you are interested, please read on.

A number of friends and colleagues, particularly Bruce Ackerman, Arnoud Boot, Michael Dooley, Mel Eisenberg, Luca Enriques, Frank Easterbrook, Daniel Fischel, Jeff Gordon, David Haddock, Henry Hansmann, Hideki Kanda, Tony Kronman, Yair Listokin, Henry Manne, Fred McChesney, Geoffrey Miller, Maureen O'Hara, Mitch Polinsky, Roberta Romano, and David Skeel served as valuable sounding boards for many of the ideas floated in this book. I am extremely grateful to them for what, in most cases, has been decades of advice and support. Most of all, I am grateful to my wife Amy for sticking by me, as well as to my "big kids" Josh and Ally not only for their support of me, but also for their support of Zachary, the new kid in our lives.

Portions of this book have been presented at faculty workshops at Columbia, Harvard, Stanford, and Yale, and I received extremely valuable comments and advice from the faculty and students who participated in those workshops. Portions of the book derive in various degrees from previous articles, particularly "'Getting the Word Out About Fraud,' A Theoretical Analysis of Whistleblowing and Insider Trading" 105 *Michigan Law Review* 1899 (2007) (chapter 12); "Too Many Notes and Not Enough Votes: Lucian Bebchuk and Emperor Joseph II Kvetch about Contested Director Elections and Mozart's *Seraglio*"; 93 *Virginia Law Review* 759 (2007) (chapter 13); "The Politicization of American Corporate Governance," 1 *Virginia Law & Business Review* 10 (2006) (chapter 8); "Positive Political Theory and Federal Usurpation of the Regulation of Corporate Governance: The Coming Preemption of the Martin Act," 80 *Notre Dame Law Review* 951 (2005); "Monitoring, Corporate Performance: The Role of Objectivity, Proximity and Adaptability in Corporate Governance," 89 *Cornell Law Review*, 356 (2004) (with Arnoud Boot); and "Corporate Governance and Commercial Banking: A Comparative Examination of Germany, Japan, and the United States," 48 *Stanford Law Review* 73 (1995) (with Geoffrey P. Miller) (chapter 14); and "A Pox on Both Your Houses: Enron, Sarbanes-Oxley and the Debate Concerning the Relative Efficiency of Mandatory Versus Enabling Rules," 81 *Washington University Law Quarterly*, 329 (2003) (chapter 7).

CORPORATE
GOVERNANCE

INTRODUCTION

CORPORATE GOVERNANCE AS PROMISE

The purpose of corporate governance is to persuade, induce, compel, and otherwise motivate corporate managers to keep the promises they make to investors. Another way to say this is that corporate governance is about reducing deviance by corporations where deviance is defined as any actions by management or directors that are at odds with the legitimate, investment-backed expectations of investors. Good corporate governance, then, is simply about keeping promises.[1] Bad governance (corporate deviance) is defined as promise-breaking behavior.

The theory that underlies the way that this book treats corporate governance is that all investors have certain reasonable expectations about what corporate managers should and should not do with their power over the corporations. These I will call investors' legitimate investment-backed expectations. Shareholders' expectations are derived from a variety of sources. They come mostly from law and contract, but market forces and social norms also inform investors' expectations about how managers should perform in very important ways. For example, it is universally understood that managers cannot steal from the companies they work for. It also is well understood that managers and directors should avoid transactions that place them in conflict of interest between their obligations to the corporation and their own personal financial objectives. Law, contract, and social norms all point the same way in this regard, making certain sorts of conflict of interest dealings, such as insider trading, illegitimate as well as illegal. Law and contract have less to say about how diligent and attentive to the interests of shareholders corporate managers must be. Here, social custom (norms) and markets play the dominant role in constraining managerial deviance. Profit maximization sometimes is expressed as a societal norm, but it sometimes also is expressed as a legal requirement, at least in the United States.

In governing the modern corporation, the more work that is done by social norms, the less heavy lifting needs to be done by contract and law. If corporate officers and directors can be deterred by social norms from insider trading or from trading with the firms they work for on excessively favorable terms, then investors will be forced to rely less on more costly enforcement mechanisms, like lawsuits, to control managerial deviance.

Corporate governance is a broad descriptive term rather than a normative term. Corporate governance describes all of the devices, institutions, and mechanisms by which corporations are governed. Anything and everything that influences the way that a corporation is actually run falls within this definition of corporate governance. Every device, institution, or mechanism that exercises power over decision-making within a corporation is part of the system of corporate governance for that firm.

The governance of an organization such as a corporation is done through a complex framework of institutions and processes, including law. Taken together, these institutions, processes, and mechanisms determine how power within a company is exercised, the extent to which investors are given a voice, and how all sorts of decisions are made.

The purpose of corporate governance is to safeguard the integrity of the promises made by corporations to investors, but investors and companies are left to their own devices (i.e., the contracting process) to define the content of the promises themselves. Generally, the baseline goal is profit maximization. Corporations are almost universally conceived as economic entities that strive to maximize value for shareholders. But the goal of maximizing wealth for shareholders is, or should be, a matter of choice.

Investors should be free to choose to invest in ventures that pursue other goals besides profit maximization. Outsiders, however, should be no more at liberty to dictate the terms of the private arrangements between companies and their shareholders than they are free to dictate the terms of other purely private contractual arrangements.

For many, particularly those in the law and economics movement, any action by managers, directors, or others that is inconsistent with the goal of shareholder wealth maximization is considered a form of "corporate deviance." Economists call corporate deviance "agency costs" to capture the notion that corporate managers and directors are agents of their shareholders. Since controlling agents is costly, it is inefficient to control all deviant behavior by managers, directors, and others. But, to the extent that investors seek to control their agents, the devices they use are the institutions and mechanisms of corporate governance. The best corporate governance systems are those that do the best job of controlling corporate deviance.

We care about corporate governance because it affects the real economy. Holding other things equal, we can improve corporate performance and provide better access to capital by improving the quality of corporate governance. However, since installing corporate governance devices is not free, we maximize value by optimizing, rather than maximizing, the extent to which corporate governance systems monitor and discipline corporate managers.

This is the baseline rule, but it is not inviolate. There is nothing sacred about setting shareholder wealth maximization as the goal for the corporation. Investors can, and do, set up corporations with many goals other than the traditional goal of wealth maximization for outside shareholders. For example, thousands of corporations, from the Boy Scouts to the Red Cross, are expressly organized as charitable, not-for-profit enterprises with social goals wholly unconnected to investors or to their interests. Even some "traditional" closely held corporations appear to be run more to provide rewarding job opportunities for family members than to generate profits for (nonexistent) outside investors. There is nothing deviant or lamentable about this sort of behavior as long as it is consistent with the legitimate investment-backed expectations of those who invest in (or donate to) these enterprises.

Shareholders and other investors are free to organize and invest in corporations that serve whatever legitimate (legal) objectives they choose from wealth maximization to wealth redistribution. There is no legitimate theoretical or moral objection to those who assert that the goals of the modern corporation should be to serve the broad interests of all stakeholders rather than to serve the narrow interests of just the shareholders, *provided that these goals are clearly disclosed to investors before they part with their money.* My response to the oft-heard critique of modern, shareholder-centric corporate governance is that the goals and objectives of the corporation should be determined by the organizers of the corporation and disclosed to participants *ex ante* at the time the corporation goes public or otherwise attracts its first outside (non-controlling) investors. After that, the group in control should act consistently with the legitimate, investment-backed expectations of investors.

In the United States, more than in any other country, the modern publicly held corporation is characterized by the separation of share ownership and managerial control of the corporation itself. This means that non-owner managers and directors control corporations' assets, and are responsible for the strategies and tactics utilized by companies to earn money. In the meantime, a largely separate group of people, the shareholders, put up the lion's share of the vast amounts of risk capital that finances the purchase of the corporation's assets and facilitates all other corporate activities, including raising money from creditors and other fixed claimants. The interlocking directorates and the ownership of control blocks of stock by families and corporate groups common in Europe and Asia are largely absent in the United States.

The more or less unique ownership structure of U.S. corporations presents unique opportunities as well as unique challenges. The ability to raise vast sums of money from widely disparate investors permits the democratization of capital. Large companies control billions of dollars in resources raised from middle-class investors, whose contributions to insurance premiums, pension funds, and mutual funds pay for the stock that capitalizes corporate America. Without an ownership structure characterized by the separation of share ownership and corporate management, it would not be possible to have both a robust middle class and a large number of powerful, multinational corporations. The U.S. "shareholder culture" remains unique in this way. In other countries, even developed countries like France, Germany, Italy, and Japan, most big companies are controlled by powerful families, other corporations via complex corporate cross-holdings of shares, large banks, and, occasionally, by governments themselves. Shareholders are generally at the mercy of these powerful interests, and shareholders' interests, not surprisingly, often are mere afterthoughts for the managers of such companies.

In the United States, by contrast, shareholders traditionally have been at the very epicenter of the corporate governance model. In the United States, as distinct from other countries, there is broad (though by no means universal) consensus that the corporation is and should be governed for the benefit of shareholders, subject only to the legal and contractual responsibilities of the company to third parties. For example, when senior managers of U.S. corporations were asked, "Who owns the large public corporation?" 76 percent responded that the corporation is owned by the shareholders. In sharp contrast, in Japan an astonishing 97.1 percent of corporate senior managers said that the corporation was owned not by the shareholders but by "all of the stakeholders" including workers, customers, suppliers, and local communities. Corporate managers in Germany and France were not far behind Japanese executives: 82 percent of German managers and 78 percent of French managers said that German and French companies are owned by all corporate stakeholders rather than just the shareholders.

Survey data about managers' views of the importance of dividends and the importance of job security for workers confirm the distinction noted here about America's exceptional approach to the governance of the corporate enterprise. In France, Germany, and Japan most managers think that their primary obligation is to provide job security for workers, while in the United States managers are much more focused on the shareholders' interests in general and on paying dividends in particular. For example, in the United States 89 percent of corporate senior managers said that providing dividends for shareholders was more important than providing job security for workers. In Japan, only 3 percent of senior managers thought that dividends were more important than job security. Similarly, a survey of 1,000 companies in Japan and 1,000 companies in the United

States by Japan's Economic Planning Agency reported that U.S. firms view their stock price as far more important than market share, while Japanese companies view market share as more important than share price.

These data are changing and will be out of date soon. Companies all over the world, including China and India, are embracing the U.S. "shareholder-centric" model of corporate governance. The recent emergence of London and Hong Kong as launching pads for initial public offerings reflects the success of companies in both Europe and Asia in convincing investors that they can receive a "fair deal" on their equity investments in non-U.S. companies. It also reflects a growing consensus around the globe that large, well-capitalized corporations can only exist in stable democracies with robust middle-class populations if the ownership structures of such companies are characterized by the separation of ownership and control.

The focus on U.S.-style ownership and control structures inevitably has led to attention on corporate governance in America, which is the subject of this book. The high-profile scandals in corporate America that occurred at the turn of the twenty-first century caused many to wonder whether the U.S. model of corporate governance was working properly. To evaluate the U.S. system of corporate governance, we must first have some idea of what corporate governance is.

In my view, corporate governance describes the various mechanisms and institutions, including law, contract, and norms, by which shareholders and other outside investors attempt to assure themselves that management will be faithful guardians of their investments. One goal of the analysis here is to present a picture of corporate governance that is consistent with the basic economic analysis of the corporation. In particular, modern scholars have never successfully reconciled Ronald Coase's famous "Theory of the Firm," which posits that the modern, publicly held corporation is a nexus of contracts, with the widely accepted notion in law and economics that corporations and their directors should maximize the value of the firm. This notion manifests itself in economics in the doctrine that maximizing shareholder value is the primary objective of the business corporation. The notion manifests itself in law in the doctrine that officers and directors of corporations owe undivided fiduciary duties of care and loyalty to their shareholders and to their shareholders alone.

After all, if Coase is correct, as he surely is, that the corporation is best conceptualized as a complex web or "nexus" of explicit and implicit contracts among the company's various constituencies, including, but not limited to, shareholders, then everything is up for grabs—or up for negotiation—including the issue of what the basic objectives and purpose of the corporation should be. Under this theory, it would seem clear that the various participants in the corporation can and should be left free to contract among themselves to establish any set of priorities they choose. The fact that corporate managers could, if they wished to do so, try to sell shares in their firms by promising to promote worker primacy, environmental protection, the elimination of poverty, or shareholder wealth in exchange for investors' money supports this conclusion. What corporate managers should not be permitted to do is to sell their shares with the implicit or explicit promise that they will maximize value for shareholders and later, after collecting the investors' money, decide to pursue some other calling that they have themselves determined should be pursued.

Shareholder wealth maximization is and should be both a norm and a default rule, but *only* a norm and a default rule. Shareholders should be, and are, basically free to invest either in companies that maximize profits or in those that do not. The choices for investors range from not-for-profit entities, which, of course, explicitly promise zero returns to shareholders, to the standard, for-profit corporations (including munitions manufacturers and cigarette companies) that typically come to mind when one thinks about investing, with socially or environmentally conscious mutual funds in between.

In May 2007, for example, the *New York Times* reported on a company called Altrushare Securities, a Wall Street broker-dealer firm that has two-thirds of its stock controlled by two charities, which the paper cited as "an example of the emerging convergence of for-profit money-making and nonprofit mission."[2] The nonprofit control of the firm resulted in a different "mission" for Altrushare, whose goal, according to Peter Drasher, the company's founder, is "to support struggling communities with our profits" rather than profit maximization.[3] Other corporations appear to be following this model of blending the efficiency of the for-profit corporation paradigm with different mixes of the social and community ideals of the not-for-profit sector. This hybrid model has not met with success outside of the closely held corporation setting because when share ownership becomes too widely dispersed it becomes practically impossible for the shareholders to agree on any goals beyond simple profit maximization.

Most people want to invest in for-profit enterprises. And the more profit, the better investors like it. This overwhelming tendency may be attributable to greed, but not necessarily. True, people generally invest to maximize their wealth. But some level of modest wealth is a prerequisite to philanthropy. Once investors have accumulated a little wealth, they can decide for themselves how much of it to contribute to charity, and which charities to support. It is not surprising that even in a country as full of beneficent, generous people as the United States, people actually choose to invest in for-profit corporations. Corporations that hold themselves out to investors as being good investments are more successful at raising investment dollars than are those that do not.

A contractual, even morally based view of the modern public corporation emerges from the Coasean, contractual perspective of the corporation presented here. Since, as Coase said, the corporation is a nexus of contracts, its purpose should be to conduct itself in a manner that is consistent with both the underlying law of the jurisdictions in which it does business, as well as the complex set of explicit and implicit promises it makes. Of paramount interest are the *promises* that corporations make to investors when selling its shares, but other agreements are relevant as well, which is why I refer to this approach as the "promissory theory" of the corporation, and it is the perspective on corporate law and corporate governance adopted in this book.

The starting point for the analysis in this book is that the corporation is a nexus of contracts, and as with other contracts, the contracts made by a corporation constitute a set of promises to investors, workers, suppliers, customers, local communities, and others. The clear, longstanding, and unambiguous default rule in corporate law is that corporations are organized to maximize value for shareholders, subject to the constraint that, in doing so, they act consistently with both applicable law and with prior agreements with other constituencies such as employees and creditors.

The law governing the corporation is consistent with the economic analysis presented here. Shareholders are distinctive in the corporation because they are residual claimants: they are entitled to the profits of the firm, but only after all of the other, fixed claimants' claims have been satisfied. As residual claimants, the shareholders are the group with the best incentives to make discretionary decisions about corporate strategy. Decisions about such things as new investments, strategic direction, and corporate strategy should be effectuated for the shareholders, because they are the group with the biggest stake in the outcomes of these decisions. In contrast, as Frank Easterbrook and Daniel Fischel have observed, "all the actors, except the shareholders, lack the appropriate incentives. Those with fixed claims on the income stream (generated by a corporation) may receive only a tiny benefit (in increased security) from the undertaking of a new project. The shareholders receive most of the marginal gains and incur most of the marginal costs. They therefore have the right incentives to exercise discretion."[4]

Business organizations in general, and corporations in particular, are standard form contracts. Corporate governance works when it encourages corporate officers and directors as well as other corporate decision-makers to act in ways that are consistent with the explicit and implicit contractual understanding between investors and the firms. Whatever else one might say about famous examples of corporate deviance, like Enron or Tyco, they represent situations in which officers and directors did not keep their legal and fiduciary promises to investors.

Starting with the premise developed in this introduction that corporate governance is about promise, this book is about what I regard to be the most important and interesting institutions and mechanisms that exist to ensure that companies that sell stock to the public keep their promises to investors. Taken together, all of these devices make up the corporate governance infrastructure that a particular economy makes available to its investors and entrepreneurs. The term "corporate governance" includes law, policy, and social norms, as well as contracts that regulate and motivate behavior within the corporation. For example, chapter 1 considers the way that contracts, in the form of a corporation's charter and bylaws, articulate the contractual relationship between a corporation and its shareholders.

While all corporations need capital to finance their various endeavors, not all capital is created equal. For many sorts of investments, particularly risky investments such as research and development, equity is vastly preferred over debt because such risky investments produce uncertain cash flows that are unsuitable for fixed claims like bank loans or bonds and there is no way to devise the schedule for the repayment of principal and interest that fixed claimants require. For this reason, corporate governance is, and should be, primarily directly toward the goal of maximizing value for shareholders.

A large and diverse array of mechanisms and institutions of corporate governance are credited with playing central roles in corporate governance. The list includes all sorts of gatekeepers, such as lawyers, investment bankers, and accountants, as well as corporate boards of directors and financial institutions, which monitor companies to which they have loaned money. Shareholders rely on the institutions of corporate governance to solve the problems inherent in the separation of share ownership and management of large public corporations. The persistent willingness of investors to purchase residual equity interests in firms controlled by others is an astonishing and distinctive feature of U.S. capital markets, which are characterized by far more widely dispersed ownership than are other capital markets throughout the world. The proclivity of investors to part with their investment dollars in far-flung ventures over which they have no practical control and no legal rights either to the repayment of their principal or to receive periodic returns (dividends) on their capital requires a lot of trust on the part of investors. This trust, in turn, depends critically on the efficient operations of the institutions of corporate governance.

In chapter 1, and throughout the book, I attempt to identify and distinguish among the three primary sources of influence over decision-making within the firm: contract, law, and societal norms and customs. Taken together, these three sources of corporate governance, intrafirm contract, legal rules, and societal norms, dictate how the corporation is governed. The interactions among these sources of governance are highly complex. Contracts, legal rules, and societal norms serve as complements for each other and as substitutes. Take, for example, something as basic as the voting rights of shareholders, the subject of chapter 13. The three sources of corporate governance, taken together, describe the various ways of affecting the policies, strategies, direction, and decisions of an organization.

The approach taken here is designed to provide a framework with which to evaluate the assertion that a particular company has "good" or "bad" corporate governance, and also with which to evaluate the assertion that a particular legal system has "good" or "bad" corporate governance. Take, for example, the thorny topic of executive compensation. The average pay for chief executives of large public companies in the United States is now well over $10 million a year. Top corporate executives in the United States are paid more than executives in any other country. They get about three times more than their counterparts in Japan and more than twice as much as their counterparts in Western Europe. A lot of people think that corporate directors are overpaid, while others think that the process by which executive compensation is determined has been corrupted by acquiescent, docile, pandering, and otherwise "captured" boards of directors (the subject of chapter 4), lax accounting rules (chapter 11), ineffective shareholder voting (chapter 13), or captured regulators (chapter 7).

These people may well be right. If, however, I am correct in arguing that corporate governance is about controlling corporations' proclivities to deviate from the legitimate, investment-backed expectations of investors, we can evaluate executive compensation in a new light. First and foremost, it seems clear that as long as a corporation is meeting its payroll, paying its suppliers, current on its taxes, and fulfilling all of its other obligations to its fixed claimants, then these corporate constituencies have no legitimate reason to complain about executive compensation. In particular, the concern that executive pay is not sufficiently linked to executives' job performance is of concern to companies' shareholders and to its shareholders alone.

And it is not at all obvious that shareholders have a legitimate complaint about executive compensation. Take the famous controversy over Jack Welch's undisclosed compensation while he was CEO of General Electric. Long criticized for his high compensation while at the helm of GE, during divorce proceedings in 2001 it was disclosed that GE had been paying for a variety of Welch's personal expenses during his retirement, including the maintenance on his $15 million apartment on Central Park

West, twenty-four-hour, unlimited access to private jets, and tickets to shows and sports events, in addition to his $9-million-a-year pension. On the other hand, as well-known compensation attorney Gerson Zweifach pointed out at a recent conference on corporate governance at Yale Law School, the value of GE stock increased by an incredible $250 billion during Welch's tenure. Shareholders who owned small stakes in GE in the 1970s literally became millionaires by the time of Welch's retirement. Suppose Jack Welch had approached each of these shareholders in 1970 and said that in return for his services as CEO of GE, which would make most long-term shareholders millionaires, he expected to receive hundreds of millions of dollars in compensation, and upon retirement to have tons of perks, including flowers delivered weekly to his Manhattan apartment. No rational shareholder would turn down this deal.

The interactions between Jack Welch (as representative of GE) and GE shareholders involved a hypothetical contract, rather than an actual promise because neither Welch nor GE had ever made an actual promise regarding such things as flower arrangements and other perks. Actual, not hypothetical or implicit, promises are the best indications of what shareholders have bargained for, but hypothetical bargains such as the one described above are also useful and illustrate the sort of work that the corporate-governance-as-promise approach suggested here might do.

Beginning in chapter 3, I discuss the various institutions and mechanisms of corporate governance and discuss which of these, in my view, function better than others. Although the book is meant to cover the broad field of corporate governance more or less in its entirety, this book reflects a particular point of view. It is not meant as a general survey.

Chapters 4 through 15 analyze what I regard as the most interesting and important institutions and mechanisms of the corporate governance infrastructure. The question I hope to answer is whether the dominant social and legal institutions are evenhanded in the way that they encourage or discourage these various corporate governance mechanisms. The argument developed here is that U.S. law is not evenhanded. Fewer constraints, and even outright encouragement and regulatory subsidies, are provided for the least effective mechanisms and institutions of corporate governance. In contrast, efforts are made to constrain and discourage the corporate governance devices that are most effective at harnessing managerial opportunism.

For example, historically, the most effective corporate governance mechanism, the market for corporate control, has been the subject of an intense regulatory backlash. This market has been crippled by statutes and regulations, rendering the hostile takeover virtually obsolete. The initial public offering is another effective corporate governance tool that is seldom used because of litigation risk and regulatory burdens. At the same time, relatively ineffective institutions, such as administrative agencies, credit-rating agencies, and even boards of directors, enjoy regulatory "subsidies."

Innovative entrepreneurs have developed new corporate governance devices to respond to those that have been rendered too costly by regulations. In particular, hedge funds and private equity funds now carry much of the corporate governance burden shouldered historically by the market for corporate control. Thus it is no surprise that these emergent corporate governance institutions are facing an increasingly loud chorus of voices clamoring for new, more, and better regulation.

The corporate-governance-as-promise approach adopted here is, from the American perspective, both normative and descriptive. That is, it describes not only what corporate governance in the United States *ought* to do but also what corporate governance *actually* does in action. Law, regulation, contract, and social norms are all *intended*, at least ostensibly, to serve the interests of investors. Norms and rules that maximize the value of the firm directly, that create incentives for others to maximize firm value, or that, at the very least, provide investors with sufficient information through corporate disclosures to enable them to decide for themselves which firms will generate the best returns for investors are consistent with the promissory theory of the corporation.

The corporate-governance-as-promise approach to corporate governance is universal and applies across borders to every economic system that purports to be guided by the rule of law. However, the U.S. approach, which styles the default corporate governance promise as shareholder wealth maximization, is by no means the only, or even the dominant, approach to corporate governance that one observes throughout the world. In many places, particularly Germany and Japan, the fundamental premise behind the corporation is not the notion of a promise to maximize value for shareholders. Instead, the fundamental corporate governance premise in many companies is that the corporation is a creation of the state, whose goals are to serve myriad and often conflicting societal interests. In places that embrace this theory of corporate governance, as a legal matter, corporations in many countries, including Germany, are not free to commit themselves contractually to maximize profits for investors, though market pressures and concerns about international competitiveness may force them to do so, despite the lack of legal pressures.

The approach taken in this book also is distinctive because it suggests that in many contexts, less rather than more corporate governance may actually be better from the point of view of investors. For example, much of the recent talk among legal scholars and regulators has focused heavily on the question of how to "improve" shareholder democracy by expanding shareholders' voting rights. The implicit assumption in this discussion is that more voting is necessarily better for shareholders. As explored in more depth in chapter 13, however, from a promissory perspective, more is not necessarily better. The real question is not how to *increase* shareholder voting but how to *limit* shareholder voting to the contexts in which the benefits associated with such voting outweigh the costs. From the corporate-governance-as-promise perspective, shareholders should be assumed to be maximizing the value of their shares. Issues about voting for other reasons, such as to engage in self-expression or to manifest one's sense of being a "citizen" of the corporation, do not factor into the promissory perspective embraced here.

Shareholders should be free to expand (or to contract) the range of issues over which they can vote. The corporation-as-promise perspective on corporate governance embraced here views the goal of shareholder wealth maximization as merely the default rule that exists for U.S. corporations. Shareholders who think that they can make themselves better-off by expanding the range and scope of the issues over which they can vote clearly should be allowed to do so. Moreover, even shareholders who believe that they will make bad decisions in the election process should be able to bargain for increased voting rights if they prefer voting to wealth. Here again, the critical issues for society should not be whether a corporation and its shareholders should be free to choose the legal arrangements to which they are subject. Rather, the critical issues are what is the default rule and what is the proper way to disclose proposed departures from the default rule.

Any time shareholders feel they need special voting rights to constrain agency costs (in this context agency costs means managerial deviations from shareholder preferences), courts should rush to their defense. For example, shareholders understandably may think that managers and directors might resist a hostile outside bid for control of the corporation to hold onto their lucrative, powerful, and prestigious positions. It is not hard to imagine that senior managers' wealth and egos might sorely tempt them to put their own interests ahead of those of the shareholders. And even the most shareholder-focused CEOs may easily deceive themselves into thinking that they can do a better job at the helm than would an outsider, despite the outsider's willingness to offer shareholders a handsome premium for their shares. For these reasons, shareholders have frequently gone to the courts to ask for greater voting rights in control contests. Generally what shareholders are asking for is the ability to approve outside offers against the wishes of their boards of directors. Specifically, shareholders often seek to prevent (or, at a minimum, to require a shareholder vote on) defensive tactics by management that can thwart outside offers.

This tension between the interests of the shareholders under the corporate-governance-as-promise approach and the law is one of the major themes of this book. Though corporate law rules and Securities and Exchange Commission (SEC) regulations *should* strengthen shareholders' contracting power within the firm, they do not always do this. As just mentioned (and as elaborated on in chapter 8), state and federal regulations thwart the market for corporate control and fail to permit shareholders to vote in control situations where such voting threatens the traditional powers of directors. Similarly, I argue in chapter 9 that despite the important corporate governance benefits of frequent public offerings, regulations have strangled the market for such offerings (known as initial public offerings [IPOs]) in the United States.

A frequent topic in international corporate governance circles is the role that banks and other lenders should play in corporate governance (chapter 14). Proponents of banks taking a lead role in corporate governance consider big financial institutions a species of über institutional investor, with the resources, sophistication, and wherewithal necessary to monitor and control managers of even the biggest and most sophisticated public companies. The popular notion that universal banks should be at the epicenter of corporate governance is driven by the view that *somebody* needs to stand guard over management's stewardship of the corporation. While unsophisticated, widely disbursed shareholders do not seem capable of monitoring and controlling incumbent managers and directors, big banks certainly do.

The problem with this view is that the economic perspective of banks is fundamentally different from that of shareholders. As detailed in chapter 14, banks' primary interest in corporations stems from their relationship as lender to these firms. As lenders, banks are concerned first and foremost with making sure that the principal and interest due on their commercial loans to corporate borrowers are repaid. Lenders' first concern is with borrowers who take big risks on new ventures or who focus on projects that are riskier than absolutely necessary. In sharp contrast, shareholders care most about generating cash (making profits) *above and beyond what is necessary to pay off fixed claimants like banks.*

The differing perspective of fixed claimants and equity claimants regarding risk creates genuine tension among these sometimes rivalrous classes of claimants about what course of action is best. Shareholders generally prefer investments that feature higher risks and higher potential payoffs than lenders, who generally prefer safer investments to maximize the probability that their loans will be repaid when they come due. As such, banks are not a perfect solution to the corporate governance problems that face shareholders, although they may be better than nothing when better alternatives are not available. In the United States, laws separating commercial banking and investment banking and commercial banking and commerce have prevented commercial banks from taking the active role in corporate governance that they take elsewhere. But generally speaking, these laws have been relaxed.

In addition to considering corporate governance devices that work well for shareholders, this book pays attention to a number of corporate governance devices that are less successful. At the same time that certain regulations are stifling a large number of the more effective and powerful corporate governance devices, other regulations are actually encouraging and subsidizing a number of the more ineffective corporate governance tools.

One highly touted, but overrated, corporate governance device is shareholder voting, which has already been mentioned in this introduction. I will argue (in chapter 13) that shareholder voting's role in corporate governance is important but rather limited. Shareholders do not have the time, expertise, incentives, or inclination to vote more than they do. For this reason, I categorize shareholder voting as an ineffective corporate governance mechanism. (See chapter 3 for my taxonomy of effective and ineffective corporate governance mechanisms.)

Other corporate governance devices have proven even less reliable than shareholder voting as mechanisms to control managerial deviance. For example, in my view, perhaps the most important contribution of this book is chapter 6, which describes the role of corporate boards of directors. Here I point out that certain theories and assumptions about the role of corporate boards of directors lie at the heart of every theory of corporate governance ever devised. In my view, each of these extant theories suffers from one or two major flaws. First, many of these theories assume, without analysis, that boards of directors can be trustworthy and reliable monitors. Failed boards, like those of Enron, WorldCom, Tyco, and Adelphia, are criticized for being too trusting of management and not sufficiently skeptical about the sorts of things these companies were doing. In fact, all of these boards had a majority of independent directors. Indeed everybody on the Enron board except one person (Ken Lay, the company's CEO and board chair) was independent of management.

Perhaps the most controversial argument in this book is contained in chapter 4, which challenges the old but untested assumption that we can improve the quality of corporate governance in public companies simply by increasing the number of independent directors on these companies' boards of directors. The problem with this assumption is that even the so-called independent directors crowding into boardrooms these days are highly susceptible to being captured by the very management teams that they are supposed to be monitoring. Chapter 5 presents a number of case studies to illustrate the problem of board capture and to drive home the argument that boards that *appear* to all the world to be paradigms of independence often end up being the most captured. Enron is a powerful, but by no means unique, illustration of this general problem.

Chapter 6 considers a new form of "super-independent" director known as the dissident director. These are directors nominated and elected outside of the traditional management-dominated nominating committee structure of incumbent boards. Such directors are not nearly as susceptible to capture as traditional directors who come to the company with the approval of the incumbent managerial group. The directors nominated by hedge funds and private equity firms (discussed in chapter 15) are the best sources of dissident directors for public companies.

Everybody agrees that boards of directors, even ostensibly independent directors, are prone to capture. Nobody has even *suggested* a test for sorting out the directors who are truly independent of management from those who merely appear to be independent. Until such a test is devised, in my view, independent directors cannot be relied on to solve the agency problem that lies at the heart of corporate governance.

What is worse, directors chosen for their independence alone often know little if anything about the actual operations or strategic challenges that face the companies on whose boards they serve. Shareholders may be better-off abandoning the myth of independent directors and moving back to boards of directors with several insiders on the board. If senior managers are superior managers but not inferior monitors, then shareholders would be wise to bring more of them onto their companies' boards of directors. The costs to shareholders of having only one senior manager on their companies' boards may be worse than the benefits.

Having identified corporate boards of directors as a rather ineffective corporate governance device in chapter 4, I attempt in succeeding chapters to identify other corporate governance tools, some of which are effective and some of which are not. To be clear, when I say that a corporate governance device is ineffective I do not mean, of course, that it is completely ineffective. Rather, I simply mean that it is ineffective relative to alternative highly effective mechanisms like the market for corporate control *and* that it does not live up to its hype. Boards of directors, shareholder voting (chapter 13), outside accountants (chapter 11), and corporate whistle-blowers (chapter 12), as well as credit-rating agencies, stock market analysts, and regulators (all treated in chapter 7), have been proven to be rather ineffective in my view.

One of the main points developed in this book is that the corporate governance mechanisms that are the least effective are the ones that are most encouraged by regulators and lawmakers. At the same time, the corporate governance devices that are the most effective, particularly hedge funds and private equity firms (chapter 15), dissident directors (chapter 6), the market for corporate control (chapter 8), and IPOs (chapter 9), are the corporate governance devices that are the most heavily regulated. The key exceptions to the generalization that regulation follows superior performance are private equity firms and hedge funds. It is not coincidental that these are the governance mechanisms most threatened with being regulated. The threats are constant, and corporate managers are hardly opposing the chorus of voices urging tighter control over hedge funds and private equity firms.

That is not coincidental either. Only occasionally, as in the summer of 2002 when Sarbanes-Oxley was passed, does corporate governance become a highly visible, salient political issue. And only when corporate governance is a visible, salient issue is legal reform possible. When, as was the case in 2002, corporate governance becomes an important issue on the political landscape and politicians believe that they must enact reforms to satisfy public opinions, they are still heavily influenced by organized special interest groups. Shareholders are not well organized into effective political coalitions; managers are. Managers will staunchly resist corporate governance reforms that put their jobs in jeopardy or threaten their ability to remain independent from outside entities such as activist hedge funds and corporate raiders or that otherwise make their lives more difficult. They will support (or decline to oppose) governance reforms that "merely" raise costs on shareholders.

High on the list of corporate governance measures that managers oppose are reforms that liberalize the market for corporate control or that make it easier for shareholders to control (or even to understand fully) their compensation. In contrast, managers are likely to find little to complain about measures that bolster their already captured boards of directors or require them to expand their already bloated central office bureaucracies.

The theory that the best corporate governance devices are taxed by regulation while the worst are subsidized by regulations is consistent with the simple theory that regulators and politicians are following the path of least resistance when they regulate. They can satisfy the public's outcry that they "do something" about corporate governance by passing laws like Sarbanes-Oxley that increase the power of "independent" directors and like the Williams Act that weaken the market for corporate control without upsetting the top managers of public companies or any other well-organized special interest group.

The main purpose of this introduction is to define the key phrase in this book, which is "corporate governance." I conceptualize corporate governance in contractual terms. By this I mean that I view the corporation as a nexus of contracts, and I see corporate governance as one of many societal, legal, cultural, and economic factors that can, if used properly, make the contracting process more efficient and more reliable. The purpose of corporate governance, in my view, is to control corporate deviance, by which I mean deviance from the terms of the contracts between the various contractual participants in the corporate enterprise and the company itself. Simply put, contracting parties should get what they pay for. I call this the "promissory theory" of the corporation because the contracts that constitute the corporation also can, and should be, viewed as a series of promises by management to investors of all types.

The particular contract that shareholders have with the firm is not more important than the contract that other corporate constituencies have with the firm—but it is more poorly specified. Non-shareholder constituencies want simple promises to be kept. These include promises about such things as terms and conditions of employment, wages, and the payment of principal and interest. In contrast, shareholders, as residual claimants, want managers and directors to maximize the value of the company in which they have invested. This far more vague promise is the promise of corporate governance. The following chapters provide my rather unromantic and perhaps idiosyncratic perspective on the various institutions and mechanisms that function to try to ensure that these promises to investors will be kept.

CHAPTER 1

THE GOALS OF CORPORATE GOVERNANCE

The Dominant Role of Equity

Corporate governance is generally about promises, while corporations themselves are about contracts. Every facet of a corporation's existence from beginning to end is organized around contracts, although the "contract" that the corporation has with its shareholders is little more than a promise.

Employment agreements (sometimes, but increasingly rarely these are collective bargaining agreements with unionized workers) specify the terms of the contract between workers and the corporations. Suppliers have contracts. Customers' purchases are contracts according to commercial law. Executives have contracts. Even directors have contracts.

The contract that the corporation has with its shareholders is the corporation's charter (sometimes known as the Articles of Incorporation). This charter, supplemented by more detailed bylaws, contains the baseline rules that govern the corporation and constitute the fundamental corporate governance rules for the corporation. The charter and bylaws describe the contours of the relationship between the shareholders and the company. Consistent with the contracting paradigm, corporate charters and bylaws vary widely from corporation to corporation.

Consistent with the idea that the relationship between shareholders and the corporation is characterized by promise rather than contract, the typical corporate charter is extremely cursory. The document will contain a statement of the purposes and powers of the corporation. (Typically, corporate charters permit corporations to pursue any lawful act or activity for which corporations may be organized and to exercise powers granted under the Business Corporation Law of the state in which they are incorporated.) The charter will specify how much stock the corporation can issue, and it may provide that the company's board of directors can issue different classes of stock. The charter may specify the respective rights of the holders of various classes of stock with respect to such matters as dividends, voting, and order of priority in liquidation and other distributions, but often the charter will delegate this power to the corporation's board of directors. The charter will provide that other things, such as the number of directors of the corporation, are to be specified in the company's bylaws. For example, the corporate charter for IBM requires that the number of directors of the corporation shall be provided in its bylaws, but shall not be less than nine or more than twenty-five.[1] These sorts of provisions, of course, give corporations a lot of freedom to operate within the constraints of the "contracts" they have with shareholders.

State law does not require that corporate charters contain very much. The only mandatory requirements are for provisions that specify the name of the corporation, the number of shares of stock that the corporation is authorized to issue, the names and addresses of the people organizing the company, and the name and address of an agent in the jurisdiction where the company is organized who can accept service of process if the corporation is sued.

Since the mid-1980s, most corporations in the litigious United States have amended their charters to reduce the risk of personal liability of directors in shareholder lawsuits. These charter amendments have come in the wake of state legislation that permits corporations to insert in their corporate charters provisions that eliminate the liability of a corporation's directors to the corporation or its stockholders for damages for negligence and breach of the duty of care. However, state statutes specifically provide that corporate charters may not eliminate directors' liability for receiving financial benefits for which they are not entitled, intentional harm done to the corporation or its shareholders, criminal acts, and payment of dividends to shareholders while the company is insolvent.

The bylaws govern the details of the internal management of the corporation. Unlike corporate charters, bylaws can be amended either by the shareholders or by the corporation's directors. The corporation is, to a large extent, a political entity. It has a chief executive who is appointed by a democratically elected group of directors. The rules governing these elections and appointments, and indeed the officials elected and appointed, are subject to the controlling law contained in the corporate bylaws and charter. The articles of incorporation are analogous to the corporation's constitution, while the bylaws are like the entity's statutes.

The primacy of contract theory in corporate governance cannot be overemphasized. Corporate governance is about the constraints on the behavior of corporate actors, and these actors, whether they are officers, directors, or controlling shareholders, are governed in the first instance by contract. The role of contract in corporate governance, and, indeed, in corporate law generally, is so pervasive that it is often not clear where contract law ends and where corporate law begins. Some prominent law and economics scholars take the entirely defensible view that corporate law is simply a specialty within the larger field of contract law.[2]

Scholars who take this view, most prominently Frank Easterbrook and Daniel Fischel, generally place little emphasis on corporate charters and bylaws, despite the fact that these are the *actual* contracts that exist between investors and their companies. Instead, the corporation is viewed as a hypothetical bargain between shareholders and managers. Under this approach, judges are directed to decide cases by determining what the parties to the disputes would have agreed to had they negotiated the question being litigated *ex ante*, that is, at the time of their original investments.

The hypothetical bargaining approach is central to the contractual approach to corporate law. But this is not because corporate charters and bylaws and other real contracts are unimportant. Rather, the opposite is true: where corporate charters and bylaws control a particular dispute among the various claimants to a corporation's cash flows, disputes do not arise among these claimants because the actual corporate contracts clearly control. Only where an intracorporate dispute arises that is not specifically covered in the actual corporate contract does hypothetical bargaining have a role to play in corporate governance. But that happens a lot.

From an economic perspective, corporations are not only organized around the idea of contract, they are most accurately described as contracts. As Ronald Coase has suggested in his seminal article "The Nature of the Firm,"[3] the corporation is best conceptualized not as an entity but as a complex web or nexus of contractual relationships. It is undeniable that every corporate constituency, including shareholders, directors, managers, workers, suppliers, customers, and even local communities, has a relationship with the corporation or other constituencies that is contractual in nature. Once these contractual relationships are unbundled from the corporation, there is nothing left. For this reason, to the extent that corporate governance is effective in controlling corporate conduct, it must control the people who actually act for the corporation and for themselves.

Contract plays such an important role in corporate governance that one must ask why there needs to be anything else. Contracts inevitably generate outcomes that are *ex ante* efficient. Participation in the corporate enterprise is voluntary and inevitably precipitated by a voluntary exchange. Unless we can identify with some precision a flaw or deficiency in the contracting process, we should conclude that corporations and corporate actors should be governed by contract rather than by statute.

At various times, three distinct (though often conflated) objections to the claim that contracts provide a sufficient infrastructure for corporate governance have surfaced. First, it is argued that contracts are necessarily incomplete and therefore something is needed to deal with the pervasive incompleteness of the corporate contract. A second, but related, reason why the contractual (or, as it is sometimes called, a "contractarian") paradigm may be considered insufficient is because contractual provisions are not sufficient to the task of protecting the claims of shareholders. Shareholders, as residual claimants, have financial interests in the firm that simply cannot be protected *ex ante* by contract. Third, and from a completely different perspective, comes the assertion that corporations simply are too important to society to be relegated to the contractual sphere of private ordering.

Each of these claims is unpersuasive. As for the first, all contracts are incomplete and many are unclear in their drafting. Most of the subject of contract law is concerned with how to deal either with the problem that contingencies arise that were never considered by the parties or with the problem that even the contingencies that were foreseen were ignored or dealt with in an ambiguous fashion.

The second claim, that contracts are insufficient, ignores the fact that *all* solutions to the contracting problems that face shareholders have costs as well as benefits. The relevant question, then, is not whether contracts are sufficient to the task of protecting shareholders but whether contracting is the best device for maximizing wealth. It may very well be the case that adding other sorts of legal "remedies" to the baseline solutions provided by contract will make investors worse-off, not better-off.

The third claim, that corporations simply are too important to society to be relegated to the contractual sphere of private ordering, fails to address the fundamental question of whose interests are at stake in the formulation of corporate governance rules. Where the issue involves the narrow question of whose interests the corporation should serve, the contracting, promissory approach taken in this book seems clearly superior to any alternatives. Of course, nobody asserts that contract is sufficient to deal with all problems, particularly the problems associated with externalities or third-party effects. Environmental law, criminal law, tort law, and so forth deal with these sorts of problems, but this fact, of course, is by no means limited to corporations or even to business organizations. Contract is not sufficient to regulate private ordering among individuals where there are clear negative effects on third parties from the agreements made by the private individuals.

The claim that corporate governance should be analyzed entirely through a contractarian paradigm can be easily dispensed with. It clearly is the case that contracts of all kinds, including corporate contracts, are incomplete. Much of contract law concerns itself with dealing with this problem. For example, commercial contracts contain "implied covenants of good faith" that require the parties to act in good faith when carrying out their contractual obligations. Courts long have allowed people to discharge their contractual obligations where they can claim fraud, unconscionability, or impossibility of performance because of the pervasive failure of contracting parties to deal with these issues satisfactorily.

Another way to approach the gap-filling function served by law is from the perspective of efficiency. To a large extent, corporate contracts are incomplete because it is efficient for them to be incomplete. State actors in the form of judges simply do a better job than private parties in ordering the arrangements among participants in the corporate enterprise. While this seems odd in light of the overwhelming evidence that government is inefficient in general and particularly inept at running businesses, it appears true nevertheless. Apparently, the fact that government has demonstrated that it cannot efficiently run businesses does not necessarily mean that the state is ineffective at assisting the private-ordering process when the entrepreneurial decisions are made by others. The state has a clear role to play in enforcing the contracts that are made in the private sector. Unbiased, professional interpretation and enforcement of contracts is a significant undertaking that adds incalculable value to business.

In fact, the role of the state goes even beyond the mere enforcement function. The state applies "off-the-rack" rules that actually serve as substitutes for the rules that investors might develop. It has long been recognized, particularly by those in the "law and economics" movement, that the corporation, along with other forms of business organization, including such modern forms as the limited liability company (LLC) and the limited liability partnership (LLP), should be viewed as a "nexus of contracts" or set of implicit and explicit contracts. The term "nexus of contracts" describes corporations and other forms of business organizations as complex webs of contractual relationships among the various participants in the enterprise: investors, managers, suppliers, workers, customers, and so forth. Under this view, business law, including corporate law, exists to economize on transaction costs by supplying sensible "off-the-rack" rules that participants in a business can use to economize on the cost of contracting.

Critically, this analysis also applies to fiduciary duties. Fiduciary duties are part of the contractual nature of the corporation and exist to fill in the blanks and inevitable oversights in the actual contracts used by business organizations. The purpose of fiduciary duties is to provide people with the results that they would have bargained for if they had been able to anticipate the problem at hand and had contracted for its resolution in advance. Thus the law of business organizations in general and corporations in particular is highly contractual in nature. The purpose of the various laws of business organizations is to facilitate the contracting process, not to displace the actual contracts reached by the parties. Business organizations need law, including fiduciary duties, because it simply is not possible for those who organize businesses to identify all of the potential problems and conflicts that inevitably will arise in a business. Specific issues and transactions invariably will present themselves that could not have been identified *ex ante*. Fiduciary duties exist to provide a framework for dealing with those issues.

Consistent with this analysis, the modern trend is inexorably toward more contractual freedom in corporate law. For example, in Delaware, the law that applies to limited liability companies explicitly permits members and managers of LLCs to expand, restrict, or eliminate fiduciary duties and other duties, other than the implied contractual covenants of good faith and fair dealing.[4] However, it is clear that the *default rule* for all other forms of business organization in Delaware, and elsewhere, is that fiduciary duties are owed to investors. Fiduciary duties exist unless the parties have explicitly and unambiguously contracted them away.

Investors can opt out of these rules in at least three ways. First, they can draft their own rules to cover a particular contingency. Where this is done properly, the agreement reached by the parties will be respected, so long as there has been no fraud or unfair dealing in the contract negotiation. Second, promoters and entrepreneurs who organize corporations can choose from among many U.S. and offshore jurisdictions when they decide where to incorporate, and thus where to "locate" their businesses for legal purposes. Simply by incorporating their businesses in a jurisdiction that contains statutory provisions that are to their liking, people organizing new business (or reorganizing existing businesses) can select or "opt into" the set of "off-the-rack" legal rules that best fit their needs. Third, even within a single jurisdiction, people organizing a business can select among a variety of different forms of business organization, such as the traditional corporate form, as well as the limited partnership, the limited liability company, and the limited liability partnership.

While contracting clearly is a significant source of governance rules for corporations, the contracting process is very costly. Take, for example, the issue of executive compensation. Many economists are of the view that the broadening gap between CEO and rank-and-file pay reflects a failure of corporate-governance practices to maintain a proper relationship between compensation and performance.[5] The specific executive compensation arrangements that we actually observe, however, simply reflect the result of a bargaining process between shareholders' elected representatives and managers. It would be possible for companies, especially companies selling their shares to the public for the first time, to design more modest compensation packages. At a minimum, it would be possible for directors to have at least a basic understanding of the compensation arrangements they are reaching with top executives. In recent years, it has turned out that directors of corporate giants like Disney and United Health did not even comprehend how much their companies might be on the hook for the multimillion arrangements they reached with top corporate officers.

The power of contract in corporate governance is profound. In theory, contractual remedies can provide complete protection for shareholders against corporate oppression. Academic writing in corporate governance has paid virtually no attention to specific features of contract design such as the buy-sell agreement. A buy-sell agreement commits either the corporation or certain of its shareholders to purchase the interest of a withdrawing shareholder upon the occurrence of contractually specified contingencies. These arrangements can solve virtually all of the problems that shareholders face in closely held corporations, from job stability for the minority, to liquidity, to oppression, and freeze-out. A buy-sell arrangement can be structured so as to give equity investors a put option that allows such investors to force the corporation, or a subgroup of its shareholders, to repurchase their shares at a negotiated, formulaically determined price.

These arrangements are used frequently in closely held corporations in order to "create a private market and give the minority shareholder an out in the event of a falling out or disagreement with the majority shareholder."[6] Buy-sell agreements are so useful that a lawyer's failure to advise a minority investor in a closely held company of her ability to negotiate to obtain such protection prior to investing probably constitutes professional negligence.

While buy-sell arrangements are extremely common, they are designed to be deployed only under very limited, clearly specified conditions. For example, buy-sell arrangements sometimes cannot be triggered until a certain date, often years after a shareholder has made her initial investment. It is extremely common for the triggering event for buy-sell arrangements in closely held companies to be the death or incapacity of the shareholder (or her heirs) seeking to exercise the contractual right to sell her shares. Such limitations are not surprising in light of the fact that buy-sell arrangements are very costly for companies. In particular, creditors understandably view such arrangements as a significant source of risk, since the exercise of a buy-sell agreement by a shareholder reduces the "equity cushion" available to creditors whose loans have not been repaid when the shareholder's stock is purchased by the company. Moreover, since buy-sell agreements often are funded by insurance policies, restricting the trigger events to death or incapacity is necessary to mitigate the problem of moral hazard.

Moral hazard refers to the problem, ubiquitous in insurance markets, that people protected by insurance coverage will engage in activities that tend to make the event being insured against more likely to occur. The term "moral hazard" also has come to refer to the increase in risk-taking

proclivity caused by contract. For example, a manager whose employment agreement calls for a generous severance package will be inclined
to engage in activities that are more likely to result in termination. Shareholders in companies also face moral hazard vis-à-vis corporate creditors.
As the proportion of debt relative to equity (leverage) goes up, so too
does the moral hazard facing shareholders. By engaging in risky activities,
companies with large amounts of debt and very little (or no) equity can
benefit shareholders at the expense of creditors. Moral hazard stems from
the fact that the shareholders' participation in any gains from the risky
activities is disproportionate and unlimited, while their losses are limited
to the amount of their initial investments.

The point here is not that buy-sell arrangements are underutilized.
There is no evidence or reason to believe that this is the case. Rather, the
use of buy-sell arrangements is probably optimal. The point is that buy-
sell arrangements that confer broad liquidity rights on shareholders are
available. The availability of these contractual rights has profound implications for our understanding of the role of contract in corporate governance. The existence (and low cost) of buy-sell arrangements provides
proof of a profound reality about corporate governance because it shows
that the limits of contract in corporate governance are not due to shortcomings in the legal system, to technological flaws, or to cultural bias in
the contracting process.

The enforceability of buy-sell arrangements and other "global" contractual corporate governance rules demonstrates the failure of contract
to dominate the corporate governance landscape availability. Thus the
fact that contractual corporate governance rules occupy such a small part
of the corporate governance landscape must be due to factors other than
flaws in the legal system or in the contracting process.

The same holds true for the arguments that technological flaws in the
contracting process or cultural bias in society impede the primacy of contract. A highly developed and sophisticated contracting infrastructure exists for buy-sell agreements. Literally thousands of articles and dozens of
books and practical guides explain how to structure these agreements,
which some attorneys have taken to calling "business pre-nups," meaning
that they are prenuptial agreements for business. Advice is also widely
available on the Internet.[7] These agreements, however, generally limit the
circumstances under which the buy-sell obligations are triggered. Such
agreements are primarily used to regulate the corporate governance and
to lower the estate taxes in small businesses where the death of a shareholder causes not only a disruption of the business but also significant tax
consequences for the heirs of the deceased shareholder.[8]

Other circumstances in which buy-sell agreements frequently are used
are bankruptcy,[9] divorce,[10] disability, and retirement[11] of designated share-

holders. The mystery is why these agreements do not go much further than they do to provide corporate governance protections for shareholders. Such agreements could, for example, provide shareholders with put options in case of any sort of disagreement among shareholders about the corporation's strategy, or even in the event that a shareholder would like to withdraw voluntarily.

Moreover, buy-sell agreements are by no means the only sort of contractual corporate governance devices available to shareholders. For example, in the early nineteenth century, it was the "usual practice" that corporations in the business of owning and operating bridges and turnpikes had corporate charter provisions that provided for mandatory dividend payments for shareholders.[12] As with buy-sell arrangements, and myriad other easy-fix corporate governance contractual devices such as employment contracts, mandatory dividend payments are underutilized because investors do not want to use them, not because they cannot be made to work.

Virtually no legal or technological impediments exist to the use of contract as the exclusive mechanism for the governance of corporations and their agents. As is well known, shareholders are free to pay their executives as much or as little as they wish. Shareholders also are free to structure these compensation plans more or less as they wish, subject only to some certain technical constraints such as those regarding corporations' inability to deduct salary payments over $1 million unless they are linked to performance and the well-accepted constraints on insider trading.

It also is the case that there are few norms or cultural biases that impede the utilization of contracts or contractual solutions as mechanisms for investors and other participants in the corporate enterprise to resolve anticipated problems. For example, while normative concerns in the form of professed moral indignation and public expressions of outrage about executive compensation are articulated among academics and members of the press, executives themselves seem hardly troubled by the problem, except to the extent that the outrage brings increased regulatory scrutiny and, possibly, increased regulation. The opposite is true. For decades now, contract has been the dominant paradigm among lawmakers and scholars of corporate governance. Indeed, the idea of the corporation as a nexus of contracts is not only descriptive but normative. The corporation is a voluntary association, and contract is viewed as providing the clearest, most direct insight into the preferences and understandings of the investors and other voluntary participants in the enterprise.

From this perspective, the role of statutory law is to provide default rules that fill in when the corporate contract is silent. The idea that statutory law serves as a contractual gap-filler is both descriptive and normative. It describes what corporate law does, as well as what it is supposed to do, illustrating the strong social consensus around the idea of corporation as contract. We can, therefore, clearly rule out the role of social norms or other societal impediments as the explanation for why corporate governance issues are not handled in a unitary, ubiquitous fashion by contract.

Interestingly, therefore, it must be the case that shareholders do not utilize contractual solutions to attain complete corporate governance protections for themselves because governing the corporation by contractual means alone is not the most efficient way to govern the corporation. Indeed, the reason is cost. It turns out that law, in the form of non-contractual rules, dominates the legal landscape of the world of corporate governance because law is more efficient than contract at providing solutions to the problems of corporate governance.

CHAPTER 2

CORPORATE LAW AND CORPORATE GOVERNANCE

The importance of corporate law for corporate governance is far from clear. Bernard Black, for example, argues that non-contractual corporate law is "trivial" because its provisions do not depart significantly from the rules that would be chosen voluntarily in corporate charters if the law did not intervene.[1] This observation tracks the standard account in law and economics that the role of corporate law is to economize on transaction costs by supplying the corporate governance rules that investors would have formulated for themselves if they had allocated the time, effort, and expense of doing so when they made their initial investments.[2] In an important extension of this analysis, Mark Roe argues that even at its most effective, non-contractual law protects participants in the corporate enterprise only against self-dealing, and not against poorly conceived business decisions, taken in the ordinary course of business, that may gravely harm the interests of stockholders. Roe argues that even if a nation's core corporate law is "perfect," the most that it attempts to do is to eliminate self-dealing. Managerial mistake and managerial negligence, along with most managerial shirking, are simply outside of the scope of non-contractual law.[3]

The analysis by Black, Easterbrook and Fischel, and Roe is right as far as it goes, but it is incomplete because it fails properly to account for the dominance of non-contractual law in two respects. First, if corporate law really is trivial, then one must ask why there is so much of it in relation to the amount of contract law that we observe. Second, the standard accounts do not give proper credit to the fact that non-contractual sources generate corporate governance rules without any reference to the actual contracts that investors have with their firms. In other words, the provision of non-contractual corporate law rules is a creative exercise that only uses the contractual paradigm as a metaphor. The paradigm of contract, or, as Easterbrook and Fischel call it, the hypothetical bargaining model, provides both a normative justification and an analytical framework that judges use to supply *ex post* solutions to disputes about how corporations should be governed. Because the corporate governance problems that emerge in the firm are very complex and highly contextual, they also are likely to vary in substance from firm to firm,[4] making a contractual approach to corporate governance appear not only advisable but inevitable, at least as a matter of judicial rhetoric.

In other words, the contracting paradigm provides a useful tool for judges to use to justify their decisions. Whether this justification is convincing or not is far from clear. It is clear, however, that the analytical framework that the contracting paradigm provides for non-contractual law is not much of a constraint on policymakers, since virtually any decision that a judge makes can be justified as being consistent with the hypothetical bargain that the shareholders would have reached had they sat down and negotiated about the issue. Since, by definition, shareholders and other parties to corporate governance disputes that wind up in litigation have not actually specified a preferred outcome *ex ante,* a court's hypothesis that a particular result is the one that the shareholders would have preferred cannot be refuted.

While there is a great deal of corporate law, both statutory and judge-made, there is precious little in the way of contract between shareholders and corporations. The judge-made law may masquerade as contract by invoking the idea of hypothetical bargaining, but that does not detract from what it is: non-contractual law.

Simply put, the non-contractual law governing shareholder rights is literally voluminous, while the actual contracts that exist are skeletal, particularly in the publicly held corporation.

One way of seeing this point is to examine the curriculum of the basic courses in corporate law, mergers and acquisitions, or corporate governance that are taught in American law schools. These courses deal with law, both statutory and, to an even larger extent, judge-made. They do not deal with contract, except to a small extent. For example, to the extent that students are taught about how to form a corporation, they are taught about how easy it is, how quickly it can be done, how little documentation is required, and how the formation of the corporation is a job for paralegals and secretaries, not for corporate lawyers. If the process of forming a corporation involved meaningful contracting, this would not be the case.

Equity investors rely on corporate governance systems far more than other participants in the corporate enterprise for the simple reason that other participants can rely on contracts to a far greater extent than can equity claimants. One of the most remarkable aspects of modern economic life is the fact that hundreds of millions of investors have been persuaded to part with hundreds of billions of dollars in exchange for residual claims on the cash flows of companies. The securities that represent these residual claims offer their owners virtually nothing in the way of formal, legal protections. Shareholders do not have the right to repayment of their principal, ever. Companies issuing the equity claims have no obligation to repurchase the shares from investors, regardless of how well or poorly the issuing companies perform. These companies are not under any obligation to pay dividends or make any other sort of payments to equity claimants.

Joseph Bishop is largely correct in noting that although U.S. law does offer some protection for investors when managers and directors engage in palpable fraud or outright stealing, there is no judicial oversight of managerial competence, and virtually no review of negligence.[5] Contracts protect equity investors to some extent. They provide for incentive-based compensation, for example, which motivates managers, and they also provide, pervasively, for protections against takeovers, which, as discussed in chapter 9, tend to have the opposite effect.

Charters and bylaws, as well as other contractual arrangements, provide only skeletal protections for shareholders. These protections fall demonstrably short of what non-contractual law is prepared to provide. Corporate law, not contract, provides the basic framework for the decision-making that occurs within the firm. For example, non-contractual law sets rules about the composition of the board of directors, the committee structure of the board, and the independence of directors. Of equal importance is the emphasis that courts, particularly in the key state of Delaware, place on the process that a board has constructed and followed in making decisions. And this law, for better or worse, focuses on something that contract law ignores completely: the form rather than substance of the decision-making process. This tendency clearly has been intensifying in recent years[6] and shows no signs of abating. Courts are focusing on what is, or what they are persuaded is, "genuine process." Indeed, process has accurately been described as a recurring and dominant theme in the corporate law of Delaware.

The landmark decision of the Delaware Supreme Court in *Smith v. Van Gorkom*[7] is the starting point for any discussion of the role played by process in the production of non-contractual rules of corporate governance. In a surprising decision that cannot be explained or even conceptualized on contractual grounds, the most authoritative court in the United States in the area of corporate governance held the directors of a major New York Stock Exchange listed company, TransUnion Corporation, personally liable for damages. The damages resulted from a lawsuit in which shareholders claimed that the directors of the company were negligent in failing to construct and to follow an adequate process for reaching a decision about whether and at what price to sell the company in a cash merger.

While some commentators believe that the decision in *Van Gorkom* has led to better decision-making in the firm,[8] many others believe that the decision has led to an excess of process in decision-making. The criticism of the all-consuming focus on process, which is now beginning its third decade at the epicenter of judge-made corporate governance, is quite convincing. The concern is that board meetings, where corporate governance is actually done, have turned into festivals of process that are little more than kabuki-like rituals at which lawyers and investment bankers choreograph ersatz discussions designed to protect foregone conclusions from being attacked by judges as being the result of a defective process.[9] Regardless, it is troubling that the focus on process is decidedly non-contractarian. Participants in the corporate enterprise do not appear to have any flexibility to determine via contract how much process to employ when making decisions.

Despite this disagreement, there is unanimity about one aspect of the watershed opinion in *Smith v. Van Gorkom*. Everyone agrees that the decision led either to the creation or to the perpetuation of a "process culture" in American corporate governance. In other words, the law has evolved to exalt the role of process and, in doing so, the role of "process entrepreneurs" such as lawyers, accountants, and investment bankers who structure and facilitate the process that judges consider so important. In doing so, the increased focus on process has diminished the role that managers, entrepreneurs, and other people whose job is running the business have to play in corporate governance.

Social Norms

The governance of corporations is effectuated not only through contracts, law, and norms but also through the complex set of relationships that exist among these three sources of corporate governance. Contracts are written under the "shadow of the state." By this I mean that when parties negotiate, their bargaining inevitably will be informed by their understanding of what legal and social sanctions will be experienced if they deviate from the agreement. To take a simple example, stock market rules in the United States on both the New York Stock Exchange and the NASDAQ generally require that listed companies must maintain a share price of at least $1 per share in order to remain listed for trading. This, in turn, will affect the number of shares that a company will issue to investors. Companies will choose to issue a smaller number of shares at a higher price per share than they might otherwise issue in the absence of such a rule.

Thus, rules, norms, and statutes inform the content of contracts that affect corporate law and corporate governance because they dictate the background factors that the parties take into account when they negotiate. Contracts inform the content of statutes and other non-contractual corporate law because of the universal acceptance of the norm that corporations themselves are contracts, and that the role of law is to strengthen and facilitate the contracting process among participants to the corporate enterprise.

Process plays a large role in American corporate governance. Thinking about, constructing, and evaluating process is the comparative advantage of lawyers and judges. Lawyers and judges, however, err on the side of injecting too much process into the realm of corporate governance because lawyers experience the economic costs of process as benefits, both in terms of income and in terms of status, as corporate actors must increasingly rely on the judgments of lawyers as procedural values come to dominate corporate governance. Procedural rules that appear to investors and entrepreneurs as burdensome and inefficient appear to the lawyers involved as well-deserved sources of revenue and of recognition of their rightful place in the governance structure of the corporation. Thus it is not surprising that the tendency to advocate a process-based approach to all problems including problems in corporate governance "is an occupational hazard of those legally trained."[10]

For better or worse, when judges and lawmakers formulate non-contractual rules of corporate governance, they inevitably import their own norms into these rules. The norms, such as strict allegiance to process-oriented values, that permeate the legal culture became inserted into the legal landscape by lawyers and judges who embraced the view that process is what entrepreneurs and investors really want and would have contracted for if only they had taken the time and effort to do so.

Thus, the strange nature of the corporate governance landscape can only be explained by understanding how the nexus of contracts metaphor for the corporation is used as a judicial tool by judges. In deciding cases, judges import their own values, in particular their devotion to form over substance, under the guise of reaching the outcomes that entrepreneurs, managers, and investors would have reached through actual bargaining.

Norms therefore play an important role in corporate governance. Judges and lawyers (who draft statutory corporate governance rules) inevitably import their own norms into the structuring of the corporate world "process." The only question is how important norms are in the governance of the corporation. The term "norm" is so vague and poorly understood that it is difficult to address this question with much precision.

To start with, a norm is something by which other things are measured and judged. A norm describes a standard or pattern of behavior that is not required by law but is generally regarded as typical (normal) and therefore expected in a particular community. This approach to norms is consistent with the definition suggested by Richard Posner, who has described a norm as "a rule that is neither promulgated by an official source, such as a court or legislature, nor enforced by the threat of legal sanctions, yet is regularly complied with."[11]

Norms, then, are important for corporate governance for at least three reasons. First, as we saw above, norms are important because they are often the source of actual legal rules. Starting with the observation that there is a complex and symbiotic relationship among the three primary sources of corporate governance rules (contract, law, and norms), we observe judges imposing the norms of the legal culture (particularly the norm that exalts process) on the rules of corporate governance. Judges use their own norms as their primary source of authority in that they justify their legal decisions and statutory rules on the basis that these (generally process-oriented) rules are consistent with the hypothetical bargaining that would occur among investors.

In other words, norms are important for corporate governance because law is important, and norms are an important source of law. The example used above, about how the process-focused norms of the legal culture can seep into corporate law, is rather subtle. Norms also influence legal rules more directly. When administrative agencies and self-regulatory organizations like stock exchanges formulate legal rules that influence the governance of the firm, they naturally look to prevailing industry and community standards (i.e., norms) as their primary reference point.

On this point, it is worth emphasizing that a primary source of corporate governance rules are the legal rules formulated by the prestigious American Law Institute (ALI) in its "Principles of Corporate Governance."[12] The Principles of Corporate Governance were initially set out to be a restatement of existing law, but ended in a highly contentious, politicized struggle between legal academics and business lawyers about whose norms would be reflected in the rules. Regulations are always shaped by politics, of course. The point here is not that the political battle over the ALI's corporate governance rules initiated any sort of new era of political influence on corporate law. Rather the difference was that the politics came out of the closet. The lawyer-factotums at the ALI were no longer able to pretend that they were acting apolitically. Their corporate clients forced them to admit the possibility that their work was furthering the interests of the corporate bar rather than the interests of justice. These corporations were unabashed in their insistence that the original ALI proposals were political. Their response was not to urge the "depoliticization" of the process. Their response was to influence the process for their own ends.

Founded in 1923 to promote the clarification and simplification of American judge-made common law, and to facilitate the adaptation of law to changing social needs, the ALI drafts, approves, and publishes restatements of the law, model codes, and other proposals for law reform.

Although restatements do not have the force of law, they are highly influential on judges and legislatures because of the prestige enjoyed by the ALI and because of the careful, incremental, and thoughtful process by which restatements are drafted.

In the past, ALI projects have been characterized by scholarly debate, restrained emotions, and a practice of "leaving clients at the door" of the meetings of advisors, counselors, and members. Only occasionally have those traditions been breached. Interestingly, it is generally acknowledged that the principles reflected in those traditions were completely abandoned. The goal of restating the law was abandoned, as lawyers refused to acquiesce in the characterization of the rules articulated in early drafts of the project as being a "restatement" of the law. The entire process became politicized. As a highly respected corporate practitioner and ALI member observed, "Many corporations plainly indicated to their outside counsel, who were members of the ALI, how they should vote on contested issues; lawyers were encouraged to join the ALI for the sole purpose of adding their voices to the chorus of criticism; and debates at members' meetings were sometimes as carefully orchestrated as the proceedings of a political convention."[13]

The controversy over the ALI's attempt at norm entrepreneurship demonstrates that norms do matter. The idea of restating the law similarly illustrates the way that norms transform themselves into law. In fact, the whole idea of formulating a "restatement" serves the purpose of formalizing, and thus incorporating into law, the prevailing norms in a particular field.

Norms also play an important role in the interpretation of contracts because judges often interpret contracts, including corporate contracts, with reference to norms. In interpreting contracts, judges must determine what is "commercially reasonable" and what is "ordinary and customary" in a particular context. This approach to the interpretation of contracts requires the direct importation of norms into judicial decision-making.

Second, norms are important in corporate governance because they begin to affect behavior even before they become formalized as law. For example, as Mark Roe has observed, the core idea of shareholder primacy is itself nothing but a norm.[14] As Roe indicates, this may be good or bad for society, depending on how competitive product markets are in the nation. And, it seems, there are wide differences among countries in terms of the extent to which they embrace the shareholder primacy norm.

In the United States and other common law countries, shareholder primacy is a broadly shared norm among managers and entrepreneurs, though less so among academics and lawyers. In the United States, shareholder wealth maximization is considered valuable, appropriate, and just.[15]

In civil law countries like France, Germany, Italy, and Japan, share-holder wealth maximization is not a norm. Shareholder primacy is not even considered particularly desirable from a social perspective, especially where the interests of shareholders conflict with the interests of non-share-holder constituencies, such as workers and local communities, or with political goals such as promoting local ownerships of strategic enterprises like banks, airlines, and manufacturing.

Because norms are a reflection of the views held by most people, survey evidence is useful in demonstrating how pervasive a norm might be among a particular subgroup of society. For example, a survey of senior managers of major companies reported by Franklin Allen and Douglas Gale generated astonishing insights into managers' views on why corporations exist and whose interests corporations should serve. It showed widely divergent views between the United States and the United Kingdom on the one hand, and Japan, Germany, and France on the other.[16]

Allen and Gale found that in the United States and the United Kingdom the vast majority of managers (76 percent and 71 percent, respectively) took the view that the corporation belonged to the shareholders. In sharp contrast, in Germany 82.7 percent of senior managers thought their company belonged to all of the stakeholders. France was not much different, with 78 percent of top managers "giving" the corporation to the stakeholders. In Japan, an astonishing 97 percent of managers thought that the company belonged to all stakeholders. Only 3 percent of senior managers in Japan thought that the shareholders were the owners of the business.

Similarly, Allen and Gale also report that job security for workers was far more important to senior managers in Japan, Germany, and France than to their English and American counterparts. Ninety percent of managers in the United States and the United Kingdom thought dividends were more important than job security. By contrast, in Japan only 3 percent of managers thought dividends outranked stable employment for workers in importance to the corporation. In Germany and France large majorities found stable employment for workers more important than dividends.

It is not for nothing that the term "shareholder culture" has emerged to describe societies characterized by broad interest in and awareness of equity markets. Clearly societal norms play a large role in determining whether a shareholder culture will emerge in a particular country, and what it will look like if it does. Thus, a second reason why norms are important in corporate governance is because they influence how businesses are actually run. Senior managers who think that dividends are more important than job security and that shareholders, not other stakeholders, own the company are going to run a company very differently than are senior managers who think that companies must maintain stable employment even if they must curtail dividends to do so and who do not think that shareholders are more special than any of the myriad other groups with claims on the cash flows generated by the corporation.

A strong shareholder wealth maximization norm leads to a business environment more tolerant of risk-taking by managers. As the firm's residual claimants, shareholders are not entitled to any distributions of corporate profits unless, and until, all of the fixed claims on the cash flows on the corporation have been satisfied. But once those fixed claims have been satisfied, shareholders are entitled to everything else. Thus, it is entirely understandable that shareholders have a preference for corporate strategies that promise high returns at concomitantly high risk, while fixed claimants prefer low-risk strategies that yield correspondingly low returns but are highly likely to result in the repayment of the corporation's fixed claimants. Accordingly, a strong shareholder wealth maximization norm is likely to translate into managers pursuing riskier projects than other corporate norms.

Note that this analysis turns on its head the oft-heard assertion that U.S. managers' concern for shareholders causes them to focus too much on the short term. In fact, the opposite is true. Fixed claimants can reduce risk and uncertainty by shortening the maturity schedule of their loans. By frequently rolling over their loans, creditors lower their risk. Shareholders, on the other hand, will have a higher tolerance for riskier, long-term projects, especially since the expected returns from such projects will be immediately reflected in the current price of their shares on a discounted present value basis.

Rank-and-file workers, along with creditors and other fixed claimants, are likely to prefer a corporate environment that generates the steady, low-risk, low variance cash flows that maximize the probability that the firm will be able to meet its fixed obligations. Shareholders, on the other hand, will prefer higher variance projects. A simple example illustrates the point. Suppose a payment in the amount of $50 million is due to fixed claimants (lenders, workers, and so forth) at the end of the year. Suppose that everything beyond the mentioned amount will go the shareholders. Fixed claimants faced with a choice between a project that is certain to generate a payout of $60 million and a second project that has 0.5 chance of generating a payout of $40 million and a 0.5 chance of generating a payment of $140 million inevitably will want to pursue the project that will generate the $60 million in revenue with certainty. In contrast, this project is worth only $10 million to the shareholders (as residual claimants the shareholders get the $10 million that remains from the $60 million after the fixed claimants are paid the $50 million that they are owed). The shareholders, therefore, will strongly prefer the second investment, which has a value to them of $45 million ([0.5 × 0] + [0.5 × $90 million]). The second project, however, is also worth $45 million to the fixed claimants, which is $5 million less than the $50 million value the fixed claimants put on the first project ([0.5 × $40 million] + [0.5 × $50 million]).

Managers in a country like the United States or the United Kingdom, where the dominant norms favor shareholder wealth maximization, are more likely to favor the second project. Managers in Japan, Germany, and France, who are more focused on non-shareholder constituencies, are more likely to favor the first project. Of course, managers' choice of projects is influenced by many factors in addition to norms like the shareholder primacy norm. The incentive structure created by executive compensation schemes, for example, clearly will influence managerial behavior as well. In the above example, for instance, an incentive compensation scheme laden with stock options and performance bonuses might incline the manager toward the riskier investment, particularly if the compensation arrangement includes a generous golden parachute or severance arrangement that could cushion the blow from a negative result. On the other hand, a compensation arrangement dominated by salary and deferred fixed compensation benefits would incline an executive to pursue strategies more in line with the interests of the firm's fixed claimants.

Significantly, it seems at least as likely that the prevailing system of norms will influence the nature of the compensation scheme awarded to managers. At a minimum, it would seem likely that the remarkably high relative levels of executive compensation that one observes in the United States (discussed in chapter 15) could not be sustained unless the prevailing social norms were supportive or at least tolerant of such high compensation.

Looking at society's norms about business failure suggests another way that norms profoundly affect the conduct of corporate managers and directors. Some businesses inevitably fail, of course. Fraud and mismanagement surely account for some of these failures. But more often, business failure is explained by benign factors like technological change, changes in supply and demand conditions in an industry, and other factors that simply are beyond the power of managers and directors to control.

Besides being attentive and honest, the only way that corporate officers and directors can affect the probability of business failure is by reducing the amount of risks that they direct the business to take. Since shareholders can limit their participation in the firm-specific risk of the failure by diversifying their equity portfolios, they may want to increase managers' proclivities to take risks on their behalf. As a consequence, inducing managers to engage in the appropriate levels of risk-taking is one of the central challenges of corporate governance.

All of our sources of corporate governance, contract, law, and social norms, address the regulation of risk-taking, albeit in different ways. The contractual approach involves the use of executive compensation packages negotiated, at least in theory, between managers and the compensation committees of boards of directors, who often are heavily advised by compensation consultants. The legal approach to regulating risk-taking adopts many forms. Tax law rules prohibit corporations from taking tax deductions for executive compensation over $1 million, unless the compensation is demonstrably performance based.

Liability rules play a critical role in regulating risk-taking proclivities. Following relevant societal norms, liability rules in the United States encourage risk-taking, while liability rules in many EU countries do not. For example, the famous "business judgment rule" in U.S. corporate law creates a strong presumption that ordinary business decisions are made in good faith, on an informed basis, and in the best interest of the corporation. The business judgment rule acts as a shield on directors' liability, precisely for the purpose of encouraging risk-taking by officers and directors.

In contrast, in many other countries, including some prominent European countries like France and Italy, there is potential civil (and, in some countries, criminal) liability for directors of failed corporations. Clearly, such a liability threat produces marked disincentives for risk-taking by corporate decision-makers. A particularly potent device for dampening risk-taking is the rule, common in the EU, requiring companies to maintain capital in perpetuity in an amount equal to one-half of the capital originally contributed by shareholders or else reorganize or liquidate. Thus, for example, if a company starts life with €100,000 in capital (generally defined as the value of assets minus liabilities of the company), should the capitalization of the company ever fall below €50,000, the directors of the company would be required to liquidate or add additional capital. If the original capitalization were not maintained, and the company failed, the directors would be personally liable for any losses suffered by the company's creditors.

These profound differences in liability regimes reflect equally profound differences in norms that critically affect corporate governance by influencing corporate decision-making. The nature of prevailing norms, for example, will determine how the careers of senior managers and directors will be affected if they are at the helm when a business fails. In the United States, it is quite common for the careers of top managers to survive not just one but several business failures; an executive can still rise to the top of a major corporation despite having been at the helm of several failed businesses. In many European countries, by contrast, being the CEO of a company that fails inevitably ends one's career.

In the United States, cultural factors create a corporate governance environment in which the personal cost of business failure is relatively low, because such failure does not involve shaming sanctions as it does elsewhere. The importance of the lack of social stigma associated with business failure cannot be overestimated. As David Skeel has interestingly observed, "corporations and corporate directors are enmeshed in communities in which reputation does indeed matter. The directors of large U.S. corporations are, in the words of one shareholder activist, 'the most reputationally sensitive people in the world.'"[17] How a business failure affects the reputation of managers is, therefore, an important determinant of how much tolerance such managers are likely to have for risk-taking. In the United States, where the social stigma and shame associated with bankruptcy are quite low, managers are likely to be more willing to pursue risky projects that managers would never consider if failure would result not only in an immediate economic loss but also in the ruination of the managers' careers and permanent social stigma in the close-knit community of corporate managers.

These norms influence the content of corporate governance rules. They also influence corporate conduct, especially risk-taking proclivities of corporate managers. Norms that encourage honesty and a strong work ethic may lead to a diminution in shirking and other inefficient corporate behavior. On the other hand, norms that encourage the creation of artificial, time-consuming, costly, and meaningless procedures, or that venerate deal-making for the sake of making deals rather than enhancing value, are inefficient and welfare-diminishing.

A third reason why norms are important is because they appear to emerge spontaneously without the intervention into markets. Contracts, including intrafirm corporate contracts like charters and bylaws, evolve through complex market processes in which contract terms emerge in response to market demand. Contract terms are priced, and innovations are highly prized as they are in other contractual settings.

As public choice theory has amply demonstrated, the contours of legal rules, including the legal rules related to corporate governance, reflect the outcome of behavior in political markets that conforms to standard economic models. Law is a product generated in a Darwinian process in which interest groups express their demand for law by offering, or withholding, political support to politicians who require such support to survive. Law comes to reflect the market-clearing equilibrium generated by the interaction of multiple interest groups. As applied to corporate governance, we see that corporate law rules benefit discrete interest groups like managers, lawyers, and investment bankers, as well as shareholders.[18]

Because markets are the source of the contractual rules of corporate governance as well as the statutory rules of corporate governance, norms are a distinctive component of the corporate governance infrastructure. Unlike private contracts and law, norms emerge in a non-market process. In other words, while norms can help or hinder the functioning of markets, it is far from clear how much influence markets have on the development of societal norms. Markets affect norms to at least some extent, as will be shown below. Markets affect law, and law affects norms, so clearly there is some feedback effect between markets and norms. But norms appear to develop and evolve spontaneously, at least to some extent.

Even the most seminal and important contemporary writings on norms, including those of Francis Fukuyama,[19] James Coleman,[20] and Robert Putnam,[21] consider norms to be an endogenous feature in society. Since Alexis de Tocqueville, who in *Democracy in America* coined the phrase "art of association" to describe Americans' propensity for civil association, it has been understood that informal norms generate for society a valuable asset that Fukuyama calls "social capital."

Social capital has a direct and important role to play in corporate governance. Social capital reflects the economic value of societal norms. Norms are a low-cost substitute for other corporate governance mechanisms, like contracts and law. As Fukuyama has observed, "the economic function of social capital is to reduce the transaction costs associated with formal coordination mechanisms like contracts, hierarchies, bureaucratic rules, and the like."[22]

More important, from a corporate governance perspective, contracts and law simply are not possible unless a sufficient amount of social capital has been generated by informal norms. Without social capital, people will not obey laws or abide by contracts when it is not in their personal interest to do so. In the absence of sufficient levels of social capital, the trust necessary for investment will not exist.

Virtually all forms of economic activity across markets, from voluntary compliance with income tax law to compliance with ordinary commercial contracts, require social capital. Not only are people more inclined to perform their part of a contract to the extent that they think that their counterparty will perform, but people also are more inclined to pay their taxes to the extent that they think that other taxpayers also will comply with the tax laws.[23] But nowhere is social capital more important than in corporate governance because of the vague, almost wholly unspecified nature of the relationship between shareholders and the companies in which they invest. Because shareholders have so few specific contractual or legal protections, their relationships with the firms in which they invest is necessarily characterized by high levels of trust. Strict enforcement of contracts in litigation can do much to remedy noncompliance with well-specified legal obligations as articulated in the provisions of the income tax code, or in a commercial contract, or even in a loan agreement or a bond covenant. In contrast, however, shareholders have little to litigate, not only because it is difficult to monitor the effort expended by management but also because even if managerial effort could be monitored, shareholders, lacking contractual payment rights, have little to litigate about if their investments languish.

In a society with large amounts of social capital in the form of what Fukuyama calls "instantiated informal norms,"[24] these social norms become important sources of corporate governance rules that not only help investors but make capital formation possible. As Marcel Kahan has observed, the way that a manager runs his company affects his power, prestige, and status. Managers of companies that perform well receive much coveted recognition, prestige, and status in the close-knit communities in which they operate.[25] Kahan, however, takes this observation as support for the proposition that norms are not important for corporate governance. His argument is that the quest for power, prestige and status, and the desire to avoid embarrassment, rather than norms, are what supplement contract and law in providing incentives for managers to perform well. The problem with this analysis is that it misses the point that norms are what create the social environment in which managers care about how they are perceived in society. In other words, doing well by shareholders does not universally confer the benefits of power, prestige, and status that Kahan describes. Rather, only in societies with a sufficient stock of social capital will managers actually perceive that there are any benefits from using shareholders' money to benefit shareholders rather than themselves or their families.

Social scientists studying development assert that a so-called radius of trust describes the size of the group whose interactions are characterized by high degrees of trust, and among whom norms of cooperation are operative.[26] People do not much care about, or trust, people outside this radius of trust. For example, as Fukuyama points out, "in Chinese parts of East Asia and much of Latin America, social capital resides largely in large families and a rather narrow circle of personal friends."[27] Not only do people distrust those outside their circle of trust, but they feel that a lower standard of moral behavior applies outside their kinship group. This, in turn, generates destructive norms that tolerate corruption. In such societies, public and corporate officials are not concerned with their reputations outside their immediate group, and group members put in positions of trust feel "entitled to steal" on behalf of their families.[28]

Thus, social capital that encompasses a large radius of trust is a necessary precondition to the organization of a publicly held firm characterized by the separation of share ownership from managerial control. Unless the shareholders of a corporation are thought by managers to be within this radius of trust, the managers will feel no obligation to maximize the value of the firm on the shareholders' behalf. Worse, such managers will steal from shareholders to the extent that they think that they can get away with it. Recognizing that they are outside this "radius of trust," rational investors inevitably respond by declining to invest in companies run by such managers.

Thus Marcel Kahan is right that incentives related to social status such as the desire for prestige and the fear of being shamed are important sources of corporate governance. He misses, however, the important idea that the system of norms in a society is what determines the extent to which managers actually *care* about being known for competence and honesty or fear being labeled as a crook. To illustrate this point, imagine that market participants consist of two groups. The first group is made up of people who are highly reputationally sensitive. They care deeply about how they are viewed by the people with whom they interact in the marketplace. They are very concerned about whether they appear on *Fortune* magazine's list of the best CEOs in America or on lists of the worst-performing managers.

The second group is made up of what we might call a deviant subculture whose members feel free to flaunt the norms of the dominant community. This group will exhibit what the members of the first group would regard as immoral behavior because they do not embrace their norms.

Norms are a valuable corporate governance device for the members of the first group, but not for members of the second. People are willing to make equity investments in companies run by members of the first, "reputationally sensitive" group, but not in companies run by members of the second group, which is populated by members of the deviant subculture. The emergence of the modern publicly held corporation depends on the emergence of what Richard McAdams describes as a shared and publicized consensus in society that certain behavior is valued and certain behavior is unacceptable.[29] Maximizing value for shareholders is the behavior that must be valued, and shirking, stealing, and engaging in other shareholder wealth-diminishing activities must be viewed as unacceptable.

In a society of any size, complexity, and diversity, it simply will not be possible for the members of a group characterized by reputational sensitivity to eliminate the deviant subculture. Since the members of the deviant subculture, by definition, do not care about how they are perceived by the dominant group, the usual shaming techniques employed to enforce norms will not succeed. However, it may be possible for a deviant subculture to eliminate the reputationally sensitive group, or at least to make it impossible for that group to succeed.

A company trying to raise capital by selling stock will be deeply concerned about whether the managers of the company are perceived as reputationally sensitive or as reputationally insensitive. Rational companies will select managers whom investors perceive as reputationally sensitive, since rational investors will not invest in companies that they think are run by people who are outside the culture embracing shareholder wealth maximization as a norm. In other words, for public companies to succeed, a sufficient amount of social capital is important to produce a managerial talent pool made up of people who are reputationally sensitive.

But the existence of a talented, reputationally sensitive pool of potential managers is a necessary, but not sufficient, condition for the emergence of a public company. In addition, because societies are populated by deviants as well as the reputationally sensitive, potential investors must have a way to be able to distinguish reputationally sensitive managers from other managers. This is not an easy task since deviants have strong incentives to masquerade as reputationally sensitive. Thus, it is not surprising that seniority and experience are heavily favored in selecting corporate officers, directors, and outside advisors since these characteristics provide assurances to investors that managers are reputationally sensitive.

This analysis goes a long way toward explaining one of the greatest mysteries in corporate governance, which is the seemingly exorbitant pay of U.S. corporate executives. If, as I posit is the case, the pool of potential CEOs is limited to people who have demonstrated that they are highly reputationally sensitive, those with proven experience as CEOs will predictably be in great demand. The existence of discrete industry subcultures will exacerbate this tendency, as shareholders in steel companies will try to recruit executives in that industry and shareholders in automobile companies will try to recruit executives in that industry. Consistent with that analysis, research by economists Xavier Gabaix and Augustin Landier shows that executive compensation in different industry sectors grows along with the role of that industry sector in the overall economy as measured by capitalization. As a particular sector of the economy grows, so too will the demand for executives in that sector, forcing executive compensation upward.[30] This explanation of executive compensation appears more plausible than the alternative hypothesis that top executives of the largest multinational corporations have skills that are highly asset specific, particularly in light of the absence of any explanation for what these details might be.

It is well known that outside advisors such as lawyers, investment bankers, and accounting firms play an important role in corporate governance. Such advisors are known as "reputational intermediaries," because they are thought to be reputationally sensitive. Their association with a group of entrepreneurs adds value by signaling a willingness by the reputational intermediaries to invest their reputational capital in the entrepreneurs' venture. An implication of the analysis here is that these "gatekeepers" are only likely to be effective to the extent that they remain reputationally sensitive. As explained more fully in the subsequent chapters, the decline in reputational sensitivity among gatekeepers goes a long way toward explaining corporate governance meltdowns like Enron.

The analysis here suggests that an important role for the various mechanisms and institutions of corporate governance is to foster the production of social capital through rules and institutions that enable market participants to distinguish between reputationally sensitive managers and deviant managers. Fraud penalties for false or misleading disclosure and SEC penalties that feature lifetime bars from the securities industry raise the costs to people masquerading as reputationally sensitive when they are not. Indeed, I will argue that a certain amount of social capital is necessary in order for administrative agencies like the SEC to function at all. This is because such agencies, which rely exclusively on weak civil penalties, coupled with shaming, have few, if any, sanctions at their disposal to deter misbehavior by members of the deviant subculture.

MARKETS, INSTITUTIONS, AND CORPORATE GOVERNANCE

As a practical matter, corporate governance is effectuated by a number of public and private institutions and mechanisms that interact to enforce (and sometimes to undermine) the contracts, laws, and social norms discussed above. These mechanisms and institutions directly and indirectly affect contracts, law, and social norms in a variety of ways that heretofore have been poorly understood.

Public corporate governance institutions include the states, which promulgate corporate law, and the SEC. Private, market-based corporate governance devices include the market for corporate control and executive compensation, and informal mechanisms and institutions like whistle-blowing and insider trading. Nongovernmental organizations like commercial and investment banks and credit-rating agencies also participate in corporate governance because their activities influence corporate conduct. The various institutions and mechanisms of corporate governance vary enormously in terms of their organizational forms and existential motivations, but they share the common characteristic of contributing to the control of agency costs faced by investors in public companies.

As we will see in the chapters that follow, the institutions of corporate governance in the United States have become dangerously politicized. This politicization threatens to undermine the extent to which these institutions support the operation of the contracts, laws, and social norms that are critical to the governance of the public corporation.

Regulations have caused the cartelization and ossification of important institutions like the accounting industry and the credit-rating industry. Other politically motivated rules have dramatically hobbled the market for corporate control, which historically has been the cornerstone of corporate governance. The observation generated by this book is that the politicization of the process of corporate governance has produced massively perverse results. Specifically, the corporate governance institutions that have performed the worst have been rewarded, while the institutions that have performed the best have been hampered by legal rules designed to impede their ability to operate. Rather than producing genuine reform, the wave of corporate governance, accounting, and capital markets scandals of the 1990s has generated political responses that benefit narrow interest groups and harm investors. Politics, not economics, determines which corporate governance devices are favored and which are not. As a consequence, the most effective corporate governance devices tend to be disfavored, while ineffective mechanisms are rewarded in the regulatory process.

CHAPTER 3

INSTITUTIONS AND MECHANISMS
OF CORPORATE GOVERNANCE

A Taxonomy

In the previous chapter, contracts, law, and social norms were identified as the three components of corporate governance. The one thing that these three components of corporate governance have in common is that they are not self-enforcing. For this reason institutions and mechanisms are required as enforcement tools.

The major corporate governance institutions include the accounting firms that audit public companies, the credit-rating agencies that determine whether their debt is "investment grade" or not, the market for corporate control that disciplines management of poorly run companies, the organized stock exchanges that promulgate corporate governance rules, the market for IPOs of company shares, and the SEC itself, which regulates markets, oversees corporate disclosure, and, increasingly, formulates corporate governance policies for public companies.

The political side of the story that emerges is sobering. Darwinian processes have conspired to produce certain perverse results that have gone unnoticed. Specifically, the corporate governance institutions that have performed the worst—the accounting firms, the SEC, and the credit-rating agencies—are thriving, shielded from the consequences of their poor performance by a regulatory system that has rewarded poor performance.

By contrast, the market institutions that have done the best and that hold the most promise for maximizing value for investors have been undermined and thwarted by decades of protectionist legislation and the perpetuation of negative stereotypes. In particular, the market for corporate control has been hobbled by statutes and judicial decisions that allow incumbent managers to escape the discipline of a hostile takeover. And short sellers, who perform an extremely valuable corporate governance role by ferreting out fraud and disciplining bad managers, are thwarted by being unjustly branded as being part of a deviant subculture within the securities industry.

It is highly unlikely that the perverse outcomes described here are entirely random. Rather, these outcomes are more likely the result of a series of unrelated individual political decisions that were made under conditions of crisis, in response to political pressure, or as a result simply of following the path of least (political) resistance. Whatever the reason for the outcomes catalogued here, however, one thing is clear: The consequence of this unfortunate series of decisions is a massive diminution in the quality of corporate governance.

On the economic side of the equation, the story is considerably brighter. Private sector entrepreneurs have incentives to create institutions and market mechanisms that address problems of corporate governance because doing so is profitable. Thus, we see that hedge funds and private equity funds are relatively recent market responses to the opportunities created by inefficiencies produced by government regulation of traditional mechanisms of corporate governance like the market for corporate control.

Measuring the quality of corporate governance systems is not an easy task. Even at their best, corporate governance mechanisms do not assure ordinary investors that they will receive adequate returns on their investments. Rather, corporate governance mechanisms, at best, increase the odds that shareholders will receive a fair deal, where "fair deal" is defined as investment returns commensurate with the risks associated with their investments. An advantage of this measurement metric for corporate governance systems is that, unlike most other approaches, which speak in terms of "assuring adequate returns," the approach focused on both risk and return gives proper respect to the critical idea that risk-taking is important.

Large returns are generally not possible in competitive capital markets without taking large risks. For this reason, corporate governance systems must be careful to penalize fraud and deceit rather than "mere" failure. Indeed, I would go further. Not only should failure not be punished, it also should not be stigmatized by society. Honest entrepreneurs and managers who fail are punished enough by the market.

Of course, hindsight bias is a problem to be reckoned with. Hindsight bias is the term psychologists use to refer to people's firmly embedded inclination to view any event that has transpired as having been predictable to begin with. This is a bias because people's perceptions of the probability of an event occurring are influenced by their knowledge of what actually occurred. In fact, however, merely because an event occurred does not mean that it was reasonable to expect that the event would occur. Hindsight bias is a particular problem for regulators attempting to fashion sanctions for corporate conduct because of the proclivity to blame entrepreneurs and managers for bad results. We should guard against the temptation to blame managers and entrepreneurs for bad outcomes because we are prone to ascribe unreasonable powers of foresight to managers after the fact. As noted at the outset, the institutions of corporate governance are numerous and varied. The list includes all sorts of gatekeepers such as lawyers, investment bankers, and accountants, as well as corporate boards of directors and financial institutions, which monitor companies to which they have loaned money. One of the goals of this book is to provide a systematic approach to analyzing the various institutions and mechanisms of corporate governance that regulate corporate managers.

First, from an economic perspective, corporate governance mechanisms can be evaluated on the basis of how effective they are in controlling corporate deviance. Second, from a legal perspective, corporate governance mechanisms can be evaluated on the basis of how they are regulated. Finally, corporate governance mechanisms can be evaluated on the basis of how they are viewed from a societal perspective: are societal norms reinforcing effective corporate governance mechanisms.

Looking at both the economic and legal characteristics of various corporate governance devices allows us to see the relationship between economic efficiency and regulatory intervention. Because different corporate governance mechanisms are regulated in different ways, we can examine whether regulation supports or discourages effective corporate governance, just as we can examine whether prevailing norms support or discourage effective corporate governance.

For both norms and regulation, the relationship between the efficiency of corporate governance devices and the extent to which they are encouraged or discouraged is complex, but it is not random. Rather, in my view, the corporate governance devices that are the most effective tend to be ripe targets for regulation, while the corporate devices that are ineffective tend to be ignored by regulators. This is sometimes, but not always, true for norms.

The process by which this takes place is, therefore, evolutionary. A corporate governance device typically will attract little or no attention from regulators at the beginning of its institutional existence. As time goes on, however, it may attract attention from regulators. This, in turn, leads to regulation that causes a concomitant decrease in the efficacy of the institution as a mechanism of corporate governance that is capable of controlling corporate deviancy (agency costs).

To provide a succinct summation of the arguments about the contract, law, and social norms affecting corporate governance that are presented in this book, the twelve chapters that follow analyze the most important institutions and mechanisms of the corporate governance infrastructure. The bottom line is clear. Social and legal institutions are encouraging the least effective mechanisms and institutions of corporate governance and discouraging those that are most effective. The recent spate of corporate governance scandals is evidence of this thesis.

For example, the most effective of these institutions, the market for corporate control, has been stifled by regulations that shift the balance of power away from bidders and target firm shareholders toward incumbent management. Another effective corporate governance tool, the IPO, is seldom used because of litigation risk and regulatory burdens. By contrast, relatively ineffective institutions, such as administrative agencies, credit-rating agencies and even boards of directors, enjoy regulatory "subsidies." Enhancements and subsidies to these ineffective institutions are presented by regulators and politicians as responses to public demand for improvements in corporate governance.

In this way, the increasing salience of corporate governance as a political issue has led to regulations that have transformed the landscape of corporate governance. Specifically, accounting firms, credit-rating agencies, and stock exchanges used to play a large and useful role in the governance of publicly held firms. Over time, however, regulation has undermined the effectiveness of these institutions. Where there once was market-driven demand for the services of auditors, rating agencies, and organized stock exchanges, the demand for these services is now a construct of complex regulatory regimes that not only require public companies to purchase the services generated by these firms, but effectively cartelize the industries that provide these services. In the case of accounting firms and credit-rating agencies, regulators have cartelized the industry by erecting barriers to entry that limit to a handful the number of firms that can compete to provide these services. In the case of the organized stock exchanges, regulations not only dramatically restrict entry, they also limit competition and innovation by coordinating the internal governance rules of the exchanges.

Hovering somewhere above this complex and depressing picture is the SEC, which has been generously rewarded for its own non-performance. Responding to political pressure from its constituents on congressional appropriations committees and among investment bankers and lawyers representing both themselves and management, the SEC has pressed for changes in corporate governance rules that are both costly and ineffectual but help the SEC expand its own constituency. The new rules regarding expanding shareholders' access to the corporate election machinery and the governance of mutual funds both fit this description. They purport to be devices aimed at improving corporate governance, but, in fact, they are likely to be highly ineffectual.

TABLE 3.1
Corporate Governance Mechanisms

Corporate Governance Mechanism	Effective?	Encouraged?
The Securities and Exchange Commission and the Organized Stock Exchanges	No	Yes
Boards of Directors	No	Yes
The Market for Corporate Control	Yes	No
Initial Public Offerings	Yes	No
The Accounting Rules and the Accounting Industry	No	Yes
Litigation Governance: Derivative and Class Action Suits	No	Yes
Insider Trading and Short Selling	Yes	No
Whistle-blowing	No	Yes
Shareholder Voting	No	Yes
Credit-Rating Agencies	No	Yes
Stock Market Analysts	No	Yes
Hedge Funds	Yes	No
Banks and Other Fixed Claimants	Yes	No

CHAPTER 4

BOARDS OF DIRECTORS

Perhaps the most basic principle of corporate law in the United States is that corporations are controlled by boards of directors, rather than shareholders. The board of directors is at the epicenter of U.S. corporate governance. Specifically, under U.S. law, corporations are managed by or under the direction of boards of directors, making the directors literally the governors of the corporation. The intuition that directors add value is strong and deeply held. That intuition is not challenged here. What is challenged is the deeply held assumption that traditional directors add value by serving shareholders as independent monitors of managers. It is more likely that directors nominated and elected through traditional board processes serve managers by supporting them. Sometimes, particularly when managers have useful and constructive strategic advice for management, directors add value for shareholders. At other times, however, such as when managers need directors to approve managers' aggressive salary requirements or when managers need insulation from the market for corporate control or pesky institutional investors, so-called independent directors at best do not reduce shareholder value, and at worst they destroy it.

Much is expected of boards of directors. The American Law Institute *Principles of Corporate Governance* provides that the directors of publicly traded corporations are responsible for overseeing and evaluating the business; selecting, compensating, and, where necessary, replacing senior executives; and reviewing the firm's financial objectives and its accounting.[1] The board has the authority to manage the business of the corporation and can initiate strategic plans and cause the corporation to pursue, or to change, its business plans. The board has plenary authority to act for the corporation in all matters not requiring shareholder approval.

Regulators, stock exchanges, corporate governance mavens, and plaintiff class action lawyers articulate very high standards for directors. And these groups point their fingers at board members when things go poorly. Strangely, however, while no one seriously thinks that boards of directors should be personally liable or even morally responsible for everything that happens in the companies on whose boards they serve, there is stunningly little agreement regarding the contours of directors' responsibility.

In the United States, directors' power to manage the business and affairs of the corporation is virtually absolute. This makes directors, along with managers, the natural focus of inquiry when companies fail or underperform. And it is indisputable that even the best-run companies can fail. Directors also are the natural focus of attention when a company is rocked, or ruined, by fraud. It is also understood that even with close monitoring by diligent and conscientious accountants and directors, fraud can occur. Thus, although there is an inexorable proclivity to blame directors, it has long been recognized that as long as directors act in good faith, directors will not be legally liable for bad outcomes. Instead, it is well established that "redress for failures that arise from faithful management must come from the markets, through the action of shareholders, and the free flow of capital," rather than from the courts.[2] As courts have made plain, directors can comply with their fiduciary duties, thereby avoiding personal liability for events that cause grave harm to the company, and still fail to satisfy what courts have described as "what is expected by the best practices of corporate governance."[3] These expectations constitute societal norms. Directors suffer when they fail to conform to these norms.

Since the mid-1980s, state legislatures have gone even further, authorizing corporations to add to their charters provisions exculpating directors (though not officers) from personal liability for breaches of fiduciary duties involving negligence and lack of due care, so long as there was no intention to harm the corporation.[4] These statutes permitting director exculpation were enacted in the wake of heightened concern about directors' personal liability. The concern about personal liability was generated by the Delaware Supreme Court's decision in *Smith v. Van Gorkom* (discussed below and in chapter 1), which held the members of the board of directors of a large public company personally liable for failing to exercise due care in recommending the approval of a takeover bid for the company. The new statutes suggest that directors will avoid personal liability even when they fail to exercise due care, as long as they are not disloyal to the corporations.

While directors are, of course, intensely concerned about their personal liability for negligence or malfeasance, this is not their only concern. They also are concerned about their reputations as leaders and their standing in the community. In other words, the prevailing norms of director behavior are stricter and less forgiving than the liability rules by which directors are evaluated.

The prevailing theory among policymakers in the United States is that increasing the quantity and improving the quality of board oversight is the key to improving corporate governance. Thus, the response of policymakers to the public concern about the Enron-era wave of corporate scandals was simultaneously to blame the Enron board of directors and to exhort future boards to perform more and better oversight of corporate managers.[5] Courts similarly have emphasized that board composition is an important factor in determining how much deference to give corporate decisions made with board approval. Reliance on the ability of future boards to outperform the Enron board are at the heart of the post-Enron corporate governance environment, as reflected in the new rules promulgated for public companies by the National Association of Securities Dealers, the New York Stock Exchange, and by Congress in the Sarbanes-Oxley Act.

Sarbanes-Oxley and related rule-making initiatives at the New York Stock Exchange and the National Association of Securities Dealers represent responses to the Enron-era corporate scandals. The new rules do not add many legal responsibilities; rather, as we would predict, they simply import more norms from the legal culture into the business culture. The new rules reflect the preference of the legal culture for rules that specify structure and process rules over substantive rules. For example, the new rules stress that boards' committee structures must follow a particular organizational framework, featuring an audit committee, a compensation committee, and a nominating committee. The rules further stress that these committees, along with a majority of the entire board, must be made up of independent directors, a term the rules define with significantly more detail than clarity.

Monitoring and Managing

It is well understood that corporate boards of directors have a dual role in corporate governance. They are simultaneously supposed to serve as advisors to senior officers about management issues and as monitors of management. Simply put, directors are supposed to serve both a management function and monitoring function. However, the policy implications of the existence of this dual role are not well understood. In particular, the issue of whether it is possible for board members to serve in both of these roles has not been thoroughly explored.

As part of their core responsibilities to shareholders, corporate directors also have several discrete obligations. Perhaps chief among these is the requirement that directors become significantly involved in management when the corporation is experiencing a crisis, such as the loss of the CEO or the emergence of a corporate scandal that threatens the corporation's survival. Directors clearly "earn their pay" during these sorts of crises and generally appear to perform well. Another traditional chore for independent directors in American corporate governance has been to approve transactions between the corporation and interested directors or officers. The job of the independent directors in this context is to ensure that the corporation is not disadvantaged by the directors or officers on both sides of the transaction. Directors also have generally succeeded in performing this limited, straightforward function.

But in recent years, directors' roles have expanded from these more traditional, episodic responsibilities to being responsible for both monitoring management and participating in management decisions in the ordinary course of a firm's business. The question addressed in this chapter is whether it is unreasonable to expect directors to perform both of these functions simultaneously because there is a fundamental and irreconcilable conflict between the monitoring function and the management function. To be sure, this problem has received some attention. For example, board members themselves have recognized that the dual role of monitoring and advising creates tension and conflict. According to one survey, "too much emphasis on monitoring tends to create a rift between nonexecutive and executive directors."[6]

The problem, however, goes beyond concerns about the personal dynamics between outside directors and senior management, though such concerns are entirely legitimate. The reason that the dual role of directors creates a fundamental, inescapable conflict for directors is because directors who are monitors inevitably are required to monitor themselves. When directors give advice in time period 1, they face a conflict in time period 2 when they are called upon to evaluate decisions made by management in time period 1, which were made wholly or partially on the basis of the earlier advice the directors themselves provided.

This time-inconsistency problem was well understood by the framers and by constitutional theorists then and now. As Madison observed in Federalist 10, "No man should be allowed to be a judge in his own cause, because his interest would certainly bias his judgment, and, not improbably, corrupt his integrity. With equal, nay with greater reason, a body of men is unfit to be both judges and parties at the same time." Unfortunately, the issue appears to be very poorly understood among academics and self-styled corporate governance experts.

The irreconcilable nature of the monitoring function and the management function is so profound that it affects the structural organization of the firm and requires important strategic choices by those organizing the corporation. Whether they know it or not, when lawmakers, stock exchanges, and other policymakers develop rules about board structure and composition, they are creating a board structure that facilitates either monitoring or managing by board members. For example, a board structure that emphasizes independent directors reflects a corporate governance policy of favoring monitoring over managing because the independent directors inevitably will have less information and therefore will be less able to contribute to managerial decision-making than will inside directors. On the other hand, a board structure designed to maximize the efficacy of board participation in strategic planning and other managerial functions will have relatively few outside independent directors. Instead, such boards will feature relatively more insiders who have sufficient information about the company to enable them to participate meaningfully in managerial decision-making.

Transnational differences in corporate governance structures can be explained on the basis of whether such structures are intended primarily to promote better governance in the form of better monitoring or better governance in the form of higher-quality advice for management. For example, the U.S. board structure, which has a unitary board of directors made up of a very small number of insiders (often only one) and a large number of outsiders, reflects an implicit policy choice promoting a monitoring corporate governance paradigm rather than an advising corporate governance paradigm. In contrast, in the United Kingdom, the board structure features a much higher number of insiders on the board. This structure reflects a corporate governance paradigm focused on forming and refining strategy and otherwise advising management, since clearly, the large number of insiders on the boards of U.K. companies undermines the capacity of the board to conduct credible outside monitoring.

The separation of the board into two separate governance structures is common in civil law companies. This board structure, which consists of a supervisory (monitoring) board and a management (managerial) board, represents a clear attempt to eliminate the problems associated with vesting the board's managerial and monitoring functions in a single group of people. This explains why shareholders sometimes prefer a dual board system to a single board system.[7]

Utilization of the committee structure has been suggested as a way of reducing conflict on single-tier boards of directors. Specifically, board committees are said to permit the separation of the monitoring function from the advisory function.[8] The assertion that board members somehow can function as independent monitors when serving on committees but then magically rejoin the management team when they are meeting as part of the full board rather than on the committee seems highly doubtful. It seems more likely that some board members, regardless of their committee affiliation, will view their distance from management, and resulting ability to contribute to the value of the corporation through monitoring, as the source of their value to the enterprise. Other board members will view their experience in and ability to work with management as the source of their value added to the business.

Financial economists have argued that management's view of whether the board is serving more as friendly internal advisor or whether it is serving as detached outside monitor will influence the quantity of information provided to the board. On this view, the corporation benefits if management reveals more information to the board because the increased disclosure enables the board to provide better advice to management. The CEO, however, has private incentives to refrain from revealing information to the board, to the extent that such disclosure allows the board to monitor management more effectively and more intensively.[9] In other words, managers who disclose more to their boards receive better advice but are scrutinized more closely. Renee Adams and Daniel Ferreira have developed a model that shows that management-friendly boards can be optimal because they increase the quality of the advice that directors provide to managers.[10]

These results, however, critically depend on the assumption that the benefits to shareholders of the increase in firm value from the better advice are greater than the costs to shareholders of the decrease in firm value from the lower-quality monitoring performed by management-friendly but information-rich directors.

Sarbanes-Oxley attempts to deal with the problem of auditor capture by corporate management by making it clear that outside auditors should be selected, compensated by, and report to the audit committee of the board of directors, rather than to management, as was previously done. Ironically, Sarbanes-Oxley, in focusing on the problem of capture, evinces a clear recognition that the capture phenomenon is a problem in corporate governance that must be reckoned with. Unfortunately, the statute addresses only the problem of auditor capture (and rather ineffectively, as discussed in chapter 11), ignoring the more profound problem of board capture, which is the focus of this chapter.

Ironically, these responses to the collapse of Enron ignore what may be the most important lesson for corporate governance offered by the Enron debacle, which is that putting more reliance on any particular corporate governance mechanism increases investors' vulnerability to any failure in that mechanism. To the extent the U.S. system of corporate governance relies more heavily on board monitoring than other corporate governance systems, it is concomitantly more vulnerable when such monitors fail, as they did with Enron.

A crucial, but wholly unexamined, assumption underlying this foundational theory of corporate governance is that boards of directors can reasonably be expected to do what is required of them. This assumption cannot withstand scrutiny. If it is not possible to design a corporate governance system capable of identifying and selecting board members competent to perform the monitoring and oversight functions expected during the course of their tenure in office, then our reliance should shift from boards of directors to other mechanisms of corporate governance.

The basic point of this chapter is that the reliance on boards of directors by U.S. policymakers is wholly misplaced. Public choice, social psychology, and historical observation all suggest that boards can be counted on to be only as honest and effective as the managers they are supposed to supervise. The problem with boards is their unique susceptibility to capture by the managers they are supposed to monitor. The problem of capture is so pervasive and acute that no board, not even those that appear highly qualified, independent, and professional, should be relied upon entirely. Other, more objective corporate governance devices such as trading (chapter 7) and the market for corporate control (chapter 8) are required to supplement the monitoring and discipline ostensibly done by boards of directors.

The problem of board capture is so acute that it simply is not reasonable to construct a system of corporate governance that relies in any meaningful way on boards of directors to improve corporate performance or prevent corporate deviance. The analysis here draws on work I have done jointly with Arnoud Boot about the trade-off between objectivity and proximity in corporate governance.[11] In this work, we analyze corporate governance systems as providing mechanisms and institutions by which outside investors monitor managers. Some mechanisms and institutions of corporate governance, such as the market for corporate control, operate objectively through markets, while others, notably boards of directors, operate at close proximity through direct, personal, intrafirm interaction.

The utilization of both proximate and objective mechanisms of corporate governance has costs as well as benefits. The benefit of objective corporate governance mechanisms is that they are not subject to capture or other biases that can affect their ability to analyze and evaluate the performance of management. The cost of objective corporate governance mechanisms is that these mechanisms lack the high-quality, real-time information about corporate decisions and corporate performance that is available to proximate monitors. Thus, participants in the market for corporate control are objective, but the information they use to evaluate corporate performance is the publicly available information available to all market participants when and if the company chooses to disclose it.

In contrast, the benefit of proximate corporate governance mechanisms, of which boards of directors are the archetypal example, is that they have access to the highest-quality information about what is occurring within the corporation whenever they want to have it. Unlike objective monitors, proximate monitors do not learn about corporate plans and strategies when those plans and strategies are executed. Rather, proximate monitors learn about plans and strategies as they are being formulated and developed. The cost of proximate monitoring is that such monitoring is far more susceptible to capture than are objective monitors. As shown below, because proximate monitors, like directors, participate in corporate decision-making, they take ownership of the strategies and plans that the corporation pursues. In doing so, these proximate monitors are rendered incapable of objectively evaluating these strategies and plans later on.

In particular, boards of directors have long been responsible for selecting and evaluating the performance of top management. After top managers have been selected, retained, and promoted, boards become committed to and responsible for these managers. For this reason, as board tenure lengthens, it becomes increasingly less likely that boards will remain independent of the managers they are charged with monitoring.

Research in public choice and psychology strongly supports the claim that the potential for capture is inextricably associated with proximate monitoring such as that performed by boards of directors. Boards inevitably have close proximity to management, and this makes it highly likely that they will become captured by management. For example, the "theory of escalating commitments" predicts that board members identify strongly with management when they begin to agree with management's decisions. Earlier decisions, once made and defended, affect future decisions such that later decisions comport with earlier decisions.[12] As such, studies of the decision-making process during the Vietnam War era reveal that U.S. leaders paid more attention to new information compatible with their earlier decisions. They tended to ignore information that contradicted those earlier assumptions.[13] These studies suggest that once ideas and beliefs become ingrained in the minds of a board of directors, the possibility of altering those beliefs decreases substantially. Thomas Gilovich argues that "beliefs are like possessions" and "[w]hen someone challenges our beliefs, it is as if someone [has] criticized our possessions."[14]

Furthermore, social psychologists show that people tend to internalize their vocational roles. Occupational choices, such as the choice to accept employment as a corporate director, strongly influence our attitudes and values.[15] In the context of boards of directors, this influence means that board members tend to internalize management's perspective, which causes them to lose their objectivity. This problem does not arise with shareholders in public markets who have little or no contact with management, and thus does not generally affect the objectivity in participants in the market for corporate control.[16]

The cognitive bias that afflicts boards of directors and other proximate monitors involves what Daniel Kahneman and Dan Lovallo have described as the "inside view."[17] Like parents unable to view their children objectively or in a detached manner, proximate monitors tend to reject statistical reality and view their firms as above average. Objective monitors, by contrast, evaluate management decisions and compare incumbent management and rival management teams dispassionately, albeit on the basis of less information than is available to proximate monitors.

Similarly, proximate monitors may be afflicted with what is known as an "anchoring bias" that leads them to establish or "anchor" their initial views and opinions of management. This generally occurs during the time that a firm retains a monitor or recruits an outside director. Once a proximate monitor develops a positive view of management, that opinion is "anchored" and does not change.

In addition, proximate boards lack objectivity from an economic perspective. Board supervision tends to make the board jointly responsible with management for the state of the firm. The degree of joint responsibility depends on the level of the board's involvement with the firm. The board may abstain from corrective action because of "cognitive biases," but also for related reputational reasons. The board then abstains because corrective action may reveal the board's failure to take the proper course of action.[18] Boards may resist action for other reasons as well. They invest considerably in the information specific to the existing management. Changing management would then potentially dilute the value of this investment. Moreover, to a large extent, boards of directors resemble legislatures with essentially one interest group constituency: management. Management not only has the time and resources to cultivate directors, it is also the group that presents the board with the information necessary to make decisions. Over a wide range of issues, all management must do is present information in a way likely to generate support or to achieve effective capture of the board. It is not surprising, therefore, that boards often lack objectivity.[19]

The idea of board capture, of course, is not new. Oddly, however, analysis of the problem that the independence of ostensibly independent outside directors might be compromised by board capture has been confined to the relatively narrow issue of executive compensation. Consistent with the idea of board capture, in their work on executive compensation, Lucian Bebchuk, Jesse Fried, and David Walker have argued that "outside directors are connected to the executives by bonds of interest, collegiality, or affinity."[20] As a consequence of the "substantial influence" of the CEO and the CEO's management team over even nominally independent directors, bargaining over executive compensation does not, according to these commentators, even "approach the arm's length ideal. Rather, executives use their power to set a high level of compensation, and outside directors cooperate with management at least to some extent."[21]

This approach to executive compensation seems accurate. There is no reason, however, why this approach should be limited to the context of executive compensation. Management's self-interest in their compensation is obvious and palpable. If directors are "strongly inclined to defer to and support the CEO's judgment" about managers' compensation, they will be even more strongly inclined to defer to them on issues that do not involve such a direct conflict of interest.

The core problem is that, over time, with regard to both executive compensation and to other issues of corporate governance, all directors, including outside directors, eventually become reputationally linked to management. When management performs well, the directors who have selected, recruited, and compensated these managers are viewed as able. When management performs poorly, its performance casts a long and negative shadow on the directors. In other words, in a very real sense, directors assume "virtual ownership" of the managers they ostensibly monitor. Nowhere is this problem more acute than when the chairman of the board of a company serves concurrently as the company's CEO. In such cases, the person in charge of overseeing the CEO is, literally, the CEO himself. It is difficult to rationalize this organizational structure on shareholder welfare grounds in light of the fact that the dual CEO/chairman roles exacerbate the problem of capture and undermine the efficacy of the position of board chairman.

The fact that directors are literally responsible for selecting competent management makes it exceedingly difficult for directors to evaluate managers with any distance or objectivity. Unlike outside observers of the company, directors are being asked to evaluate their own decisions when they evaluate the decisions of managers. This may be literally true, as when directors are required to evaluate the results of strategic plans that they themselves have participated in formulating and developing. It may also be indirectly true, as when directors are required to evaluate the performance of managers whose competence they have already repeatedly endorsed over the years through their retention and promotion decisions related to those managers.

The problem of board capture is exacerbated by the fact that managers are, of course, fully aware that they are being evaluated by the directors. As such, managers have extremely high-powered incentives to present themselves, and their work, to directors in the most favorable light possible. This, in turn, strongly suggests that the flow of information from management to the board will be biased in ways that put management in the most favorable light possible and undermine the effectiveness of dissident or uncooperative directors.

For example, boards of directors frequently must make decisions under tight time constraints. Directors who challenge management's recommendations or who simply demand more information risk being branded as ineffective or accused of impeding the company's ability to respond to new opportunities efficiently. Donald Langevoort has summarized the situation as being one involving a trade-off between collegiality and commitment, claiming that "the more dissension there is in a group, the less committed members become to it." At the same time, Langevoort claims that research studies support the finding that "[t]he most productive boards are ones that have enough diversity to encourage the sharing of information and active consideration of alternatives, but enough collegiality to sustain mutual commitment and make consensus-reaching practicable within the tight time frames in which boards must operate."[22]

Another way of putting all of this is that a trade-off exists between true board independence and board productivity. Truly independent boards are willing to sacrifice the goal of consensus building so that they can roundly criticize management when necessary or appropriate. The sustained mutual commitment necessary to create a truly collegial board will be highly productive, but it will not be a hospitable environment for board members who want to dissent or even challenge the group consensus.

Similarly, managers also have strong incentives to develop close personal ties with directors, "wining and dining" them and urging upon them the idea that collegiality is an important part of a director's work. While directors are, of course, encouraged to ask tough questions, to meet among themselves independent of management, and to avail themselves of outside, independent sources of information about corporate performance and director competence, many directors face conflicting social norms that may make it difficult for them to perform the tough oversight function that they are theoretically supposed to perform. In particular, directors are supposed to be "team players" who "get along" with senior executives and their fellow directors, and perform their duties in an atmosphere of comfortable collegiality.

As Renee Jones has observed, "the prototypical director conduct is attributable to the social phenomenon of conformity: a willingness to comply with the wishes and opinions of others to avoid embarrassment or discomfort. This tendency toward conformity perpetuates many undesirable director traits which stand impervious to outside influence without external feedback and intervention."[23] The dilemma faced by directors appears to be intractable because any board that is too collegial is likely to be ineffective in monitoring managers, and any board that is insufficiently collegial is likely to be unproductive because it will be unable to reach needed consensus within the tight time constraints in which boards are required to operate.

In other words, certain widely embraced social norms that are generally highly important and constructive in most social and business contexts can be quite inefficient in the context of corporate boards of directors. These norms include not only that of collegiality discussed in the preceding paragraph, but also other fundamental norms such as loyalty, civility, transparency, and deference to authority.

The conflict between the operation of these norms in the boardroom and the aspirational view of directors as independent, objective monitors of senior management has gone almost wholly unrecognized. Challenging senior management can easily be construed as disloyal. Engaging in adversarial dialogue and suggesting that the performance of senior management be discussed in closed sessions may appear to be uncivil and non-transparent. Moreover, in the United States, where the board chairmen of 70 percent of public companies serve concurrently as CEO of the company, challenging senior management may be viewed as insubordinate.

Because boards of directors are group enterprises, board members also face collective action problems in decision-making that make it even more difficult for individual board members to challenge management or otherwise to act independently. Where a CEO makes a proposal to a group of board members, the first board member to raise questions or to disagree with management bears the greatest risk of being branded uncooperative or non-collegial. With this in mind, even when a board member disagrees with management, he has an incentive to remain quiet, hoping that another board member will speak first, thereby relieving the pressure on the remaining board members. Famed corporate gadfly Warren Buffett captured the problem well in a 2002 letter to shareholders of his company, Berkshire Hathaway. Note that Buffett uses the term "boardroom atmosphere" when he refers to the social norms that permeate the boardroom. Consistent with the analysis here, Buffett suggests that breaching these norms simply is not done be well-mannered people.

> Why have intelligent and decent directors failed so miserably? The answer lies not in inadequate laws—it's always been clear that directors are obligated to represent the interests of shareholders—but rather in what I'd call "boardroom atmosphere." It's almost impossible, for example, in a boardroom populated by well-mannered people, to raise the question of whether the CEO should be replaced. It's equally awkward to question a proposed acquisition that has been endorsed by the CEO, particularly when his inside staff and outside advisors are present and unanimously support his decision. (They wouldn't be in the room if they didn't.) Finally, when the compensation committee—armed, as always, with support from a high-paid consultant—reports on a megagrant of options to the CEO, it would be like belching at the dinner table for a director to suggest that the committee reconsider.[24]

Of course, it is widely understood that a lack of objectivity undermines the efficacy of directors as corporate governance mechanisms. Even special interest groups representing business, such as the Business Roundtable, have joined the SEC, the stock exchanges, and institutional investors in championing the idea of the ideal director as an independent director. Typical approaches to boards of directors advise that board members should "have a substantial degree of independence from management."[25] At precisely the same time that companies are being exhorted to become more independent, they also are being required to do more actual work with management and to take on more responsibility for decision-making within the company. Thus, boards of directors in the United States are being asked to be more independent at precisely the same time that they are being asked to interact more with management.

The problem of capture suggests that it may be very difficult for a board of directors to attain this goal because the risk of capture increases as the board becomes more closely linked—and aligned—with the managers they ostensibly are monitoring. While the core function of the board of directors remains that of overseeing and providing guidance to management, the job descriptions of directors have expanded significantly. Directors are now required to provide far more than the broad and rather vague oversight and guidance services they traditionally provided. In the post–Sarbanes-Oxley regulatory environment, directors must review the key risks in the company's businesses, supervise the company's management of those risks, and ensure the adequacy of the company's risk management programs. Traditional tasks, like reviewing and approving major transactions, have become significantly more time-consuming and involved as directors are required to establish that these reviews have followed adequate procedures.

As the hands-on management responsibilities of boards has increased, so too has the frequency of board interaction with management. In other words, boards of directors are being asked to become a much more integral part of the decision-making and financial reporting processes within firms at the same time that they are being asked to provide more objective evaluations of the quality of these decisions and processes. These expectations are unrealistic. Boards cannot be expected to be more objective in their evaluations of senior management at the same time that they are being required to become increasingly involved with senior management in the decisions about strategy and financial reporting.

In sum, the cognitive biases leading directors to identify with management are exacerbated by the increased expectations to manage the company that modern corporate governance regulation places on directors. All directors of modern public companies are supposed to be highly diligent and closely involved with the management of the firm. Directors who are doing their jobs properly are expected to have regular, if not almost daily, contact with management. Thus, board members are increasingly being asked literally to police themselves to the extent that they are being required to police management because directors are deeply involved with management in formulating strategy and in making important decisions about the direction of the company.

In addition to these problems of cognitive bias that lead to board capture, a second problem with constructing a corporate governance system that relies primarily on boards of directors to monitor managers is that it is virtually impossible to identify, much less to monitor and control, the myriad ways that board independence can be compromised. Personal relationships, which are far more difficult to monitor and evaluate, are as likely to compromise a director's independence as a professional relationship. In other words, it often is impossible to determine whether a board is independent. This means that often it is extremely difficult, if not impossible, to distinguish a company with an independent board from one in which subtle relationships between board members and managers and among board members causes the board to lack independence from management. This point was made quite powerfully by former SEC commissioner Cynthia Glassman, who observed that "personal relationships with the CEO—living in the same community, kids at the same school, moving in the same social circle—are just as likely to undercut independence" as the financial relationships that a director may have with the company.[26]

The highly subjective nature of the concept of an independent board member is a result of the fact that there are myriad ways that board members can be captured by management. This problem is concretely manifested in efforts by regulators to make boards more independent. For example, the New York Stock Exchange (NYSE) recognizes that it is impossible as a practical matter to draft standards that provide guidance for when a board member is independent and when he is not. The problem is that "[i]t is not possible to anticipate, or explicitly to provide for, all circumstances that might signal potential conflicts of interest, or that might bear on the materiality of a director's relationship to a listed company."[27] Consequently, the NYSE rule provides that the issue of whether a director is independent must be determined not by any objective standard but by the business judgment of the directors' colleagues on the board. Thus, according to the NYSE, a director qualifies as independent when the board of directors "affirmatively determines that the director has no material relationship with the listed company (either directly or as a partner, shareholder, or officer of an organization that has a relationship with the company)."[28] The rule promulgated for directors in public companies traded over-the-counter is virtually identical to the NYSE's rule.

The NASD rule, which applies to the corporate governance of companies whose shares trade over-the-counter, provides that the board must determine whether a particular board member is independent based on whether he has a relationship that, "in the opinion of the company's board, would interfere with the exercise of independent judgment in carrying out the responsibilities of a director."[29]

In practice, however, courts clearly do not evince much faith in the ability of boards of directors to identify the subtle conflicts of interest that directors face. In the context of corporate decision-making, this suggests we will observe two types of errors in evaluating board independence. In addition to the obvious problem that a conflicted or a captured board will appear to be independent, there is the problem that an independent board will be wrongly construed as captured.

Recent shareholder litigation involving Oracle Corporation provides a vivid illustration of the difficulty of regulating director independence. The Oracle litigation began with a shareholder lawsuit against Larry Ellison, Oracle's CEO, Jeffrey Henley, its CFO, and Donald Lucas and Michael Boskin, two of its board members, claiming these officers and directors had harmed the company by engaging in improper insider trading.

The lawsuit was filed in Delaware, where Oracle is incorporated. Delaware, like every other state, treats lawsuits of this kind (known as derivative lawsuits) as the property of the corporation who allegedly was harmed, rather than as the property of the shareholder bringing the suit. The corporation—which of course really means the board of directors of the corporation—has the right to make its own determination about whether proceeding with the lawsuit is in the best interests of the corporation.

Derivative lawsuits typically name some or all of the existing board members as defendants, alleging that their malfeasance or negligence somehow has harmed the corporation (the effectiveness of these sorts of lawsuits as a corporate governance device is discussed in chapter 10). To deal with this obvious conflict of interest involved in having directors determine whether the corporation would benefit from proceeding with a lawsuit in which they themselves are named as defendants, judges have developed an elaborate procedure that enables the corporation to respond to derivative lawsuits. The procedure calls for the board to appoint a special litigation committee (SLC) of independent directors to conduct a good faith investigation of the merits of the case being brought on the corporation's behalf, and to make a recommendation to the court that the lawsuit be dismissed.

In theory, of course, the SLC does not have to recommend that the plaintiff's lawsuit be dismissed. An SLC could recommend the plaintiff be allowed to continue the lawsuit. As a practical matter, however, this is virtually never done. SLCs uniformly recommend that derivative lawsuits brought by outside shareholders be dismissed. When the SLC recommends dismissal of the suit in Delaware, the Court of Chancery, sitting without a jury, reviews the SLC's recommendation.

The critical determination regarding how much deference to give the recommendation of the SLC to dismiss the lawsuit will depend on the Chancery Court's evaluation of the independence of the SLC members. If the court determines the SLC is not sufficiently independent of the officers and directors whose conduct it investigated, it will decline to accept the SLC's recommendation of dismissal. In a decision that stunned the corporate world, a Delaware Chancery Court judge determined that the SLC appointed to investigate the Oracle officers and directors involved in trading Oracle shares was not sufficiently independent.

Oracle chose two Stanford professors, Joseph Grundfest and Hector Garcia-Molina, to the SLC investigating the claims against Ellison, Henley, Lucas, and Boskin. These professors were not implicated in the alleged trading improprieties. In fact, they were not even on the board when the trading occurred. By objective measures, the directors were clearly independent. As the court noted, they were "distinguished tenured (Stanford) faculty members whose current jobs would not be threatened by whatever good faith decision they made as SLC members." The members of the SLC had no "economically consequential" relationships with the defendants and could, therefore, reach a decision independent of pressure from the defendants. At least this is what the SLC and its lawyers thought.

However, the SLC members were linked to some of the defendants by significant ties to Stanford. The two Stanford professors on the committee were investigating another Stanford professor (Boskin), a major Stanford donor (Lucas), and a potentially major Stanford donor (Ellison). The web of Stanford connections proved too much for the judge, who indicated a willingness to evaluate independence much more strenuously than had other courts.

> [T]he SLC focuses on the language of previous opinions . . . that indicates that a director is not independent only if he is dominated and controlled by an interested party. . . . [M]uch of our jurisprudence on independence focuses on economically consequential relationships between the allegedly interested party and the directors who allegedly cannot act independently of that director. Put another way, much of our law focuses the bias inquiry on whether there are economically material ties between the interested party and the director whose impartiality is questioned, treating the possible effect on one's personal wealth as the key to the independence inquiry.

The chancellor took the position that the traditional focus on the economic interests and conflicts of SLC members would serve only to fetishize much-parroted language, at the cost of denuding the independence inquiry of its intellectual integrity. . . . Delaware law should not be based on a reductionist view of human nature that simplifies human motivations on the lines of the least sophisticated notions of the law and economics movement. Homo sapien is not merely homo economicus. We may be thankful that an array of other motivations exist that influence human behavior; not all are any better than greed or avarice, think of envy, to name just one. But also think of motives like love, friendship, and collegiality, think of those among us who direct their behavior as best they can on a guiding creed or set of moral values.

Nor should our law ignore the social nature of humans. To be direct, corporate directors are generally the sort of people deeply enmeshed in social institutions. Such institutions have norms, expectations that, explicitly and implicitly, influence, and channel the behavior of those who participate in their operation. Some things are "just not done," or only at a cost, which might not be so severe as a loss of position, but may involve a loss of standing in the institution. In being appropriately sensitive to this factor, our law also cannot assume—absent some proof of the point—that corporate directors are, as a general matter, persons of unusual social bravery, who operate heedless to the inhibitions that social norms generate for ordinary folk.

In other words, the court found that the social norms of the directors on the SLC, coupled with the web of connections between the SLC members and the defendants, rendered the SLC incapable of evaluating the conduct of the defendant directors. In the words of the judge,

[A] person in Grundfest's position would find it difficult to assess Boskin's conduct without pondering his own association with Boskin and their mutual affiliations. Although these connections might produce bias in either a tougher or laxer direction, the key inference is that these connections would be on the mind of a person in Grundfest's position, putting him in the position of either causing serious legal action to be brought against a person with whom he shares several connections (an awkward thing) or not doing so (and risking being seen as having engaged in favoritism toward his old professor and . . . colleague).

Interestingly, the court acknowledges that it is unable to tell whether the existence of the relationships it was evaluating would lead the members of the SLC to be tougher or laxer than they might be otherwise.

Still more problematic is that there is no indication of the limits of the court's analysis. The societal norms and the "there but for the grace of God go I" issues that plagued the Oracle SLC will plague directors any time they are called upon to evaluate senior officers or director colleagues in any context. As one commentator trenchantly observed, "[I]f it is difficult for two Stanford professors to investigate another Stanford professor, when there are over 1,700 Stanford professors, how much more difficult must it be for two directors to investigate three directors on a ten-person board? Social and institutional bonds, as well as economic bonds, can be much stronger between directors than between professors at a large university."[30]

To date, the entire infrastructure of board conduct is based on the idea that the board is a collegial decision-making body. It would be possible, of course, to imagine replacing the current highly collegial norms of board behavior with an adversarial model. Human nature being what it is, it is not plausible to imagine directors simultaneously being collegial and adversarial, or shifting seamlessly between these two patterns of interaction with management. To do so would require unrealistic assumptions about human behavior.

Although boards of directors are rarely adversarial, other corporate governance mechanisms and devices employ an adversarial model. Sometimes adversarial corporate governance works, and sometimes it does not. It is not for nothing that outside bidders in hostile takeovers are called "hostile" bidders. And few corporate governance mechanisms are as effective as the market for corporate control.

Another adversarial corporate governance mechanism is the litigation system, which, of course, is built on the adversarial idea that sharply opposing interests interacting before an impartial fact finder generates a truthful outcome. In the context of corporate governance, however, there is no independent and impartial judge to decide contentious issues, rendering the applicability of the adversarial model somewhat dubious, unless one is comfortable putting directors in the singular position of serving both as advocates for and against, as well as judges of managerial behavior.

CHAPTER 5

CASE STUDIES ON BOARDS OF DIRECTORS IN CORPORATE GOVERNANCE

Operating at a fairly high level of abstraction, we have considered the fundamental question of whether corporate boards of directors are effective mechanisms of corporate governance, or whether the problem of capture compromises the efficacy of corporate boards. Summarizing, the argument to this point has touched on four themes.

(a) the existence of cognitive biases and information asymmetries that make boards susceptible to capture by management and constrain the capacity and effectiveness of boards to monitor and control managerial conduct;

(b) the inability of outside investors to distinguish objective boards from captured boards;

(c) the nature and limitations of the collegial model that defines the scope of acceptable board conduct;

(d) the dominance of a collegial model of board behavior that appears to dominate the alternative adversarial model of board conduct, despite the fact that the prevailing norms of collegiality undermine the capacity of boards of directors to serve as effective monitors of managerial pathologies.

These points are reinforced in the subsections below, which present accounts of board of director conduct in corporations that experienced real or perceived corporate governance meltdowns. These accounts, which take the form of four case studies, provide concrete support for the theory of board capture articulated here. All of these companies were large, publicly traded firms whose shares were listed for trading on the NYSE. The companies had brand-name CEOs and directors with sterling resumes drawn from a who's who of corporate America. Two of the corporate governance meltdowns, those of TransUnion and Disney, involved monumentally bad decision-making and defective board process rather than fraud. The corporate governance meltdowns of the other two companies studied here, Equity Funding and Enron, involved two of the most infamous corporate scandals in modern history. In both of the latter cases, the corporate scandals rendered the companies insolvent.

In *Smith v. Van Gorkom,* the directors' decision to sell TransUnion generated a landmark Delaware Supreme Court holding. This case presents a classic example of board capture by the CEO. In *In re Walt Disney Litigation,* the directors' acquiescence in the corporation's hiring of Michael Ovitz at the behest of his best friend, Disney CEO Michael Eisner, reflects the same problem of board capture as seen in *Van Gorkom.*

Director capture went beyond bad decision-making and resulted in outright fraud at both Enron and Equity Funding. Directors in these companies trusted management to the end. The outside directors were independent and able. Yet, consistent with the analysis here, they were unable to detect any governance problems in these firms. There was no participation in the outside frauds by the independent directors. The directors did not benefit from the self-interested actions perpetrated by management. But they did nothing to stop them. Thus, these case studies, taken together, strongly support the following point: competent, independent directors may provide corporate governance benefits in the form of improved managerial decision-making, but they are unlikely to provide much value to shareholders as independent monitors.

These case studies tend to show that the more directors become engaged with management in making strategic decisions the more likely they are to become firmly convinced that their decisions, and the decisions made by their managers, are correct. It is the entrenchment of this conviction in management's infallibility that I call "capture."

The proclivity of directors to become captured by the managers they ostensibly are monitoring is not a problem that can be remedied easily or costlessly for two reasons. First, capture arises, in part, from having directors deeply involved in managerial decision-making. Particularly where directors are talented and experienced in business, however, there are tangible benefits from having directors deeply involved in managerial decision-making because such involvement improves the quality of the decisions made by management. Second, directors are inevitably involved in decisions about the selection, retention, promotion, and compensation of management. This, in turn, makes it more difficult for directors to criticize management because any such criticisms negatively reflect on the directors involved in such decisions as well as on all prior retention, promotion, and compensation decisions related to such managers. In other words, any criticisms that board members might make of management reflect badly on the very directors making such criticisms. While the capacity for objective self-evaluation is a laudable personality trait, it is rare and difficult to detect with any reliability. It is, therefore, not one that rational investors should rely on when designing a system of corporate governance.

The implication of this analysis—and of the case studies presented below—is that the institution of the board of directors, as we know it, is not a reliable corporate governance device. Boards of directors will not inevitably fail in the task of objectively monitoring management. They cannot, however, be expected to succeed reliably.

What these case studies reveal is that boards of directors face a sort of corporate governance catch-22 with respect to their responsibility to monitor management. Specifically, boards of directors are supposed to trust management while simultaneously acting as if they *don't* trust management. A common element in the cases discussed below is apparent: boards of directors that appeared on paper to be not only highly qualified but also professional and independent of management demonstrated clear evidence of capture by the CEO and top managers of the companies on whose boards they served.

The purpose of these case studies is twofold. First, they illustrate the nature, extent, and apparent inevitability of board capture. Second, and more important, they strongly suggest that recruiting an independent board of directors does not guarantee independence. The strong proclivity of board members to become captured by management implies that a board member who is independent when he is appointed may not be independent a year or so later, after he has actively participated with senior officers in the managing and strategic planning for the company.

This analysis also implies that, to the extent that independent directors are perceived as a threat to senior management, senior managers may be reluctant to cooperate with such directors and to provide them with the information needed to make decisions, particularly where such information could be interpreted to mean that incumbent managers have underperformed. Thus, the costs of independence, which come in the form of weaker managerial input from directors, may be greater than the benefits, which come in the form of improved monitoring.

The cost of misperceiving the value of independent boards of directors is likely to be significant. The analysis below suggests that the prestige and authority of a "marquee" board of independent directors, such as the Enron board, may actually empower managers to take more risks and to engage in more aggressive accounting practices than they otherwise would dare to do. Similarly, the Enron debacle also illustrates that, to the extent that potential outside monitors such as credit-rating agencies, stock market analysts, hedge funds, and regulators perceive that a company already is being monitored effectively by an independent board of directors, those outside monitors are likely to reduce their own monitoring. The reduction in monitoring by other corporate governance entities is the predictable result of the fact that outside monitoring is a costly and scarce resource that must be marshaled effectively.

The perception that outside directors are effective may cause a misallocation of scarce monitoring. A more realistic view of the efficacy of outside directors as monitors would lead to a more optimal allocation of monitoring resources.

SMITH v. VAN GORKOM

The opinion of the Delaware Supreme Court in *Smith v. Van Gorkom* is probably the most discussed legal opinion in the history of corporate law. Criticism of the opinion was literally simultaneous with its publication, as the two dissenters in the three-to-two opinion of the Delaware Supreme Court described the majority's analysis as a "comedy of errors."[1] Academics, journalists, and other commentators predicted "dire consequences" for Delaware, and characterized the outcome as "dumbfounding" "atrocious"[2] and "surely one of the worst decisions in the history of corporate law."[3]

Smith v. Van Gorkom provides a now infamous example of the cognitive bias to which directors are subject. In that case, the entire TransUnion board of directors was held personally liable for failing to follow adequate procedures when considering (and approving) a tender offer unfavorable to shareholders.[4] The holding in *Smith v. Van Gorkom* ultimately revolutionized the deliberative process in corporate boardrooms.

The basic facts of the case are as follows: Jerome Van Gorkom, a board member and TransUnion's CEO, recommended to his board of directors a bid for the company from the Pritzker Group. Notwithstanding the fact that many suspected that Jerome Van Gorkom, who was nearing retirement, engineered the merger agreement to serve his own interests rather than those of the shareholders, the board of directors approved the deal with seemingly little thought or analysis.[5]

The sale of the company to the Pritzker Group no doubt served the private interests of the retiring CEO in that it enabled him to liquidate his shares of the company just before his retirement. A large group of shareholders, however, was adamantly opposed to the transaction. The opposition was in large part due to the adverse tax consequences of the deal. In the years before the Pritzker bid, TransUnion had acquired a series of companies in tax-free transactions in which TransUnion stock was exchanged for stock in the acquired companies. TransUnion had made a total of forty-two such tax-free transactions in the decade prior to the sale of TransUnion to the Pritzker Group. These transactions, which ranged in size from $36,000 to $24 million, accounted for over one-third of TransUnion's 12.5 million outstanding shares (about 4.3 million shares). The holders of these 4.3 million TransUnion shares would incur large and unavoidable taxable gains when their shares were converted into cash upon the merger of TransUnion into the Pritzker Group. As one commentator noted, these shareholders would have preferred "if they had a choice to defer their rendezvous with the tax man as long as possible. They would much rather see TransUnion acquired in a transaction similar to the ones in which their companies were acquired—a nontaxable reorganization, where shares of the acquiring company would be exchanged for . . . TransUnion shares."[6]

The TransUnion directors, however, did not consider the interests of these shareholders. Despite the fact that the directors were elected by the shareholders, and ostensibly represented them, their true allegiance appeared to be to Van Gorkom, the CEO, with whom they shared managerial responsibilities.

The disputed transaction was agreed to in discussions between Jerome Van Gorkom and Chicago financier Jay Pritzker. Pritzker agreed to a $55 per share cash-out merger of TransUnion into a company controlled by the Pritzker Group. The $55 price offered by Pritzker had a short time fuse—it was conditioned on acceptance by TransUnion within three days.

The fact that Van Gorkom agreed to such a short time fuse without consulting his board strongly suggests the extent to which he *himself* viewed his board as captured. He was confident that the board would do what he wanted it to do, which was to acquiesce to the sale of TransUnion to Pritzker. Van Gorkom's confidence was built on both his strong relationship with his board and the fact that the $55 offering price represented a substantial premium for the company, whose stock had traded at prices ranging from $24 1/4 to $39 1/2 per share during the five-year period preceding the merger.

Van Gorkom and Pritzker reached their agreement on Thursday, September 18, 1980. Van Gorkom called a special meeting of TransUnion's board for Saturday, September 20, but did not disclose the purpose of the meeting to his fellow directors. He told his colleagues on the senior management team about the proposed transaction for the first time only an hour before the board meeting. This sequence of events adds further support to the theory that Van Gorkom knew that he was dealing with a captured board.

The board meeting at which Van Gorkom presented the terms of the proposed merger lasted only two hours. The meeting began with a twenty-minute presentation outlining the terms of deal. The terms called for TransUnion to have the right to consider, but not to solicit, other offers for a ninety-day period. On the basis of this provision in the proposed transaction, Van Gorkom told the board that the free market would judge whether the company should be sold for the $55 million proposed. He advocated that the board give TransUnion's shareholders the opportunity to accept or reject the offer.

The directors approved the transaction on the basis of Van Gorkom's recommendation and their own knowledge and experience about the company. The merger agreement was signed by Van Gorkom during a performance of the Chicago Light Opera later the same day. None of the directors had read the agreement before Van Gorkom signed it. On February 10, 1981, the board members overwhelmingly approved the proposed transaction.

As a result of this decision to approve the TransUnion–Pritzker merger, several shareholders, including the named plaintiff Alden B. Smith, brought suit against the TransUnion directors alleging that their decision to sell the company was grossly negligent and did not constitute an exercise of informed business judgment. The defendant directors claimed that the expertise, "collective experience, and sophistication" of the company's outside directors compensated for the lack of deliberation. TransUnion's outside directors were four CEOs of major corporations (who, as the court noted, had "78 years of combined experience as chief executive officers of major corporations")[7] and an economist who was a former dean of the University of Chicago Business School and chancellor of that university.

The court rejected the defendants' claim, however. The court viewed the directors' experience as irrelevant because of evidence of board capture. According to the court, the board had relied too much on Van Gorkom, on the market premium, and on Van Gorkom's dubious assertion that the price would be subjected to a market test. Similarly, the court found that the shareholder vote to ratify the deal was void due to deficiencies in the board's disclosure to the shareholders. In particular, there was no disclosure of the board's "failure to assess the premium offered in terms of other relevant valuation techniques, thereby rendering questionable its determination as to the substantiality of the premium over an admittedly depressed stock market price."[8]

Unquestionably, "[b]y today's standards, the board's procedures seem woefully inadequate."[9] Indeed, the TransUnion board "did not read the merger agreement, much less discuss and deliberate in any detail."[10] Arguably, the board in this case exhibited an "inappropriate reliance on Van Gorkom's judgment and negotiating" and did not sufficiently oversee managerial decision-making.[11] Furthermore, the board failed in "that it did not properly monitor Van Gorkom's negotiations with the acquirer."[12]

Significantly, the board's decision in this case was not tainted by self-dealing or conflict of interest, nor was the board inept, lazy, or corrupt.[13] The problem was not *corruption* but *capture*. While the TransUnion board may have been quite effective in helping manage the business, they were ineffective as monitors—they exercised no control or constraint on management. Thus, the actions of the TransUnion board illustrate the point that proximate monitors may become biased, and that boards of directors in particular are susceptible to becoming too reliant on and captured by the judgment of the management of the firms they ostensibly oversee.

Obviously, the *Van Gorkom* court believed that there was a severe corporate governance problem at TransUnion. That is why the entire board of directors of TransUnion (save one whose illness had precluded his participation in the critical decision) was found to have been grossly negligent in approving the sale of the company. Unfortunately, because the court failed to perceive the problem of capture or the incompatibility between the role of the board as monitors and the role of the board as managers, their proposed solution to the corporate governance problems at TransUnion was not at all constructive.

The court did not base its decision on the ground that the board was captured. Instead, the decision was based on the ground that the board was ill informed. The court did not—or would not—perceive that the reason that the board did not inform itself as thoroughly as they should have was because the board was captured by management to such an extent that it did not think that it needed an independent source of outside information. As an article in *Barron's* magazine published shortly after the decision in 1985 pointed out, the TransUnion directors voted for the proposed acquisition because the CEO "announced with conviction that [the] proposed acquisition was a good deal."[14] In essence the court ultimately held that directors are negligent if they approve a transaction simply because the CEO says so.[15]

The problem is that the Delaware court decision in *Smith v. Van Gorkom* reflects the assumption that the critical corporate governance problem of board capture somehow can be solved by requiring directors to deliberate more when making a decision. In reality, however, the lack of deliberation by the TransUnion board was only a symptom of a larger disease. That disease was board capture by management. The court confused this symptom for the actual disease and, in doing so, inevitably formulated an ineffective remedy. The remedy devised took the form of requiring more deliberation and a more structured process by boards of directors when making important decisions, particularly decisions involving changes in corporate control. This remedy is inefficient because it is directed at the symptom—the board's lack of process—rather than at the disease, which was the capture of an ostensibly professional and independent board of directors by management.

DISNEY

The landmark 1985 decision of the Delaware Supreme Court in *Smith v. Van Gorkom* was followed by protracted litigation by plaintiff class action lawyers in a suit brought against the board of directors of the Walt Disney Company. The Disney lawsuit is noteworthy because it provides a strikingly complete depiction of the nature of the relationships and interactions between boards of directors and management. The facts generated in the course of the legal battle also provide evidence of the deeply entrenched phenomenon of board capture. Finally, the case is important because it provides a very clear lesson in the extent to which corporate law can be used to promote effective corporate governance.

The Disney litigation grew out of the unilateral decision in the summer of 1995 by Disney CEO Michael Eisner to hire his close friend of twenty-five years, Michael Ovitz, as company president. Eisner hired Ovitz to replace the highly successful former president and CEO, Frank Wells, who had died tragically in a helicopter crash in April 1994.

Eisner single-handedly recruited Ovitz to Disney from his former position as president and founding partner of the hugely successful Creative Artist Agency (CAA), long known as the premier talent agency in the United States. In a telling reversal of the textbook chain of command, Irwin Russell, Disney director and chairman of the board's compensation committee, "assumed the lead role in negotiating the financial terms of the contract" between Disney and Ovitz per *Eisner's* direction.[16]

The negotiations resulted in Ovitz's joining Disney with one of the most excessive employment contracts in the history of corporate America. Ovitz was to receive $1 million in annual salary (the highest fixed salary a corporation can pay that is deductible as a business expense on the corporation's tax returns), and a five-year contract loaded with stock options and "performance" bonus payments.[17] The bonus payments, which were characterized by the defendants in the litigation as discretionary, were not contractually required. Nevertheless, Irwin Russell sent Ovitz a written memorandum telling him that his bonus would be approximately $7.5 million annually.

The contract had two tranches of options. The first tranche consisted of options to buy three million shares of Disney stock vesting in the third, fourth, and fifth years of Ovitz's employment with Disney. This tranche was worth at least $50 million, as evidenced by the fact that the employment agreement called for Disney to make up the difference of the value of the options had they not appreciated to $50 million by the end of five years. It is thus hard and potentially misleading to characterize these options as an incentive or performance-based compensation arrangement.

The second tranche consisted of two million options that would vest immediately if Disney and Ovitz decided to renew their contract. Importantly, the contract also provided that if Ovitz was fired by Disney for any reason other than gross negligence or malfeasance, he would be entitled to what was described in his employment contract as a "non-fault" termination payment that consisted of all salary remaining on his contract, $7.5 million a year for any unaccrued bonuses, the immediate vesting of all of the options in the first option tranche provided for under the contract, as well as an additional $10 million cash payment for the value of the second tranche of options.

Immediately after the terms of the contract were agreed to, the compensation committee added several other items to the agenda for the meeting at which Ovitz's contract was discussed. Interestingly, among the items on the agenda for that meeting was compensation for Irwin Russell, the chair of the compensation committee for negotiating the Ovitz deal. Also on the agenda were compensation packages and stock option grants for over one hundred other Disney employees. Despite the large number of issues on the agenda, the compensation committee managed to finish its work in just one hour. The compensation committee did not even trouble itself with a copy of the actual contract between Disney and Ovitz, satisfying itself with a spreadsheet summarizing the terms.

In Ovitz's first week on the job in October 2005, Eisner lauded his performance. He told Ovitz that theirs was a "partnership" that was "born in corporate heaven."[18] Eisner crowed that Ovitz's "instincts were right in coming to the Walt Disney Company and mine were right in suggesting it."[19] This self-congratulatory atmosphere, however, did not last.

In less than a month the corporate infighting began. Disney's in-house lawyer and chief financial officer had a difficult time accepting Ovitz into the Disney fold. By 1996 it was clear that Ovitz had, as the court put it, "failed to ingratiate himself in the group" at Disney,[20] committing such sins as declining to participate in group activities and riding in limousines to corporate events when other Disney executives were taking a bus. By the end of 1996 Eisner decided that Ovitz would have to go.

Unfortunately for Disney, Ovitz's compensation arrangement made it extremely expensive for the company to fire him without cause. Doing so would trigger the non-fault termination provisions of the Ovitz employment contract that required Disney to make an immediate cash payment to Ovitz of $39 million and to give him stock options worth over $101 million for just fourteen months' work.

Reviewing the facts, corporate governance blogger Steven Bainbridge concluded that Eisner "cut very lucrative deals for his friend Ovitz both on the way in and on the way out, all the while railroading the deals past a complacent and compliant board. The story that emerges is one of cronyism and backroom deals in which preservation of face was put ahead of the corporation's best interests."[21] The trial court characterized the corporate governance of Disney as one in which Eisner had "enthroned himself as the omnipotent and infallible monarch of his personal Magic Kingdom" to install his good friend Michael Ovitz as president of Disney.[22]

The parallels between the Disney case and the TransUnion case (i.e., *Smith v. Van Gorkom*) are clear. On the surface, it is obvious that both cases involved imperial CEOs, leading ostensibly independent but clearly captured directors to hastily ratify hastily made decisions already made by the CEOs. Beyond these superficial parallels there is another similarity. Ironically, despite the complete lack of process involved in these two decisions, both the sale of TransUnion and the hiring of Ovitz appear to have been good for shareholders from an *ex ante* economic perspective.

TransUnion was sold for a record share price that represented a huge premium for shareholders over the preexisting market price of the firm's shares. Similarly, immediately after Disney announced that Michael Ovitz had been hired, standard event-study methodology showed that the market value of Disney's stock increased by over $1 billion in value in a single day.[23] Thus, in the Disney case, despite the lack of board deliberation, the board's domination by CEO Eisner, and the giant size of Ovitz's excessive pay package and termination payout, the prospect of luring what the market viewed as a much-needed and highly talented executive to the Disney board provided significant value for shareholders.

One of the most depressing aspects of the Disney case is buried in footnote 373 of the trial court's opinion, which describes "the contrast between ideal corporate governance practices and the unwholesome boardroom culture at Disney."[24] The court said that the testimony in the case "clarified how ornamental, passive directors contribute to sycophantic tendencies among directors and how imperial CEOs can exploit this condition for their own benefit, especially in the executive compensation and severance areas."[25]

Despite the abject failure of the Disney board to exert any meaningful constraint on the company's CEO, Delaware judges at both the trial and the appellate level had no difficulty determining that the board acted consistently with their fiduciary duties in the process of hiring and firing Ovitz. On June 8, 2006, after ten years of litigation, the Delaware Supreme Court rejected claims by plaintiff class action attorneys that the directors of Walt Disney Company had breached their fiduciary duties and affirmed the long-held rule that directors enjoy wide insulation for liability for most decisions, regardless of defects in the process by which those decisions are made.[26] So long as directors do not act self-interestedly, courts will not second-guess their decisions. An exception to this business judgment rule occurs when the directors are found to have intentionally harmed the corporation, to have been grossly negligent, or to have been intentionally and consciously derelict in their duties as directors.

The Disney decision clarifies two widely misunderstood dimensions of the relationship between corporate law and corporate governance. First, both the Delaware Supreme Court and the Delaware Court of Chancery made it plain that, whatever corporate law is supposed to do for share-holders, it does not impose liability on directors for failing to satisfy what are viewed as the best practices of corporate governance. Companies like Disney are free to have very bad corporate governance practices and their directors will nevertheless remain free of legal responsibility if their decisions turn out badly.

Second, the Disney decision makes it very clear that board capture is not a concern of the courts. The court in Disney recognized that the board was captured, even that the boardroom was an "unwholesome" place populated by "passive directors" with "sycophantic tendencies." None of this, however, mattered to the courts. Rather, consistent with the analysis here, the courts were quite realistic in their limited expectations of directors. If, as is argued here, board capture is generally inevitable, there is little reason to punish directors for succumbing to capture. In fact, the analysis here suggests that the harm from doing so likely would outweigh the benefits. Imposing by judicial or legislative fiat a rule requiring true independence and objectivity would undermine the board's ability to participate actively with management in the operation of the company.

ENRON

By now Enron has become a metaphor for corporate governance failure. The story of Enron's collapse has been catalogued in hundreds of articles and books. It is probably the most-chronicled collapse in corporate history. When Enron declared bankruptcy on December 2, 2001, it was ranked as the seventh largest publicly traded company in the United States. Disturbingly, the company went from being *Fortune* magazine's pick for America's best-managed company in 2000 to bankruptcy in less than a year. Even more telling for our purposes is the startling fact that in 2000, the year before the company collapsed, Enron's board of directors was identified by *Chief Executive* magazine as among the best boards of any U.S. corporation.

The failure of Enron's board of directors to monitor the company effectively, combined with the parallel failures of the credit-rating agencies, stock market analysts, outside auditors, accountants, attorneys, bankers, the NYSE (the stock exchange that listed the company's shares for trading), and government regulators assigned to the company, has created a crisis of confidence and identity for U.S. corporate governance and regulation that persists today.

The most important corporate governance lesson to be learned from Enron is that it is unwise to place too much trust and reliance on a company's board of directors. Unfortunately, it appears that this lesson has not been learned. Commentators have been virtually unanimous in criticizing the poor performance of the Enron board. Echoing the typical views expressed, one law professor observed that "as the Enron board starkly demonstrated, boards often fail to live up to our expectations, and ineffectual boards cast doubt on the entire corporate governance system."[27]

These sorts of observations are of interest for two reasons. First, the recognition that boards often fail to live up to expectations should, one would hope, inexorably lead investors to wonder whether it is sensible to continue to rely on a demonstrably faulty corporate governance institution. Yet analysis that concludes with palliatives such as "[b]oards of directors should not simply rubber-stamp management's decisions and certainly should not fall asleep at the wheel"[28] do not provide any concrete guidance about how we might structure a corporate governance system on which investors could justifiably rely.

Second, the observation that the Enron board was "ineffectual" is of great interest because of the timing of the observation. Accurate though the observation may now be, the fact that the commentators did not begin to describe the Enron board as ineffectual until after the complete collapse of the company speaks volumes. That it was not until after the conviction of the CFO and the indictment of the president and the CEO that commentators routinely began to describe the Enron board in such terms signals that investors are not served by such *ex post* descriptions. One wonders where these astute observers were *before* the crash of the company, when their prognostications about the deficiencies in Enron's corporate governance might have actually done some good for investors.

Far from being the target of suspicion before the company collapse, the Enron board was widely lauded as a shining example of good corporate governance. The company had fourteen directors, twelve of whom were outsiders. The board included luminaries like Norman Blake, CEO and chairman of Comdisco and secretary general of the United States Olympic Committee; Wendy Gramm, former chairman of the Commodities Futures Trading Commission; Robert Jaedicke, former dean of Stanford's Graduate School of Business and former chair of the Department of Accounting at Stanford's business school; and Johan Wakeham, former U.K. secretary of state for energy and leader of the Houses of Commons and Lords. Enron directors were also directors in a combined total of almost fifty other public companies. Thus, if the Enron board was defective, a whole passel of other companies was certainly infected with defective directors.

In addition to being highly independent and populated with luminaries from the corporate and academic world, the board met frequently. For example, in an attempt at crisis management, the board met almost daily from the moment that the company began to experience severe problems in October 2001 until the company filed its petition for bankruptcy protection on December 2, 2001.

The organization and structure of the Enron board was also viewed as a paradigm of good corporate governance. As one commentator put it, "[T]he [Enron] board had all of the committees one would hope to see, including an executive committee, finance committee, audit and compliance committee, compensation committee, and nominating and corporate governance committee."[29]

The Enron audit committee, the committee universally acknowledged as playing the central role in monitoring, "had a model charter and was chaired by a former accounting professor who had served as the Dean of the Stanford Graduate School of Business."[30] Even more impressive was the fact that investigators found that all of the members of the audit committee save one had extensive familiarity with complex accounting principles. Two members of the committee, Professor Jaedicke and Lord Wakeham, had formal accounting training and professional experience in accounting.[31]

In a show of independence that surpassed the then-existing standards of conduct for audit committees, the Enron audit committee received regular presentations on Enron's financial statements, accounting practices, and audit results from the company's outside auditors. The audit committee chair would report on the presentations to the full Enron board after the audit committee had received the presentations outside of the presence of management.

Consistent with best corporate governance practices and as mentioned above, the members of the audit committee, the compensation committee, and the nominating committee all were made up of outside directors unaffiliated with management. Indeed, one of the great ironies of the myriad new corporate governance rules passed by courts, legislatures, administrative agencies, and stock exchanges in response to the collapse of Enron is that Enron itself met or exceeded the higher standards ostensibly promulgated to prevent future "Enrons." Oddly, if Enron survived to this day, it would not have to change its corporate governance structure at all to conform to the requirements of the Sarbanes-Oxley Act (SOX).

Any honest observer who opines that the Enron board performed poorly in retrospect must also acknowledge that "by all appearances Enron's board looked great"[32] before the company's collapse. Indeed, Enron would be considered now, as it was then, a model of corporate governance. This, it seems, strongly suggests that we need to change the extent to which we rely on board independence as our main proxy for high-quality corporate governance.

A new approach should do three things. First, it should reflect an understanding that it is wholly unrealistic to think that the same people can simultaneously serve a monitoring function *and* a management function in the same company. Next, it should leave to the board the responsibility for improving the quality of managerial decision-making. Finally, the new model of corporate governance should rely on distant and objective market mechanisms as monitoring agents rather than on proximate agents such as directors. As we have seen, directors have shown themselves to be uniquely subject to capture by the very managers they are supposed to be monitoring.

Consistent with this analysis, the Enron board was not only a model of professionalism, it also was a model of board capture by management. Only a capture hypothesis can explain the complete trust in management reflected in the board's acquiescence to the now-infamous related party transactions that ultimately played the pivotal role in Enron's demise. For example, Enron's annual reports (which are filed with the SEC on Form 10-K) showed that Enron closed deals with three thousand related entities in 1999 and 2000 alone. Hundreds of these transactions were with Enron affiliates that operated out of post-office boxes in the Cayman Islands. The Enron board acquiesced in high-risk accounting practices, inappropriate conflict-of-interest activities, and undisclosed off-the-books transactions. It also approved executive compensation packages that were, at least in retrospect, clearly excessive in light of the companies' poor performance.

The most-heralded governance failures of the Enron board were its decisions, on three separate occasions, to waive the company's code of conduct to allow Enron CFO Andrew Fastow to organize and manage limited partnerships, called special purpose entities, designed to do business with Enron. The transactions that Fastow envisioned and conducted involved the purchase and sale of assets to and from Enron by these special purpose entities in which Fastow had interests. A waiver was required because the company's code of conduct prohibited Enron employees from obtaining any personal financial gain from any company doing business with Enron, but Fastow made millions in profits as a result of these transactions. The conflict of interest was so palpable that Benjamin Neuhausen posed the following unanswerable question to his Arthur Andersen colleague David Duncan: "Why would any director in his or her right mind ever approve such a scheme?"[33]

Of course the corporate governance failures of the Enron board did not end with the approval of these inappropriate transactions. After approving the deals, the Enron board failed to monitor the terms of the deals between these entities and Enron, to manage the compensation that Fastow received from running these limited partnerships, and to determine whether appropriate internal controls were in place to regulate the business being conducted between Enron and the businesses controlled by Fastow.

While the Enron board had a wealth of information about Enron at its disposal, and the unfettered capacity to demand more, the information actually received by the board was confined exclusively to the information supplied to it by management. Relying on management for information is the norm on virtually all boards, except in times of grave crisis or intense outside scrutiny. Most of the time board members do not have any other source of information about management other than management itself available to them.

In the case of Enron, it appears that management often decided not to supply the board with the information it requested. For example, in October 2000, Enron board member Charles LeMaistre, who at the time was the chair of the board's compensation committee, attempted to obtain information about Andrew Fastow's compensation from the special purpose entities he controlled that were doing business with Enron. LeMaistre ultimately testified to a Senate subcommittee investigating the collapse of Enron that he wanted information about Fastow's compensation but did not want to start office gossip about Fastow. Thus, he asked Mary Joyce, the Enron senior officer in charge of compensation, to provide him with information on the outside incomes of all of Enron's senior officers. LeMaistre made two requests for this information. The information was never supplied to him despite these requests. Rather than move the issue to a confrontation, LeMaistre "let the matter drop."[34]

A year later, the board was still wholly uninformed about Fastow's compensation, despite the fact that the SEC had commenced an inquiry into Enron's relationships with these special purpose entities and into the accounting treatment of the transactions between Enron and the entities. The board remained uninformed until October 2001, when a *Wall Street Journal* article appeared, titled "Enron CFO's Partnership Had Millions in Profit," alleging that Fastow had received more than $7 million in compensation from the Enron-related special purpose entities he controlled.

Generally speaking, management's control of the flow of information to the board of directors creates a dynamic in which management is able to capture its board of directors by controlling the nature of the information available to directors when making decisions. In the extensive literature on the economic theory of regulation, it is widely known that well-organized special interest groups with limited resources can influence political outcomes by controlling the flow of information to legislatures and to voters.[35] Senior managers in public companies have interests and agendas parallel to the interests and agendas of special interest groups in the realm of politics. Senior managers have an interest in influencing the selection of projects, the compensation of managers, and the choice of strategies. The ability of managers to control the flow of information to the board of directors greatly facilitates their ability to achieve their private objectives, often at the expense of investors. This dynamic goes a long way toward explaining the fact that Enron's apparently sophisticated and engaged board indicated that "they were as surprised as anyone by the company's collapse."[36]

Less than a week after former Enron chairman Kenneth L. Lay was convicted of fraud by a jury in Houston, Texas, Charles Walker, a long-time director of Enron, told the *Washington Post* that he was still unable to believe that Lay actually knew about the fraudulent accounting practices that caused the company's collapse in 2001. He also expressed his disbelief of the claim that Lay had lied to conceal the true financial condition of Enron. Walker even expressed continued confidence in Lay's integrity, saying, "I'm convinced he didn't know what was going on. . . . I just can't bear the picture of him going off to jail."[37]

The board of directors of Enron provides a vivid example of the following point: even boards that appear from the outside to be independent, professional, and highly qualified are susceptible to board capture. Worse, directors tend to be judged only in retrospect. The directors of Enron, though lauded before its collapse, are now viewed as bad directors not because of any particular misdeeds of the group but because the company on whose board they served collapsed so publicly and ignominiously.

As mentioned, strengthening the independence and oversight provided by directors of publicly traded companies is the primary solution offered to avoid the occurrence of future "Enrons."[38] This response is misguided for three reasons. First, the proposed solution fails to appreciate the fact that improving board independence may weaken the capacity of boards to do what they are actually good at—providing managerial support to senior officers. Second, the appeal for more independence unjustifiably and inexplicably assumes that it is indeed *possible* for those in charge of their selection to identify directors who will reliably think and act independently of management after they have become directors. Third, the assumption that directors can be relied upon to prevent future "Enrons" creates a false sense of security in unwitting investors who believe that this truly is the case.

When Enron collapsed dozens of other companies were faced with the interesting dilemma of what to do with the Enron directors who were simultaneously serving on *their* boards of directors. Some Enron directors like Wendy Gramm, who sat on the Invesco Mutual Fund board, and Robert Jaedicke, who sat on the California Water Service board, took matters into their own hands by resigning from these boards as soon as Enron collapsed.

Labor unions went after the remaining Enron directors with varying degrees of success. The AFL-CIO Investment Fund launched a campaign against all former Enron board members who served on other boards. The labor union announced that "the colossal failure of these directors to protect shareholder interests in the Enron case disqualified them from being re-nominated to any future public board service. . . . In cases in which the board re-nominated those directors, we urged shareholders to vote no."[39]

In 2002 Enron director Frank Savage was reelected to the boards of Lockheed Martin Corporation and Qualcomm Corporation over the objections of shareholder activists including the AFL-CIO and other labor groups. The campaign to remove Savage from the Lockheed Martin board convinced only 28 percent of Lockheed Martin shareholders to withhold their votes. Savage thus remained a valuable member of Lockheed Martin's board long after Enron's collapse, although he did resign from the Qualcomm board voluntarily in 2004 at the age of sixty-five.

While the vast majority of Enron board members resigned or were removed from the other boards on which they served, some companies vigorously defended their Enron directors. A spokesperson for Lockheed was reported by the *New York Times* to have said that former Enron director Frank Savage "is a valued director with a long and distinguished association with the company."[40] Similarly, Enron board member Norman Blake, the former chairman of Comdisco, remained on the board of Owens Corning after Enron's collapse. The *Washington Post* reported that Owens Corning responded to inquiries about Blake's board service by observing that "[o]ur board reviews our director's independence and effectiveness as a part of good governance practices. Mr. Blake has capably met the requirements."[41]

The above discussion shows that capture runs both ways. Not only are boards of directors loyal to the management teams they have installed, but management is similarly loyal to their boards.

EQUITY FUNDING

On April 2, 1973, Equity Funding Corporation of America was charged by the SEC with scheming to defraud investors by manipulating the price of its stock. On that same day, the *Wall Street Journal* described the case as "one of the biggest scandals in the history of the accounting industry."

As the Equity Funding scandal unraveled, government agencies and investigators piled on. Ultimately, the SEC was joined in its investigation by the U.S. Department of Justice, the Federal Bureau of Investigation, the United States Postal Service, and the Insurance Departments of both California and Illinois, the states in which Equity Funding was licensed to do business.

The scope and scale of the fraud was staggering. Well over half of the life insurance policies on the books of Equity Funding's life insurance subsidiary (approximately 64,000 of the 100,000), were fraudulent—the company was falsely claiming to have written over $2 billion in insurance policies. Compounding the fraud, the company had issued $25 million in counterfeit bonds and claimed to have $100 million in assets that could not be accounted for.

Equity Funding has been described as "an embarrassment to the securities industry, the insurance regulatory agencies, and the auditing profession,"[42] all of whom failed to notice the warning signs that management was engaged in massive fraud. The same analysis, of course, holds true for the Equity Funding board of directors. Three of the nine directors, Stanley Goldblum (founder, president, and chairman of the board), Fred Levin (director of marketing and president of the insurance company subsidiary), and Samuel Lowell (executive vice president and CFO), were directly involved in the fraud. The six remaining directors were uninvolved and apparently completely unaware of the fraud.

The sheer magnitude of the fraud, the brazenness required to fabricate transactions with other insurance companies, and the shameless audacity required to fake insurance policies suggests a massive failure of oversight by the company's internal watchdogs.

Like Enron, the roots of the scandal at Equity Funding began with innovations. Equity Funding was an innovator in the burgeoning business of combining and jointly packaging insurance policies together with other financial products. In particular, Equity Funding customers would be encouraged to invest in mutual funds sponsored by the company, and then to borrow against the mutual fund's assets to fund the premiums on a life insurance policy. The cash values accumulated on the life insurance policies would also be used to repay the loans used to buy the insurance.

The business proved extremely popular and Equity Funding began to experience rapid growth. CEO Stanley Goldblum embarked on a campaign to acquire other companies. Since Goldblum financed these acquisitions with Equity Funding shares, he was acutely sensitive to share price fluctuations. In 1965, the fraud began when Goldblum instructed CFO Samuel Lowell to inflate the company's reported income and accounts receivable.

As is typical in the insurance industry, Equity Funding often sold all or part of the insurance policies that it had underwritten for cash to other insurance companies in a process known as reinsurance. Reinsurance generates an immediate cash payment from the insurance company selling the policy to the insurance company buying the policy, and the buyer then receives a portion of the premiums paid in future years by the people insured. Of course, when an insurance policy is fabricated as were the policies sold to reinsurers by Equity Funding, there are no clients to make premium payments in the future. This, in turns, means that there is no source of income to fund the future payments to reinsurers that these reinsurers are counting on to earn a positive return on their investment in the original policy purchases. Equity Funding dealt with this problem by creating a massive Ponzi scheme in which the premiums from selling fake insurance policies were used to pay premiums to reinsurers. Equity Funding generated additional cash by falsely claiming that some of the fictitious people whose policies it had sold had actually died, which, in turn, generated a payment from the reinsurance company that had purchased the policy.

In other words, the creation and maintenance of the fraud at Equity Funding involved an extensive organization engaged in a concerted effort first to fabricate insurance policies and sell them, and then to fabricate still more policies to fund payments to the purchasers of the fake policies that were sold first. Then those participating in the fraud periodically fabricated the deaths of some of the fictitious policyholders to generate payments from the reinsurers. Finally, of course, the financial records of the company had to be falsified to reflect all of these fraudulent transactions.

As one commentator observed,

> Creating phony accounting entries is relatively easy, but creating the documentation for 64,000 phony policies was too big a challenge, even for Equity Funding. Management wanted to be able to satisfy the auditors, who would ask to see a sample of policies for review. The auditors would examine the policies' documentation on file, and then cross-check for premium receipts and policy reserve information. However, in all but a handful of cases, there were no policy files available. To solve this problem, management created an in-house institution—the forgery party.
>
> At Equity Funding, the policy files the auditors requested would often be "temporarily unavailable." That night, a half-dozen to a dozen employees would work to forge the missing files to have them ready the next day. As one participant said, "It takes a long time and you have to be careful about date stamps and other details. But I had fun being the doctor and giving the guy's blood pressure and all that."

The Equity Funding scandal was a massive scheme, concocted by management and supported, on at least a passive basis, by a number of employees who knew or could have reasonably suspected that something was wrong.[43]

It is important to note that if today's rules were applied, the board of directors would be expected to assess the system of internal controls used to monitor the company. The company's CEO and CFO would have to attest to the quality of these controls. Similar to the situation at Enron, however, none of these new rules would have made a difference for the investors in Equity Funding in light of the fact that both the CEO and the CFO were deeply involved in the fraudulent activities.

As was the case at Enron, Disney, and TransUnion, the directors at Equity Funding were completely captured by management. The board of directors of Equity Funding did not demand the resignations of the three primary architects of the fraud until the SEC said that it would put the company into receivership unless the old management was ousted. Incredibly, according to the authoritative history of the Equity Funding scandal by Raymond Dirks and Leonard Gross, even with the SEC's promise to close the company if the senior officers were not dismissed, a majority of the board continued to support incumbent management.[44] As mentioned above, three of the nine directors at the time of the meeting, Stanley Goldblum, Fred Levin, and Samuel Lowell, were insiders deeply involved in the fraud. These three were pitted against three others, insider Yura Arkus-Duntov, business school professor Robert Bowie, and corporate counsel Herbert Glaser, who were innocent of the fraud, and who wanted the three inside fraudsters fired at once.

The three other outside directors, Judson Sayre, a retired Bendix Corporation executive, Gale Livingston of Litton Industries, and Nelson Loud, an investment banker at a firm called New York Securities that had managed Equity Funding's initial public offering of its shares, all felt intensely loyal to the soon-to-be indicted incumbent management and were inclined to stay loyal to the executives who had recruited them to the board. It was not until Goldblum, the mastermind of the fraud, refused to promise that he had not put his "fingers in the cookie jar" that the directors seriously considered removing him.[45]

The directors appeared to turn decisively against management only when they refused to agree to give testimony to the SEC about the fraud at Equity Funding. *Even then*, a number of directors, including outside director Loud and corporate counsel Glaser, apparently considered rehiring the directors and paying them on a per diem basis as consultants after their resignations had been accepted to appease regulators.

The Equity Funding scandal reveals one additional human element in the theory of board capture by management developed here—replacing management is hard work. Even when the fraud at Equity Funding was almost fully revealed, the main fraudsters, Goldblum, Levin, and Lowell, were able to argue with a great deal of conviction that the company simply could not run without them. Clearly, dismissing top executives requires boards to drop all of their other activities and devote themselves to full-time crisis management. Outside directors, who often have their own companies to run, not surprisingly find this extremely difficult to do.

Consistent with the theory of board conduct developed here, the Equity Funding board of directors was an abject failure in management. This does not mean that the board was wholly ineffective, of course, because boards of directors are responsible for managing as well as monitoring the corporation.

CHAPTER 6

DISSIDENT DIRECTORS

THe problem of director capture stems from director participation in managerial decision-making, including strategic planning and decisions about the recruitment, retention, and promotion of senior executives. The argument to this point maintains that although involvement by directors in these affairs does not *guarantee* capture, it does make capture highly likely. The social norms of collegiality and cooperation that apply to directors' behavior increase the probability of capture. These norms are reinforced by the fact that directors often socialize among themselves and with management during meetings. Management, of course, has strong private incentives to develop close bonds of trust and friendship with directors.

One particular group of directors, so-called dissident directors, is a striking exception to the general rule that non-management directors are highly susceptible to capture. The dissident director emerged during the late 1990s as an invention of activist professional money managers who became frustrated by the lack of independence of ostensibly independent directors. These money managers nominated their own slate of candidates for director as a means of pressuring incumbent management and the directors supporting them to be more responsive to the interests of outside investors.

The traditional sequence of events leading to the nomination of a dissident director begins with an activist institutional investor acquiring a substantial minority block of shares in a company and then calling on management to make changes to enhance shareholder value. For example, as discussed more fully in chapter 14, in late 2005 and early 2006, activist investor Carl Icahn made a $2 billion investment in Time Warner, acquiring 120 million shares or a 2.6 percent stake in the world's largest media company. Noting Time Warner's languishing share price (the company's share price traded in the $17–$18 range prior to Icahn's massive investment in the company), down from a high of $94 per share in late 1999, Icahn and other activist investors commissioned a study of the company by the investment banking firm Lazard Freres. During the period immediately prior to Icahn's investment, Time Warner's financial performance had been extremely disappointing. In January 2000, Time Warner acquired America Online (AOL) in a merger widely thought to be the most ill-conceived transaction in the history of corporate America, on account of both the high purchase price and the lack of synergies among the various parts of the resulting conglomerate.

At the time of the acquisition, the combined market capitalization of Time Warner and AOL was $280 billion. A scant four years later the combined market capitalization of the enterprise was down to $84 billion. In fiscal year 2002 the company reported a $99 billion loss, resulting from $100 billion in charges, most of which were incurred in a write-down of the goodwill (intangible asset) from the 2000 merger.

Icahn called on Time Warner to initiate immediate share repurchases totaling about $20 billion. Icahn also suggested that Time Warner break itself into four separate companies: Time Warner Cable; the AOL Internet business; the Time Inc. publishing business; and the content business consisting of the Warner Bros. studios and cable channels such as HBO and CNN, with the ultimate goal of moving the value of the stock to $27 per share. As to why Time Warner was unwilling to consider these changes prior to Icahn's prodding, consistent with the analysis concerning the natural proclivity of ostensibly independent non-management directors to become captured by management, during his Time Warner campaign Icahn observed that often corporate "board member are cronies appointed by the very CEOs they are supposed to be watching."[1]

In response to the perceived capture and entrenchment of the Time Warner board of directors, as well as its lack of interest in restructuring the company or taking other actions to increase shareholder value, Icahn proposed nominating a slate of dissident directors to run against the management slate. Rather than face a proxy contest, Time Warner decided to make changes suitable to Icahn in exchange for his agreement to drop his plans. The company agreed to a $20 billion stock repurchase plan and to spin off a substantial part of its cable business to stockholders. Time Warner management also agreed to appoint two new independent board members, chosen in consultation with Icahn, and to identify $1 billion in cost-cutting initiatives over the next two years. For himself, Icahn enjoyed the gains associated with the fact that Time Warner shares increased in value by $2 per share, or 12 percent, on the basis of his efforts.

The Time Warner drama was a recent and widely followed episode in the history of corporate governance illustrating the power of the dissident director. In Time Warner, the activist investors were able to use the threat of appointment of a dissident slate of directors to exert pressure on management and achieve important changes in the operation of the company. The reason the dissident director is such a powerful weapon in the arsenal of outside investors is because dissident directors are far less likely than other directors to be captured by managers. They come in as outsiders.

They are not expected to socialize with the other directors or to use their positions to gain access to other board appointments. By definition, their allegiance lies with the shareholders, and thus their success is determined on the basis of how independent they are, not how cooperative they are. In other words, dissident directors fit the monitoring model of directors rather than the managerial model that applies to directors appointed through traditional channels.

The dissident slate proposed for Armstrong World Industries, a building products and furniture manufacturer, provides another useful illustration of the power of dissident directors. In this case, a dissident slate of four candidates was proposed by the Belzberg family to fill four vacancies on the fourteen-member board of Armstrong World Industries. Of the four Belzberg nominees, one, Harvard Business School professor Michael Jensen, was elected. After assuming his board seat, it was reported that Jensen persuaded the board to replace the management team, and the company experienced a dramatic increase in the value of its shares.

Dissident directors are able to have these effects because they operate under an entirely different set of norms than do traditional directors. Such directors are, by definition, acting against the interests of the senior management of the companies on whose boards they are seeking to serve. Agreeing to act as a dissident director brands the director-nominee as a maverick and virtually eliminates the possibility that the director will be called upon to serve as a traditional director.

The analysis to this point leads to the conclusion that directors, with the notable exception of the dissident directors just described, are susceptible to capture in ways that have not been appreciated by policymakers. The biggest deficiency in policy has been an unrealistic, and wholly unjustified, reliance on the ability of the mythical outside director to solve the corporate governance problems of the public company.

The myth is that outsiders, since they lack a connection to the CEO or to other senior managers, will serve as effective, independent sources of monitoring for management. It may well be true that reducing the number of "management cronies" on boards of directors is a good idea. But the case studies presented above, particularly the Enron case, clearly demonstrate that even boards completely dominated by independent outsiders are not immune from capture. Because board members are required to monitor management, directors often end up evaluating their own decisions, and always end up evaluating the performance of their own, hand-chosen designees whose performance reflects directly on their own abilities as directors.

When selecting directors there appears to be a trade-off between directors who are able to participate with and assist management in decision-making, and directors who are able to provide effective, objective monitoring of corporate performance.

The corporate governance approach to boards of directors raises the question whether alternative approaches to populating boards of directors should be considered. A number of paradigms already exist. As noted above, in Europe, two-tiered boards of directors, where a supervisory board is concerned with monitoring and a managerial board is concerned with providing strategic advice, offer a governance structure that implicitly confronts the conflict between the simultaneous role of boards in both management and monitoring. The problem here is that while management boards may provide useful strategic advice, supervisory boards of directors have never displayed much of an inclination to intervene energetically to displace ineffective managers.

CHECKS AND BALANCES: THE LEGISLATIVE MODEL

In analyzing boards of directors it is important to distinguish the institutional features of boards from analogous governance mechanisms that serve both a monitoring and a management function. Legislatures are a prime example of such a governance mechanism. Congress, for example, both manages governmental affairs when it legislates and monitors the executive and judicial branches as part of the system of checks and balances in the separation of powers. Indeed, when the French political thinker Montesquieu coined the phrase "checks and balances," the "checks" was specifically intended to refer to the monitoring function that each of the three branches of government would perform on the other branches.

Many of the powers routinely exercised by legislatures are directly analogous to the inherent powers of corporate boards of directors. The legislative power to promulgate law is analogous to the board's powers to draft corporate bylaws and to manage the corporation. The legislature's power to confirm executive appointments (exercised under the U.S. constitutional system by the Senate) is analogous to the power of boards to appoint senior corporate officers. Both legislatures and boards of directors have the power to set the budget for the state or the company and to remove executive officers from their posts.

However, legislatures are likely to be far more successful at monitoring than are corporate boards of directors for several reasons. First, officials in the legislature generally do not feel that they owe their jobs to the executive in the same way that members of boards of directors feel that they owe their positions to management. The fact that directors owe, or feel that they owe, management for their positions as directors is an important source of board capture.

A second important difference between legislatures and boards of directors is that boards are more reliant on executive office officials for critical information on which decisions are based. It is common for legislatures to generate the information necessary for making decisions by themselves by holding hearings and conducting their own investigations. Boards are distinct from legislatures in that they lack both the inclination and the capacity to generate information for themselves through a process that is independent of management. One of the most remarkable political innovations since the founding of the American Republic has been the emergence of a distinct, professional congressional bureaucracy that provides Congress with the capability to generate information independent of the administrative agencies associated with the executive branch. When Congress wants to evaluate proposals offered by the executive, it can consult members of its own specialized, full-time, professional staff. This, in turn, inevitably reduces the susceptibility of the executive branch to capture Congress in the way corporate executives can capture boards of directors by controlling the flow of information to the board.

Third, unlike boards of directors, legislatures are generally made up of a variety of political parties that are vigorous rivals for political power. This competitive environment provides those members of the legislature who do not share the executive's party affiliation with strong incentives to monitor the executive to identify corruption or spot flaws in the executive's performance that the minority party can turn to its own political advantage. Similarly, while legislatures often are training grounds for politicians who aspire to displace the leader of the executive branch, boards of directors are almost never populated with competitors for corporate CEOs.

This analysis raises the issue of whether the organizational form of corporate boards of directors should be altered to make boards resemble legislatures even more closely than they do now. Some small steps have been taken to ensure that directors are less beholden to management. Specifically, the effort to make boards more structurally independent culminated in new requirements, imbedded in the corporate governance rules that stock exchanges impose on public companies, which require the nominating committees of the boards of directors of public companies to be independent of management. It is conceivable, but highly unlikely, that the new rules will lead to a diminution in the extent to which the board selection process is used to select members loyal to incumbent management.

Regulatory changes such as this are unlikely to eliminate the problem of board capture for several reasons. For example, there is no restriction on management's ability to nominate directors, and management is likely to remain the primary and most influential source of nominees for board positions for public companies. In addition, even if management's influence over the selection of particular board members declines, senior management retains the ability to influence board members after they are selected. Senior management has elevated the process of cultivating board members to an art form. And, after all, the competitive process by which CEOs are selected naturally produces senior executives who are capable of cultivating strong social and working relationships in situations in which it is in their interests to do so.

The reforms that have been made to the nominating process also do not change the fact that CEOs and other senior managers remain the most important influence on board retention, maintaining virtually plenary control over whether board members are renominated to the board after serving their terms. Knowledge of this fact inevitably effects board behavior. As long as directors continue to owe, or to feel that they owe, their positions as directors to management, board capture is likely to remain a serious governance problem for public corporations.

Since the Enron-era wave of corporate governance scandals there has been a steady increase in the use of professional search firms to identify and recruit board members to their positions. While this undoubtedly can produce directors with impressive credentials and experience, there is no theory or evidence to suggest that the use of professional search firms can improve board independence. In fact, if the process is not carefully structured, using such firms can actually undermine the process of identifying independent directors.

Because search firms rely on repeat business, they have incentives to choose directors with reputations satisfactory to management, rather than directors with reputations for challenging management. And, of course, the search firms are aware of the fact that their bills are processed and their payments are authorized by management, which controls the corporate coffers. The directors chosen by search firms are not free from blame either. Such directors want other directorships, and they want to assimilate well into the boards they are on. This creates a culture of congeniality and cooperation that is not going to be solved simply by using independent nominating committees to select directors.

As a matter of perception, as Michael Jensen and Joe Fuller have observed, "For all intents and purposes, the directors at most companies are employees of the CEO. The CEO does most of the recruiting for the board and extends the offer to join the board. And, except in unusual cases, board members serve at the pleasure of the CEO."[2]

Thus, the structural features defining the ways that board members interact with management are likely to lead to the continuation of the close ties that bind directors and management. The distance we observe

representatives in legislatures and board members is un-
ize the board-management relationship.

ile changes have been made to the way directors are
address the problem of board capture, little has been done
ange the fact that management is generally the only source of information about the company to which board members have access.
Consequently, boards of directors continue to rely disproportionately
on executive office officials for critical information on which decisions
are based than do other institutions with monitoring responsibilities,
such as legislatures.

The asymmetry of information problem has long been recognized as an
impediment to the ability of boards of directors to monitor management
effectively. In the mid-1960s former Supreme Court justice Arthur Goldberg recommended that boards of directors have their own professional
staffs. When Justice Goldberg was a member of the board of TWA, he
tried unsuccessfully to obtain funding for a staff that would provide the
board of directors with information from outside experts, including lawyers, financial economists, and accountants. After Justice Goldberg's request was denied he left the company's board.

The obvious problem with giving boards of directors their own budgets
for generating information about the company from outside sources and
for purchasing the advice of outside experts is that the costs of generating
and analyzing this information would be substantial. Other, more subtle
costs also plague this approach. Often the success of a corporate strategy
depends critically on the ability of the company to develop the plan confidentially and to implement the strategy quickly. Boards that attempt to
mimic management's decision-making process are likely to undermine the
ability of the company to act quickly. And of course, at the end of the
day, the board either will agree with management or will not agree. And,
when the board has a different view than management, there will be no
a priori way to determine which approach should be pursued. Thus, it is
likely that for most, if not all, firms, the costs associated with replicating
management's information-generating process at the board level are likely
to be greater than the benefits.

The Sarbanes-Oxley Act of 2002 does contain a provision explicitly
addressing the problem of board capture caused by pro-management bias
in the flow of information to corporate boards. Section 301 of Sarbanes-
Oxley was designed to ensure that board audit committees, rather than
management, have responsibility for the audit process. Section 301 authorizes the audit committees of boards of directors to engage outside advisors at the corporation's expense to help them oversee the audit function.

Section 301 requires that audit committees be directly responsible for
the appointment, compensation, retention, and oversight of the work of

the accounting firm that has been engaged as the company's independent auditor. The audit committee is responsible for resolving any disagreements that arise between management and the auditor regarding how the company's financial condition and financial results should be reported.

The new provisions of Sarbanes-Oxley also require that the independent auditor report directly to the audit committee rather than to management, as traditionally had been done. The SEC has issued regulations expanding and clarifying the provisions of Sarbanes-Oxley related to the audit committee's oversight. These regulations provide that audit committees have the authority not only to hire the company's auditors but also to terminate the independent auditors. The audit committee also has the authority to approve all audit fees charged by the auditing firm, including both audit engagement fees and any significant fees for non-audit work done by the auditor.

The SEC rules require companies to provide for appropriate funding, as determined by their audit committees, for compensation of the company's outside auditors and any outside advisors that the audit committee decides to engage. The SEC further requires that audit committees be given authority to engage outside advisors, including lawyers, as needed. The SEC's premise is that the advice of outside advisors may be necessary to identify potential conflicts of interest and assess the company's disclosure and other compliance obligations with an independent and critical eye.

By empowering the board to obtain information necessary to monitor management without management's participation in the information-production process, these rules represent the most ambitious attempt to date to deal with the problem of board capture. While there undoubtedly are significant benefits associated with this reallocation of power to audit committees, there also are significant costs. The new audit costs associated with Sarbanes-Oxley have been estimated at around $2 million per year for every company subject to Sarbanes-Oxley. However, the benefits of these regulations may well exceed the costs if the new rules improve the quality and reliability of the financial reporting of public companies. Nevertheless, board capture is likely to remain a problem as long as directors and managers continue to work together to manage public companies.

A similar corporate governance innovation in the United States is the trend toward appointing one outside director as "lead" or "presiding" director. Few companies had designated such a director at the turn of the century, but by 2003, 36 percent of S&P 500 companies had a lead director. By 2004 the percentage was up to 85 percent, and by 2005, 94 percent of S&P 500 boards had designated a lead director. Clearly, one factor driving this trend is the implementation of stock exchange rules requiring that non-management directors preside over board executive session meetings of non-management directors. This rule encourages the appointment of a lead director to preside over executive sessions, but it does not compel the appointment because the same director is not required to preside at every session.

More important, in all likelihood, is the pressure applied by corporate governance advocates for greater board independence. This pressure, however, is not being applied by groups actually desiring the appointment of a lead or presiding director. Rather, the appointment of directors to these positions is in response to groups who actually want companies to separate the job of chief executive officer from the role of board chair.[3] For example, the Council of Independent Directors advocates that boards be chaired by independent, non-management directors. Moreover, institutional investors generally are of the view that the CEO and chair roles should not be combined.[4]

From the point of view of those who see the board of directors as a mechanism for monitoring management, few issues in corporate governance are as troubling as the deeply embedded American tradition of corporate CEOs playing the dual role as chairmen of the boards of the companies they lead. To the extent that boards of directors monitor management, it is indeed perverse to have the monitors led by the leader of the executive groups they ostensibly are monitoring. On the other hand, of course, if the board is supposed to play a managerial role and provide strategic support for the company, as maintained by the managerial model of boards, then combining the CEO function and the function of board chair makes perfect sense.

In 70 percent of large U.S. companies, the CEOs serve simultaneously as board chairs. A study of proxy statements from 2005 by the executive search firm Spencer Stuart revealed that when one includes in the calculation board chairs who have formal connections to management or are former CEOs, only 9 percent of big U.S. companies have board chairs who are truly independent of management.[5]

Lead or presiding directors can serve a symbolic function. Such directors also can add value during times of crisis, scandal, or transition. It is completely erroneous, however, to think outside directors who play an episodic role as lead or presiding directors have the same authority as directors who actually chair their boards. The difference is clear. Board chairs are at the top of the organizational charts of their companies. The CEO and the rest of management report to the board chair. In contrast, presiding and lead directors step in occasionally to run meetings, but they lack the ongoing authority of people with the actual power over boards of directors.

In this respect, there may be some distinction, though not much, between the job of lead director and the job of presiding director. Generally speaking, the choice is made to designate a director as "presiding" rather than "lead" in order not to suggest that one director has any more authority or prestige than any other. The term "presiding director" is thought to connote more equality among directors according to surveys of directors.[6] Further, to emphasize the director equality norm, many companies rotate the position of presiding director.

Those arguing that appointment of lead and presiding directors represents a move toward enhancing the monitoring function of boards neglect the reality that splitting the CEO and chair functions would be a much more important step toward achieving a meaningful monitoring function for the board. By way of example, in a stark departure from the U.S. model, U.K. companies are advised in their Codes of Best Practice not only to separate the roles of CEO and board chair but also to have "senior independent directors" who are charged with representing the views of independent directors.

Perhaps the most deeply rooted distinction between boards of directors and legislatures is that, unlike legislatures, boards of directors lack any "opposition party." Deeply imbedded in the culture of legislatures is the notion that members of the legislature are in rivalrous competition with the executive. Even the most radical conception of the role of independent directors does not go so far as to envision directors committed to the removal of incumbent management in the way members of opposition political parties are committed to the removal of presidents, prime ministers, and other political chief executives.

One feint in the direction of meaningful independence is the relatively new requirement contained in stock exchange corporate governance rules for listed companies that independent directors meet without management in regularly scheduled "executive sessions" to promote open discussion among non-management directors. These rules properly can be described as mere feints in the direction of independence because attendance at these executive session meetings does not depend on true independence: former executives, relatives of current executives, and directors with material financial relationships with the company all participate in these executive sessions.

The distinction between legislatures and corporate boards brings into sharp focus the radical structural and organizational changes in the institution known as the board of directors necessary to make the board truly and meaningfully effective as a monitor of corporate management. Not only would the entire concept of board service be radically altered but the value of the board as a strategic ally of management inevitably would be lost. In other words, from a corporate governance perspective, we must choose between organizing corporations so they have boards that are trusted advisors, and organizing corporations so they have boards that are meaningful monitors.

Perhaps the best way to conceptualize the critical difference between boards of directors and other monitoring institutions such as legislatures is from a transaction costs perspective. Constitutional theory teaches that the system of checks and balances, of which the separation of powers is a part, is designed to *increase* the transaction costs involved in formulating policy.[7] The core problem to which the organizational design of government is directed is that lawmakers would be captured by interest groups who would trade political support in exchange for narrow, special interest, anti-majoritarian legislative "deals." As Madison pointed out in Federalist 10, "among the numerous advantages promised by a well-constructed Union, none deserves to be more accurately developed than its tendency to break and control the violence of faction."[8] The desirability of adopting the Constitution as a means to control interest groups by raising the transaction costs of government was a dominant theme of the sustained defense of the newly proposed Constitution contained in *The Federalist Papers*.

Designing a governance system for government that raises transaction costs is wise because, as Hamilton put it in Federalist 78, the will of the legislature sometimes "stands in opposition to that of the people."[9] As James Buchanan and Gordon Tullock show in their classic work, *The Calculus of Consent*,[10] the constitutional system of checks and balances created what is, in effect, a supermajority voting requirement raising the costs of decision-making, thereby slowing down and reducing the incidence of all sorts of legislation, particularly legislation favoring special interest groups.

From this perspective, the problem with simply exporting the constitutional framework designed for a public law system into the corporate governance system for private sector, publicly held companies is clear: In the private sector, the goal is designing a system in which the decision-making process is more efficient, not less efficient. In the public sector, deliberation is valued as a mechanism through which people can consider what the appropriate goals for public policy are. In the private sector, there is no need for such deliberation because all investors share only one goal: profit maximization. Moreover, in the public sector there is no consensus about how to evaluate the performance of government officials. Eliminating poverty, reducing the budget deficit, protecting the environment, and improving education are all legitimate, competing goals for government. In other words, the goal of corporations is to maximize profits for shareholders. That is the purpose for which corporations are formed and the premise upon which equity capital is raised from investors.

The goal of profit maximization yields results at odds with the broader interests of society only to the extent that the activities associated with profit maximization generate negative externalities, that is, uncompensated costs to third parties. Pollution is the paradigmatic negative externality. Where such externalities exist, government regulation is necessary to cause the polluter to internalize the costs of its profit-making activities.

Recent corporate governance initiatives, including Sarbanes-Oxley, are misguided because they erroneously assume corporate boards can be organized or incentivized successfully to monitor and manage the corporations they serve. All of the available theoretical and empirical evidence suggests this is not the case. In other words, when designing a corporate governance system, it is necessary for contracting parties to choose whether they prefer that their companies be managed by a board that is focused on monitoring management or by a board that is focused on working with management in designing and implementing policies. Recognizing the necessity of choosing between a "managerial" board and a "monitoring" board produces four important insights about the nature of corporate governance.

First, the analysis here provides theoretical support for the empirical fact that independent boards do not improve corporate performance and that boards with too many non-management directors may actually have a negative impact on corporate performance.[11] As Roberta Romano has observed in her exhaustive economic analysis of the effects of Sarbanes-Oxley, none of the numerous studies using a variety of accounting and market performance measures, as well as measures of investment strategies and of the productivity of assets, has found any relation between board independence and performance.[12] In fact, the best social science research suggests the current move in the direction of removing all but one or two insiders from boards may be counterproductive. Sanjai Bhagat and Bernard Black, for example, find evidence that companies with a "moderate number" (three to five) of inside directors on an average-sized board (eleven directors) tend to be more profitable than firms with only one or two directors.[13]

This finding is consistent with the theory of board capture presented in this book. Outside directors on boards with three to five inside directors will have access to more sources of inside information than will outside directors on boards with only one or two inside directors. Having more inside directors reduces the ability of the CEO to ration or slant the information disseminated to the board. The presence of several top managers also enables outside directors to evaluate first-hand the personal dynamics among the management team, and puts the outside directors in a much better position to make decisions about CEO succession, since the outside directors will have observed first-hand the likely internal candidates.

The analysis here is not intended to suggest that having truly independent outside directors is a bad idea. Rather, the point is subtler. The argument is that the current trend of touting independent directors as some sort of corporate governance panacea is misguided. The intense focus on directors deflects attention from market-based solutions to the monitoring problems that are likely far more effective. The theoretical and anecdotal evidence presented here strongly suggests boards are not only highly susceptible to capture, they are also insulated from any serious threat of personal responsibility for their actions. This, it turns out, is not all bad. Protecting directors from liability insulates them from hindsight bias, that is, from being held responsible for honest business decisions that turn out badly. Recognizing that boards are likely to be ineffective at monitoring management, the U.S. system of corporate governance treats boards of directors as what they generally are: close friends and confidants of management. Despite the packaging of corporate governance mavens from academia, not to mention managers, stock exchange officials, and politicians, boards of directors simply are not the fiercely independent outside monitors upon which investors can justifiably rely for strict supervision of corporate management.

Ironically, "the more outside directors the better" is the conventional wisdom regarding best corporate governance practices. The trend has been toward having "supermajority-independent" boards with a single or at most two independent directors. The analysis here supports the empirical findings that having such "supermajority boards" does not improve corporate performance.

Second, focusing on the comparative advantage of boards as managers will clarify and sharpen our understanding about what directors should do and how their performance should be evaluated. If one is of the view that directors are to be effective monitors of corporate performance, then preventing fraud and eliminating conflicts of interest transactions should be the board's focus, as well as the focus of our evaluation of directors' conduct. Alternatively, if one is of the view that directors are partners with management in running the business, then the value added by directors should be manifested in the form of higher-quality strategic decision-making.

The trade-offs involved here are quite tangible. For example, the renewed emphasis on the monitoring function of boards of directors at the expense of the managerial function led to what has been described as a "seismic shift" in board composition, characterized by, among other things, a dramatic reduction in the percentage of CEOs sitting on the boards of directors of companies other than their own.[14] Prior to the Enron era, directors were expected to help CEOs manage their firms, and CEOs from other firms were thought to be the best source of expertise for senior management. In the pre-Enron era, "at least half of the directors of a typical corporation were active CEOs. Highly valued for their general management experience, big picture view, and knowledge of current business challenges, sitting CEOs were the inevitable 'ideal' candidate in nearly every board search."[15] New legislation in the form of Sarbanes-Oxley and new exchange listing requirements urging greater independence and greater board monitoring responsibility have made board membership less attractive to CEOs. As CEO recruitment experts have observed, "This is bad news for companies, which benefit from the exposure their CEOS get to other industries, business issues, and leadership styles through outside board experience."[16]

The post-Enron generation of directors is likely to be less capable than their predecessor directors in performing the *managerial functions* of directors. But there is no particular reason to believe that the new generation will be any more successful in their performance of their *oversight responsibilities*. The new generation of directors is being recruited from farther down the organizational charts of companies, and from the ranks of retired rather than active CEOs, who may lack the confidence or the wherewithal to confront the CEOs of the companies on whose boards they serve.

Third, recognition of the monitoring-managing trade-off makes clear the important role of shareholder choice in determining the appropriate corporate governance of public companies. Because not all firms are the same, and different companies have different corporate governance needs, some firms undoubtedly will be better-off with a board structure favoring directors who specialize in monitoring, while other boards will be better-off with a board structure that favors directors who specialize in management. This, in turn, strongly implies that private contracting, rather than one-size-fits-all government regulation, should determine the job description of corporate directors.

Along these lines, an advantage of private sector ordering in determining the composition of boards is that private ordering can adjust board composition to reflect the efficacy of complementary corporate governance mechanisms. For example, companies that receive substantial outside scrutiny from the markets (because their shares are widely held and control is highly contestable) may need less monitoring from directors than companies whose shares are closely held, making control less contestable. This, in turn, suggests that companies that have substantial anti-takeover protective mechanisms, such as poison pills (described in the subsequent chapter) and staggered boards of directors, are likely to have more independent, outside directors than companies lacking an arsenal of anti-takeover devices.

Finally, and most important, recognition of the managerial-monitoring trade-off and the ubiquitous problem of capture suggests that it may be entirely rational for shareholders to prefer a board that excels in providing managerial support for executives at the expense of ongoing monitoring. In particular, to the extent that outside shareholders are able to rely on objective market mechanisms such as the market for corporate control, arbitrageurs, hedge fund managers, and others to perform the task of monitoring, the costs of having a managerial board rather than a monitoring board may be quite low. Such alternative monitoring mechanisms are less susceptible to capture because they operate at a greater distance from management. With this greater distance comes greater objectivity, which, in turn, makes for better monitoring.

According to conventional wisdom, the board of directors is at the epicenter of corporate governance. Two of the most respected figures in the international corporate governance movement, Adrian Cadbury and Ira Millstein, have described the board of directors as "the foundation of the entire corporate governance paradigm."[17] The analysis in this chapter explains why it is not surprising that managers have not resisted the calls for greater board independence and for the strengthening of board audit committees, compensation committees, and nominating committees promulgated by the stock exchanges at the urging of the SEC. Put simply, these initiatives have not reduced the incidence of board capture. They have failed to increase the constraints on CEOs or to improve the quality of monitoring, and they certainly have not led to any reductions in CEO compensation.

What the intense focus on boards has done is to increase managerial autonomy and draw attention away from other potentially more effective solutions to the challenge of providing reliable, objective monitoring of corporate management. For example, as the following chapter illustrates, the assumption that directors can function simultaneously as monitors and as managers provides the implicit justification for the current regulatory regime in which directors have been given virtually plenary authority to determine what sort of defensive maneuvering a company should be allowed to engage in when faced with a hostile offer for control. This power stems from an assumption that directors are not only good managers, in the sense that they can evaluate outside offers for the company, but also good monitors, in that they can evaluate the prospects of incumbent management as objectively as outside bidders.

CHAPTER 7

FORMAL EXTERNAL INSTITUTIONS
OF CORPORATE GOVERNANCE

The Role of the Securities and Exchange Commission, the Stock Exchanges, and the Credit-Rating Agencies

This chapter considers the extent to which we can reasonably rely on formal governmental and quasi-governmental institutions to provide truly useful corporate governance rules. The major institutions of corporate governance are the Securities and Exchange Commission (SEC), the stock exchanges, and the credit-rating agencies. All three have been a major disappointment. Unfortunately, the reasons for this disappointment appear to be structural, and thus hard to fix now that they are broken. In particular, none of these institutions faces meaningful market incentives to promulgate corporate governance rules that would tend to maximize value for shareholders. As bureaucracies, they have incentives to protect their turf and to increase their budgets. The inevitable proclivity for such groups to be captured should not be ignored either.

THE SECURITIES AND EXCHANGE COMMISSION

The SEC is playing an increasingly active role in corporate governance. For example, in late 2005, the SEC put three high-profile corporate directors on notice that the commission was considering filing suit against them for failing to spot fraud by Conrad Black at Hollinger Corporation. The three executives, James R. Thompson, Richard R. Burt, and Marie-Josée Kravis, constituted the audit committee of Hollinger's board of directors from 1998 to October 2003.[1]

As the *New York Times* reported in its account of the SEC's activities, "[i]f the S.E.C. does file a civil suit against Mr. Thompson, Mr. Burt, and Mrs. Kravis, it would be an unusual attempt to hold independent directors to account for not being vigilant enough about a suspected fraud. None of the three directors received any of the money from payments that are the subject of various actions against the Hollinger co-founder Conrad M. Black and his associates."[2] An internal report by a special committee of Hollinger's board, written under the direction of Richard C. Breeden, a former SEC chairman, said that the audit committee was characterized by an "inexplicable and nearly complete lack of initiative, diligence, or independent thought," which led to "self-righteous and aggressive looting" of the company.[3]

The SEC's aggressive pursuit of these directors in a civil action clearly illustrates the commission's shift from its traditional role of policing the capital markets and promoting full disclosure by public companies to its new, if unauthorized role of corporate governance watchdog.[4] The SEC has found that emphasizing corporate governance is an effective political strategy. Despite the deficiencies in the commission's own corporate governance[5] and its lack of success in regulating, the SEC in recent years has been hugely rewarded in the only two ways that matter for regulatory agencies: massive budget increases and significant new powers.

The commission's performance can be most charitably characterized as anemic in every aspect of its mission during the wave of scandals that rocked corporate America and Wall Street. The SEC failed to anticipate or to deal decisively with the wave of corporate governance scandals (such as, inter alia, Enron, WorldCom, Global Crossing, Adelphia, Tyco, Waste Management, and Sunbeam). The SEC similarly failed to regulate in its own core areas of expertise—disclosure and capital market regulation— as evidenced by the mutual fund market timing and late trading scandals, the scandals involving securities analysts' conflicts of interest, the spinning and laddering of initial public offerings, and the breakdown in the corporate governance of the securities exchanges. In each of these areas, the SEC was motivated to act not on its own initiative but in pallid response to the more energetic activities of the New York attorney general, Eliot Spitzer.

Despite its failures, the SEC's budget more than doubled during the period from 2001 to 2004, increasing from $422.8 million to $913 million, including a sizable $100 million budget increase in fiscal year 2003. Although the SEC was not the only agency to receive a budget increase during this period, the commission was the only federal agency to receive substantial budget increases in both 2003 and 2004.[6] Testifying before the House Commerce-Justice-State Appropriations Subcommittee, then-SEC chair William Donaldson said President Bush's request for $841.5 million in fiscal 2004 "recognizes that the Commission's needs are growing and ongoing."[7] That funding, which was provided to the SEC, would, according to Donaldson, "enable us to meet the remaining fast-approaching deadlines of the Sarbanes-Oxley Act, hire over 800 new staff [and] advance initial start-up funds to the Public Company Accounting

Oversight Board."[8] The 2005 budget request of $893 million for the SEC, an increase of $81 million, was 10 percent above the 2004 level.[9] The president's fiscal year 2004 budget for the SEC was the largest increase in the history of the agency, nearly doubling the SEC budget relative to fiscal year 2002 levels. The resources were used to hire new accountants, lawyers, and examiners "to protect investors and combat corporate wrongdoing."[10] These huge budget increases were strongly supported by the Investment Company Institute (ICI) and the Securities Industry Association (SIA), which are the principal interest groups representing, respectively, the mutual fund industry and the securities industry.

SEC staff received the largest pay increases of any administrative agency in the U.S. government when Congress enacted the Pay Parity Act in 2001. The House Financial Services Committee voted to increase the SEC's pay at its first markup session, elevating SEC staff members to the same pay scale as employees of the Federal Reserve Board and the Comptroller of the Currency.[11]

From a corporate governance perspective, these gigantic budget increases and large pay raises seem highly anomalous, to say the least. According to most observers, the SEC's performance was dismal.[12] Eliot Spitzer even remarked that "heads should roll" at the SEC for its failure to detect and act on abuses in the mutual fund industry and elsewhere.[13] This criticism, of course, seems highly inconsistent with the increases in pay and power that characterize Congress's response to the SEC's failures.

More generally,

> Firms that are subject to market forces at best shrink and sometimes shrivel and die when they under-perform. In other words, the market punishes rather than rewards failure in the private sector. The recent spate of scandals, particularly among mutual funds and market analysts, can hardly be viewed as a success story for the Securities and Exchange Commission. In case it were needed, this recent wave of scandals can be viewed as additional evidence that administrative agencies are not subject to the same Darwinian pressures as firms in the private sector. . . . [T]he crisis of confidence in U.S. capital markets was clearly beneficial to the SEC in general.[14]

The unwarranted budget expansion and pay increases at the SEC are two more examples of the increasing politicization of institutions of corporate governance, a process that has richly rewarded poor performance. Whatever one might say about the increases in salary and power enjoyed by the SEC, these changes most emphatically do not represent pay for performance. At best, one can say that the SEC, like the accounting industry and the credit-rating agencies, is being rewarded in spite of its failure to protect investors or to promote the public interest.

Most emphatically, the point here is not that activist attorney generals such as Eliot Spitzer are good guys and the SEC is full of bad guys. Rather, the point here is that both are political institutions that respond in their own ways to political pressures and constraints. Eliot Spitzer's entrepreneurial activism changed the old rules of the game under which the SEC had been operating. For many years the SEC's chosen strategy was to operate quietly and to refrain from doing much, other than helping to cartelize the securities industry and to increase the demand for securities lawyers and other SEC constituents. All of this was done by an agency that preferred to operate outside of the limelight. Spitzer's contribution to the capital markets was to force the intense Klieg lights of politics onto the work of the SEC. Spitzer's activism made it clear that if the SEC was not going to respond to populist sentiments, then he would respond. Embarrassed and stunned, the SEC responded with a new era of activism. The SEC sought to take away, or at least to share, Eliot Spitzer's bully pulpit. Spitzer's temporary success inspired imitators, from New York's own Andrew Cuomo, who succeeded Spitzer as the state's attorney general, to other aspiring politicians across the nation.

The SEC's Shareholder Access Proposal

In 2003, the SEC proposed Rule 14a-11,[15] representing a major change in the ability of outsiders to gain access to corporate voting machinery. If enacted, this rule would permit qualifying outside shareholders to require the corporations in which they own shares to place their nominee on the corporation's ballot alongside the company's own nominees.[16] Companies subject to the rule also would be required to publish the nominee's supporting statement.

The rule would give shareholder groups this access to the corporate proxy machinery only if one of two triggering events were to occur. The first triggering event is majority shareholder approval of a shareholder proposal to authorize shareholder nominations that has been placed on the ballot under SEC Rule 14a-8. The second triggering event is the casting of 35 percent or more of the total votes in a corporate election by shareholders electing to withhold proxy authority from the incumbent board of directors.[17] If one of these two triggering events occurs, then at the following annual meeting at which directors are to be elected, shareholder nominees must be included in the company's ballot and accompanying proxy statement.[18] As I have observed before, this ineffectual proposal reflects the SEC's "desperate attempt to regain control of the regulatory agenda"[19] in the field of capital markets regulation.

The SEC could, if it were so inclined, enact voting rules improving the quality of corporate governance by reducing the ability of incumbent

managers to bypass shareholders' efforts to vote on management proposals, such as poison pills, that impede the market for corporate control.
Specifically, the SEC has withheld vigorous support of the shareholder
rights bylaw, which would allow investors to enact corporate bylaws requiring directors to permit shareholders to vote on whether a company
should nullify anti-takeover devices, such as the poison pill, when a company receives a fully funded cash takeover bid for all of its outstanding
shares at a substantial premium to market.[20]

Along these lines, the explicit provisions in the SEC's proposed rules
that make it impossible for shareholders to replace a majority of incumbent directors are critical to understanding the SEC's proposal regarding
director nominations. According to the proposal, any candidate nominated by the shareholders must be an independent director under listing
standards applicable to the issuer, and must also be independent of the
nominating shareholders. This means that a nominee, no matter how
much support he or she has from the shareholders, cannot be affiliated
with an outside group seeking to gain control of the board. Moreover,
only one candidate can be nominated if the board has fewer than nine
members. Two candidates may be nominated if the board consists of nine
to nineteen directors and votes are withheld from two management nominees. The number of nominees increases to a maximum of three if the
board is composed of twenty or more directors and votes are withheld
from three management nominees.[21] Thus, under the SEC's proposal,
shareholders can only replace two-ninths of the board, far less than the
majority necessary for control. And even with this pale version of a control, contest is diminished further by the fact that it takes two election
cycles before any shareholder nominees can be elected, because the first
election is needed to obtain the votes necessary to trigger an election the
following year. The time lag extends still further because to nominate a
candidate for the board, shareholders and shareholder groups must have
held over 5 percent of the issuer's securities for at least two years.[22]

Thus, the SEC's proposed rule cannot be construed as bolstering the
faltering market for corporate control because it cannot be used to facilitate a control transaction. Rather, as I have previously observed, the SEC's
proposed new rule is a "poorly disguised attempt [by the SEC] to link itself
to a new constituency: public interest pension funds and other 'activist'
shareholder groups, whose preferences and agendas are unlikely to reflect
the profit-maximization motive that is embraced by the average investor."[23]

The SEC's Mutual Fund Board Chairman Independence Rule

In another example of the new, post-Enron SEC, on June 23, 2004, by a
vote of three to two, the SEC voted to require that the chairs of mutual

funds' boards of directors be independent of the advisors of such funds.[24] Commissioner Cynthia Glassman commented on the complete lack of empirical or theoretical justification for this proposal.

> It is a fact that many of the top-rated funds today based on high performance and low fees have inside chairs. Why should we tell shareholders they can no longer have the form of governance that produced this high level of performance? And further, why should we require them to pay for it? There can be no doubt that this requirement will add to fund expenses. An independent chair cannot be expected to have—and in most cases, will not have—hands-on knowledge about fund operations. Therefore, to be effective, the chair would have to hire a staff. Shareholders will bear that expense as well as the likely additional cost of the independent chairman. In sum, the benefits are illusory, but the costs are real.[25]

Commissioner Glassman also noted the lack of empirical evidence for the assumption inherent in this rule that mutual funds with independent chairs have either higher returns or lower overhead and administrative costs than mutual funds chaired by insiders.[26] As I have previously noted,

> As with the SEC's proposed shareholder ballot-access rule, it appears that in promulgating the chairman independence rule, the Commission is clearly less concerned with shareholder welfare and the quality of U.S. capital markets than it has been in the past. The public interest concern with the quality of U.S. investors and capital markets appears to have been replaced by a regulatory agenda that includes rulemaking oriented toward special-interest groups.[27]

In the post-Enron world, the SEC, always a bureaucracy interested in maximizing political support, is guided by political considerations rather than policy considerations in its determination of which new corporate governance rules should be promulgated, and in determining how its existing rules should be enforced. Rather than use its interpretive and regulatory powers to promulgate regulations that improve the functioning of the market for corporate control or encourage initial public offerings, the SEC has chosen to allocate its resources toward cosmetic measures, like shareholder ballot access and independent board chairs for mutual funds. The only bottom line that will be improved by passage of these measures is the SEC's own.[28]

The SEC's success in procuring more resources in the form of higher budget allocations does not necessarily mean that the SEC's power and prestige have increased in the wake of the corporate scandals that rocked Wall Street. Also, the SEC's budget increases do not reflect heightened public recognition of the SEC's relevance or effectiveness. Rather, the SEC's success in the budgetary process reflects the need for federal officials

TABLE 7.1
SEC Budget History vs. Actual Expenses

Fiscal Year	Budget Authority	Actual Obligations	Percentage Increase from Previous Year
1990	$166,633	$165,211	—
1991	189,083	187,689	13
1992	225,792	224,281	19
1993	253,235	251,871	12
1994	269,150	266,249	6
1995	300,437	284,755	12
1996	300,921	296,533	0
1997	311,100	308,591	3.4
1998	315,000	311,143	1.3
1999	341,574	338,887	8
2000	377,000	369,825	10
2001	422,800	412,618	12
2002	513,989	487,345	22
2003	716,350	619,321	39
2004	811,500	—	13
2005	913,000	—	13

Note: $ in thousands; data from Securities and Exchange Commission, "Frequently Requested FOIA Document: Budget History—BA [Budget Authority] vs. Actual Obligations," http://www.sec.gov/foia/docs/budgetact.htm. See also Jonathan R. Macey, "Positive Political Theory and Federal Usurpation of the Regulation of Corporate Governance: The Coming Preemption of the Martin Act," *Notre Dame Law Review* 80 (2006): 951–74, at 969, table 1, and my own calculations.

to appear to be "doing something" in the wake of the crises that have emerged on Main Street (Enron, Global Crossing, Adelphia, Tyco, Waste Management, and Sunbeam), and in the wake of the scandals that the SEC's main rival, Eliot Spitzer, uncovered on Wall Street (i.e., financial analysts and market timers at mutual funds).

As an economic matter, corporate governance rules can be categorized as either effective or ineffective. As a political matter, corporate governance rules can be categorized as either favored or disfavored. Strikingly, this book has shown that the corporate governance rules that seem to be most favored in the political realm are precisely the rules that are least effective in practice. By contrast, the corporate governance rules that are the most effective, as measured by the extent to which they reduce agency costs and enhance shareholder wealth, are those that are least favored in the realm of politics. These observations do not bode well for the future of the U.S. economy.

The Organized Stock Exchanges

Organized stock exchanges, particularly the New York Stock Exchange, used to play an important role in U.S. corporate governance. When a public corporation listed on a stock exchange, that corporation was making a credible commitment to abide by a set of corporate governance rules designed to maximize shareholder wealth.[29] The commitment was made credible by the threat of delisting, which, historically, had draconian effects on companies because of the lack of alternative trading venues for shares in public companies. Over time, however, advances in technology and the development of markets have weakened the primacy of the traditional exchanges. A whole host of competitors for the traditional stock exchanges have emerged.

Traditionally, firms have not listed on more than one venue. When firms changed from one trading venue to another, it was usually because they had grown and were promoted from the over-the-counter markets to the NYSE. Decisions by highly successful companies, such as Google and Microsoft, to remain in the over-the-counter markets, along with the ability of firms such as Hewlett-Packard to be simultaneously listed on both the NYSE and NASDAQ, illustrate the change in the traditional ordering.

The modern stock exchange is subject to vigorous competition from a variety of sources, including both rival exchanges and alternative trading venues, such as Electronic Communications Networks (ECNs) and Alternative Trading Systems (ATSs). This competition has strained the exchanges' capacity for self-regulation and undermined their incentives to regulate in the public interest with respect to issues related to the corporate governance of their members. Moreover, the available evidence indicates the organized exchanges do not even act as stand-alone regulators anymore. Instead, they are better understood as conduits for the SEC, which coordinates the corporate governance regulations that ostensibly are promulgated under the exchanges' authority as self-regulatory organizations.[30] As the *Special Study on Market Structure, Listing Standards and Corporate Governance* has pointed out, "the SEC had adopted a practice of encouraging the exchanges 'voluntarily' to adopt given corporate governance listing standards and in the process has urged the exchanges' listed companies and shareholders to reach consensus on those standards."[31] The SEC now coordinates the regulatory price fixing among the exchanges' self-regulatory organizations with respect to every facet of the exchanges' relationships with listed companies. Thus, the SEC has undermined the traditional way that exchanges competed with one another to provide efficient corporate governance rules.

A cogent example of this phenomenon is the one-share, one-vote listing requirement. During the 1980s, the managers of several firms listed on the NYSE were concerned about the possibility of a hostile takeover and wanted to adopt a particularly potent defensive strategy, which involved recapitalizing the firm with additional classes of voting stock, to be held by management, which would have significantly greater voting rights than the shares held by other shareholders. The problem with this recapitalization strategy was that it clearly violated a longstanding NYSE rule providing that all shares of common stock of listed companies could have one, and only one, vote.[32]

The SEC was deeply concerned that several high-profile listed firms, notably General Motors Corporation and Dow Jones, Inc., wanted to engage in these so-called dual-class recapitalizations. The NYSE was alarmed when both of these firms decided to proceed with their plans to offer dual classes of voting stock, in flagrant violation of the NYSE's rules. For the NYSE, delisting these firms would have caused a significant loss of both prestige and revenue. But for GM and Dow Jones, the consequences would have been negligible. Delisting would have meant that shares in the two firms would have been traded in a competing forum, such as the American Stock Exchange or the NASDAQ, both of which permitted dual-class recapitalizations.

This episode illustrates the NYSE's inability to enforce its own corporate governance rules in today's new world of competing trading venues. Ultimately, the NYSE was forced to relax its listing requirements to avoid losing two of its most valuable listings. In order to avoid a recurrence of this embarrassing episode, the NYSE then petitioned the SEC to impose a uniform voting rights standard for all publicly traded firms. Although the SEC granted the NYSE's request, the SEC's uniform voting rights standard was ruled invalid as an impermissible extension of the commission's regulatory authority into the realm of corporate governance, which traditionally is the domain of the states.[33]

THE CREDIT-RATING AGENCIES

Credit ratings from credit-rating agencies such as Moody's and Standard and Poor's provide predictive opinions on an isolated characteristic of a company—the likelihood that the company will be able to repay its rated debt in a timely manner. Credit-rating agencies attempt to downplay the role they play in corporate governance, claiming that because their ratings are grounded on analysis of information generated by the companies themselves, they are not in the business of searching for and exposing fraud.[34] This claim is somewhat disingenuous. It is generally accepted that the uninformed investors inhabiting financial markets clearly rely on the ratings generated by the major credit-rating agencies. Why this is the case is something of a mystery.

Moreover, as Frank Partnoy has observed, there is a great deal of evidence indicating that the product generated by the rating agencies, that is, information, is both stale and inaccurate.[35] The truly abominable performance of the credit-rating agencies in their ratings of a whole host of debt issues, including Orange County, Mercury Finance, Pacific Gas & Electric, Enron, WorldCom, and, most recently, General Motors and Ford, amply illustrates this point, as do a plethora of academic studies showing that changes in credit ratings lag the market.[36]

In particular, the Enron case provides a rather illustrative example of the credit ratings' lag behind the market.

> Neither Standard & Poor's nor Moody's downgraded Enron's debt below investment grade status until November 28, 2001, four days before the firm's bankruptcy, when the company's share price had plunged to a paltry sixty-one cents. . . . For Enron, the corporation's $250 million in rated senior unsecured debt had declined in value from ninety cents to thirty-five cents on the dollar in the month preceding its downgrade. In other words, the market rejected the investment grade rating on Enron's debt before the credit rating agencies exercised their power to downgrade it.[37]

As with accounting firms, credit-rating agencies have not lived up to their promise as important components of the corporate governance infrastructure. And, as with accounting firms, public choice theory and the economic theory of regulation provide the best explanation for the failure of credit rating in American corporate governance. Historically, companies that utilized the public markets for debt and equity utilized credit-rating agencies for the same reason they utilized the services of accounting firms: they wanted their financial condition to be verified by a credible, independent source. Demand for the services of rating agencies derived from the fact that companies lowered their capital costs when they subscribed to the services of credit-rating agencies, and the savings from such lower capital costs were greater than the costs of the subscription fees charged by the credit-rating agencies for assigning a rating to a company's securities.

The historical evolution of the demand for the services of credit-rating agencies is identical to that of the accounting firms. Genuine demand fueled by market forces was displaced by ersatz demand fueled by regulatory requirements. This, in turn, led to the cartelization of both industries, as the number of accounting firms auditing large public companies dropped to four, and the number of credit-rating agencies enjoying the coveted status of an SEC-sanctioned Nationally Recognized Statistical Rating Organizations (NRSROs) has dropped to three. As cartelization has occurred, we also have observed a marked diminution in the quality of the services provided to investors and markets in both industries.[38]

SEC regulation, in the form of the NRSRO designation, has created an artificial demand for ratings, despite their lack of usefulness to investors.[39] These regulations require that investors limit their investments in companies to those whose debt is rated by one of the three companies designated by the SEC as an NRSRO. The SEC uses NRSRO credit ratings to determine how much capital broker-dealer firms must maintain when they hold debt securities under Rule 15c3-1 of the Securities Exchange Act of 1934 (the "Exchange Act"). The ratings of NRSROs are also used to measure the credit risk of short-term instruments in the regulation of money market funds under Rule 2a-7 of the Investment Company Act of 1940 (the "1940 Act"). Issuers of certain debt securities that receive an investment-grade rating from an NRSRO are entitled to register under the Securities Act of 1933 (the "Securities Act") on the shorter Form FS-3. Banking and other regulators similarly rely on NRSRO credit ratings to protect the capital of financial institutions. Therefore, many regulated financial institutions can only purchase certain types of securities if they have received an investment-grade rating from an NRSRO.[40]

Thus, the best explanation as to why credit-rating agencies simultaneously enjoy great success while providing no information of value to the investing public is that the SEC inadvertently created an artificial regulatory demand for the services of a small number of favored ratings agencies when it misguidedly invented the NRSRO designation. This designation has, over time, caused an artificial demand for ratings, despite their lack of usefulness to investors.

Responding to decades of inaction by the SEC and growing alarm at the poor performance of credit-rating agencies, the Credit Rating Duopoly Relief Act was enacted and signed into law in the summer of 2006. The bill is aimed at eliminating the SEC's ability to determine which credit-rating agencies qualify for the NRSRO designation, and limits the SEC's power over credit-rating agencies to inspecting the agencies and instituting enforcement actions against them if they violate the securities laws. The statute requires that credit-rating agencies register with the SEC, but it also removes the SEC's discretion to register such agencies as NRSROs if they have been in business for three years.

It is not clear what effect, if any, the new statute will have on credit-rating agencies' role in corporate governance. It seems clear the big ratings agencies never had to worry about competition before, but the world is different now. One possible manifestation of the new competition will be a race to quality among the credit-rating agencies in which each competes to develop a reputation as the best, most reliable, and most accurate corporate overseer. This, of course, would be wonderful for corporate governance, but it is by no means clear that this will happen.

Another possibility is that companies, with greater choice, will cause a "race to the bottom," in which issuers who must have their debt rated by an NRSRO retain NRSROs based on which is the most malleable and the most liberal with the investment-grade rating. As between these two possibilities, the early evidence is not particularly promising. From a theoretical perspective, credit-rating agencies have an obvious conflict of interest. As one 2003 analysis of the ratings industry by two economists from the Board of Governors of the Federal Reserve pointed out, this conflict stems from the fact that "they have a financial incentive to accommodate the preferences of bond issuers because they are selected and paid by the issuers. This incentive conflicts with the agencies' stated goal of supplying independent and objective credit-risk analysis to investors."[41] Of course, this conflict is tempered by reputation concerns, which may lead the credit-rating agencies to act in ways that benefit investors because concern for their reputation provides incentives to generate accurate, timely ratings and rating adjustments. As the following anecdote suggests, the new Credit Rating Duopoly Relief Act may exacerbate this traditional conflict of interest. It simply is too soon to know whether the conflicts of interest will dominate or be dominated by the reputational concerns of credit-rating agencies as they enter a new, unprecedented environment of intrafirm competition.

In March 2007, the Oregon utility Portland General Electric (PGE) filed for approval from the Oregon Public Utility Commission for a 9 percent raise in the rates it charged for electricity. By law, without such regulatory approval, the company would not be permitted to raise its rates. As the Pulitzer Prize–winning investigative reporter Nigel Jaquiss pointed out in his column in the *Willamette Weekly*, one of the key pieces of evidence that PGE used to support its request was a report prepared by the credit-rating agency Standard & Poor's (S&P). PGE had hired S&P to rate its bonds, so the company was a paying client of the rating agency. S&P assisted its client by issuing a report saying that without a rate increase, the company's "financial position will be in jeopardy."[42] Even worse, as Jaquiss points out, it appears the credit-rating agency actually allowed the utility to edit its report. Specifically, the utility "redlined" or edited three drafts of the S&P report, apparently in an effort to make PGE's financial condition look worse and therefore bolster its rate-hike request.[43]

Though the PGE official who did the actual editing claimed all of her comments "were suggestions that PGE could accept or reject,"[44] such editing would have violated S&P's own internal code of conduct, which provides that "to maintain Ratings Services' independence, objectivity, and credibility, Ratings Services shall maintain complete editorial control at all times over Ratings Actions and all other materials it disseminates to the public, including . . . reports, research updates, studies, commentaries . . . or any other information relating to its ratings."[45] The report goes on to say that "rating services and its analysts shall use care and analytic judgment to maintain both the substance and appearance of independence and objectivity."[46]

Clearly, the Credit Rating Duopoly Relief Act will affect the competitive environment in which the credit-rating agencies operate. Unfortunately, it is possible that the new statute will make credit-rating agencies less effective mechanisms of corporate governance by exacerbating the conflicts of interest existing between rating agencies and their clients. It also is possible that the new competition engendered by the statute will make credit-rating agencies more effective at corporate governance by providing them with incentives to issue timely, high-quality ratings to garner business by improving their reputation among investors. While it is far too soon to tell, the early anecdotal evidence is not promising.

CHAPTER 8

THE MARKET FOR CORPORATE CONTROL

The most important market-inspired component of the U.S. corporate governance infrastructure is the market for corporate control.[1] An efficient, vibrant market for corporate control deters managers from shirking by running the firm below its full performance potential. Because running a firm below its firm potential would make it more likely that the company's incumbent management would be replaced in a hostile acquisition, a robust market for corporate control is vitally important as a corporate mechanism for monitoring and disciplining managers.[2]

Ironically, however, as the scientific evidence about the importance of the market for corporate control became so overwhelming as to be incontrovertible,[3] regulations impeding the market for corporate control became ubiquitous.[4] This confluence of events was not random. Rather, the law reflects the private interests of corporate managers, a discrete, well-organized interest group whose preferences are championed by organizations such as labor unions and the Business Roundtable.[5]

As my colleague Roberta Romano has observed, a massive number of empirical studies have found uniformly and unanimously that regardless of the time period or acquisitive form, there are statistically significant positive abnormal returns on the investments of shareholders in companies that receive takeover bids.[6] Clearly political theory, not economic theory, is required to explain the regulatory burdens that impede the market for corporate control. The following section describes the relationship between the goals of corporate governance and the operation of the market for corporate control. This section is followed by an analysis of the legal impediments that have arisen to thwart the market for corporate control.

CORPORATE GOVERNANCE, POLITICS, AND THE MARKET FOR CORPORATE CONTROL

The market for corporate control is a pure market process. Government intervention is not needed to correct structural defects in this market. Rather, regulatory intervention, when it occurs, reflects the efforts of special interest groups such as managers and labor unions to impede the market process to protect incumbent management at firms that are either actual or potential targets.

The market for corporate control is simply risk arbitrage on a very grand scale. Risk arbitrage involves the time-honored process of "buying low and selling high." Unfortunately, the response by corporate managers to efforts by entrepreneurs to enter this market has been to "buy law" to prevent takeover professionals from buying low.

In efficient capital markets, poor performance is hard to hide. When firms fare poorly, such poor performance is reflected in the firm's share prices and in a host of other indicators, including accounting data, particularly reported earnings, and sales performance in comparison to rival companies. All of these indicators are highly accessible and visible to a whole host of sophisticated outsiders, such as analysts, arbitrageurs, and venture capitalists watching the company. When these indicators lag relative to industry and sector competitors, potential acquirers have strong incentives to notice: by acquiring the shares of a poorly managed firm at a depressed price that reflects the firm's poor performance, the acquirer can institute the changes necessary to restore top corporate performance. Generally, these changes require that the top management of the company being acquired be displaced by a new management team.

A properly functioning market for corporate control clearly then provides benefits for the shareholders of companies whose shares are purchased by the outside bidder. Such shareholders receive a substantial premium, generally around 50 percent of the price at which the target firm's shares had been trading before the bid.[7] Moreover, even non-selling shareholders benefit when there is a hostile acquisition of a public company in which they own shares. Such non-selling shareholders benefit when the new management team takes over, reorganizes the target company, and does what successful bidders do: provide better discipline for management, seek strategic synergies with other companies, and sell assets, subsidiaries, divisions, and other components of the target that are not adding value to shareholders. In efficient capital markets, share prices for non-selling shareholders go up when these strategic changes are announced by competent bidders.

It is quite clear that takeovers provide benefits for target firm shareholders, whether they sell their shares or not. Absent regulatory distortions, the best strategy for target management to avoid being ousted in a hostile takeover is to keep share prices high. Higher share prices deter hostile bids by making such bids more costly because they destroy the arbitrage potential that exists when shares are undervalued relative to their true potential.[8]

Because share prices represent the best available—and indeed the only—real-time, unbiased assessment of a company's performance and future prospects, by providing strong incentives for target managers to keep such share prices high, the market for corporate control is an elemental component of any corporate governance system in which the owners of residual claims in the company are not in positions of management. Improved corporate governance is a by-product of an efficient market for corporate control. Such improved governance, however, is not limited to firms that actually receive premium bids from outside acquirers. Rather, the genius of the market for corporate control as a corporate governance device is that it improves the quality of the corporate performance at all publicly held firms whose shares are "contestable."[9]

The reason that the benefits of the monitoring provided by potential bidders are not limited to the shareholders in firms fortunate enough actually to receive a bid from a hostile bidder is because managers who want to avoid being displaced in a hostile takeover must keep the prices of their firms' shares high. Because managers and boards know that they will be ousted following a successful hostile acquisition, they will work harder to maximize shareholder value. Thus, a takeover threat will not only discipline management, but also discipline the non-monitoring board.[10]

The tender offer was invented in the 1960s, and fundamentally changed the economic landscape for American corporations. As Theodor Baums and Kenneth Scott recently observed, prior to the introduction of the tender offer, launching a proxy fight for the election of directors was the only way that a challenger could hope to oust an underperforming incumbent management team.[11]

As a corporate governance device, proxy fights suffer from two distinct disadvantages relative to takeovers. First, incumbent management enjoys a number of structural advantages over outsiders in proxy contests. Incumbent management controls the timing of the contest and can charge election expenses to the company. The incumbents also have better information about who the company's shareholders are and about what issues are likely to appeal to particular cohorts of shareholders. Moreover, when a company is involved in a proxy fight, shareholders are required to choose between the incumbent management team, which is a known quantity, and a group of unknown outside raiders.[12]

But the second, more profound deficiency in proxy contests as corporate governance devices is that those launching proxy contests lack credibility relative to those launching takeover contests in the form of tender offers. Potential acquirers making tender offers for a controlling block of a company's shares have enormous credibility because they are risking their own capital to acquire the controlling block. Having gained control of the company, tender-offerors stand to benefit by managing the business in such a way as to increase the value of their shares, and the shares of their fellow shareholders.

By contrast, an entrepreneur who launches a proxy contest need not, in theory, own any shares in the target company whose board she seeks to displace. Rather, the outside "raider," as they are called, asks that shareholders take it on faith that a successful proxy battle will lead to improvements in corporate governance. Thus, it is not surprising in the least that proxy contests are rarely successful unless organized and conducted by raiders who have very significant investments in the shares of the target firms. Only raiders who also are large block holders at the time they launch their proxy contests can make a credible commitment to the target firm shareholders that their goal is to maximize the value of the entire firm, rather than simply to loot the firm to obtain the private benefits of control.

Thus, the emergence of the hostile tender offer in the 1960s should be viewed as a major innovation in the history of corporate governance. It provided the first large-scale, self-effectuating corporate control devices. The hostile tender offer is large scale because it affects all shareholders and because it involves the deployment of massive resources by outside bidders. These resources are required to monitor potential target companies, to evaluate which incumbent management teams are operating so inefficiently that they warrant being displaced in a hostile bid, to effectuate the hostile acquisition, and to implement the strategic plan to redeploy the target company's assets to higher-valuing uses.

The market for corporate control is self-effectuating because it emerges spontaneously from market forces without the need for any action taken or resources deployed on the part of the subject company. An efficient market for corporate control is such an effective corporate governance device that it dramatically facilitates the separation of equity ownership and managerial responsibility in unique ways not replicable by other corporate governance devices. In particular, the tender offer, which is the pivotal device in the market for corporate control, obviates the need for target company shareholders to make comparisons of the relative merits of competing management teams before deciding whether to approve a proposed change in control transaction. Rather, as Baums and Scott have observed, "With the development of the tender offer in the 1960s, [shareholders] didn't have to make a comparison between alternative management teams but merely a comparison between the price being offered by the acquirer and the market price under current management."[13]

Under this system, acquirers seeking control of target companies began to fare much better than they had when the principal strategy available to them was the proxy contest, but target management fared worse. As the market for corporate control became more effective as a governing device, life became less comfortable for incumbent management, who felt increasing pressure to maintain high share prices to reduce the probability that they would face a hostile tender offer for control.

LEGAL IMPEDIMENTS TO THE MARKET
FOR CORPORATE CONTROL

In addition to simply being more responsive to the needs of shareholders, management resorted to a number of additional tactics in response to the tender offer era. First, in 1968 management registered its strong negative reaction to an unfettered operation of the market for corporate control by supporting the passage of the Williams Act, which deterred corporate takeovers by dramatically increasing both the out-of-pocket costs and the legal risks that bidders face when launching a tender offer.

Specifically, the Williams Act appropriates valuable property rights in information belonging to bidders by requiring such bidders to disclose such information to the financial markets. Among other things, the Williams Act requires that individuals, groups, and firms making tender offers supply the markets with their identities, their plans for the target firm, and their sources of financing.[14] The requirements of the act made it easier for target firm management to entrench themselves by giving them "earlier warning" about an outside bid, as well as more time to resist.[15] As a consequence of the Williams Act and other anti-takeover efforts, hostile takeovers began a steady decline from 14 percent to 4 percent of all mergers and acquisitions activity in the decade after the statute was passed in 1968.[16]

Second, managers championed a number of changes to their charters and bylaws designed to impede the market for corporate control. As Baums and Scott have observed, managers and their attorneys implemented staggered boards of directors; abolished the right of shareholders to remove directors without cause, to hold special meetings, or to act by written consent without meeting; and employed supermajority shareholder vote requirements to approve clean-up mergers that members of the prior board had not approved.[17]

Two factors prevented managers from being able to accomplish very much to retard the market for corporate control. First, fundamental changes to a company's corporate governance structure require that a company change its books of incorporation (corporate charter), which, in turn, requires shareholder approval. Rational shareholders would not approve proposed changes to the governance structure of a company that would make them worse-off by impeding the operation of the market for corporate control. Second, there were important innovations in the market for corporate control, particularly the emergence of the leveraged buyout and junk bond financing, that facilitated the takeover market and tended to counteract the pernicious effects of managerial entrenchment efforts.[18]

The Delaware judiciary struck a grave blow to shareholders and to the free operation of the market for corporate control when it upheld the use of a radical new anti-takeover device, the poison pill, in *Moran v. Household International*.[19] This case deserves to be counted as the worst opinion in the history of corporate law. Countless trillions of dollars in shareholder wealth have been lost by the failure of state court judges, particularly in Delaware, to protect the interests of shareholders during corporate control contests.[20]

The Poison Pill

Technically called a "shareholder rights plan," the term "poison pill" is the nickname for a particular device utilized by public companies to avoid a hostile takeover by making themselves unattractive to the investor who wants to make the hostile acquisition. Poison pills prevent hostile take-overs by increasing the costs of acquiring a large block of shares in a target company whose board has installed a poison pill. A poison pill involves the issuance by a company of a new class of stock, usually pre-ferred shares, that provides holders with the rights to purchase additional shares, either in the target company ("flip-in" pills) or even in the acquirer ("flip-over" pills), whenever certain triggering events occur. The most common triggering event is the acquisition of a certain threshold percent-age (often 30 percent) of target firm shares by any acquirer that the target company board finds unacceptable. Should an outside bidder make acqui-sitions that exceed the designated threshold without the permission of the target firm's board of directors, the target firm's shareholders are able to purchase additional shares at hugely discounted prices. The device is called a poison pill because these discount purchases have the intended effect of diluting the ownership interests of the outside bidder, who is specifically precluded from participating in the discount purchases permit-ted to the other investors.

Because poison pills have been technically evaluated as representing merely the issuance of a new class of shares, which most companies can do without shareholder approval, poison pills may be implemented by corporate boards without any shareholder action. When adopted, the rights initially attach to the corporation's outstanding common stock, cannot be traded separately from the common stock, and are priced so that exercise of the option would be economically irrational. As men-tioned above, the pill or "rights" become exercisable and can trade sepa-rately from the common stock only when a triggering event occurs.

A pill's flip-over feature typically is triggered when the target is merged into the acquirer or one of its affiliates after the acquirer obtains the specified percentage of the target's common stock. When this triggering event occurs, the target firm's shareholders become entitled to purchase common stock of the acquiring company, typically at a deeply discounted price. These purchases have the effect of impairing the acquirer's capital structure and drastically diluting the interest of the acquirer's previous stockholders. Where flip-over pills are triggered by the merger of the acquirer and the target, flip-in pills are triggered merely by the acquisition of a specified percentage (usually 20 percent) of the issuer's common stock. When a flip-in pill is triggered, all target firm shareholders except the acquirer are permitted to buy shares in the target at a deeply discounted price.

Poison pills impede the market for corporate control by eliminating the possibility of hostile takeovers in firms with poison pills in place. Significantly, the shareholder "rights" distributed by companies as poison pills can be redeemed by the target at little or no cost to the issuing company. Redeeming the rights eliminates the poison pill and permits an acquisition to proceed. In other words, the consequence of the poison pill is to require acquirers to obtain the approval of target company boards of directors before proceeding. The harm to acquiring firm shareholders from the triggering of a poison pill is so severe that the poison pill has never been intentionally triggered.[21]

Thus, the poison pill has effectively destroyed the hostile takeover. Companies with the most venal management teams are immune from ouster in a hostile takeover. Only companies with benign, other-regarding boards of directors will redeem their poison pill rights plans and permit outside acquirers to effectuate a change in control.

The Delaware Judiciary

In a key passage in *Moran*, the Delaware Supreme Court observed that permitting companies to implement poison pill rights plans without shareholder votes would not have deleterious corporate governance effects because such plans would be subject to intense scrutiny by the courts. In particular, with respect to the poison pill rights plan adopted by Household International, the court asserted that "the Rights Plan is not absolute. When the Household Board of Directors is faced with a tender offer and a request to redeem the Rights, they will not be able to arbitrarily reject the offer. They will be held to the same fiduciary standards any other board of directors would be held to in deciding to adopt a defensive mechanism, the same standard as they were held to in originally approving the Rights Plan."[22]

Unfortunately, state courts in general and the Delaware courts in particular have not lived up to their obligation to protect shareholders by policing the implementation, if not the adoption, of poison pills.[23] Instead, the requirement that the decision to use the pill be evaluated by state courts to determine whether the decision is consistent with the directors' fiduciary responsibilities has "turned out to be of little substance."[24] Subsequent decisions have permitted target company boards of directors to thwart outside acquisition attempts by leaving their poison pill rights plans in place on the basis of highly dubious justifications. For example, in *Paramount Communications v. Time, Inc.*,[25] the court was persuaded not to act to force management to redeem its pill on the thin reed of management's highly self-serving claim that it had a "strategic plan" that it thought would lead to greater returns to shareholders than the acquirer was offering.[26] The decision in *Time* is particularly troubling because the bid was all cash and was made for 100 percent of the target company's shares.[27] The only coherent justification for defensive tactics such as the poison pill is that they protect shareholders from coercive two-tiered bids, in which shareholders are induced to sell their shares to a bidder offering to purchase less than 100 percent of the company's outstanding shares, because they are concerned that the bidder will obtain control of the firm and mismanage it, thereby driving down the value of any remaining shares.[28] These sorts of two-tiered offers are coercive because target firm shareholders face a collective action problem similar to a prisoner's dilemma: the best outcome for all shareholders would be for none to tender in the first stage of a coercive two-tiered offer, but the best outcome for any individual shareholder would be to be able to sell her shares for cash, particularly if the coercive bidder's bid succeeds.

In *Moran* itself, the court justified allowing the target firm to retain its poison pill because the pill was adopted "in reaction to what it perceived to be the threat in the market place of coercive two-tier tender offers."[29] Later court decisions have ignored the fundamental distinction between two-tier bids and cash bids for 100 percent of the stock in the target company.[30] For example, in *Time*, the Delaware Supreme Court permitted the firm to retain its poison pill despite the fact that the bidder was offering all cash for 100 percent of the target firm's shares, thereby obviating any argument that the pill was needed to protect target firm shareholders from the coercive effect of a two-tier bid.[31]

Thus, courts have failed to live up to their promise to protect shareholders from the use of the poison pill to insulate incumbent management from the salutary effects of the market for corporate control. In addition, courts have failed to restrict the use of poison pills to their proper context—the regulation of coercive two-tier tender offers. Moreover, courts have ignored the chilling effects that poison pill rights plans have on the market for corporate control, and hence on the governance of the publicly held corporation. Specifically, by making hostile acquisitions more costly and more difficult, poison pills impose significant disincentives on acquirers. Not only are acquirers deprived of incentives to make bids, they also are deprived of incentives to engage in the costly search process necessary to identify undervalued firms.

In *Moran*, the Delaware Supreme Court appears to have gone out of its way to ignore these incentive effects. The court blithely observed that the target firm's poison pill was not suspect merely because it did not prevent stockholders from receiving tender offers, failing to understand the plaintiffs' cogent argument that allowing the poison pill would cause shareholders to "lose their right to receive and accept tender offers."[32] Unable or unwilling to see beyond the banal technicality that bidders retain the power to make a hostile tender offer for firms with poison pill rights plans, the court failed to acknowledge that such plans destroy bidders' incentives to do so unless they can engineer a way to get the approval of the target firm's board of directors (in which case, of course, the bid is no longer hostile).[33]

Thus, by judicial fiat, the Delaware courts have removed from the marketplace the hostile tender offer, which is the most powerful corporate governance device in the shareholders' corporate governance arsenal. As Baums and Scott presciently have observed, "Delaware jurisprudence seems to be willing, in substance . . . to give management something approaching an absolute veto over hostile tender offers despite overwhelming evidence that they confer large benefits on target shareholders."[34] Again, just as courts and legislatures have undermined the vitality of credit-rating agencies and accounting firms, they have undermined the market for corporate control.

The only way to make sense of the laws that govern the market for corporate control is by recognizing the nature of the political forces that shape the regulation of this market. The shareholders who would benefit from the high premiums and more rigorous scrutiny of management associated with a robust market for corporate control from more intense monitoring and are widely disbursed and disorganized. On the other hand, the managers who want to be free of the intense market discipline associated with a robust market are a small, discrete, well-organized group that constitutes an effective political coalition. This coalition, aided by management lawyers and investment bankers who benefit from a sclerotic market for corporate control that is run by lawyers and bankers rather than entrepreneurs, can be credited for the regulations we observe.

CHAPTER 9

INITIAL PUBLIC OFFERINGS AND
PRIVATE PLACEMENTS

Capital markets are another poorly understood institution of corporate governance. Capital markets operate in three contexts: initial public offerings (IPOs), private placements, and ordinary secondary trading. Well-functioning secondary markets provide investors and other corporate constituencies with a succinct, accurate, unbiased real-time measure of a company's performance and competitive position. This measure comes in the form of the company's share price, which is set on an ongoing basis in the trading markets.

Thus, the value from a corporate governance perspective of robust secondary trading markets for a company's corporate governance is incalculable. From the corporate-governance-as-promise perspective taken in this book, a public company's stock price provides the measure by which we can tell whether a company is delivering on its promises to investors.

A very similar analysis applies when a company makes a public offering or a private placement of securities. Whenever a company goes to the public or private capital markets for funds, it commits itself to rigorous monitoring by a cadre of lawyers, investment bankers, and financial analysts, all of whom face reputational and legal risks for failure to do an adequate job of protecting investors. This process serves as a gatekeeping function.[1]

The gatekeeping function in IPOs and private placements revolves around the due diligence investigation that routinely occurs in connection with the offering. The term "due diligence" is legal-speak for the activities that the underwriters and placement agents who sell securities engage in to avoid legal liability. Securities laws exempt from liability investment bankers and others who reasonably believed, after "reasonable investigation," that no disclosure violations occurred in the offering. The securities law protects underwriters and placement agents who exercise "reasonable care" and did not know or could not have known of such violations.

Some say that due diligence is the legal equivalent of "kicking the tires" on a used car before buying it. But this is not entirely true. Proper due diligence requires a bit more. It requires actually looking under the hood to see if anything is wrong with the vehicle. Investors rely on underwriters and placement agents to discover and ensure the disclosure of the essential facts relevant to the financing and to the company engaged in the transactions. Banks conducting due diligence investigations not only should meet with the top management of the issuer in order to establish their "due diligence defense" under the securities laws, they also must independently verify the accuracy of statements made by management as well as those contained in offering documents.

Bankers whose investigations are deficient are not entitled to take refuge in a due diligence defense. For a due diligence investigation to succeed in insulating underwriters and placement agents from liability, the banks performing the due diligence cannot simply blindly rely on management. They must independently verify the information given. Courts have recognized that independent verification is a critical step in the due diligence process.

The point of this description of the due diligence process is to illustrate how companies subject themselves to monitoring by outsiders when they decide to go public.

Unfortunately, a variety of factors are conspiring to reduce the incentives of firms to go public. In particular, while civil liability is necessary to provide incentives for investment banks and other gatekeepers to monitor, where liability is imposed willy-nilly, without regard to the efforts made by investment banks to investigate, firms will respond by declining to go public or by selling their shares far less frequently.[2] This results in less interaction between the company and its gatekeepers, with a concomitant reduction in monitoring, leading, in turn, to a diminution in the quality of corporate governance for the firm.

As Frank Easterbrook has explained, we observe the strange phenomenon of companies simultaneously disbursing cash to investors by paying dividends and raising cash from investors by making initial public offerings of equity on the same class of securities.[3] The best explanation for this apparently odd behavior is that it is in investors' interest for companies to submit themselves regularly to the monitoring function of the due diligence process associated with IPOs.

From this perspective, the recent changes in the tax code that dramatically reduce the tax rates on dividend payments can be viewed as strengthening the corporate governance infrastructure in the United States by removing an impediment to paying dividends. This reduction, however, is scheduled to expire.[4] The reduction should be made permanent, and additional regulatory changes should be implemented to encourage companies to make regular offerings of their equity securities in public offerings.

Not surprisingly, corporate and management interests, who want a pretext for hoarding cash in the company and for engaging in empire building, prefer that dividends be taxed at a high rate. High taxes on dividends give corporate interests an excuse for not paying dividends to shareholders and using the money that might have gone to dividend payments to fund managers' pet projects like acquisitions, expansion, remodeling, and, of course, executive compensation.

There is more than a little bit of tension between the description of the legal framework for the due diligence process, which is driven by legal rules and efforts to avoid liability for civil securities fraud, and Easterbrook's economic view of the due diligence process, which is driven by market forces. The legal description suggests that due diligence is conducted because the law requires it in order to avoid liability. The economic description of due diligence presumes that private incentives provide sufficient motivation for bankers to conduct due diligence investigations.

Under Easterbrook's view of the due diligence process, it seems clear that reputable investment banking firms would be driven by market forces to agree voluntarily to assume responsibility for conducting due diligence investigations. As noted above, according to Easterbrook's account, issuing companies commit to "submit themselves" to the monitoring function of the due diligence process. But for this commitment to be credible, some price must be paid by an underwriter who does not perform an adequate due diligence investigation. It is possible, though unlikely in my view, that in the absence of civil liability for failure to perform adequate due diligence, the reputational loss suffered by underwriters of unworthy issuers would provide a sufficient incentive to do adequate due diligence. Concerns about capture of individual investment bankers within a firm, and last period problems, suggest that some reasonable, fault-based liability should attach to underwriters' failed due diligence investigations.

CHAPTER 10

GOVERNANCE BY LITIGATION

Derivative Lawsuits

With the possible exception of corporate boards of directors, litigation in the form of class actions and shareholder derivative actions is conventionally believed to be the most important corporate governance mechanism available to U.S. investors. This belief is both inconsistent with the corporation-as-promise approach taken in this book and wrong.

It is highly unlikely that shareholders would voluntarily agree to opt into an expensive private litigation system such as the one that exists in the United States that allows plaintiffs' class action attorneys to extort billions of dollars from companies, and requires that shareholders acquiesce in lawsuits in which massive amounts of money are transferred from one group of investors to another or, worse still, from investors to lawyers.

Just as the goal of the early chapters of this book was to show that boards of directors are a wildly overrated feature of the corporate governance landscape, the goal of this chapter is to show that litigation is part of the corporate governance problem, not part of the solution. Plaintiffs' lawyers and the lawsuits they bring on behalf of investors are fraught with conflict of interest and agency problems and likely do more harm than good.

Of course, there is an argument on the other side. Plaintiffs' lawyers call themselves "the first line of protection against corporate greed." Lawyers and regulators generally are of the view that litigation is an important tool shareholders can use to hold management accountable for intentional misconduct and gross negligence. Harvard's Reinier Kraakman, for example, takes the view that "shareholder suits are the primary mechanism for enforcing the fiduciary duties of corporate managers."[1] Former SEC chairman Arthur Levitt has called private litigation "crucial to the integrity of our disclosure system because [it] provide[s] a direct incentive for issuers and other market participants to meet their obligations under the securities laws."[2]

Supporters of shareholder suits brought by private attorneys argue that they solve the significant collective action problem that widely dispersed shareholders in U.S. public corporations face in attempting to exercise control over management. The problem arises because even when negligent and corrupt management of public companies causes massive losses, these losses often are spread widely over hundreds of thousands of investors. This, in turn, means that the economic harm to particular individuals generally is quite small in relation to the costs that would be required for an individual investor to monitor or investigate corporate misconduct. Class action and derivative litigation can overcome these collective action problems by allowing a single representative shareholder and a plaintiffs' attorney working on a contingency fee basis to sue on behalf of all of his or her similarly situated peers without consulting them, thereby greatly lowering the costs of action.

It would be highly irrational for individual investors to spend significant resources on corporate governance because the expected payoff any individual shareholder stands to gain from ensuring good management performance is so small in relation to the required investment. In other words, it is rational for investors to remain ignorant about how their companies are being run, particularly when investors can rely on mechanisms that do not require their participation—such as the market for corporate control discussed in chapter 8—to discipline management.

Moreover, to the extent that an individual shareholder or other small investor acting alone is able to improve corporate governance, any gains realized from such improvements must be shared with all the other shareholders. This, in turn, leads to the collective action problem known as "free-riding," which describes what happens when economic actors are able to enjoy their share of benefits from some costly activity, such as investing in corporate governance, without shouldering their share (or any) of the costs of the activity. In the absence of procedures that either require all shareholders to bear their fair share of the cost of engaging in active corporate governance activities or provide disproportionately large private rewards for individual shareholders who engage in these activities, economic theory predicts that rational actors would refuse to provide them as a result of the free-rider problem. Class action and derivative lawsuits ostensibly are justified on the grounds that they eliminate the collective action problems faced by widely dispersed, small-stakes investors.

The class action lawsuit is a procedural mechanism used to obtain legal redress for large numbers of similarly situated people whose legal grievances involve common questions of law and fact. As with other direct lawsuits by investors, class action lawsuits are typically brought to enforce the fiduciary duties of officers and directors, often for securities fraud, and any recovery is distributed to the individual plaintiffs.

The derivative lawsuit is brought by a shareholder on behalf of a company in which he or she owns shares to deal with harms done to the corporation that management and the board of directors refuse to redress. Through the derivative lawsuit, shareholders can exercise control over management and prosecute the corporation's claim on behalf of the company even over their objections. The most obvious reason why management or the board would refuse to redress such harms is because the claim involves misconduct by the managers or members of the board of directors or both. Shareholders benefit indirectly from the resulting increase in share price and the general deterrent effect of the threat of litigation. The derivative lawsuit overcomes free-rider and collective action problems because it allows a single shareholder to bring a suit on behalf of the entire corporation and because the cost of litigation to a shareholder represented by a law firm working on a contingency fee basis is arguably negligible. In theory at least, the derivative lawsuit serves a valuable role in corporate governance by providing a mechanism to address wrongs that a corporation's insiders can inflict upon it. Some sort of mechanism for addressing wrongs by insiders is vital, of course, because managers and directors are insiders themselves and obviously cannot be counted on to police themselves or even to evaluate themselves objectively.

The first part of this chapter provides an overview of class action and derivative lawsuits as corporate governance tools before engaging in an in-depth consideration of their common pathologies. These are problems that ironically take nearly the same form as the corporate governance difficulties that these litigation techniques were intended to address.

CLASS ACTIONS

Shareholder class actions have historically been viewed as an important supplement to the SEC's enforcement authority[3] because they allow investors to overcome collective action and free-rider problems by aggregating their claims. Federal Rule of Civil Procedure 23 allows a representative plaintiff to file an action and seek class certification if she can meet several requirements, such as establishing the existence of questions of law or fact common to the class and showing that their claims are typical of the claims of the class generally.[4]

Because the economic stakes for most shareholders in these suits are so small, investors do not have powerful incentives to initiate suits. Plaintiffs' counsel, in contrast, stands to gain a great deal financially through the awarding of attorneys' fees. That fact, combined with the reality that law firms, rather than individual investors, are often the economic actors with the ability to bear the costs of bringing a suit, creates the risk that plaintiffs' lawyers will bring meritless "strike suits." Concern over strike suits seems justified by the fact that most class actions are initiated by plaintiffs' attorneys rather than shareholders, and suits are often filed very quickly, "within days of the events giving rise to . . . litigation."[5] Indeed, studies of shareholder class actions paint a picture of passive shareholder-plaintiffs, revealing that often "plaintiffs are poorly informed about the theories of their cases, are totally ignorant of the facts, or are illiterate concerning financial matters."[6]

The individual investor's small economic stake in the case's outcome translates into low incentives for the investor to monitor plaintiffs' counsel during litigation. Furthermore, "even if plaintiffs wanted to monitor the litigation, they would experience severe difficulties in doing so because they are often entirely unaware that the litigation is pending until after a settlement has been reached."[7] If a member of the plaintiff class in a direct suit did approach the class attorney with a request relating to the prosecution of the suit, it is not clear how responsive the attorney would or should be "because the attorney must act for the benefit of the class as a whole and therefore is not obliged to follow the unilateral wishes of any individual class member."[8] Attempting to improve communication between the class attorney and class members is unlikely to be fruitful since the costs associated with communicating with a vast and widely dispersed group of shareholders are likely to be high, and devising a decision-making procedure that would allow class members to have input as to legal strategy is likely to be unworkable.[9]

The absence of meaningful client monitoring is particularly worrisome in light of the conflicts of interest between class members and class counsel. A conflict of interest inevitably arises in deciding how far to pursue litigation and when to settle. Shareholder plaintiffs in class actions want to pursue litigation until the point at which their gross recovery minus attorneys' fees is the largest.[10] Plaintiffs' counsel, however, will want to end the lawsuit when "the difference between his or her fees and costs— which include not only the money that the lawyer spends in advancing his or her client's cause but also the opportunities for other work that the lawyer gives up by pursuing it—is greatest."[11] As the court in *In re Cendant* notes, the results of these calculations "rarely converge."[12] This chapter considers the problems of client monitoring, attorneys' fees, and decisions concerning settlement in more detail below.

DERIVATIVE SUITS

A derivative suit is a complicated legal device, used almost exclusively in the United States. A derivative lawsuit is a claim brought by shareholders purportedly "by or in the right of the corporation" to redress some harm done to the enterprise, usually by high-ranking officers and some or all of the board of directors. In derivative lawsuits, the attorneys representing the shareholders must engage in two analytically distinct legal actions. First, the attorney sues the company and its board of directors to obtain the power to displace the legal authority of the board of directors and management in corporate governance for the limited purpose of deciding whether to litigate on behalf of the corporation. This means persuading a court, virtually always over the vehement objections of the directors and the counsel for the corporation, that authority over the administration of the lawsuit should be taken away from the board of directors and given to a plaintiffs' attorney who claims to be representing the corporation "derivatively" on behalf of investors.

In most states, a derivative suit plaintiff must usually make a demand on the directors for the initiation of the lawsuit.[13] In such "demand required" cases, the recommendation of the board of directors will be evaluated by the court under the standards of the business judgment rule.[14] Absent fraud or lack of good faith, as long as the board's decision can be attributed to any rational business purpose, it will be upheld. Demand is justified by the assumption that directors have a significant stake in the corporation and that their interests are therefore usually aligned with those of the shareholders.[15] In addition, directors have more information and expertise about the company than most shareholders or plaintiffs' attorneys and are usually in a better position to determine whether pursuing litigation is in the company's best interest.[16]

In some cases, shareholders may believe that making demand on the board of directors would be futile. Such situations arise "where the directors have a personal interest in the litigation that is adverse to the corporation."[17] In such cases, a court may excuse demand. An example of a demand excused case might be one in which the suit claims that the company's directors have breached the duty of loyalty. In such a case, directors who are potential defendants "could use their powers under the demand rule to derail the litigation, by, for example, delaying their response to the demand, taking over the litigation and then dismissing it, or compromising it on terms favorable to their own interests."[18] When plaintiffs can raise reasonable doubt as to the disinterestedness of the majority of the board, or about whether the challenged transaction was protected by the business judgment rule, demand may be excused.[19] While the demand excused derivative lawsuit allows shareholders to exercise control over management, obtaining excuse of demand from a court does not necessarily end managerial involvement in the lawsuit.

If demand is excused, management may reenter a derivative suit by organizing a special litigation committee "to investigate the plaintiff's allegations, prepare a thorough written report, and almost invariably seek dismissal of the derivative action."[20] In *Zapata v. Maldonado*,[21] the Delaware Supreme Court devised a two-part test to determine whether a special litigation committee should be permitted to dismiss a derivative suit. First, the court must determine whether the committee acted independently and whether its conclusions "had reasonable factual basis."[22] Second, the court must apply its own business judgment to determine whether the corporation's motion to dismiss the lawsuit should be granted.[23] However, it is unclear what standard a trial court should use in applying its own business judgment. This poses a risk that the trial court may find "the *Zapata* test a convenient means for disposing of cases on the merits, even though conceptually the business judgment analysis should not reflect the court's evaluation of the case on the merits but rather whether the control of the litigation should be left in the derivative plaintiffs' attorney's hands."[24] In addition, trial judges are not business experts and are unlikely to effectively exercise business judgment. Arguably, trial judges "will naturally feel an inclination to defer to the views of corporate directors."[25]

A recent study of all corporate litigation in Delaware over a two-year period found that plaintiffs almost never make demand but rather plead demand futility.[26] Empirical research shows that defendants are frequently successful in challenging plaintiffs' futility claims.[27] Relative to the number of state class actions or federal securities fraud class actions, the number of derivative suits brought on behalf of public companies is small.[28] This may be because the demand requirement and the possibility of reentry into the suit by management through a special litigation committee discourage plaintiffs from bringing derivative suits.[29]

In light of the questionable utility of derivative suits,[30] commentators have suggested various reforms to strengthen their efficacy as tools of corporate governance. Given that institutional investors who hold large stakes in a company may be more willing to initiate derivative litigation than smaller investors, some have recommended that demand be excused when a shareholder who owns 1 percent or more of the outstanding shares brings suit.[31] Because such shareholders have significant financial holdings in the corporation, it is unlikely they would act against their own self-interest by bringing frivolous suits against the companies they own.[32] One way of making sure the availability of managerial reentry into a lawsuit via a special litigation committee does not undermine the efficacy of the derivative suit as an instrument of corporate governance would be to change the standard of review so that courts are not asked to apply their business judgment to the decision of a special litigation committee. A better rule would ask trial courts to determine "whether the benefits to the corporation of continuing the litigation exceed the costs of doing so."[33] Corporate management would have the burden of showing that the costs of pursuing the lawsuit in question exceed the potential benefits.

Another way of strengthening the demand excused derivative suit would be to change the way the costs of the special litigation committee are paid. Special litigation committees usually retain counsel to investigate the value of the litigation, and such investigations can result in sizable legal bills.[34] If a court determines that the committee has not acted independently but rather "as a tool of the defendant directors, it would be appropriate to require the defendants to pay the costs of the committee in the event they are eventually held liable."[35] Some commentators have suggested appointing a guardian ad litem as a representative of the class during settlement. The guardian would act as a sort of devil's advocate and "would be expected to object to settlements almost as a matter of course, or else to provide the court with a statement of why, in the guardian's opinion, the settlement is fair to the plaintiff class."[36]

If the derivative attorney prevails in the initial phase of the derivative litigation, he can then proceed with an action to redress some substantive harm that was done to the corporation. Since this part of the case proceeds against managers or directors as third parties who are alleged to have harmed the corporation, in the rare situations in which a derivative lawsuit actually generates a recovery, that recovery is paid to the corporation, rather than directly to the shareholders. This, of course, further attenuates the interest that individual plaintiffs have in bringing suit, since even if a recovery is paid to the corporation, there is no guarantee that its proceeds will be paid out to the shareholder or otherwise used to benefit the investors in whose name the suit was brought.

THE PROBLEM OF AGENCY COSTS

The common difficulty with class action and derivative litigation as corporate governance devices is that they merely take the governance problems shareholders face when they try to monitor and control management and supplement them with an even more intractable set of problems of the same type: the problem of monitoring and controlling the plaintiffs' lawyers directing the litigation. The governance problems associated with derivative lawsuits range from the tactics used in selecting which cases to pursue to decisions about whether to settle or to litigate. Taken together, the process too often resembles a thinly veiled shakedown of corporations whose shares recently have suffered from steep declines in value, regardless of whether such declines are properly attributable to poor management or not.

Both class action and derivative lawsuits allow a lawyer for a "representative plaintiff"—in the case of the derivative lawsuit the representative plaintiff is always a shareholder—to commandeer the litigation process.

The problem is that the broader population of real plaintiffs—who are usually investors of some kind, and most often shareholders—must rely on the representative plaintiff's lawyers. And these lawyers are at least as likely as corporate managers to place their own interests ahead of the interests of the broader class. In other words, investors face exactly the same collective action problems of free-riding and rational ignorance when relying on lawyers suing on their behalf as they face when relying on managers investing on their behalf. This problem is one of agency costs.

Like managers, lawyers have incentives to pursue their own private interests, including big fees or increasing their reputation within the plaintiffs' bar, instead of advancing the interests of investors. Just like monitoring managers and directors, monitoring lawyers is very costly and requires a significant amount of expertise. Any investor/client who makes this investment must share any eventual payoff with all of his fellow investors—giving rise, once more, to the free-rider problem. Moreover, because it is so costly to invest in monitoring lawyers and the expected payoff to each investor is so small, rational investors will refrain from doing so in the first place (the rational ignorance problem).

Indeed, the problems clients face when they attempt to monitor their lawyers is even more acute than the problem investors face when they try to monitor the managers and directors of public companies. As noted in chapter 9, monitoring of managers and directors in public corporations is greatly facilitated by the ready availability of stock prices, which provide a measurement variable that is reliable and unbiased—at least in the sense of not reflecting the inherent bias of over-optimism that plagues managers and directors.

In other words, a reliable and effective market pricing mechanism exists that investors can use to evaluate the performance of the managers and directors of the corporations in which they have invested. Unfortunately, nothing remotely similar to this market pricing mechanism exists for the clients of the plaintiffs' attorneys who represent investors in class action and derivative lawsuits. Even if one could find out how much money the lawyers are making, that would tell us no more about how good a job lawyers are doing for their clients than knowing about executive compensation would tell us about how good a job a top manager is doing.

For an empirical indication of how very difficult it is for clients to monitor their lawyers in the corporate context, one need only consider the existence of massive offices of in-house counsel at major corporations. While these general counsels provide assorted legal services, at many corporations, their main function is to monitor outside counsel. Unfortunately, investors typically cannot afford to hire sophisticated lawyers for the purpose of monitoring the other lawyers who are ostensibly acting in their interest by bringing class action and derivative lawsuits.

THE MILBERG WEISS SAGA

An unusually clear window into the unseen life of the corporate class action plaintiffs' firm began to open in May 2006 when a federal grand jury in Los Angeles indicted the law firm Milberg Weiss, Bershad and Schulman—formerly the largest, most prestigious class action law firm in America—as well as two of its name partners for what journalists called "an alleged conspiracy of staggering proportions."[37] Allegations include the distribution of over $11 million in "secret kickback payments" to induce people to act as lead plaintiffs in class action suits, as well as bribery, fraud, obstruction of justice, and perjury charges.

According to the indictment, partners at Milberg Weiss allegedly obtained ready access to cooperative representative plaintiffs in lucrative class action suits against major corporations by cultivating a small handful of "professional plaintiffs." Milberg Weiss would allegedly encourage these individuals to hold or purchase small amounts of stock in many public corporations—in particular, companies that looked as though they might imminently admit to wrongdoing, either as a result of demands arising from internal oversight measures or government investigation. When damaging evidence of corporate misconduct in one of these companies emerged, Milberg Weiss would already have a ready and willing representative plaintiff, which would allow Milberg Weiss to file a class action lawsuit immediately. This provided the firm with an advantage over competing law firms in becoming lead counsel.[38]

Although cultivating readily available lead plaintiffs is not in itself illegal, federal prosecutors claim Milberg Weiss broke the law when it secretly provided compensation to these representative plaintiffs, which the firm tried to conceal under the guise of referral fees that it sent to the plaintiffs' personal attorneys. The details of these alleged payments provide a vivid illustration of the dominant role that plaintiffs' attorneys and their interests frequently play in driving this species of litigation: the $11.4 million in payments the indictment alleges went to only three individuals, who together served as lead plaintiffs in 180 cases.[39] A federal judge presiding over a 1993 securities class action case involving one of these lead plaintiffs had sardonically noted that the plaintiff was "one of the unluckiest and most victimized investors in the history of the securities business."[40] The phenomenon of these serial plaintiffs—a practice that is at present entirely legal, so long as the law firms representing the plaintiffs do not provide them with compensation—suggests the degree to which the initiation and conduct of many class action and derivative suits is motivated by the interests of law firms rather than bona fide investors.

Why is the class action system structured so as to allow plaintiffs' lawyers to so easily commandeer a process that was intended to promote the interest of litigants rather than that of the lawyers who represent them? The Milberg Weiss affair suggests a ready answer: Milberg Weiss was not only the most important plaintiffs' class action law firm in the corporate area; it also has been a major force in the Democratic Party. Milberg Weiss leads the trial lawyers' bar, which is the most important source of contributions to Democrats. Indeed, soon after Milberg Weiss was indicted, some of the largest recipients of the firm's fund-raising largesse, Democratic congressional representatives Charles Rangel, Gary Ackerman, Carol McCarthy, and Robert Wexler, produced and signed a half-page ad, paid for by Milberg Weiss, but appearing under the misleading headline "Congress of the United States: Statement on the Indictment of Milberg Weiss, Bershad & Schulman." The ad sharply attacked the decision of the Justice Department as a "thinly veiled attempt of the Bush Administration to accomplish by bullying and intimidation what it has not been able to do by law—to end class-action lawsuits, one of the few tools remaining to safeguard the American consumer."[41] According to the Center for Responsive Politics, during the five years prior to its indictment, Milberg Weiss and its lawyers gave $4 million to Democratic candidates, Democratic Political Action Committees (PACs), and other political donation vehicles.[42] The primary lobbying group for the plaintiffs' bar, the Association of Trial Lawyers of America, donated $23 million to Democrats, dwarfing the $2.7 million they gave to Republicans during this period.[43]

The political reality of class action and derivative litigation suggests that successful reform is unlikely. The beneficiaries of meaningful reform are highly dispersed and disorganized, whereas the existing system's beneficiaries—including the organized bar—are highly concentrated and well organized. The bar benefits from increasing litigation and, of course, increasing attorneys' fees. And plaintiffs' lawyers, such as Milberg Weiss, can easily afford their political largesse. Representing the plaintiffs in a single high-profile case can generate tens of millions of dollars in legal fees. For example, the WorldCom corporate governance and accounting scandal yielded $94 million in legal fees for Lerach Coughlin, a firm that split off from Milberg Weiss in 2004 and whose name partner William Lerach remains under federal investigation. Considering the rich rewards corporate governance litigation produces, it is completely unsurprising that this context has given rise to a powerful combination of deep-pocketed interests and close political connections that make litigation reform very difficult.

MOTIVATIONS FOR LAWYERING
IN THE CORPORATE CONTEXT

Although not all plaintiffs' attorneys may be as flagrant in their conduct as Milberg Weiss, that firm's story provides an important reminder concerning the motivation of plaintiffs' attorneys in the corporate setting. In other contexts in which class action litigation may be used, attorneys dedicated to the cause of social justice for disenfranchised plaintiffs will work for very little other than the satisfaction of advancing causes such as equal rights for the disabled or the right to free speech.

But corporate litigation is about the money. The plaintiffs on whose behalf corporate and class action plaintiffs' attorneys ostensibly are acting are unorganized and unknowledgeable, but they are not exactly poster children for the poor and downtrodden. As such, there is little reason to think that plaintiffs' attorneys in the corporate context are motivated by a desire for justice, and every reason to believe, despite their protestations to the contrary, that they are prototypical rational economic actors: they are in it for themselves. As a result, investors need to be as wary of their attorneys as they are of other economic actors with whom they interact.

Depending on the fee arrangement, plaintiffs' attorneys will have different incentives that cause their preferences concerning the management of a case to diverge from their clients' interests. If the attorney is to receive a percentage of the judgment, he has an incentive to settle early, possibly for an amount that is less than what the plaintiffs might receive at trial, to maximize his profit.[44] If the attorney is to be compensated according to the lodestar method of awarding fees, which takes into account the number of hours counsel has spent developing the case, he has an incentive to stretch out litigation and delay the negotiation and acceptance of reasonable settlement offers to run up the number of billable hours that will enter into the compensation calculation.[45] These interest calculations also reveal the two main areas that present the primary difficulties with regard to client control of plaintiffs' attorneys in the corporate context—attorneys' fees and settlement.

ATTORNEYS' FEES

One of the distinctive features of the American litigation system is the high cost of lawyers and litigation, and this problem is particularly acute in the area of plaintiffs' class actions for corporate and securities fraud. Class action and derivative lawsuits require significant financial resources to launch successfully. It is very expensive to mount a major case against a deep-pocketed corporate defendant. Plaintiffs' class action corporate and securities law firms must have prodigious resources, not only because the direct costs of litigating are so high, but also because payment comes only when the litigation is over. Plaintiffs' lawyers have to possess the resources to "go the distance"—or at least to credibly threaten going the distance—in litigation that can take years or even decades to conclude.

The capital required to maintain corporate class actions creates powerful barriers to entry into the business. A few firms, such as Milberg Weiss and Bernstein Litowitz Berger and Grossman, control most of the market. This in turn means that there is little pressure on the firms to control fees, and even less need to be responsive to client concerns.

Horror stories abound. In early January 2007, the Archdiocese of Milwaukee, the largest plaintiff in a shareholder class action against Halliburton, made the unusual move of asking the judge in its case to remove the lead attorneys for the class from their position as lead counsel. The archdiocese voiced several complaints with the firms that the court had appointed to be "their lawyers," including the plaintiffs' attorneys' failure to keep them informed about the status of the case, in violation of not only a pretrial order from the judge but also both federal and state law.

The archdiocese also voiced concerns about the negative impact on the litigation from the proliferation of media attention surrounding name partner William Lerach of Lerach Coughlin and the Department of Justice's ongoing criminal investigation of him and his former firm, Milberg Weiss and Bershad, and two of his former partners. The archdiocese was worried as well about what it thought were "insurmountable" conflicts of interest that continued to mount as the plaintiffs' lawyers scrambled to retain their position as lead counsel in the face of ongoing scrutiny into their conduct.

Or consider the Delaware Court of Chancery's fee award to plaintiffs' counsel in the 1997 case *In re QVC, Inc. Shareholders Litigation,*[46] which Jill Fisch cites as a striking yet not uncommon example of the enormous fees lawyers can extract from clients through the class action system.[47] The plaintiffs in the underlying suit were QVC shareholders who had launched an assortment of class action suits in response to the disclosure of tentative merger terms between QVC and CBS. The case ended after CBS withdrew its merger offer and QVC subsequently negotiated a tender offer with Comcast and Liberty Media at a price of $46 per share, an improvement from Comcast and Liberty's original offer of $44 per share. While the tender offer was being negotiated, the various groups of plaintiffs and their attorneys consolidated and amended their actions so as to be applicable to the new offer and made attempts to promote a higher offer price by jawboning the QVC board and threatening to request an injunction against the new offer. However, the Delaware court found that the QVC board and Comcast and Liberty had agreed to the final terms prior to negotiating with plaintiffs' counsel, and as a result "the class action litigation had a minimal impact on the terms of the revised Comcast/Liberty offer."[48]

The plaintiffs' law firms applied for $5.5 million in fees—nearly 10 percent of the total value of the increased share price resulting from the more favorable merger terms—and the court granted an award of $1.1 million. As Fisch notes, in making this award, the court held that plaintiffs' counsel did not have to prove that it actually contributed anything concrete in terms of the results of the settlement or the new merger. The court found only "indications" that counsel's work might have provided some undefined measure of bargaining power that led to more favorable merger terms and that the hours the various law firms billed furthermore involved "substantial duplicative effort" and no "substantial risk."[49] Instead, the court appears to have primarily based its award on the 1,500 billable hours that plaintiffs' counsel spent going through "the appropriate motions and maneuvers with requisite professional skill."[50]

What is astonishing about the case was that $1 million in legal fees was awarded despite the plaintiffs' attorneys having done nothing that the court could point to that provided a benefit to the actual plaintiffs who were, at least ostensibly, their clients. It appears that, as a matter of professional courtesy, the court awarded plaintiffs' counsel for their lawyerly "motions and maneuvers" regardless of whether such machinations actually provided any value to anybody.

The generous fees the court permitted in *In re QVC, Inc. Shareholders Litigation* despite the meager or nonexistent benefits provided by the attorneys are by no means unusual. State court judges, particularly in Delaware, are extremely generous with fees. This generosity is not surprising. Judges are successful members of the legal culture and naturally tend to think that lawyering and the law are of value, since it is their life's work. In addition, modern procedural rules give plaintiffs wide discretion as to forum, particularly where the defendants are large corporations who do business in many states. Thus, even if all courts are not generous, those that are, such as Delaware, inevitably will attract the lion's share of litigation since lawyers will file in the fora that they expect will be the most generous in terms of fees.[51] Thus, selection bias alone keeps fees high.

Finally, certain states clearly want to attract corporate litigation because it can contribute to their economies, particularly in a small state like Delaware, where fees from nonresident companies make up a major share of the state's annual revenues. Not surprisingly, other states, such as Maryland, Nevada, Pennsylvania, and Virginia, have made it clear that they want to participate in the jurisdictional competition for the fees associated with attracting corporate chartering and corporate litigation. Thus it is noteworthy that Delaware not only leads the jurisdictional competition in terms of the numbers of charters it attracts; it appears to have an even bigger lead over its rival states in terms of offering itself as a hospitable forum for litigation.

The "entrepreneurial" attorneys bringing cases against corporations have the initial choice of where to file. These attorneys are acutely aware that in class actions and derivative lawsuits, it is the courts, rather than the clients, who authorize their fees. So they are attracted to states, like Delaware, that have a strong record of unusual generosity. Attorneys' fees in Delaware are awarded not just on the basis of the number of hours that an attorney has spent on a matter—though this is surely relevant—but also on the basis of the benefit conferred on the plaintiffs by bringing the litigation.

This approach to fees may appear at first blush to harm plaintiffs' attorneys because it is based on the relief actually obtained for clients rather than on the actual work done. But as the QVC case demonstrates, some courts are generally extremely generous not only in the amount of fees that they award but also in their interpretation of when litigation against a company benefits its investors. According to Delaware corporate law, as interpreted by the *In re QVC* court, such benefit need not even be monetary or proprietary. *In re QVC*, which did not produce any recovery for investors, is typical in this regard, but there are even more egregious cases.

One prominent example is the case *In re Caremark Int'l Inc. Derivative Litigation*,[52] in which the Delaware Court of Chancery awarded fees of $816,000 above and beyond expenses to plaintiffs' counsel for their role in settling a derivative lawsuit with Caremark, a large managed health care services provider. The suit was initiated after the corporation was investigated by the Office of the Inspector General of the U.S. Department of Human Services. Caremark was ultimately charged with violating the provisions of 42 U.S.C. § 1395(m), which makes it illegal for health care providers to provide any form of compensation in exchange for obtaining Medicare or Medicaid patient referrals.

The government alleged that Caremark had given research grants and consulting contracts to doctors, who had in turn recommended counseling services or prescribed products provided by Caremark. It is important to note that these research grants and consulting contracts were not illegal under any federal law, including the Anti-Referral Payments Law. The problem was one of optics: it might *appear* that the doctors' recommendations or prescriptions were made in response to kickbacks from Caremark, which would have been illegal if proven.

Caremark was indicted in 1994, three years after the government's investigations began. The case was ultimately settled. No senior officers or directors of Caremark were charged with wrongdoing in the Government

Settlement Agreement or in any of the indictments. Instead, the company agreed to plead guilty to a single count of mail fraud and to pay a criminal fine and civil damages to the government in the amount of $250 million. Under the terms of the settlement, Caremark was permitted to continue to participate in Medicare and Medicaid programs, as well as to provide doctors with research grants.

The derivative suit came three years after the Office of Inspector General had begun issuing subpoenas, and followed in the wake of investigations by the Department of Justice and other federal and state agencies that were included in the settlement described above. Thus, the derivative suit involved no original investigation or discovery of wrongdoing by the plaintiffs, and appears to be best described as "piling on" by fee-hungry lawyers.

The defendants in the Caremark derivative litigation were not in any way personally implicated in the alleged wrongdoing. They were the individual members of Caremark's board of directors who allegedly breached their duty to monitor and supervise the enterprise in an appropriate manner. The case, like virtually all such cases, settled out of court. Approval of the proposed settlement as "fair and reasonable" was required, however, before the settlement could be finalized.

The Delaware Court of Chancery approved the settlement and the attendant application for attorneys' fees, despite the fact that the court found "a very low probability that it would be determined that the directors of Caremark breached any duty to appropriately monitor and supervise the enterprise."[53] Indeed, the court noted that "the record tends to show an active consideration by Caremark management and its Board of the Caremark structures and programs that ultimately led to the company's indictment and to the large financial losses incurred in the settlement of [the government's] claims."[54]

Given that the court found that the derivative suit would have had a very low probability of success on the merits, it is not surprising that the litigation did not generate any recovery. The proposed settlement did not require any monetary payment whatsoever. It did not even require the defendant directors to relinquish any of their Caremark stock options. Instead, the settlement principally required Caremark to do the following: (1) to "take steps to assure that no future violations of the Anti-Referral Payments Law occurred; (2) to advise patients in writing of any financial relationship between Caremark and a health care professional or provider who made the referral; and (3) to create a Compliance and Ethics Committee composed of four directors, including two non-management directors to monitor future conduct."[55]

It is hard to see how this lawsuit, much less the settlement, could possibly have benefited the corporation in whose name it ostensibly was brought. As is typical, the resolution of the litigation seemed entirely cosmetic, designed to provide a cover for the settlement agreement. To be more precise, the payment of the attorneys' fee award cannot be justified under any view of the case. If the directors really were involved in wrongdoing, then the settlement was far too gentle. And if they weren't, then the settlement was far too harsh with regard to its consequences for the corporation. It is hard to imagine an informed group of investors agreeing to a settlement that imposed substantial compliance costs on the corporation, on top of the compliance initiatives required in the company's settlement with the government.

SETTLEMENT

The majority of class action and derivative litigation is settled.[56] Because settlements are unreported and often subject to confidentiality agreements among the parties, comprehensive data is hard to come by, but disturbing anecdotes abound. For example, in the early 1990s, securities class action lawyers sued Occidental Petroleum Company for fraud when the company cut its dividend by $1 from $3 to $2 per share. A settlement was reached in which the company agreed not to reduce its dividend below $2 per share unless, "in the judgment of the company's board of directors, the dividend should be reduced." The company agreed to a $2,975,000 attorneys' fee for arranging the settlement, which appears to have contributed absolutely nothing of value to the corporation or its investors.[57]

Both sides of a lawsuit face incentives to settle that may cause them to act in conflict with the best interests of the corporation. Defendants have incentives to settle even strike suits of dubious merit. Insurers of directors and officers (D&O) reimburse both plaintiffs' and defendants' expenses in a settlement, and therefore neither party is forced to internalize the costs of litigation.[58] Worse, since most settlements are paid out of D&O insurance, shareholders are hurt by the cost of the deductible and any increases in insurance premiums that result from litigation.[59] Defendants are further motivated to settle because court approval of a settlement stops other shareholders from bringing similar claims against the defendant.[60]

Many detractors claim that class action and derivative lawsuits merely try to persuade courts that the discovery and correction by a company of an error in corporate governance or financial reporting is the same thing as intentional wrongdoing. These lawsuits also are criticized as involving nothing more than "fishing expeditions." In such fishing expeditions, plaintiffs' lawyers hope that they will stumble on a corporate official who broke the law or that the expedition will become so costly for the company to defend against that it capitulates by offering a favorable settlement.

Because litigation costs are high, it is often in the corporation's interest to settle claims, even those lacking in merit. Imagine a lawsuit that will require $1 million in defense costs, a modest fee in any major litigation. Even if the plaintiffs have a zero percent chance of success, it will be cost-effective from the corporation's perspective to settle the suit for any sum less than $1 million. And the settlement value goes up considerably when we add to direct legal fees the time and distraction for directors and management, bad publicity, and other intangible factors. The value of acceding to a settlement goes up still further if we introduce the specter of error costs, and the related specter that judges and juries will use the litigation as an opportunity to redistribute wealth from corporate defendants to investors (and their lawyers). Specifically, even if the corporation assigns a low, say 10 percent, chance of success to the plaintiffs' case, this will add $1 million dollars to the rational settlement figure for every $10 million in damages claimed. This figure will be higher still if we assume, as we probably should, that corporations and their directors are risk-averse.

A further reason so many apparently frivolous lawsuits end in settlement arises from another manifestation of agency costs. Just as agency costs exist between plaintiff-investors and their lawyers, they also exist between these same investors and the corporate officers and directors being sued in derivative and class action securities litigation. Because settlements generally are paid by corporations or insurance companies, and not by individual defendants, even an extremely remote chance that a lawsuit will result in a recovery that a director's insurance company will refuse to pay or that the company will refuse to indemnify provides individual defendants with a very strong motivation to settle.

At the limit, these two agency problems together raise the specter of collusive settlement. A collusive settlement in the context of derivative or securities class action litigation is one in which the defendants and their lawyers collude with the plaintiffs' lawyers to reach a settlement that furthers their joint interests at the expense of the investors. A simple example illustrates the problem. Imagine that a board of directors or a corporation has engaged in misdeeds that impose $25 million in damages. Imagine that in a perfectly competitive world with perfect information and zero agency costs, the case would settle for $25 million and $5 million in attorneys' fees would be paid to the plaintiffs' attorneys. In the real world, both the defendants and the plaintiffs' lawyers would be better-off by simultaneously decreasing the size of the $25 million settlement and increasing the $5 million in attorneys' fees so long as the resulting two numbers (settlement and fees) is less than $30 million. Imagine, for example, a settlement of $15 million with $10 million in attorneys' fees. This settlement would make the defendants (or the company indemnifying or insuring them) better-off by $5 million since the overall settlement was reduced from $30 million to $25 million, and the plaintiffs' attorneys would be better-off by $5 million, since their fee—which in such cases is paid by the company so long as the plaintiffs' attorneys conferred a substantial benefit on the corporation—increased from $5 million to $10 million.

INSTRUMENTS AND PROPOSALS FOR IMPROVING CORPORATE GOVERNANCE LITIGATION

The next three sections consider three potential methods for reducing the agency problems arising from class action and derivative litigation in the corporate context: auctions for lead counsel, the Private Securities Litigation Reform Act of 1995, and judicial oversight of settlements. Although none of these measures is likely to completely solve the inherent flaws of class action and derivative litigation, they are worthy of consideration given the political barriers that render a total overhaul of the system implausible.

Auctions

One mechanism that may mitigate the agency costs associated with the lawyer-driven model of litigation is the use of auctions to select plaintiffs' lead counsel.[61] Imagine that a corporation or certain of its officers and directors were alleged to have engaged in some sort of wrongdoing. In an auction, competing plaintiffs' attorneys would bid for the right to represent the plaintiffs. The money paid at the auction would then be distributed to the injured investors (or to the corporation in the case of a derivative suit), and then the winning law firm would pursue the litigation and have the right to retain any eventual recovery to offset the amount initially bid.

Thus, for example, suppose that the winning bid for a particular cause of action was $50 million. This amount would be immediately distributed to the shareholders or other injured investors, allowing them to obtain something they virtually never get under the present system: an actual monetary recovery. If the litigation eventually produced a judgment or settlement of only $10 million, the bidding law firm would lose $40 million plus its time and expenses. On the other hand, if the litigation produced a judgment or settlement of $100 million, the law firm would make $50 million, less time and expenses.

Competition among law firms during the auction process would drive the returns to law firms down to competitive levels. Firms could band together to bid on big cases as a consortium. Lawyers could mitigate the risk associated with any particular piece of litigation by holding a diversified portfolio of lawsuits.

A major advantage of this auction framework, which Geoffrey Miller and I proposed in a previous joint work,[62] is that it would, for the first time, create a system in which the competence of the lawyers involved would be rewarded. Under the historical selection procedures for choosing lead counsel in class action securities and derivative litigation, courts pick lead counsel based on the factors that they can observe readily, such as when the lawsuits were filed, and what fees the lawyers estimate will be charged. Judges currently lack either any inclination or any legitimate process to determine whether a particular law firm should be compensated more because it is qualitatively better than another. In contrast, under the auction system proposed here, higher-quality firms would be able to garner higher fees from larger judgments and settlements. This, in turn, would enable the better lawyers to outbid their less able rivals, holding anticipated compensation equal.

Auctions are by no means a panacea for the agency costs associated with shareholder litigation, and critics have commented on their weaknesses. In cases where the right to act as lead counsel is awarded to the lowest bidder, courts may award the lead counsel position based merely on the monetary amounts of the bids without performing the kind of analysis of the cost and quality of services that a client would perform.[63] In addition, "bids in large, potentially high-recovery, cases are likely to be quite complex and it may be difficult for courts to assess their relative costs to the class."[64] Defining the scope of the claims being auctioned may also prove difficult at the outset of litigation.

In addition, if bidding lawyers engage in collusion to keep prices high, the effectiveness of the auction approach will of course be undermined. Collusion is a real risk given that the plaintiffs' securities class action and derivative bar is highly concentrated and dominated by a very small number of legacy law firms. The auction procedure could also be ineffective if there are too few bidders or if there is a capital markets failure that generates too few bidders with the financial resources to bid competitively.[65]

The Private Securities Litigation Reform Act of 1995

Reacting to the abuses in securities class action lawsuits by powerful plaintiffs' firms, in 1995 a Republican Congress passed the Private Securities Litigation Reform Act (PSLRA), and then overcame a veto by President Bill Clinton to see the legislation enacted into law. Congress was concerned about the proliferation of strike suits filed "not because plaintiffs or their class action lawyers had any persuasive evidence of fraudulent conduct on the part of defendants," but as a means of extracting settlements from defendants.[66] Legislators worried that frivolous suits threatened to undermine the international competitiveness of U.S. capital markets and "unnecessarily increase the cost of raising capital and chill corporate disclosure."[67]

Prior to the passage of the PSLRA, the first law firm to file a complaint usually controlled the litigation and as a result "there developed a 'race to the courthouse' mentality that discouraged the plaintiffs' counsel from conducting reasonable factual investigations before initiating a class suit."[68] Congress came to believe that the real winners of strike suits were members of the plaintiffs' bar, "whom Congress perceived to be richly rewarded without commensurate risk."[69] From the perspective of rationally self-interested plaintiffs' lawyers, there were "no compelling reasons not to initiate speculative class action lawsuits."[70] Defendants, as noted above, had strong economic incentives to settle, particularly in cases where several defendants were named in the same action and the specter of joint and several liability created potentially huge losses for firms and individuals only peripherally responsible for allegedly fraudulent misstatements or omissions.[71]

Congress's concern that many baseless lawsuits were being brought by entrepreneurial plaintiffs' attorneys found substantial support in empirical studies of shareholder suits. One study of shareholder suits brought between 1960 and 1987 found that plaintiffs won in only 6 percent of adjudicated cases and did not win any judgments for damages or equitable relief.[72] Awards were paid to attorneys more often than to shareholders in settlements, and in 8 percent of the cases that settled, the only awards were attorneys' fees.[73]

The PSLRA was intended to make litigation more client-driven. For the first time, rather than having attorneys seek out potential shareholder-plaintiffs when a company's stock dropped, dissatisfied shareholders could choose their counsel for themselves. The legislation created a rebuttable presumption that the investor with the largest financial stake in the case's outcome would be designated the "lead plaintiff" for the litigation. The idea was that sophisticated institutional investors would become lead plaintiffs, which would facilitate better monitoring of plaintiffs' counsel.

An important provision of the PSLRA entitles the lead plaintiff to select lead counsel subject to the approval of the court. A large institutional investor with a significant economic stake in the outcome of litigation would presumably engage in aggressive negotiations to obtain high-quality, reasonably priced attorneys. Lead plaintiffs also would monitor lead counsel's activities during the course of the litigation. To avoid the situation in which "[a]ll too often, the same 'professional' plaintiffs appear as name plaintiffs in suit after suit,"[74] the PSLRA includes a provision prohibiting the same plaintiff from bringing more than five securities class actions in any three-year period.[75] The act also establishes proportionate liability, reducing the undesirable settlement pressures that resulted from joint and several liability.[76]

In a post-PSLRA case, *In re Cendant Corporation Litigation*, the Third Circuit Court of Appeals reviewed a lower court's approval of a $3.2 billion settlement of a securities fraud class action that included an attorneys' fee award of $262 million.[77] The magnitude of the economic stakes involved were noted by the Third Circuit, which observed that "[t]he enormous size of both the settlement and the fee award presages a new generation of 'mega cases' that will test our previously developed jurisprudence."[78] The Cendant litigation arose after two companies merged, but accounting fraud in one company was discovered after the merger had been effectuated. As a result, the resulting corporation's stock price fell and shareholders lost approximately $20 billion in value.[79] In accordance with the PSLRA, the district court selected a lead plaintiff, a group of three institutional investors led by CalPERS, the California Pension Fund. The CalPERS group then negotiated a fee agreement with two law firms it had selected to prosecute the class action.

Although the PSLRA provides that the lead plaintiff "shall, subject to the approval of the court, select and retain counsel to represent the class,"[80] the district court did not agree to the appointment of the firms chosen and recommended by the CalPERS group. Instead, the court decided to hold an auction for the position of lead counsel.[81] The qualified firm that submitted the lowest bid would win. The district court gave the firms chosen by CalPERS a chance to match the lowest bid, which they did. When the parties agreed to settle, plaintiffs' counsel was awarded a fee based on the percentage determined through the auction. The resultant fee of $262 million was $76 million more than had been negotiated initially by the CalPERS group.[82] On appeal of the settlement and award of attorneys' fees, the Third Circuit upheld the settlement but reversed the award of attorneys' fees, holding that the PSLRA did not permit the use of an auction to determine lead counsel under the circumstances of the case.[83] Other courts have used alternatives to auctions that can reduce attorneys' fees in derivative and class action litigation while posing less tension with the lead plaintiff's ability to choose its own counsel. For example, a court may require the proposed counsel for the putative lead plaintiffs to submit their fee proposals and if the court determines that any of them appear excessive, the court may give the firm a chance to revise and resubmit its proposal.[84]

In other jurisdictions, however, courts have found a lead counsel auction to be reconcilable with the PSLRA.[85] In the decision *In re Lucent Technologies Securities Litigation*, the court observed, "It is interesting that in a matter consolidated from eighteen separate complaints and involving thousands of plaintiffs, not a single party has opposed either the Motion for Lead Plaintiff or the Motion for Lead Counsel or proposed other counsel. This apparent apathy suggests possible collusion or a 'too comfortable' arrangement among counsel who appear to be directing this litigation."[86] Suspecting that the negotiations between the lead plaintiff and proposed lead counsel had not been conducted at arm's-length, the court went on to order selection of lead counsel through a competitive bidding process. The court reasoned that such a method would better achieve Congress's goal of preventing lead counsel from choosing "itself as lead counsel by selecting a plaintiff and initiating litigation."[87] Under a broad reading of the court's statutory authority to approve lead counsel, courts retain the power to resort to a competitive bidding process if such a selection mechanism would best serve the PSLRA's client-empowerment goals.

Judicial Scrutiny of Settlements

The judiciary is the last bastion of defense for investors against the runaway litigation and collusive settlements that characterize corporate class action securities and derivative litigation in the United States. The historical regulatory response to the conflict of interest problem between class action and derivative lawsuit plaintiffs and their attorneys has been to require that judges scrutinize and approve any proposed settlement. Even before the passage of the PSLRA, class actions and derivative litigation, once filed, cannot be dismissed or settled without judicial approval. Notice of any settlement or dismissal must be given to all shareholders or members of the class.[88]

The PSLRA, by introducing the concept of the lead plaintiff, recognized, at least implicitly, that the requirement of judicial approval of proposed settlements is not a complete solution to the agency cost problem that plagues derivative and class action litigation. In fact, the requirement of judicial scrutiny has not been much of a constraint at all on the problem of collusive settlement or the other problems with litigation as a corporate governance tool.

Judges simply cannot be relied on to turn back inadequate or collusive settlements or to monitor the job that plaintiffs' attorneys do for three reasons.

First, judges' self-interest is decidedly on the side of approving settlements. Judges are overworked. Judicial dockets are overcrowded. And if more cases were litigated to conclusion rather than settled, this problem would increase. In other words, whenever a judge approves a settlement she succeeds in removing a burden from her already overburdened docket.

Second, judges care about their reputations and they do not hurt their reputations by approving settlements. They do, however, put their reputations at risk when their decisions are appealed and they are threatened with the possibility of reversal by an appellate court. Because settlements are, by definition, consensual, there are no appeals and, consequently, no reversals. In contrast, if a judge rejects an agreed-upon settlement, there will definitely be an appeal, with both of the parties to the settlement protesting the rejection.

Besides being reversed, another factor that harms judges' reputations is tardiness. Judges that keep up with their case loads and move their dockets along tend to have better reputations than those who fall behind. Securities class actions and derivative suits are unusually time-consuming and complex. It is hard to imagine a judge who regularly chose to reject settlements that would resolve such cases standing a chance of keeping up with her docket.

Thus, settlement accomplishes both of the judicial goals of reducing reversal rates and maintaining control of a burgeoning docket. Thus it is not surprising that judges who can "guide the parties to settlement" are viewed as good judges. It is also no surprise that the adage "even a bad settlement is better than a 'good trial'" is commonly heard around courthouses and in judges' conversations with their clerks. In a nutshell, judges are "heavily conditioned by the ethos of their jobs to view settlements as desirable."[89]

The third reason court approval of settlements is an inadequate corrective relates to the severe information asymmetries that confront even the most well-intentioned judge who wants to scrutinize a proposed settlement. Trial courts lack the information they would require to make an informed evaluation of a settlement's fairness because judges must rely on the information provided to them by the parties when evaluating a proposed settlement. This information, of course, is likely to be highly biased, since both of the parties will at this point favor the proposed settlement and the materials they submit will reflect their desire for its approval. In other words, settlement hearings typically lack the truth-generating capacity of ordinary adversarial trials, where the rival parties can be expected to contest disputable facts and point out weaknesses in the other side's arguments.

Any additional time a court spends generating additional information is likely to promote more advocacy by the parties in favor of settlement, since they will realize that their proposed settlement is being questioned. Moreover, any such additional information that the clients are required to produce will be costly not only to the lawyers involved but also to the judge, who must evaluate the new information.

For this reason, settlement hearings in class action and securities litigation have been characterized as "typically pep rallies jointly orchestrated by plaintiffs' counsel and defense counsel."[90] Plaintiffs' lawyers explain to the judge how difficult their case was, and how little chance they had of winning to justify their fees, while defendants praise the plaintiffs' experience and counsel. As the factors on which a judge must predicate her decision to reject a proposed settlement are imprecise and subjective, such rulings would be difficult even in the context of an adversarial proceeding. Given the one-sided presentations that constitute settlement hearings, issuing a convincing rejection is nearly impossible in the absence of an objection to the settlement.

Objections to proposed settlements are quite rare, so it is not surprising that settlements are almost always approved. When objections arise, they generally come from lawyers whose arguments are heavily discounted because they have had a falling out with the other plaintiffs and they still want to share in any fees approved by the court. Courts not only are effusive in their praise for named counsel—they frequently go so far as to "lambaste anyone rash enough to object to the settlement."[91]

CONCLUSION

This chapter's analysis of the efficacy of class action and derivative lawsuits as tools for improving corporate governance strongly indicates that litigation has little to contribute. Indeed its effect is more likely negative than positive, as the threat of litigation—along with the large settlements that frequently occur—impose costs on investors by raising insurance premiums. These more-or-less direct, out-of-pocket costs are by no means the only, or even the largest, costs associated with derivative and class action securities litigation. The specter of such litigation has led to a crisis that threatens to damage the United States' reputation as a business-friendly environment—except perhaps in the eyes of managers who like big legal fees and want to see a lot of lawyers. The litigation crisis makes it harder for new businesses to raise capital from outside investors and leads to suboptimal levels of risk-aversion among managers and directors.

Reform is theoretically possible. In particular, judges could require that plaintiffs' securities class action and derivative lawyers bid for the right to pursue cases and collect damages, allocating the money paid directly to the allegedly injured parties. It is, however, highly unlikely that the theoretical solution of adopting an auction approach to securities class action and derivative claims ever will be implemented on a widespread scale. The enormous amount of money that lawyers have made from class actions has allowed them to expand their influence. Plaintiffs' attorneys contribute enormous amounts to federal and state political campaigns. In fact, such contributions now rival the political contributions made on behalf of the interests of large publicly held corporations at all levels.

These political contributions are at least sometimes paying off for the plaintiffs' bar. Congress has thwarted efforts to reduce the statute of limitations for these sorts of cases, culminating in the addition of Section 27(a) to the Securities and Exchange Act of 1934, which actually overruled judicial curbs on how much time could elapse before a cause of action was barred.[92] Law firms specializing in bringing class action suits against corporations and their managers and directors also poured millions into sponsoring and promoting a California ballot initiative, Proposition 211, which was designed to make it even less burdensome to file securities class actions.[93] The initiative was placed on the ballot but ultimately defeated.

This political reality suggests that it is highly unrealistic for those in search of meaningful reform of the corporate governance system to look to derivative lawsuits or to securities class action lawsuits as a source of positive change. These lawsuits are part of the problem, not part of the solution.

CHAPTER 11

ACCOUNTING, ACCOUNTING RULES,
AND THE ACCOUNTING INDUSTRY

Because corporate governance is about promises, it is critical that we have some metric for gauging whether companies are living up to the promises they make about their financial performance. The metric is share prices. Accounting is, in my view, not particularly important to investors, *except to the extent that accounting information is useful in the formation of share prices and in the allocation of economic resources* that share prices facilitate.

For public companies in places like the United States that have well-developed capital markets, share prices provide the best lens with which to evaluate corporate performance. Share prices are less biased and they are more credible than other information about corporate performance, including accounting data that is manufactured and provided to investors by the company itself. Unlike accounting information, share prices reflect people's actual willingness to buy and sell stakes in the companies whose shares are traded. And, because traders in shares can profit both when stock prices go up and when stock prices go down, they provide an objective measure of corporate performance.

One of the most interesting and important issues in the burgeoning field of corporate finance is the role that accounting data plays both in the formation of share prices as well as in the allocation of economic resources. While share prices are important, the financial information contained in accounting reports constitutes an important element in the mix of data that market participants utilize when they engage in the buying and selling of shares that determines share prices. For this reason, at least to some extent, the old adage "garbage in, garbage out" applies to the stock price formation process that is critical in enabling people to evaluate corporate performance. If the accounting data that market participants use to calculate share prices is not reliable, then share price will not be reliable either.

For private companies and for public companies located in places with undeveloped markets, accounting data is even more important, since it is the only information available that can be used to value and evaluate corporations. The point here is that one way or another, directly or indirectly, accounting data is important to corporate governance. Without accurate, reliable accounting information, it would be very difficult, if not impossible, to tell whether corporations are keeping their promises to investors.

Strangely, the policy debates about accounting tend to confuse concerns about the proper way to *format and package* accounting information with concerns about the actual *content* of information. Unfortunately, regulators sometimes seem to be more concerned with the format in which accounting information is presented than they are with whether the accounting information that is presented is useful to investors. To a large extent, the obsession with form over substance in American accounting reflects the relative power of the accounting industry. For example, debate has long raged about whether non-U.S. public companies should be permitted to list their shares on U.S. trading venues like the NYSE without changing the formatting of their financial statements to comply with U.S. standards.

Those who argue in favor of uniform formatting focus, obsessively in my view, on the concern that uniform presentation of accounting information is necessary to permit investors to make "apples and apples" comparisons of financial results across various companies. This argument fails to comprehend that competition among rival methods of presenting accounting information would be a good thing, and that deviation from conformity with existing norms sometimes reflects useful innovation rather than harmful obfuscation.

Worse, those focused on uniformity of format to the exclusion of all else fail to comprehend the capacity of the capital markets to sort out what's important, which is the content of financial reporting, not the format. Our obsession with the format used to present accounting information draws attention away from more important questions about substance. Efficient capital markets will take accounting information and process it regardless of the format in which it is presented. Firms that present valuable information in clear ways will be rewarded by market participants. Firms that fail to present important data or that present it in ways that are difficult to comprehend will be punished with share prices that reflect the uncertainty in the firms' accounting data. Of course, firms that present material financial information in false or misleading ways should be held accountable under the broad anti-fraud provisions of the securities laws regardless of the format used to present the information.

One of the most enduring issues among students of securities markets is whether regulation should compel the reporting of certain financial results through the promulgation of mandatory disclosure rules or leave the decision about whether and how much information to disclose to investors to the realm of contract. University of Chicago economist and Nobel Laureate George Stigler was the most prominent exponent of the free market view that mandatory disclosure rules are of little use to investors because private contracting would produce more finely tailored, flexible disclosure. Stigler reasoned that private contracting and capital market incentives would punish companies that failed to generate reliable financial data for investors and that mandatory disclosure would produce too much useless information and not enough important information. Recently Michael Greenstone, Paul Oyer, and Annette Vissing-Jørgensen rigorously analyzed the effects on share prices of the last major imposition of mandatory disclosure requirements in U.S. equity markets, which came in 1964 and took the form of amendments to the 1964 Securities Acts that extended the applicability of four important disclosure requirements to large firms traded over the counter that had applied to exchange listed firms for the previous thirty years, since 1934. Specifically, Greenstone, Oyer, and Vissing-Jørgensen looked at new 1964 rules that required firms to do the following: (1) register with the SEC, (2) provide periodic updates on their financial condition in the form of audited balance sheets and income statements, (3) issue detailed proxy statements to shareholders, and (4) report on insider holdings and trades.

Interestingly, Greenstone, Oyer, and Vissing-Jørgensen found that over-the-counter firms that started complying with all four forms of mandatory disclosure had statistically significant positive returns net of general market returns of between 11.5 and 22.1 percent when compared to firms that were already listed on major exchanges and thus were already required to provide all of this information. According to the authors, the results of their study are consistent with the hypothesis that mandatory disclosure laws are good because they induce corporate managers to work harder to improve shareholder value.[1]

Disclosure is clearly important. What is titillating about the Greenstone, Oyer, and Vissing-Jørgensen results are their findings that *mandatory* disclosure is important. After all, if the disclosures that were required for over-the-counter firms after 1964 created lots of value for investors, then market forces should have prompted firms to make such disclosure long before, as they did for many other firms prior to the passage of the securities laws. In other words, nothing prevented companies from voluntarily complying with the 1964 act's mandatory requirements. In the wake of the interesting research results by Greenstone, Oyer, and Vissing-Jørgensen, strong believers in markets (and I am one of them) need to explain why companies did not voluntarily elect to provide investors with the information contained in the 1964 law before they were compelled to do so.

In my view, the 1964 act benefited investors because it solved a credible commitment problem. The new disclosure rules provided better information to the capital markets and induced managers to focus more intensely on maximizing value for shareholders. Prior to these rules becoming law, firms whose shares were not listed on any organized exchange had a problem. They could unilaterally promise to provide information to markets and investors in the future, but there was nothing to prevent them from reneging on these promises in the future. Managers or directors who adopted a generous disclosure policy in time period 0 could elect to withdraw that policy in time period 1. In other words, what the 1964 mandatory disclosure rules did was to allow firms whose shares traded over the counter to make the same credible commitment to abide by their promises to disclose that exchange-traded securities long had done. The firms affected by the 1964 laws were either too small to be eligible to list on the organized exchanges or else too thinly traded to make listing on an organized exchange cost-effective.

In other words, consistent with the corporate-governance-as-promise theme pursued throughout this book, mandatory disclosure makes sense when, and only when, it solves intrafirm contracting problems. It simply cannot be true that mandatory disclosure of any and all information is valuable. It has to be the case that at some point there are diminishing returns to increased disclosure. If firms in search of capital really could lower their capital costs by making additional disclosures or by promising to make additional disclosures, they would do so voluntarily if they could. To the extent that regulation solves contracting promises within firms that makes it difficult or costly to make and keep their promises to investors, regulation can improve shareholder value, as Greenstone, Oyer, and Vissing-Jørgensen trenchantly observe.

The demand for reliable accounting data creates, in turn, a demand for reliable external auditors. Here competition has a clear and beneficial role to play. In theory at least, companies demand external auditors as a signal to potential sources of capital that the accounting information on which valuations are largely based is accurate.[2] This demand is particularly acute in light of the strong incentives that managers have to misstate a company's earnings and other indicia of a company's financial performance.[3]

[A]uditors' reputations are central to the standard economic theory of auditing. Only auditors with reputations for honesty and integrity are valuable to audit-clients. The idea is that, absent a reputation for honesty and integrity, the auditor's verification function loses its value. In theory, then, auditors invest heavily in creating and maintaining their reputations for performing honest, high quality audits. High quality audits by external auditors who have good reputations are assured. The quality assurance is derived from the fact that performing poor-quality audits diminishes the value of the audit firm's investment in reputation.[4]

The so-called pre-Enron view of the auditing industry, embraced by the law and economics movement,[5] held that auditing firms compete in a "race-to-the-top" that provides incentives to produce high-quality audits.

> There was a time that the audit function was carried out in a market environment that induced high quality financial reporting. In that era, accounting firms were willing to put their seal of approval on the financial records of a client company only if the company agreed to conform to the high standards imposed by the accounting profession. Investors trusted accountants because investors knew that any accounting firm that was sloppy or corrupt could not stay in business for long. Auditors had significant incentives to "do superior work" because "auditors with strong reputations could command a fee premium," and high fees "signaled quality in the auditing market."[6]

Under this pre-Enron paradigm, auditing firms had incentives to provide high-quality services because they sought to protect their reputation for independence and integrity.[7] Indeed, years before the scandal at Enron, Judge Easterbrook opined in *DiLeo v. Ernst & Young* that an auditing firm's "greatest asset is its reputation for honesty, followed closely by its reputation for careful work."[8] As Theodore Eisenberg and I previously observed, "In a world in which auditors have both invested in developing high quality reputations and in which no client represents more than a tiny fraction of total billings, high audit quality seems assured. Under these conditions, any potential gain to an auditor from performing an insufficient audit, much less from participating in a client's fraud, would be vastly outweighed by the diminution in value to the auditor's reputation."[9]

In sum, even though companies can and do audit themselves, they obtain external auditing firms to enhance their financial reputation and credibility among a wide range of current and prospective claimants on their cash flows, including investors, suppliers, customers, and prospective employees. Under this reputation model, companies require external auditing firms to attract outside capital on the prevailing assumption that auditing firms that discover problems would insist on corrections or, ultimately, oust clients. While being ousted by an auditing firm entails serious implications for clients,[10] economic theory holds that auditing firms that oust clients would, at worst, only lose the ousted clients. Indeed, such losses would likely be offset by new clients drawn by the elevation in reputation that might result from ousting clients.

The "law and economics 101" approach to auditing thus embraces the view that though companies can and do impose internal financial controls and audits, they obtain external auditing firms to capitalize on their reputation for probity. Under this theory, hiring an auditing firm allows clients to "rent" an auditing firm's reputation, borrowing its reputation for care, honesty, and integrity to its clients. As one observer has characterized the market for auditing firms' services, "Public accountants knew they had a lot to lose if their clients' information turned out to be false or misleading. Auditors who did a superior job would reduce the chance of their clients' issuing unreliable information and so reduce their own risk of being sued by aggrieved investors. Such suits are costly to auditors; even unsuccessful suits damage their valuable reputations."[11]

This pre-Enron theory, however, is flawed. First, the auditing firm industry is not characterized by robust competition. Collectively called the "Big Four," four auditing firms—Ernst & Young, Deloitte, PricewaterhouseCoopers, and KPMG—presently audit nearly all large companies. They audit 99 percent of public company sales taken as aggregate, 97 percent of public companies with sales exceeding $250 million, and 78 percent of all public companies. A half-dozen much smaller firms audit the remainder.[12]

Consider the Herfendahl-Hirshman Index (HHI), a measure of industry concentration.[13] An industry HHI score below 1,000 means that it is unconcentrated, while a score above 1,800 indicates high concentration. Measured in 2002, the auditing industry's HHI stood at an astonishing 2,500.[14]

Moreover, consider that each of the Big Four has expertise in certain industries, while lacking requisite expertise in others. In 2004, three audited the oil and gas industry and two audited 88.2 percent of the casino industry, with similar results in air transportation, coal, and other industries.[15] Thus, one often dominates the market for clients in specific industries, and often two share more than 70 percent control in other industries.[16] Because smaller firms are constrained from servicing companies that routinely obtain one of the Big Four, a large company looking to obtain an auditing firm often has one alternative—and, in some cases, no alternative at all.[17] Consider Sun Microsystems, which uses three of the Big Four for non-auditing purposes. Because Sarbanes-Oxley prohibits Sun Microsystems from obtaining auditing from auditing firms that provide it non-auditing services, and because no auditing firm outside of the Big Four can service a company of Sun Microsystems' magnitude, the company has no choice in choosing an auditing firm.[18]

The General Accounting Office has noted that smaller auditing firms face "significant barriers to entry" and that "market forces are not likely to result in"[19] new entry. The Economist has observed that the American Electronics Association, an outspoken critic of Sarbanes-Oxley that represents 2,500 companies, maintains that lack of competition "is significantly increasing the costs of section 404 certification,"[20] a provision in

Sarbanes-Oxley that holds managers accountable for maintaining "adequate internal control structure and procedures for financial reporting," and requires external auditing firms to attest to the management's appraisal of such controls by disclosing any "material weaknesses."[21]

The highly concentrated nature of the auditing industry and the small number of auditing firms available to service the largest companies suggests that the industry is susceptible to implosion.[22] Given that only four auditing firms can service the largest companies, significant problems at any one could entail substantial systematic consequences. Only three auditing firms would remain, able to service the myriad large companies that can only depend on four; many companies would be unable to obtain the services required by Sarbanes-Oxley.

In addition to a lack of robust competition in the auditing industry, the pre-Enron theory is flawed because investors have little confidence and faith in the numbers generated by auditing firms.[23] As Eisenberg and I have shown, there are no statistically significant distinctions among the big auditing firms with respect to quality. Rather, they produce similarly unimpressive results and, contrary to the assumptions of economic theory, it is simply impossible for companies to signal probity and honesty in accounting standards through auditing firm selection.[24] This lack of distinction in quality is exacerbated by the lack of competition—not only do four large firms enjoy an enormous competitive advantage over second-tier firms, but they are lumped such that no single member benefits from performing better than the other three.

Many explanations exist for this decline in auditing quality. These range from declines in civil liability and changes in organizational form, which diminished incentives for auditing firms to monitor themselves,[25] to immense changes in the complexity of financial transactions, which made auditing more difficult.[26] Somewhat more controversially, provisions dealing with consulting services by auditing firms upset the traditional balance of power between issuers and auditors, contributing to the capture of auditing firms by clients.[27]

The essential point in this chapter is not simply that auditing firms have failed to distinguish themselves in their role as gatekeepers; this is well known. Rather, consistent with the theory advanced in this book, the essential point is that America's response to the scandal at Enron and the dismal performance of auditing firms was not what it should have been. The appropriate response would have been to address the real problems of "capture" cartelization that plagued—and continue to plague—the auditing industry and to improve competitive conditions in, or to facilitate entry into, the auditing industry. Sarbanes-Oxley's response failed on both fronts.

Sarbanes-Oxley dramatically increased demand for the Big Four, thereby imposing massive costs on investors without any clear concomitant benefits. As *The Economist* observed in 2005, an association of top financial executives found that companies paid an average of $2.4 million more for auditing in 2004 than they had anticipated prior to the passage of Sarbanes-Oxley (and far more than Sarbanes-Oxley's designers had envisaged).[28] *The Economist* further observed that Sarbanes-Oxley has "provided a bonanza for accountants and auditors—a profession thought to be much at fault in the scandals that inspired the law, and which the statute sought to rein in and supervise."[29] Deloitte reports that, on average, large auditing firms have spent nearly 70,000 added work hours to comply with Sarbanes-Oxley.[30] In a sample of 97 companies, auditing firm fees increased, on average, from $3.5 million to $5.8 million—all attributed to Sarbanes-Oxley.[31]

In response, non-American companies warn that they no longer plan to list on American stock exchanges, while other non-American companies have delisted in part because of Sarbanes-Oxley.[32] One law firm reports that at least 20 percent of public companies listed on American stock exchanges have considered going private to avoid Sarbanes-Oxley[33]—only to enter a lightly regulated market, an ironic result given Sarbanes-Oxley's goal to improve financial information for investors. Indeed, *The Economist* noted in 2006 that "[t]he Sarbanes-Oxley legislation, passed after the collapse of Enron in order to stiffen up corporate governance, has put off foreign companies from listing there. The London Stock Exchange . . . has been the big beneficiary. Foreign firms have flocked to list on its main market and AIM, a less regulated market that it established in 1995.[34] London's "continuing tradition of 'light-touch' regulation . . . proved to be another essential ingredient" in its "remarkable transformation to become a global financial centre."[35]

Not surprisingly, the large auditing firms are strong Sarbanes-Oxley proponents, just as any firm would be of legislation permitting price increases and output decreases. The chief executive of Pricewaterhouse-Coopers is an "an enthusiastic advocate of the new law."[36] The head of KPMG's U.S. business unit recognizes the price increases associated with Sarbanes-Oxley, but predicts they will fall in the future, as significant costs from acclimating to Sarbanes-Oxley decrease.[37]

Turning to the substance of Sarbanes-Oxley, the fundamental problem with the statute is that individual auditors who make up the engagement teams that audit public companies are highly susceptible to capture by their clients—that is, highly susceptible to the "caring and feeding" of their clients. Such auditors typically audit one firm at a time. The capture problem, coupled with reduced incentives to provide impeccable audits, was exactly what generated the problems that Arthur Andersen encountered when servicing Enron.[38] Auditing is a service business and client satisfaction is as important in auditing as it is in all service businesses. Increasingly, auditor careers depend entirely on the "caring and feeding" of solitary clients. Sarbanes-Oxley did nothing to address this problem. Although it could have fixed the problem by requiring that public companies change auditing firms periodically, such a radical change was not implemented. Instead, as a "compromise," Sarbanes-Oxley requires individual auditors within auditing firms to rotate clients every five years.[39]

This rotation provision is likely to be extremely costly and highly ineffectual—costly because individual new auditors will incur substantial billable start-up costs as they begin new engagements every five years, and ineffectual because it will not reduce auditor tendencies to be captured by clients. In fact, the provision exacerbates those tendencies: new auditors rotated onto new accounts certainly will not want to receive lower client satisfaction ratings than their predecessors. Put differently, the provision may trigger a destructive "race to the bottom" among auditors working for companies that are aggressive about their financial reports. Those auditors willing to use the most creative auditing techniques will receive the highest ratings for customer satisfaction.

In sum, Sarbanes-Oxley's provisions provided demonstrable benefits for a discrete interest group—the largest auditing firms. The benefits that the biggest auditing firms provide to investors are not at all clear, given the unreliable nature of the financial certifications they provide. Nevertheless, demand for their services remains strong—not because of market forces, but because of regulation.

SEC regulations have effectively cartelized the auditing industry by requiring that large, public companies be audited by auditing firms that obtain only a small proportion of their revenues from any one client. This, in turn, means that large public companies can only be audited by very large auditing firms. In my view, this is what led to the massive consolidation and concentration experienced by the auditing industry in recent decades. Sarbanes-Oxley has further entrenched the regulatory cartel for the largest auditing firms without doing anything to improve the quality of the work so vitally important to investors and capital markets.

Using event-study methodology, Ivy Xiying Zhang estimates that Sarbanes-Oxley's net private cost is $1.4 trillion,[40] or about $460 for every person in the United States. This figure, characterized as "astonishing" by *The Economist*, is an econometric estimate of shareholder wealth lost because of Sarbanes-Oxley. Put differently, the study measures Sarbanes-Oxley's direct costs to investors. Some costs undoubtedly are deadweight social losses associated with the highly inefficient statute. Another significant portion of the costs, however, reflects wealth transfers from widely dispersed, politically weak shareholders to well-organized, highly concentrated interest groups—like the biggest auditing firms. Sarbanes-Oxley must suppress $1.4 trillion in fraudulent losses before it begins to benefit investors.

In other words, as it relates to auditing firms, Sarbanes-Oxley appears to provide a straightforward application of the important, public choice insight that narrow interest groups tend to dominate political processes.[41] Interest groups, their lobbyists, and other agents interact with government officials in markets for political support. To survive, regulators and politicians are constrained to generate results (in the form of statutes, regulations, and administrative agency actions) that typically benefit highly concentrated groups able to overcome free-riding and rational ignorance collective action problems. In this way, they harm less well-organized groups—such as consumers and, of course, private investors—through price increases and output decreases.

CHAPTER 12

QUIRKY GOVERNANCE: INSIDER TRADING, SHORT SELLING, AND WHISTLE-BLOWING

This chapter considers the sorts of promises companies should make about their policies regarding insider trading, short selling of company stock, and whistle-blowing. The common theme among all of these apparently disparate topics is that they all deal with the thorny topic of how to uncover negative information about corporations. Insiders who dump their shares, short sellers who sell shares they don't yet own, and whistle-blowers are all people who engage in ways of bringing information—especially negative information—about corporate performance and corporate conduct to light.

It is more than passing strange, in my view, that these various sources of valuable information about corporate conduct are treated so differently by regulators and under the law. Insider traders, of course, are considered crooks. Short sellers, though they provide valuable information about corporations gone bad, are viewed with deep suspicion. In contrast, whistle-blowers, clearly the least effective of this triad, are venerated in the popular press, in Hollywood movies, and by regulators. Still, as I will point out in more detail in this chapter, whistle-blowers have not been embraced by companies as a particularly legitimate corporate governance mechanism. If they were, whistle-blowers would be awarded bounties for bringing important information about fraud or other illegal behavior to light. But this has never happened, at least in the private sector.

Recently whistle-blowers have become fashionable in corporate governance circles. Whistle-blowers, traditionally considered tattletales and generally viewed with suspicion,[1] have enjoyed a distinct rise in general popularity in recent years as well. According to *Salon* magazine, "In recent years, aided in part by movies like 'The Insider,' whistleblowers have attained the status of folk heroes. 'It's become popular to protect whistleblowers—that's never happened before,' says Danielle Brian, executive director of the Project on Government Oversight, a nonprofit public interest group dedicated to exposing governmental corruption and mismanagement that works closely with whistleblowers and that advocates for them."[2]

Time magazine even went so far as to dub 2002 "The Year of the Whistle-blower," honoring "inside do-gooders who risked their careers"[3] by exposing, among other things, how the FBI let a key terrorist suspect slip through its fingers before September 11, 2001, and how Enron misled investors through phony accounting treatment of off-balance sheet transactions. There is now a National Whistleblower Center, a nonprofit group dedicated to helping whistle-blowers in their efforts "to improve environmental protection, nuclear safety, and government and corporate accountability."[4]

Whistle-blowing is "a form of organizational dissent,"[5] although the recent positive publicity for whistle-blowers suggests that whistle-blowing is now viewed with less suspicion, and whistle-blowers as less politically motivated and more altruistic than was the case in the past. Whistle-blowers are now thought of as an integral component of the recently re-regulated system of corporate governance that is supposed to result in better monitoring and control of managerial misconduct (agency costs) in large publicly held corporations.[6] Tip-offs from insiders have been described as "by far the most common method of detecting fraud."[7]

The purpose of this chapter is to explore whistle-blowing, insider trading, and blackmail and their possible roles in corporate governance. Why don't firms do more to promote whistle-blowing? Can any sort of insider trading ever, under any circumstances, aid shareholders in ferreting out corporate fraud? I argue here that one particular kind of insider trading—insider trading on the basis of information about corporate corruption, corporate fraud, or other illegal corporate conduct—and whistle-blowing are analytically and functionally indistinguishable as responses to corporate pathologies such as fraud and corruption.

When giant businesses like Enron, Adelphia, and WorldCom are brought to their knees by whistle-blowers, innocent people are harmed. The innocent employees, small suppliers, local communities, and philanthropic organizations that depended on these firms suffer as much as, if not more than, the firm's largely diversified investor base, and these groups single out the whistle-blower as the source of their trouble. Revelations by whistle-blowers can be embarrassing to regulators, prosecutors, and others who are supposed to be on the lookout for fraudulent corporate activity.

Conversely, it also is the case that inside traders sometimes have fared surprisingly well in the courts. In particular, in cases where insider trading leads to the same revelations about insipient fraud as whistle-blowing would, courts can be remarkably accepting of such trading.

In this chapter, I advance the theory that both whistle-blowing and insider trading are best analyzed as involving rights in the same inchoate intellectual property: valuable information. The issue of whether one has the right to blow the whistle on somebody else, like the issue of whether one has the right to trade on the basis of nonpublic information, ultimately depends on whether the person engaging in the conduct has a rightful property interest in the information he or she is using. If so, then the conduct, whether it is characterized as whistle-blowing or as insider trading, should be not only legally permissible but also affirmatively encouraged. By contrast, in situations where the person doing the trading or whistle-blowing has no legitimate property interest in the information because somebody else has a right to keep it confidential and/or to use it as they see fit, the behavior should be illegal.

This chapter begins with a definition of whistle-blowing and a history of the government's efforts to encourage the practice. Part I also includes an analysis of perhaps the most famous case of whistle-blowing: Sherron Watkins and Enron. Part II compares insider trading and whistle-blowing. This comparison explains the traditional antipathy and suspicion toward whistle-blowers. In part III, I explore whistle-blowing and insider trading as phenomena that often occur in tandem. Part IV demonstrates why whistle-blowers lack credibility and explains that verifying the assertions of non-trading whistle-blowers is likely to be very costly. In part V, I discuss the implications of a property-rights regime for insider trading and whistle-blowing, as well as the legal regimes dealing with each. In this part, I show how insider trading on negative information, when properly regulated, is a superior substitute for whistle-blowing. The argument here is not that inside trading should be generally permitted or that such trading is universally beneficial to shareholders, companies, or society. Rather, it is that the limited and tightly regulated ability to sell short can credibly signal to the market that the trader has negative information about a company.[8] Part VI provides a consideration of why, in light of this analysis, we observe such radically different treatment of whistle-blowers and inside traders. In part VII, I look at the distributional concerns of insider trading and of whistle-blowing for the investors of a company, exploring who actually pays for these practices and their effects on the company. Part VIII explains why the private contracting process within firms is not likely to permit the sort of trading advocated here, thereby making it necessary to accomplish the result by regulation rather than by intrafirm contracting. Part IX briefly discusses blackmail as a method for reacting to confidential or secretive information about corporate fraud and compares this reaction to whistle-blowing and insider trading.

I. Whistle-blowing

Defining Whistle-blowing

A whistle-blower is an employee or other person in a contractual relationship with a company who reports misconduct to outside firms or institutions, which in turn have the authority to impose sanctions or take other corrective action against the wrongdoers. While some definitions of whistle-blowing require that misconduct be reported to people outside of the organization, others include reporting misconduct up the chain of command within an organization.[9] Where one is blowing the whistle against an entire way of doing business or against people at or near the very top of a company, as was the case with Enron, reporting the behavior up the chain of command is not actually whistle-blowing. After all, it is hardly whistle-blowing to report misconduct to the very people engaged in the misconduct. On the other hand, where the misconduct involved is committed by public officials, instead of individuals in the private sector, disclosure to those outside the organization may constitute a crime if the information is classified pursuant to administrative action or subject to an executive order of confidentiality.

Our Venerable Tradition of Compensating Whistle-blowers

The origins of whistle-blowing legislation in the United States can be traced to the False Claims Act, enacted in 1863 to reduce the incidence of fraud among the suppliers of munitions and other war materials to the Union government during the Civil War.[10] The act authorizes payments to whistle-blowers of a percentage of any money recovered or damages won by the government in cases of fraud that the whistle-blower's evidence helped expose. The act allows whistle-blowers, called "relators," to bring *qui tam* actions on behalf of the government against those alleged to have submitted false claims to the government.[11] As with modern whistle-blower statutes, the False Claims Act also provides protection for whistle-blowers for wrongful dismissal.

The False Claims Act was not widely utilized until far-reaching amendments to the act in 1986 made it an attractive weapon to combat fraud in virtually any program involving federal funds. Although originally intended to deter the submission of fraudulent invoices by defense contractors, the False Claims Act now covers every industry that deals with the federal government, and it is sometimes used even in ordinary commercial contract disputes. The act provides for whistle-blowers to be reinstated to their jobs with seniority, double back pay, interest on back pay, compensation for discriminatory treatment, and legal fees.

Additional federal legislation bars reprisals against those who expose government corruption.[12]

Congress adopted further whistle-blower protection for public employees in 1989 when it passed the Whistle-blower Protection Act (WPA). The WPA is an anti-retaliation statute that prohibits the federal government from retaliating against employees who blow the whistle on public sector misconduct and provides a means of redress for employees. The Office of the Special Counsel and the Merit Systems Protection Board are charged with upholding the WPA. Employees can obtain protection as whistle-blowers by making disclosure to a special counsel, the inspector general of an agency, another employee designated by an agency head to receive such disclosures, or any other individual or organization.

Thus, employees who work for companies that deal with the government or who are themselves in government jobs have incentives to disregard internal channels, such as the internal audit function, and file whistle-blower actions in court because the so-called *qui tam* provision of the federal False Claims Act allows an individual with knowledge that someone has filed a false claim involving payment by the government to file a *qui tam* action in court. When such an action is filed, the government takes responsibility for investigating the allegation.

Where the fraud is successfully prosecuted, the whistle-blower is eligible to receive a bounty of at least 15 percent of the final recovery, which for large frauds can amount to tens of millions of dollars merely for having brought a false claim to the government's attention. The burden of proving the false claim must be met by the government: "The whistleblower has to do nothing other than file the *qui tam* action."[13]

Thus, while it is tempting to distinguish whistle-blowing from insider trading on the grounds that the motivations of whistle-blowers are more "pure," this does not appear to be the case. Here, the point is not that insider traders are particularly virtuous. Of course they aren't. Rather the point is that whistle-blowers are often motivated by the financial returns associated with whistle-blowing in the same way that insider traders are motivated by the financial returns associated with trading. Consistent with this intuition, the federal statutes regulating whistle-blowing for public corruption are specifically designed to provide economic incentives for whistle-blowers. And, at least some whistle-blowers have profited richly from *qui tam* actions. In fiscal year 2005, for example, federal whistle-blowers were awarded $166 million, up from $108 million in 2004.[14] In one case, the various government settlements from the myriad investigations into HealthSouth Corporation's alleged fraud against Medicare and other federally insured health care programs yielded $327 million in fines payable to the U.S. government.[15] Of this amount, $76 million in recoveries was attributable to four *qui tam* lawsuits. Five relators received

$12.6 million for their contributions to the HealthSouth litigation.[16] More generally, recoveries resulting from all *qui tam* and non–*qui tam* cases brought under the False Claims Act from 1986 to 2004 totaled $13.5 billion. Whistle-blower rewards for *qui tam* cases exceeded $1.4 billion during this period.

Self-Interested Behavior and Whistle-blowing

Even where whistle-blowers do not engage in whistle-blowing for money, often there are other self-interested motivations behind this ostensibly altruistic behavior. Disgruntled employees are more likely to engage in whistle-blowing than other employees are, and revenge is a common feature in whistle-blower cases. Thus, it does not appear possible to distinguish whistle-blowing from insider trading by citing differences in the motivations of whistle-blowers and inside traders.[17] As noted above, a whistle-blower is someone who observes criminal behavior and alerts a competent authority. The term naturally conjures up images of concerned citizens frantically blowing whistles to thwart muggings and bank robberies on Main Street, USA.[18]

Sherron Watkins—A Paradigmatic Whistle-blower?

Sherron Watkins, the iconic whistle-blower, does not remotely fit the traditional definition and imagery associated with a whistle-blower.[19] She did write a memorandum articulating some of her concerns about the "suspicions of accounting improprieties" at Enron. But she gave this document to the company's CEO, Kenneth Lay, now a criminal defendant in various fraud and insider trading cases related to Enron's collapse. Then, on the basis of Lay's vague assurances that he would look into the wrongdoing, she did nothing, and her memorandum was not made public until congressional investigators released it six weeks after Enron filed for bankruptcy—long after the company and its stock price had collapsed.

Critical to understanding Watkins' role as a self-interested whistleblower is to understand her objectives in writing the whistle-blower letter. To do this, it is necessary to parse the letter that Watkins anonymously e-mailed to Lay. The opening line makes it clear that Watkins' objective is to retain her employment and to protect her pension savings. The letter begins by asking, "Has Enron become a risky place to work? For those of us who didn't get rich over the last few years, can we afford to stay?"[20] Far from whistle-blowing, the letter suggests ways that the company can unwind its problems, without the need to notify investors or regulators of the massive improprieties going on in the company. She adds, "I am incredibly nervous that we will implode in a wave of accounting scandals.

My eight years of Enron work history will be worth nothing on my resume, the business world will consider the past successes as nothing but an elaborate accounting hoax."[21]

Moreover, Watkins clearly identified herself with the management team that created the scandal as much as with the Enron investors who were devastated by the collapse of the company. For example, she expresses concern that unhappy employees were aware of the company's improper accounting practices and could possibly seek revenge on the company by exposing the fraud. Watkins observes that many shareholders "bought [Enron common stock] at $70 and $80 a share looking for $120 a share and now they're at $38 or worse." She also observes that she and other employees "are under too much scrutiny and there are probably one or two disgruntled 'redeployed' employees who know enough about the 'funny' accounting to get us in trouble."[22]

Watkins' letter reveals that she was well aware that the company was engaged in accounting shenanigans and that the financial statements of the company did not fully represent to investors and regulators the true condition of the company. For example, Watkins observes, "[W]e have had a lot of smart people looking at this and a lot of accountants including AA & Co. have blessed the accounting treatment. None of that will protect Enron if these transactions are ever disclosed in the bright light of day."[23]

This suggests that Watkins was not only self-interested but also realized that there were material accounting issues that had not been disclosed. Rather than disclose these issues, she advocated attempting to correct the problems secretly, which she analogized to "robbing [a] bank in one year and trying to pay [the money] back two years later." In other words, the Watkins letter is more consistent with an effort by Watkins to distance herself from the fraud, while declining to go the authorities, in hopes that the entire mess would somehow blow over and life could return to normal.

Acting in a manner entirely consistent with the model of rational self-interested behavior, Watkins attempts to quantify the risks and rewards of continuing to mask the company's ongoing fraud by assessing the probability of getting caught. She points out that if "the probability of discovery is low enough and the estimated damage too great; then therefore we [should] find a way to quietly and quickly reverse, unwind, write down these positions/transactions."[24] Alternatively, she advises that if "the probability of discovery is too great, the estimated damages to the company too great; therefore, we must quantify [and] develop damage containment plans and disclose."[25] Her biggest concern is detection. She fears that "too many people are looking for a smoking gun,"[26] and she fully understood that Enron was "a crooked company."[27]

Analyzing Sherron Watkins' Actions

The point here is not to vilify Sherron Watkins. Rather, the purpose of this detailed review of her "whistle-blowing" is to emphasize that she did not do anything to expose the ongoing financial irregularities and accounting fraud. It is doubtful that Watkins properly can be characterized as a whistle-blower. As I observed earlier, reporting fraud to the very people engaged in the misbehavior is hardly whistle-blowing. Even if Watkins could be thought of as a whistle-blower, she must be described as an unsuccessful one.

More important, regardless of whether Watkins' activities technically constitute whistle-blowing, it is impossible to describe her motives as being more altruistic or other-regarding than those of inside traders. Clearly, there were many motivations for her actions, including concerns about self-preservation, her savings, her reputation, and the undiversified human capital investment she had made in Enron.

The complexity that characterizes Sherron Watkins' motives is probably quite typical. Whatever distinctions one might be able to draw between whistle-blowers and inside traders, it is not possible to distinguish these two activities on the basis of the motives of the actors. Because the activities cannot be distinguished on the basis of *motive*, and they cannot be distinguished on the basis of *consequences*, one is left to wonder what fuels our intuition that whistle-blowing is desirable while insider trading on the same set of information is so abhorrent.[28]

Most, but not all, whistle-blowing is tolerated. There is an exception to the general rule favoring whistle-blowing where a whistle-blower reveals confidential information that she has a legitimate legal duty not to disclose. But this, as shown below, is precisely the context in which insider trading is illegal. Insider trading should be prohibited only in cases where whistle-blowing is also prohibited, that is, in cases where the would-be trader has a legitimate legal duty to keep the information confidential and otherwise to refrain from acting on it.

But while the legal system ostensibly excoriates inside traders, the law protects whistle-blowers from retaliation by their employers by making it illegal for any public company to "discharge, demote, suspend, threaten, harass, or in any other manner discriminate against an employee" because of any lawful provision of information about suspected fraud.[29]

II. Insider Trading as Whistle-blowing

Insider trading involves buying or selling securities (or derivatives, such as puts, calls, or futures) on the basis of material, nonpublic information.[30] In this chapter, I limit my discussion of insider trading to the narrow context in which such trading occurs in a situation where whistle-blowing could also occur.[31]

In this context, insider trading occurs when the potential whistle-blower has bad news about a company. The conduct that replaces the whistle-blowing involves selling shares short, selling single-stock futures contracts, and purchasing put options or selling call options—all strategies that permit traders to profit on the basis of price declines.

Insider trading on the basis of information about an ongoing fraud necessarily leads to the exposure of that fraud. It is not profitable for an inside trader simply to sell or to sell short shares in the company involved in the fraud without revealing or causing the underlying information to be revealed. While it might seem that mere selling without disclosure might be a profitable strategy for insiders because such selling drives share prices down, this is not the case.[32] In efficient capital markets,[33] transacting in financial assets (whether it involves buying or selling) will not affect the underlying values of those assets unless such transactions reveal information. The prices of securities and other financial assets reflect all publicly available information relevant to the price of that asset. Consequently, new information, not mere trading, is what moves security prices.[34]

Because trades that lack information content will not affect prices for very long, insiders cannot profit merely by selling—they must also reveal information for prices to adjust. As with whistle-blowing, insider trading on whistle-blower information must result in the exposure of information about a fraud. If the information turns out to be unreliable, prices will not adjust, and the insider will lose the transaction costs associated with his investment. These costs can be substantial if the insider is selling short as well as liquidating his current holdings.[35] For this reason, short selling is likely to be a far more credible signal than whistle-blowing because the talk involved in whistle-blowing is cheap, while the trading involved in short selling is costly to the short seller whose information about the underlying company is erroneous.

Such short selling can create perverse incentives, particularly the incentive that top managers might have to cause harm to their firms to make private gains on the following declines in the company's shares. But these perverse incentive effects do not pose a problem in cases where inside trading is done by employees who have no power to affect the strategic decisions of the firm, either because they no longer are employed by the company or because they work in a low-level capacity that does not involve strategic decision-making. For this reason, regulation should be enacted that permits low-level insiders such as rank-and-file employees to trade on the basis of material nonpublic information under certain conditions.

As with whistle-blowing, insider trading requires that the person engaged in the conduct have a preexisting relationship with the company. In fact, liability for insider trading requires that there be a preexisting relationship of trust and confidence that the defendant-insider has breached by trading.[36] To be a whistle-blower requires a similar sort of relationship. And, of course, at a bare minimum, both whistle-blowing and inside trading require that the whistle-blowers and the traders actually have some information not generally known that is of interest to others.

Tying these strands together, we see that whistle-blowers and insiders share the same basic defining characteristics: (a) they are informational intermediaries; (b) they have information not widely known or not already reflected in share prices; and (c) they are in a preexisting contractual or quasi-contractual relationship with the source of the information.[37] As a descriptive matter, the only meaningful difference between inside traders and whistle-blowers lies in how the information possessed is used by the trader or by the whistle-blowers' talk rather than trade. This distinction may appear vast but, when analyzed realistically, it is far from clear that this is a difference with much, if any, moral significance. And, as shown below, it also is far from clear that these activities can be distinguished on the basis of their economic impact on third parties.

Dirks v. SEC

The starting point for any analysis of the relationship between whistle-blowing and insider trading is *Dirks v. SEC*.[38] This case is interesting for two reasons. First, the case involves the efforts of a failed whistle-blower. Raymond Secrist, the Equity Funding employee who provided the tip about the company's fraud to the defendant, Ronald Dirks, only resorted to Dirks because his repeated efforts to act as a whistle-blower were unsuccessful. Second, *Dirks* is interesting because it suggests that whistle-blowers and inside traders are likely to have similar motivations for their behavior. Whether their underlying motivation is revenge, profit-seeking, or some complex combination of reasons does not appear relevant to our analysis of the social desirability of the attendant behavior.

In *Dirks*, the Supreme Court examined the insider trading liability of Ronald Dirks, who received valuable information from a disgruntled employee of fraud-ridden Equity Funding. Dirks then passed the information along to his clients, a group of institutional investors, who in turn traded on the basis of the information in advance of the public disclosure of the fraud.

A brief review of the facts of the case will help our analysis. On March 6, 1973, Raymond Dirks, a securities analyst at the investment bank Hawkins Delafield, received a tip from Ronald Secrist, a disgruntled former officer of Equity Funding of America. Secrist's tip alleged that the assets of Equity Funding, a diversified corporation primarily engaged in selling life insurance and mutual funds, were vastly overstated as the result of a massive, ongoing series of fraudulent corporate practices. Secrist also told Dirks that he and others had tried to convey information about the fraud to various regulatory agencies, including the SEC, the California state securities commissioner, and the Illinois state securities commissioner. None of the agencies followed up on these accusations. Secrist urged Dirks to verify the fraud and to disclose it publicly. Secrist did not attempt to blackmail Equity Funding.

At oral argument in the Supreme Court, the SEC took the position that Dirks's obligation to disclose would not be satisfied by reporting the information to the SEC.[39] In its brief to the Court, the SEC took an inconsistent position, arguing in favor of a "safe harbor" rule under which an investor would satisfy his obligation to disclose by reporting the information to the commission and then waiting a set period of time before trading.[40] However, as noted by the Court, because no such safe harbor rule was in effect, "persons such as Dirks have no real option other than to refrain from trading."[41]

The prohibition on insider trading in *Dirks* was unfortunate. If the legal restrictions against insider trading had been successful in deterring Raymond Dirks from acting on the tip he had received from Ronald Secrist, it would have prolonged a massive ongoing fraud. Clearly, prohibiting insider trading would have been inefficient in this context, which is why the Supreme Court rejected the SEC's legal theory and overturned the commission's sanctions against Raymond Dirks.

Lessons from Dirks

The *Dirks* case illustrates that insider trading has at least one clear advantage over whistle-blowing: it provides a significantly more credible signal of the veracity of the information. Talk is cheap. When, as is often the case, the whistle-blower is a disgruntled employee, people are less inclined to believe the whistle-blower's story. People are particularly disinclined to believe whistle-blowers when they are reporting about companies like Equity Funding or Enron, which were corporations with significant resources with which to respond to the whistle-blower's allegations. In *Dirks* (and there is no reason to assume that this result should not be generalized), insider trading worked where whistle-blowing did not.

The constellation of facts that produced the litigation in *Dirks* demonstrates that insider trading on negative information has certain decisive advantages over whistle-blowing. One such advantage is that insider trading does not require that the person in possession of knowledge of the wrongdoing be able to persuade a government official to take action before the wrongdoing can be confronted. The insider need only convince herself that she is right in her own assessment of the situation. This, of course, means that insider trading on whistle-blower information obviates whistle-blowers' credibility problem.

It is true that in the important subset of cases involving government corruption, whistle-blowers can bring their own lawsuits in the form of *qui tam* actions. But litigation is costly and time-consuming, and plaintiffs in *qui tam* actions must confront the bureaucratic hurdles of court procedure, hurdles that need not be confronted by those who simply trade.[42] Thus, at least in some cases, insider trading has the advantage of involving a faster and more certain payoff for the insider in possession of whistle-blower information than whistle-blowing does. Unlike whistle-blowers, inside traders do not have to rely on the competence of government officials, who are often poorly motivated or inept, to profit from the information they have acquired. Similarly, unlike whistle-blowers, inside traders do not have to wait for the litigation process, which may take years to produce a recovery or settlement, to run its course.

III. INSIDER TRADING AND WHISTLE-BLOWING: IS THE COMBINATION THE NORM?

Dirks v. SEC involved the simultaneous use of both whistle-blowing and insider trading (via tipping) in a very effective manner, where effectiveness is measured by success in revealing the fraud. The claim that insider trading and whistle-blowing are closely linked is bolstered by the extent to which these activities are conducted simultaneously. Insider trading and whistle-blowing both require possession of material, nonpublic information, and both trading and whistle-blowing are consistent with the rational self-interest of the people engaging in these activities. Thus it should not be surprising that we observe in cases such as *Dirks* that these activities are carried on simultaneously.

For example, Sherron Watkins, "the whistleblowing Enron vice president who has been portrayed as a kind of white knight among a cast of self-serving charlatans," engaged in trading on the basis of the information contained in her whistle-blower memorandum and, as a result, was described as being "at risk for having violated insider trading laws."[43] During her congressional testimony about her role in uncovering the financial and accounting fraud at Enron, Watkins revealed that soon after warning Enron CEO Kenneth Lay that the company was about to "implode in a wave of accounting scandals," she sold a large block of her shares to avoid impending losses. That sale violated the current interpretation of SEC Rule 10b-5, the regulation prohibiting insider trading, which makes it illegal to buy or sell securities "while in possession of material, nonpublic information about the security," where doing so involves the breach of a preexisting duty of trust to maintain the confidentiality of such information.

Of course it is not possible to acquire data on the specific incidences of insider trading by people with whistle-blower information given that people trading on the basis of material nonpublic information do not advertise their transactions. However, Watkins' near incrimination under the laws prohibiting insider trading is not without precedent.

In addition to the Watkins and the *Dirks* examples, the classic insider trading/whistle-blower sequence (and even accusations of blackmail) is reiterated in the example of Ted Beatty at Dynegy, another Houston energy company. Beatty, who was angry at Dynegy because he was overlooked for a promotion, resigned from the company. When he left, he took with him incriminating documents that suggested questionable accounting at the company in a transaction called Project Alpha. The information revealed by Beatty caused several high-ranking Dynegy officers to resign almost immediately, led to fraud investigations of energy traders at several companies, and resulted in an SEC suit against Dynegy for securities fraud. Dynegy ultimately suffered the complete collapse of its equity and consented to a $1 million SEC civil fine, selling all of its major assets to survive.

Following a pattern of conduct virtually identical to the one followed by Ronald Secrist in the *Dirks* case, Beatty tipped his information about Dynegy to another analyst, Jack Pitts, of the New York investment fund Steadfast Capital. Steadfast, like Raymond Dirks's firm, Hawkins Delafield, sold Dynegy's stock short. Shortly before trading, Pitts, the tippee, wrote an e-mail to his tipper, Beatty, observing that "any sign of dubious accounting at Dynegy would make investors' fears go crazy and take the stock into a tailspin."[44] Again, a combination of whistle-blowing and insider trading led to the exposure of fraud.

IV. Credibility, Payoffs, and Reliance on Other Mechanisms of Corporate Governance

The *Dirks* case and the Beatty incident both illustrate the parallels between insider trading and whistle-blowing where the information being used pertains to fraud or other corporate misconduct. Both insider trading and whistle-blowing can be used to expose fraud. In both cases, it appears that trading was more successful than whistle-blowing in revealing the fraud. Given the complexity of whistle-blowers' motives, their inability to make a credible commitment about the veracity of their information, and the necessity for bureaucratic intervention and investigation of the information being disclosed, it is not surprising that whistle-blowing is often unsuccessful.

Another important distinction between whistle-blowing and insider trading relates to how each of these activities interacts with other informational gatekeepers and institutions of corporate governance, particularly Wall Street industry analysts and the SEC. Whistle-blowing, to be effective, requires that other institutions of corporate governance also function effectively, because whistle-blowing is not self-effectuating. Specifically, unlike inside traders, whistle-blowers must first convince regulators, financial analysts, or some other corporate governance intermediary of the validity of their claims before their actions can gain traction. Thus, the effectiveness of whistle-blowing largely depends on the integrity and efficacy of these other institutions. In light of the historical unreliability of institutions of corporate governance, the need to rely on these institutions is a serious disadvantage for whistle-blowing relative to insider trading. Again, the *Dirks* case provides a useful illustration.

The Failure of External Corporate Governance Mechanisms

Stock market analysts were quite bullish on Equity Funding, the company about which Ronald Secrist was attempting to reveal fraud. Shortly before Equity Funding collapsed, an analyst at the investment banking firm Cowen & Co. issued a report recommending that investors buy Equity Funding "for aggressive accounts."[45] An analyst at Burnham & Co., Inc. opined that Equity Funding was "an excellent value" and rated the company "a Buy."[46]

Analysts were not only touting Equity Funding, they also engaged in active efforts to defend the stock against Secrist's efforts at whistle-blowing. On March 26, 1973, the day before the New York Stock Exchange halted trading in Equity Funding, the analyst at Hayden, Stone, Inc. who was responsible for covering the company circulated a memorandum announcing that "rumors have been circulating which have affected Equity Funding's stock." The analyst reported that his well-regarded investment bank had "checked these rumors, and there appears to be no substance to any of them."[47] It turned out that the analyst had checked with insurance regulators in various states and each one said they had no present intention of conducting any inquiries into Secrist's allegations.[48] The SEC showed a similar lack of interest in investigating Equity Funding until investors tipped by Secrist began trading on the information he gave them. Secrist testified that Equity Funding employees who had attempted to notify the SEC of the wrongdoing at the company had been "brushed aside with a comment that that's a ridiculous story." Worse still, whistle-blowing employees also found that the information was sometimes relayed back to Equity Funding and that "they were placed in personal jeopardy as a result of having gone" to the SEC.[49]

Attempts by Dirks to tip Equity Funding's outside auditors were similarly ineffective. During the course of his investigation of Equity Funding, Dirks met with the company's auditors "in an attempt to spread word of the fraud and bring it to a halt."[50] When Dirks learned that Equity Funding's auditors were about to release certified financial statements for the company, he contacted them and apprised them of the fraud allegations, hoping that they would withhold the release of their report and seek a halt in the trading of the company's securities. Instead, the auditors merely reported Dirks's allegations to management.[51]

Despite the fact that whistle-blowers had contacted the SEC and state insurance officials as early as 1971, Equity Funding's chairman, who was one of the principal architects of the fraud, testified that prior to March 1973, when Secrist's insider trading caused Equity Funding's stock price to collapse, he had "received no questions from auditors, state regulatory authorities, or federal regulatory authorities that suggested they suspected there was a fraud at Equity Funding."[52]

The Failure of the Media to Expose Corporate Fraud

Journalists often perform no better than regulators in facilitating the efforts of whistle-blowers. In fact, the rationale given by the *Wall Street Journal* for declining to write a story about the fraud at Equity Funding usefully reveals a general problem for journalists seeking to publish information tipped by whistle-blowers: namely, the lack of means to verify the credibility of the information being provided.

> During the entire week that Dirks was in Los Angeles investigating Equity Funding, he was also in touch regularly with William Blundell, the *Wall Street Journal*'s Los Angeles bureau chief. Dirks kept Blundell up to date on the progress of the investigation and badgered him to write a story for the *Journal* on the allegations of fraud at Equity Funding. Blundell, however, was afraid that publishing such damaging rumors supported only by hearsay from former employees might be libelous, so he declined to write the story. . . . Dirks provided Blundell with "the substance of all he knew," including his "notes" and the "names" of all witnesses. Nevertheless, given the "scope of the fraud," Blundell doubted that it could have been "missed by an honest auditor" and discounted the entire allegation.[53]

Whistle-blowers' Failure to Communicate

The cautious reactions to information provided by whistle-blowers are not necessarily a result of sloth or venality on the part of regulators, market analysts, journalists, or others. Rather, the suspicion attached to whistle-blowers is justified by the dubious motives that often accompany their actions. For example, Raymond Secrist, the tipper who pointed Raymond Dirks to the Equity Funding fraud, was reported to have tipped Dirks because he was "upset over his small Christmas bonus."[54] Similarly, Ted Beatty, the Dynegy tipper, began his whistle-blowing because Dynegy failed to give him "the promotion he felt he deserved."[55]

In addition, it is by no means clear that highly cautious reactions are particularly inefficient responses to whistle-blowing. To gauge the efficiency of ignoring whistle-blowing, one must compare the costs of ignoring the information with the benefits, which come in the form of conserving resources that otherwise would be wasted in pursuing the false charges of disgruntled employees and other malcontents. The question of whether the costs of such caution exceed the benefits of investigating the merits of the allegations remains an empirical issue for which data are scarce if not nonexistent. One thing that is known, however, is that the cost-benefit calculations associated with ignoring whistle-blowers may be different for bureaucrats and financial intermediaries than for society as a whole. Bureaucrats are inherently risk-averse. They benefit little from validating a whistle-blower's complaint, and risk a lot if they make a blunder. Thus, bureaucratic incentives may lead to whistle-blowers' claims being met with an excess of caution.

Of course, when analysts and other corporate governance intermediaries have incentives to bias their recommendations and analyses in favor of companies and to ignore fraud, whistle-blowers will face even greater obstacles in trying to convince people that what they are saying is true. As I have observed in a previous work, "The problem with the analysts' recommendations is not difficult to grasp. Investment banks pressure the analysts they employ to give positive ratings on companies tracked by issuers, because positive ratings boost stock prices and generate capital for their investment banking clients."[56] Thus gatekeepers such as stock market analysts and bureaucrats have much to lose and little to gain from crediting whistle-blowers' accusations.

The Effects of These Failures on Whistle-blowing: The Relative Payoffs of Whistle-blowing and Insider Trading

This analysis reveals a major defect with whistle-blowing. Besides providing a more credible signal than whistle-blowing, insider trading does not rely on other institutions of corporate governance to be effective. As these other corporate governance institutions become more effective, however, the need for whistle-blowing itself also declines. This, in turn, indicates that whistle-blowing is least effective when it is most needed, which is during times when the basic institutions of corporate governance are not functioning independently or effectively.

Predictably, the market's response to whistle-blowing and insider trading reflects the higher value associated with trading than whistle-blowing. The Beatty incident at Dynegy and the *Dirks* case both suggest that the monetary payoff for trading is higher than the payoff for either whistle-blowing or tipping, at least in the private sector, where there are no statutes that provide monetary incentives for whistle-blowers. In both cases, it appears that the tippees receiving the information and trading on it fared much better than the tippers who provided them with the information and attempted to inform regulators of the problems they had discovered. Beatty was assured by the people he approached with his information about Dynegy that his assistance in their trading activities "would earn him big money." Subsequent press reports of Beatty's activities, however, reveal that "no such payout has materialized" and that Beatty is now "unemployed and in financial stress."[57] Raymond Dirks, meanwhile, became a celebrity. Ironically, his efforts to cooperate with the SEC led to his being prosecuted by the SEC for insider trading.[58] If he had confined his activities to trading and had not attempted to inform the SEC of his concerns about Equity Funding, it is likely that he would have avoided prosecution.

V. Insider Trading, Whistle-blowing, Property Rights, and Law

Insider trading can accomplish the same socially desirable results as whistle-blowing. An important difference between insider trading and whistle-blowing is that whistle-blowing is strictly regulated and constrained by the need for whistle-blowers to have their claims validated by some sort of public institution like an administrative agency or a prosecutor. This required mediation by an outside organization is a controlling mechanism to ostensibly restrict the flow of frivolous or inappropriate whistle-blowing. As shown above, the problem with this process is not so much that it may generate too many whistle-blower complaints, but that it may generate too few; and those that are generated are sometimes still inappropriately discounted.

The Law of Insider Trading and Its Foundations in Property Rights

By contrast, there is no mediating public institution in place to monitor and control insider trading on whistle-blowing information. There are, of course, legal restrictions on insider trading, but these restrictions are aimed at eliminating insider trading and do not have the intention of facilitating insider trading on whistle-blower-type information.

Completely eliminating or even relaxing the rules against insider trading would predictably result in an oversupply of insider trading. Some mechanism or interpretive rule is needed to distinguish among various sorts of inside (material, nonpublic) information and to permit market participants to determine what sort of information may be utilized in trading and what sort of information must remain confidential.

Current court interpretations of the SEC rules related to insider trading provide a very promising starting point for developing an interpretive rule about when insider trading is appropriate in the whistle-blowing context. Here the argument proceeds in three steps. First, the legal prohibition against insider trading does not bar all trading that occurs when one trader has an informational advantage over her counterparty. Rather, the rule requires that the trading on an informational advantage be the result of a breach of fiduciary duty for it to be illegal.

Second, basing legal responsibility for insider trading on the breach of fiduciary duty serves as a basis for establishing and allocating property rights in nonpublic information. Information belongs to somebody, usually the company that is the source of the information. Where trading on this information involves the misappropriation (or theft) of such information, a breach of duty occurs. Conversely, trading does not involve the breach of a duty when the trader is not violating the property rights of any other person or entity by trading.

Third, applying the above analysis of fiduciary duties and property rights to trading on the basis of whistle-blower information suggests that there is no basis upon which to ban such trading. Information about an ongoing fraud or other criminal activity should not be considered the property of the firm that is engaged in the fraud. Trading on the basis of such information, therefore, should not be considered a breach of fiduciary duty. Put simply, while companies clearly have a valid interest in maintaining the confidentiality of legitimate corporate information, such as their strategic plans, their earnings, their acquisition plans and other activities, they have no valid interest in maintaining the confidentiality of information about fraud or other illegal activities that might be used in whistle-blowing.

The rules against insider trading are meant to protect public companies and investors from theft of information that properly belongs to them. Insiders such as executives or directors, and "temporary insiders" such as attorneys, accountants, financial printers, and investment bankers, routinely obtain confidential information about a company in the course of their work. The insider trading rules are intended to prevent both these permanent and temporary insiders from abusing their positions of trust by trading in violation of their legal duties of confidentiality.

The Supreme Court clearly articulated the fiduciary underpinnings of insider trading regulations in *Chiarella v. United States*.[59] The defendant in this case, Vincent Chiarella, was a financial printer whose employer, Pandick Press, was routinely hired by companies seeking to acquire other companies. These acquirers required the services of a printer to manufacture the disclosure documents that would accompany their offers to acquire other companies. Chiarella traded on the basis of his advance knowledge of the information contained in the disclosure documents that he was printing. In so doing, he breached a fiduciary duty not to his trading partners—he owed no fiduciary duties to them—but rather to the bidding firms that were the sources of the information and to his employer, both of whom had relied on Chiarella to keep the information in his possession confidential. In the court's view, unless Chiarella had a fiduciary obligation requiring him to keep the information he had acquired confidential, his trading did not constitute insider trading despite the fact that he clearly possessed advantageous nonpublic information.[60]

Legal Lessons for Trading on Whistle-blower Information: Creating Incentives

Here the parallel to whistle-blowing is clear. Insider trading is regulated for the purpose of *maintaining* the confidentiality of legitimate corporate information. Whistle-blowing is encouraged to *prevent* information about fraud and corruption from remaining confidential. In both the insider trading context and the whistle-blowing context, the key issue is the extent to which the applicable law provides the appropriate incentives for people. In the case of insider trading, the focus is on providing incentives for people to maintain the confidentiality of legitimate corporate information that is meant to be used only for a corporate purpose and not for the private benefit of inside traders. In the case of whistle-blowing, the focus is on providing incentives for people to reveal information about wrongdoing.

No rational person would consider the disclosure of some material nonpublic information about a company's strategic plans to be legitimate whistle-blowing. It is, therefore, mysterious why anyone would consider information about an ongoing corporate fraud to be bona fide corporate information that a company could legitimately require its employees to keep confidential. Since it seems irrational to prevent people from disclosing such information, it also seems irrational to prevent people from trading on the basis of this sort of "whistle-blower" information.

From a legal perspective, insider trading is illegal only when such trading is based on material nonpublic information and the person doing the trading has breached a fiduciary duty by trading. From a property rights perspective, the same inquiry into whether a person owes and has breached fiduciary duties by trading defines and allocates the nature of the property interest in the information being exploited through trading. The reason that someone may owe a fiduciary duty such as a duty to refrain from trading or to keep information confidential is to protect the value of property rights in information.

Consistent with this analysis and going back at least to Locke, information acquired through legitimate means, such as one's own labor, is the property of the person who has acquired it.[61] One has a presumptive right to use information acquired in this way.[62] As Hernando de Soto has powerfully illustrated, the economic justifications for clearly defining property rights, as well as for extending such rights to people who have made legitimate acquisitions, is that doing so provides the best set of incentives to maximize the value of such information. As Locke was concerned with the underutilization of land enclosed by England's landed gentry, De Soto's is with "dead" assets, a term he uses to describe the undisclosed and unregistered assets of those operating outside the highly corrupt, overbureaucratized formal economies of undeveloped countries.[63]

The implications are clear: failure to allow insider trading on the basis of whistle-blower information will lead to the same sort of underutilization of assets as the failure to legalize property rights in underdeveloped sectors of the world. Just as in the case of ill-defined property rights in De Soto's Peru, the failure to recognize the rights of people in possession of corporate whistle-blower information to profit from that information will lead to underutilization of such information and to inefficiency.

Thus, applying this analysis to the legal restrictions on insider trading yields at least three reasons why certain insiders should be permitted to trade on whistle-blower information. First, insider trading is only illegal when it involves the breach of a fiduciary duty, and there is no fiduciary duty to maintain the confidentiality of information about an ongoing fraud. Second, from a property rights perspective, a company committing fraud cannot claim a legitimate corporate interest in maintaining the ongoing confidentiality of information relating to its fraud. Finally, applying the sort of economic analysis that De Soto applies in the development context yields the conclusion that insider trading on whistle-blower information should be encouraged because, just as it is socially desirable to encourage the efficient utilization of assets in the economy, it is also efficient to encourage activities that will not only lead to the exposure of corporate fraud but also actually discourage such fraud by raising the probability that it will be exposed.

Still another incentive-based justification for permitting insider trading on the basis of whistle-blower information is that doing so is likely to decrease the time required for the information to be revealed to the public.

Insiders may trade knowing that the information they are using will come out eventually. As long as insider trading is illegal, however, there exists a powerful disincentive to reveal that they are trading. Legitimizing their property rights in whistle-blower information by making insider trading on the basis of such information legal not only would have the obvious effect of encouraging more such trading; but it also would encourage traders to disclose or otherwise take steps to make public the information in their possession. This in turn would accelerate the exposure of the fraud and other wrongdoing that was the subject of the trading.

What Kind of Information Qualifies as Whistle-blower Information?

In addition to limiting the identity of who can trade on whistle-blower information, there remains the issue of what sort of information is the proper subject of trading and what is not. Here the analysis is greatly facilitated by analogy to protections afforded to corporate whistle-blowers by the Sarbanes-Oxley Act. Sarbanes-Oxley provides protection for information "regarding any conduct which the employee reasonably believes constitutes a violation . . . of any provision of Federal law relating to fraud against shareholders."[64] Thus, just as not every disclosure by self-proclaimed whistle-blowers is protected activity, neither should every trade by an insider be subject to the defense that it involved protected whistle-blowing. Nevertheless, the category of protected activity is broad for whistle-blowers,[65] and it should be no less broad for inside traders.

Whistle-blower disclosures to nongovernmental agencies including the news media have long been protected by the Department of Labor under statutory provisions that are virtually identical to the provisions protecting whistle-blowers in Sarbanes-Oxley.[66] Permitting whistle-blowers to communicate in a slightly different way, by trading, seems like a modest extension of this current policy.

Sarbanes-Oxley contains protections for whistle-blowers who mistakenly believed that their employers were engaged in illegal conduct. Specifically, an employee's whistle-blower disclosures are protected as long as they are based on the employee's "reasonable belief" that the employer has engaged in fraudulent or illegal conduct. Under Sarbanes-Oxley, the employee is under no obligation to show that her allegations are meritorious.[67]

The problem associated with the transmittal of erroneous information pertaining to a corporation's activities is far less acute in the whistle-blower context than for insider trading for two reasons. First, where an insider engages in trading on the basis of whistle-blower information— regardless of whether that trading consists of short selling, selling call options, single-stock futures, or buying put options—the insider must risk her own capital, betting that there will be a decline in the value of the company's share price when the whistle-blower information is revealed. This means that, regardless of whether the insider is acting in good faith, it is costly for an insider to trade on the basis of erroneous information because doing so involves a substantial risk that the insider will suffer trading losses. Second, whistle-blowing involves moral hazard problems that do not exist in the insider trading context. Specifically, because it is illegal for employers to retaliate against whistle-blowers, employees have an incentive to invent issues about which they can whistle-blow to obtain job security that they would not otherwise have. Employers will be reluctant to fire whistle-blowers because doing this risks not only civil penalties, but also criminal sanctions under Section 1107 of Sarbanes-Oxley.[68]

In addition, Congress, to make it "easier for an individual to prove that a whistleblower reprisal has taken place," has declared that for a whistleblower to obtain relief in the form of reinstatement or damages for alleged retaliation, he need not show that "the whistleblowing was a factor in a personnel action." Indeed, the whistle-blower need not even show that the whistle-blowing was a substantial motivating or predominant factor in any action taken against him.[69] Instead, he need only show a tenuous correlation: merely that the official taking the action knew that whistleblowing had taken place and acted within a time period after such whistleblowing that "a reasonable person could conclude that the disclosure was a factor in the personnel action."[70]

The analysis up to this point has demonstrated that there are built-in incentives that limit the extent to which people will engage in insider trading on the basis of erroneous whistle-blower information. These safeguards do not similarly constrain whistle-blowers. The analysis also indicates that only certain information should be the subject of insider trading. This information, which is the same information that might assist in an investigation of a violation of law, is the sort of information that we should encourage whistle-blowers to disclose. The fact that we are able to determine the sort of information that qualifies for whistle-blower protection demonstrates that we can also determine the sort of information that is the proper subject for protected insider trading.

However, the analysis here does not yield the conclusion that anybody in possession of material information about an ongoing corporate fraud should be able to trade on such information. As suggested above, the information must have been obtained in some legitimate manner. Thus it is necessary, as Locke puts it, that such property rights be allocated to information and other assets that are the product of one's "honest industry."[71] This suggests that the right to engage in insider trading on the basis of whistle-blower information ought not be allocated to people who actually are participating in the fraud, because those who generate or participate in generating information about an ongoing fraud have not acquired such information as the result of their "honest industry" and are not entitled to profit from exploiting such information.[72] Similarly, from an economic perspective, permitting participants in a fraudulent scheme within a corporation to trade on such information could have the undesirable effect of providing additional incentives for miscreants to commit fraud.

VI. WHISTLE-BLOWERS AND INSIDER TRADING: SOME DIFFERENCES

Whistle-blowing and insider trading are complements, not substitutes. A system that permitted both whistle-blowing and insider trading on whistle-blowing information would do a better job of ferreting out wrongdoing than a system that permitted only one practice and not the other. The legitimacy of payments to whistle-blowers is well established and uncontroversial. The legitimacy of insider trading is, of course, far more contested.

The previous section stressed certain advantages that insider trading has over whistle-blowing. Insider trading is self-effectuating. Inside traders receive prompt compensation for revealing corporate fraud. By contrast, private sector whistle-blowers are merely protected from retaliation. Even in the public sector, where statutes provide for payments for whistle-blowers, compensation for whistle-blowing is highly uncertain and requires the whistle-blower to wait for years, if not decades. However, insider trading on whistle-blower information is not without problems of its own. Thus, as discussed below, insider trading will never replace whistle-blowing as a device for dealing with corporate wrongdoing.

The Need for Public Securities Markets

One problem with insider trading as a corporate governance device is that it is only effective in companies whose shares are publicly traded. There may be no insider trading opportunities for whistle-blowers where the fraud or wrongdoing discovered by the whistle-blower took place in government agencies or in privately held businesses. However, this shortcoming of insider trading can be easily overstated. First, the observation that it is not possible to engage in insider trading in firms and agencies with no publicly traded shares does nothing to undermine the argument that insider trading on whistle-blower information can be of value in revealing fraud in companies whose shares are publicly traded. Second, drawing from what Ian Ayres and Joseph Bankman have observed, when insiders cannot trade in their own company's stock, they may be able to use the information to trade instead in the stock of their firm's rivals, suppliers, customers, or the manufacturers of complementary products.[73] Ayres and Bankman refer to this form of trading as trading in stock substitutes. These scholars observe that trading in stock substitutes may be quite profitable, and Heather Tookes has shown that insider trading in competitors' shares often is a more profitable trading strategy for insiders than trading shares in their own firm.[74]

Ayres and Bankman do not consider the possible role of insider trading as a substitute for whistle-blowing. Clarifying the law to permit insider trading in stock substitutes would dramatically expand the usefulness of insider trading on whistle-blower information. For example, where a municipal worker has information about fraud in the allocation of construction contracts, she could sell stock in the contractor prior to blowing the whistle.[75]

The Timing Problem

An additional theoretical problem with insider trading is that the ability to engage in insider trading on any sort of information, including (but not limited to) whistle-blower information, may create perverse incentives for the person in possession of the whistle-blower information to delay revealing the information to complete her trading. Legalizing insider trading in material nonpublic information about corporate fraud, or any other whistle-blower information, is inefficient to the extent that such legalization provides incentives for traders to delay disclosure until the point at which the information would otherwise be disclosed.[76]

The question of the extent to which such delays would occur is an empirical one for which no data are available. However, while delays in the disclosure of whistle-blower information do represent potential social costs inherent in the proposed regime, there are significant benefits on the other side of the ledger that are very likely to outweigh such costs.

Foremost among these advantages is the great likelihood that permitting insider trading on whistle-blower information would lead to the disclosure of information that otherwise would not be divulged at all. Since complete non-disclosure of whistle-blower information is clearly worse that a mere delay in disclosure, it is highly probable that the benefits of permitting insider trading on the basis of whistle-blower information outweigh the costs.

Even if there is a delay in disclosure while insiders trade, this delay must be evaluated in light of the fact that there also is an inevitable delay in disclosure whenever a whistle-blower engages in whistle-blowing without concomitantly engaging in insider trading. Moreover, as described in more detail below, insider trading tends to push prices in the "correct" direction even before the revelatory disclosures are made. In contrast, when whistle-blowing occurs unaccompanied by trading, there may be no change in share values prior to the public disclosure of information.

VII. Who Pays for Whistle-blowing and Insider Trading: Fairness Worries and Distributional Issues

The above discussion has presented an analysis favoring allowing insider trading on the basis of whistle-blower information from instrumentalist and efficiency perspectives. Insider trading also raises important distributional concerns. In particular, at first blush it might appear that one advantage whistle-blowing has over insider trading is that, because its impact is distributed more evenly over a corporation's population of shareholders, it is more "fair" than insider trading.

Fairness

At the outset, I wish to emphasize that no claim is being made here that those who trade on the basis of an informational advantage are particularly virtuous. These folks are not heroes. No claim is made that they are. Rather, the claim is simply that those who trade on the basis of inside information about an ongoing corporate fraud cannot be said categorically to be morally inferior to someone like Sherron Watkins who engages in self-serving whistle-blowing. This, of course, is not because those who engage in inside trading are commendable, but rather because those who engage in whistle-blowing are not. Nevertheless, it is far from clear that insider trading of the sort described here should be banned on fairness grounds.

It is important to recognize at the outset that the traders being discussed here deserve to be able to sell their shares ahead of other shareholders. From a fairness perspective, perhaps the best way to conceptualize the issue is by analogizing the shareholders in a company riddled with fraud to the ethical dilemma that confronts the crew of a sinking ship with a grossly insufficient supply of life rafts. Selling shareholders are a bit like crew members who learn about a crisis some time before their fellow passengers. Should the crew members be able to use this information to save themselves by securing a place on a life raft before the passengers?

Focusing on the differences between the employees (crew) and the outside investors (passengers) suggests that in the corporate context, the answer to this question generally will be yes. Unlike outside investors, the rank-and-file employees are unable to diversify their investments in the companies in which they work, and thus they suffer disproportionately from the effects of major corporate scandals. In particular, workers, unlike outside investors, have undiversifiable investments in their own human capital. Trading on the basis of inside information related to an ongoing corporate fraud that will destroy the company at least permits an employee to recoup some of this lost investment.

When corporations like Cendant, Enron, and Equity Funding implode, the rank-and-file workers are often the hardest hit. When Enron filed for bankruptcy protection, more than 4,500 workers lost their jobs.[77] In the fall of 2001, as the problems at Enron gradually revealed themselves, "the company swiftly collapsed, taking with it the fortunes and retirement savings of thousands of employees."[78] The Enron rank-and-file employees have had a very difficult time securing comparable employment elsewhere, even years after the collapse of the company.[79] In contrast with the executives at the top, who participated in the fraud and made millions, "most former Enron employees who had nothing to do with the fraud at the company," have not fared well at all.[80]

Like 25.6 percent of companies with 5,000 or more employees, most (60 percent)[81] of Enron's employees had their retirement money in undiversified investments in Enron stock,[82] despite the fact that these employees had other alternatives.[83] Like many other public companies, Enron matched pretax 401(k) contributions with its own stock and limited the ability of employees to sell that stock.[84] Given the undiversified nature of employees' investment in Enron stock and the inability of Enron employees to diversify, it does not appear to be unfair to permit these employees to sell and to sell short when in possession of material nonpublic information about their company. Other investors can avoid the firm-specific risk of an implosion by holding a diversified portfolio of securities. Workers cannot avoid this risk. The only way for them to mitigate the risk is by trading on the basis of inside information.

Permitting certain rank-and-file insiders to trade on the basis of their informational advantage about ongoing fraud would be entirely fair. Workers are at a disadvantage relative to other shareholders because they are unable to diversify their human capital investment in their companies. Rules enabling these people to trade would be consistent with John Rawls's idea that legal rights ought to be arranged so that they inure "to the greatest benefit of the least advantaged."[85] Rawls, therefore, endorses precisely the sort of involuntary disadvantage that results from insider trading when such a disadvantage benefits the worst-off.

Another Rawlsean perspective, the veil of ignorance, generates the same conclusion about the fairness of insider trading. Rawls's methodology for generating principles of justice is to imagine what rules of social ordering rational, self-interested people would choose from behind a veil of ignorance. It seems clear that rational shareholders in large public companies would agree *ex ante* to permit innocent insiders to trade on the basis of whistle-blower information. From the contract-as-promise perspective taken here, it is worth noting that self-interested investors would agree to permit insider trading that reduces the probability that fraud will occur in the first place by increasing the probability that such fraud would be found out.

It is undeniable that insider trading, by definition, involves unequal treatment. To the extent that fairness is defined as equal outcomes, then the insider trading I describe, along with all other trading, would be banned. More troubling is the fact that the trading I describe also involves inequality of *opportunity*, because the insiders have access to whistle-blower information that is not available to their trading partners. However, as Frank Easterbrook and Daniel Fischel ably have explained, in the corporate context at least, fairness does not mean equal treatment because fairness and equality are not the same thing.[86] Fairness, for investors, requires the pursuit of policies that maximize the value of investments *ex ante*.[87] Easterbrook and Fischel illustrate the point as follows: given a choice between two ventures, one that provides a payoff of $10 to every one of a firm's ten investors, and one that provides a payoff of $40 to five of the ten investors but nothing to the remaining five, a firm's board should choose the latter venture. Boards prefer the latter venture because the total expected return from that investment is $200, while the expected return from the former investment is only $100. As Easterbrook and Fischel observe, if unequal distribution is necessary to make the overall returns higher, then the company is *required* to choose inequality.[88] This illustration maps perfectly onto the whistle-blower issue. Barring insider trading on whistle-blower information would eliminate the inequality that results from the insider's trading on an informational advantage, but it also would eliminate the substantial gains to all investors associated with the *ex ante* reduction in the incidence of fraud. Thus, because shareholders "unanimously prefer legal rules under which the amount of gains is maximized, regardless of how the gains are distributed,"[89] insider trading on the basis of whistle-blower information is fair to investors under any coherent notion of the meaning of the term "fair."

Finally, with respect to fairness, I hasten to acknowledge that the "pure" whistle-blower (should such a thing exist) is a Good Samaritan.[90] Insiders, on the other hand, decidedly cannot be accurately described as Good Samaritans. Nevertheless, nobody has ever seriously suggested that one is legally required to be a Good Samaritan. The issue, in other words, is not whether insider trading on whistle-blower information should be applauded; the issue is whether the conduct should be considered criminal. At a minimum, this decision should be left to investors themselves, who, after full disclosure, should be allowed to decide for themselves whether they want to invest in a public company that permits insider trading on the basis of whistle-blower information.

Distribution Effects of Insider Trading Regulation About Corporate Misconduct

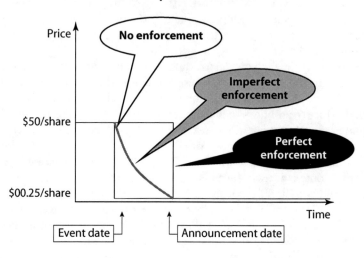

Distributional Concerns

Intuitively, whistle-blowers' impact is uniform across all shareholders, while insiders' trading differentially effects those (buying) shareholders who are unfortunate enough to be the counterparties of the insiders who are selling on whistle-blower information. However, this intuition is wrong because it falsely assumes that those trading with insiders in possession of whistle-blower information are harmed. In fact, the outsiders who are the whistle-blower information traders' counterparties likely benefit from the insider trading here. Selling by insiders in possession of whistle-blower information will, to the extent that it has any effect at all on share prices, drive down those prices, thereby benefiting their counterparties by driving down their acquisition costs.

The downward pressure on share prices caused by insider trading will benefit ordinary investors, whom I define as investors who do not purport to trade on information not already impounded in share prices, but instead buy and sell shares either to adjust their portfolios or because of changes in patterns of consumption and investment over their life cycle. The critical point here is that such traders are not induced by insider selling to buy: they would have bought anyway. As such, they are made better-off, not worse-off, by any informed sales by insiders because such sales drive down the price at which the insiders' counterparties are able to buy. This effect is depicted in figure 12.1.

The argument is that, all else being equal, in the absence of any prohibition on insider trading there will be more such trading than there would be otherwise. This greater incidence of insider trading would cause share prices to fall more precipitously than they would otherwise. Alternatively, if enforcement of the law is "perfect" in the sense that all inside traders are caught and punished, there will be no such trading, and share prices will adjust only when the fraud or other corporate misconduct is revealed to the public, at which time there will be a dramatic drop in share prices. Finally, where there are prohibitions on insider trading on the basis of whistle-blower information, but those prohibitions are imperfectly enforced, share prices will respond to insider trading, but less dramatically than they would respond if such trading were condoned.

As depicted in figure the above, because share prices fall most dramatically when insider trading is permitted, this is the legal regime that most benefits buyers. It is also clear that people who trade prior to the commencement of the fraud are not affected. And, of course, people who trade after the fraud is announced are similarly unaffected by the insiders' trading.

This discussion of the distributional effects of insider trading on whistle-blower information is incomplete because it ignores the real possibility that if insider trading on whistle-blower information were permitted, then insiders might delay exposing an ongoing fraud to allow themselves time to trade. This possibility, as noted above, also affects the analysis of the efficiency characteristics of trading on whistle-blower information. However, from a distributional perspective, it is by no means clear that a delay in revealing an ongoing fraud or other corporate misconduct hurts a company's existing shareholders. Rather, such shareholders benefit as long as the conduct goes undetected, because as long as this is the case, share prices remain high. Shareholders who manage to use any extra time to sell their shares clearly benefit.

It is also the case that if insider trading is illegal and the only avenues that insiders have for dealing with fraud or corporate misconduct are blackmail and whistle-blowing, the delay in the release of information about corporate misconduct is likely to be even longer than it will be if insiders are permitted to trade. Most important, from both an efficiency standpoint and a distributional standpoint, insider trading on whistle-blower information is likely to lead to less corporate misconduct because the possibility that such insider trading will occur increases the probability that corporate fraud will be detected, thereby leading to a reduction in the incidence of such fraud.

This reduction in fraud makes all shareholders better-off, whether viewed from a distributional perspective or an efficiency perspective. Thus, while there is some ambiguity about the distributional effects of insider trading on whistle-blower information, the argument that insider trading has distributional *benefits* for true outsiders, which is the class of shareholders thought most deserving of protections, is quite compelling.

VIII. Whistle-blowing and Insider Trading: Corporate Governance and Contracting Issues

Whistle-blowing has long been encouraged to reduce the incidence of fraud against the government. At common law, insider trading was tolerated: managers and other insiders were permitted to trade on the basis of nonpublic information unless specifically forbidden to do so by contract.[91] Corporate charters are surprisingly silent both on the issue of insider trading[92] and on the issue of whistle-blowing. It is surprising that corporate charters do not bar trading on inside information, and it also is surprising that corporate charters do not encourage whistle-blowing by offering monetary rewards to whistle-blowers like the ones provided for in federal whistle-blower statutes such as the False Claims Act.

However, the foregoing analysis explains both of these phenomena. As for insider trading, the analysis here suggests that it is not in shareholders' interests to bar all insider trading. Insider trading on whistle-blower information should not be banned: indeed, it should be encouraged. On the other hand, where insider trading involves the misappropriation of information that is the property of shareholders or the company itself, insider trading must be banned, as is the case where there is insider trading in advance of the announcement of a tender offer or of corporate earnings. Suppose, for example that a corporate officer accepts a bribe in exchange for information that a company was about to repurchase a large block of its own shares at a premium above the current market price. This information is then used by the person paying the bribe to purchase stock in the company, thereby driving up the price that the company must pay to acquire its own shares.[93] This sequence of events involves the theft of valuable information that is in the nature of a property right.

Current law permits insider trading when, and only when, such trading is consistent with traders' fiduciary duties of care and loyalty to the company. Fiduciary duties are the mechanisms employed by the law to identify and allocate property rights in the information that provides the basis for trading. Fiduciary duties therefore replace contractual rules where contracting is too costly. Since insider trading can arise in a widely divergent set of circumstances, and because corporations and their agents do not have perfect foresight and thus are unable to anticipate all future situations in which insider trading might occur, it would be extremely costly to draft a corporate contract that specified with precision what sorts of trading are banned. So instead of trying to specify *ex ante* every possible situation in which insider trading should be banned, we have a rule that prohibits trading that involves breaches of fiduciary duties and theft of intellectual property.

The "contracting cost" explanation of why we do not observe provisions in corporate charters or bylaws barring insider trading does not explain why we do not observe provisions in corporate contracts that specifically permit whistle-blowing, providing protections and authorizing monetary rewards for whistle-blowers. One possibility is that venal and corrupt corporate managers prevent these sorts of charter provisions from being implemented because they want to discourage whistle-blowers from revealing their illegal acts. This explanation is highly unlikely for the simple reason that there are, undoubtedly, at least *some* corporate managers who are honest and would like to see fraud and other wrongdoing uncovered. These honest managers would be able to signal their integrity by providing job security and bounties for whistle-blowers. In other words, while venal and corrupt managers might oppose rewarding whistle-blowers, honest managers would not, particularly since they would welcome a mechanism to distinguish themselves from dishonest managers. Thus, it might not be surprising that some firms decide not to provide such protections, but it is quite curious that no firms did until Sarbanes-Oxley required them to do so.

The Sarbanes-Oxley Act of 2002 contains two sets of provisions addressing issues involving corporate whistle-blowers. One set of provisions includes the whistle-blower procedures mandated by Sarbanes-Oxley Section 301, which requires audit committees to establish internal whistle-blowing procedures pursuant to Securities Exchange Act Rule 10A-3. The second set of provisions is contained in Sarbanes-Oxley Section 806, which adds a panoply of whistle-blower protections to Title 18 of the U.S. Code.

Rule 10A-3 of the Exchange Act requires the New York Stock Exchange, NASDAQ, and other stock market self-regulatory organizations to compel the audit committees of listed companies to establish formal procedures for responding to whistle-blowers' complaints regarding accounting and auditing issues. Audit committees must establish procedures for dealing with both external complaints from any sources and internal complaints from employees. Companies must provide a mechanism for receiving and processing confidential, anonymous submissions by employees of concerns regarding questionable accounting or auditing matters.

Section 806 of Sarbanes-Oxley establishes safeguards for employee whistle-blowers who report certain sorts of corporate misconduct. It provides protections for any employee who does either of the following: (a) files, testifies, participates in, or otherwise assists in any proceeding relating to an alleged violation of the mail, wire, bank, or securities laws; or (b) provides information or assists in an investigation regarding any conduct that the employee "reasonably believes" constitutes a violation of the mail, wire, bank, or securities laws. Employees are protected by Section 806 if they report information to a federal regulatory or law enforcement agency, any member or committee of Congress, any person with supervisory authority over the employee, or any other person who has "the authority to investigate, discover, or terminate misconduct." Additionally, Section 806 prevents employees who file complaints with the secretary of labor from being discharged, demoted, suspended, threatened, harassed, or discriminated against as a result of that involvement. Civil remedies for violations of Section 806 include reinstatement, back pay with interest, and attorneys' fees.

It is also curious why firms emerging from bankruptcy, firms going public for the first time, or firms for which the original financing came from venture capitalists did not try to improve their access to the capital markets and the terms of their initial financing by introducing whistle-blower protections such as those contained in Sarbanes-Oxley. In all likelihood, such provisions were not adopted by companies because they do not enhance shareholder welfare. It would be an exaggeration to say that providing protections for whistle-blowers is devoid of benefits. Rather, the point is simply that it appears likely that companies generally decide on their own not to provide for protections for whistle-blowers because the cost of maintaining such provisions outweighs the benefit.

One significant cost of installing whistle-blower protections of the kind described in Sarbanes-Oxley is the cost of evaluating a whistle-blower complaint. Particularly where bounties are involved, as noted above, there are likely to be several false complaints for every valid one. The risk of receiving false complaints is compounded when one takes into account that disgruntled former employees, especially those who have been terminated, are likely to bring whistle-blower complaints to try to obtain reinstatement and/or back pay.[94] It is also likely that terminated employees will attempt to extract a measure of revenge on former supervisors, particularly those responsible for their termination.[95]

Evidence of concern about false whistle-blower complaints is contained in the provisions of Sarbanes-Oxley Act itself, which requires OSHA to dismiss any whistle-blower complaint without conducting an investigation unless the complainant can make a "prima facie showing" that his or her whistle-blowing activities constituted at least "a contributing factor" in any alleged unfavorable personnel action. Even if the complainant succeeds in making this prima facie showing, Sarbanes-Oxley does not permit OSHA to investigate "if the employer demonstrates, by clear and convincing evidence, that the employer would have taken the same unfavorable personnel action in the absence of that behavior."

The high costs of investigating a whistle-blower's complaints and the problems of false and retaliatory complaints, coupled with what may, in fact, be a low incidence of corporate fraud, make it likely that the costs of whistle-blower provisions outweigh the benefits. These costs appear to be the best explanation for why companies did not adopt whistle-blower protections such as the ones mandated by Sarbanes-Oxley before they were required to do so by statute.

IX. Whistle-blowing and Insider Trading are not Blackmail

Like whistle-blowing and insider trading, requests for blackmail payments reflect an effort to traffic in intellectual property. In particular, in all three cases, there is information that somebody wants to conceal, and somebody else wants to bring it to the light of day. Scholars have gone to great lengths to try to explain the harm in blackmail.[96] My goal here is not to add to the existing theories of how blackmail is different from or similar to other crimes. The primary reason that blackmail has posed such an analytical problem for scholars is that it involves the combination of two acts: threatening to reveal a secret and demanding money (presumably) to keep the secret, neither of which, standing alone, is illegal. Rather my point is simply that blackmail does not share the benign, welfare-enhancing characteristics that link insider trading and whistle-blowing. In particular, whereas whistle-blowing and insider trading inevitably lead to the discovery and exposure of pathological behavior, the payment and acceptance of blackmail lead to the continued concealment of the unacceptable behavior. This suggests that blackmail is a less desirable practice than either insider trading or whistle-blowing. While insider trading and effective whistle-blowing lead to the exposure of wrongdoing, successful blackmail leads to continued cover-up.[97]

Blackmailers are accurately perceived as sleazy and corrupt. Their conduct is clearly illegal. By contrast, whistle-blowers are occasionally viewed as brave and altruistic, and inside traders, viewed somewhat more ambivalently than whistle-blowers, seem to hold a position in the moral order somewhere between blackmailers and whistle-blowers.

Insiders who know or suspect corporate wrongdoing can respond in one of three ways: by whistle-blowing, by insider trading, or by blackmailing the wrongdoers. Insider trading on the basis of information about corporate wrongdoing is more like whistle-blowing than it is like blackmail. Unlike blackmail, in order for insider trading on information concerning corporate misconduct to be successful, the information that underlies such trading must be revealed, or else the share price of the company engaged in the wrongdoing will not fall and the insider will not profit. By contrast, a successful blackmail strategy will result in a payoff to the blackmailer that will keep the information quiet forever. Thus, insider

TABLE 12.1
Functional Comparison of Whistle-blowing, Insider Trading, and Blackmail

Definition	Whistle-blowing	Insider Trading	Blackmail
Preexisting contractual or quasi-contractual relationship of trust/confidence	Yes	Yes	No
Trading/whistling/blackmail demand involves breach of duty	No	No	No
Information becomes reflected in securities prices	Yes	Yes	No

Motivations of actor	Highly Varied	Highly Varied	Venal
Informational intermediaries	Yes	Yes	No
Actions impose distributional harm	Yes	Yes	No
Actions lead to corrective measures	Yes	Yes	No
De minimis problem	No	Yes	Yes
Verification problem	Yes	No	Yes

trading on whistle-blower information, like whistle-blowing itself, results in the release of information about corporate misconduct.

The argument here is not that all insider trading should be condoned. In fact the opposite is true. The analysis applies only to a very narrow subset of inside information—information about corporate misconduct that would be the proper cause for whistle-blowing. Trading on nonpublic information about legitimate corporate news, whether the news is good or bad, is and should be illegal. The prohibition of this sort of insider trading is efficient because it protects valuable property rights in information. By contrast, corporations and corporate miscreants have no legitimate property-based expectation in keeping information about an ongoing misconduct confidential. Permitting insider trading on the basis of such information would, in a variety of contexts, provide the strongest incentives for people to seek out and expose such corporate wrongdoing.

CHAPTER 13

SHAREHOLDER VOTING

Along with boards of directors and the market for corporate control, the ability of shareholders to vote in corporations, albeit occasionally, has oddly been heralded as a source of improved corporate governance, at least potentially. According to this view, which is the dominant view among academics and policymakers, if shareholders were only given more and better voting rights, then corporate performance and accountability would have the capacity to improve even further.[1] But there are strong dissenters, with some claiming that shareholders probably vote too much,[2] and others taking the position that voting rules are efficient just as they are.[3]

This chapter begins with a brief description and analysis of the rules governing shareholder voting. I will argue that while shareholder voting probably does not do shareholders much harm, it doesn't do them much good either. Voting serves shareholders well in takeover contests and in expressions of shareholder disapproval in salient high-profile instances of corporate governance breakdown. However, it is irrational in my view to think that expanding shareholder voting can possibly improve the daily governance and operation of a large public corporation. Shareholders simply do not have the requisite information, or the inclination, to become sufficiently knowledgeable about what is going on within a public company to be useful to management in this way. Quite significantly, nearly all shareholders, even large institutions like pension funds, mutual funds, and insurance companies, hold highly diversified portfolios of securities. It is not only illogical for such shareholders to immerse themselves in the business operations and strategies of the companies in which they invest sufficiently to make informed business decisions, it is impossible. With modern funds holding shares in thousands of companies, the costs to their clients of emerging in corporate governance would make their funds noncompetitive.

Since mutual funds and pension funds own shares in such a vast number of companies, it makes sense for them only to become well informed about very major issues, such as takeovers or other fundamental corporate changes. In order for large, sophisticated investors to take the time to become sufficiently informed about their portfolio companies, they must reduce the number of companies in their portfolios. Most hedge funds and private equity funds pursue exactly this strategy, as we will see in chapter 15. Hedge funds and private equity firms own bigger blocks of shares in fewer companies than mutual funds, and this ownership structure makes it rational for them to become involved in corporate governance. But even with hedge funds and private equity funds, formal voting is not useful. Instead, it is far more sensible and efficacious for such funds to immerse themselves in real-time decision-making. When the time comes to vote to ratify a major decision such as an acquisition or a divestiture, it's too late for investor input to add value. As the available evidence shows, when sophisticated outside investors do become involved in corporate governance, they do not express themselves by voting; rather, they inject themselves into the corporation's quotidian decision-making on an ongoing basis.

The argument here is that the basic infrastructure of the law of corporate voting is not in need of repair. To be sure, the system is far from perfect and some major details need fixing. For example, the ability of management to control the timing of elections and the federal rules governing proxy solicitations do not serve the interests of shareholders and should be reformed.

More important, the point that shareholders are not likely to be effective at corporate governance simply by exercising their voting rights merits two important analytical qualifications. First, it is important to clarify that the relevant policy issue is not how effective shareholders are at corporate governance in some abstract way. Rather, the question is how effective shareholders are *relative to* alternative corporate governance institutions such as boards of directors and management. Thus, while shareholders are ill informed and inexpert at making managerial and strategic decisions about the firms in which they have invested, they do have the virtue of having the right incentives.

Shareholders do not face the same conflict of interest problems that plague decision-making by management and what earlier chapters have shown is their systematically docile nature and captured boards of directors. On issues where the choice is between the shareholder's lack of information and management's self-interest, corporate law should choose the shareholders by giving them the deciding voice in corporate governance. Takeovers are perhaps the paradigmatic example of a corporate governance issue that forces us to "decide who should decide" as between shareholders and management.

Second, it is important to distinguish between "generic" and "firm specific" corporate governance issues. The argument that diversified shareholders are unlikely to find it efficient to inform themselves sufficiently to assist in the corporate governance of the firms in which they have invested applies only to "firm specific" corporate governance issues, that is, issues that are unique to the specific circumstances of a particular company or its securities. For example, issues such as whether a particular CFO or CEO should be retained, or whether a company should buy or sell a particular asset such as a subsidiary or a division, are specific to particular firms. As a general matter, voting by shareholders is not likely to be an effective corporate governance mechanism for making decisions about these sorts of issues.

In contrast, a generic corporate governance issue is an issue concerning broad policy that is likely to affect the value of all of the companies in a particular portfolio. For example, the answer to the question of whether a particular anti-takeover device such as a poison pill (discussed in chapter 8) should be adopted by a company is likely to be the same for all companies. For such generic or market-wide corporate governance issues, it will likely be efficient for diversified shareholders to become well-informed because the resources spent in learning about the relative merits of various anti-takeover devices can be distributed across all of the public companies in an investor's portfolio.

Law and Economics of Shareholder Voting

Stephen Bainbridge of UCLA has succinctly summarized the law of shareholder voting as "so weak that they scarcely qualify as part of corporate governance."[4] Consistent with this analysis, the list of items about which shareholders have voting rights is remarkably short. Shareholders vote annually on director elections, amendments to the corporate charter, and fundamental corporate changes, such as mergers, dissolution of the corporation, and the sale of all or substantially all of the assets of a corporation. Confusingly, shareholders and directors both hold the power to vote on changes to corporate bylaws. This, in turn, raises difficult legal questions about whether a shareholder vote on bylaws can trump a decision on bylaws made by the company's board of directors.

While shareholder voting is limited to just a few issues, this is not the only or perhaps even the most significant restriction on the impact of shareholder voting. An important additional constraint on the practical efficacy of shareholder voting is the problem of *screening* by boards of directors. Before an issue even gets to the shareholders for their approval, it must almost always first pass through the board of directors for its approval. The only exceptions to this rule are the provisions for electing directors and for amending the bylaws, which do not require board approval prior to action by the shareholders. Some avaricious managers have even tried to impose greater constraints on the election process by attempting to screen nominees of outside groups. While this practice is probably illegal, it is nevertheless accomplished by requiring that all candidates proposed as nominees for directorships must first be approved by the nominating committee of the incumbent board. Given their questionable legality, these provisions illustrate the extent to which some companies are willing to go to deter outside efforts to gain control.

Perhaps the most important corporate governance feature of shareholder voting rights is the central role that they play in facilitating the market for corporate control.[5] This, by itself, provides an explanation for why shareholders value the right to vote. Shareholder voting facilitates takeovers in several ways. When an outside bidder makes a tender offer for the stock of a target company, he is only interested in acquiring shares with the votes attached. It is through exercising the votes attached to the acquired shares that the buyer attains the power to assume control of the target company.[6] Thus, any action that dilutes the voting power of shares concomitantly reduces the chances of shareholders receiving the substantial premium associated with a tender offer, and therefore reduces share value.

In addition, shareholder voting has become increasingly important as the modern arsenal of takeover defenses, particularly poison pills, often makes hostile tender offers for shares much more difficult to win. Outside bidders have increasingly turned to takeover strategies that simultaneously involve both a tender offer for the shares of the target company and a proxy contest for control of the board. By achieving even a minority of board seats, the outside bidder can at least make arguments about improving firm value and can agitate for removal of the poison pill. Clearly, shareholder votes are critical to gaining the board seats that provide a takeover platform.

WHEN SHOULD SHAREHOLDERS VOTE: GENERIC ISSUES, MAJOR ISSUES, AND PUBLIC GOODS

Internal rules of corporate governance that restrict proxy contests between rival slates are easy to defend. Talk is cheap, and the shareholders of a corporation have no way of verifying whether a new management team selected by a victorious group of outside candidates for board seats will be better or worse than the incumbent management team. Tying voting rights to share ownership solves this problem, which, from an economic point of view, exists because voting in proxy contests is a public good. As a result, outside candidates for office have few credible incentives to improve the operation of the company on whose boards they serve except to the extent that they own shares in the company. These candidates and their sponsors bear all of the costs associated with making an outside bid, but capture none of the benefits, except in their capacity as shareholders.

Incumbent shareholders face collective action problems that mirror the public goods problem that plagues bidders. In most U.S. public corporations, ownership is widely dispersed. As such, no individual shareholder can count on his or her vote being determinative of the outcome. Thus, even if a particular election will have a large effect on each shareholder's wealth, no individual shareholder has very strong incentives to invest in information about the election because the outcome of the election will be the same whether or not any particular voter chooses to participate at all.[7]

Frank Easterbrook and Daniel Fischel extend this basic point by observing that if a given election has a value of $1,000 per share, the owner of a single share of stock will have no incentive to invest more than $1,000 in obtaining and processing the information necessary to become informed about the election.[8] If the company has 1,000 shareholders, the optimal aggregate investment in information will be $1 million, so our marginal shareholder's $1,000 investment is likely to be insufficient.

Of course, a number of factors mitigate these collective action problems. Large investors with concentrated interests in the target company have more incentives to invest, both because the outcome of any election will be monetarily more important to them and because their votes are more likely to matter. Thus, it stands to reason that shareholders, particularly large shareholders, will want to vote on major issues affecting the corporations in which they have invested.

Current corporate law is generally consistent with this analysis. Corporate law uniformly provides that only fundamental corporate changes be voted on by the shareholders. Shareholders do not get to vote on matters of ordinary business judgment. These legal rules reflect the economic reality that it is not economically rational for shareholders to vote except on very large issues, on which it is worth their while to make the necessary investment required to make an informed decision.

However, this analysis is seriously incomplete because it ignores the very real fact that voters often are called upon to vote repeatedly on the same issues and the same candidates across several firms in which they have invested. When a voter can amortize the investment cost of his or her vote across a number of other votes, either because the same candidates keep appearing or because the same major issues are at stake, the voting calculus changes dramatically. Indeed, it becomes efficient for individual voters to inform themselves over even small issues where such issues are generic and will pertain to many, many firms. For example, in Easterbrook and

Fischel's well-known example, utilized above, in which a given election will have an effect of $1,000 on each share, they assume that "a single investment of $10,000 worth of knowledge may be adequate."[9] If this is the case, then not only shareholders who own ten or more shares, *but also any holder of a single share, who has a similar investment in nine other companies in which this issue is likely to arise,* will have the incentive to invest an adequate amount in the information necessary.

Recognizing the significance of recurring issues and candidates, we need to reformulate the famous rational ignorance or voter apathy models of theorists such as Anthony Downs, Mancur Olson, and Joseph Schumpeter[10] in the corporate context to take into account both repeat candidates (candidates who serve on multiple boards of directors simultaneously), as well as repeat issues. Of particular interest in my analysis are issues like anti-takeover devices such as poison pills that are generic to all corporations. Here it is easy to see that the classic voter apathy model does not apply, particularly to investors like mutual funds and pension funds that own shares in hundreds and sometimes thousands of companies.

For this reason, shareholder efforts to gain greater voting power in the takeover arena should be met with less skepticism than they have to date. Delaware courts, for example, not only have validated the use of the poison pill, but they are also highly reluctant to restrain their use even in egregious cases.[11] State courts also appear hesitant to grant to shareholders the right to vote on the initial adoption of poison pills, or even let shareholders vote to nullify or rescind a poison pill that a board has adopted.

Since 1998, shareholders have been trying to get courts to adopt bylaw provisions, known as "shareholder rights," that impose limitations on the use of poison pills, usually by requiring a shareholder vote. For example, in an early version of the poison pill, activist investor Guy P. Wyser-Pratte, who held shares in Pennzoil, proposed that shareholders adopt a bylaw provision under which Pennzoil's poison pill would become invalid after ninety days unless management got a shareholder vote approving the continued use of the pill to block an acquisition. At the time of this proposal, Pennzoil had vigorously fought a tender offer that it had received from Union Pacific Resources Group, Inc. The Pennzoil board used the poison pill to "just say no" to the offer, maintaining the pill for an extended period of time until the offer eventually terminated. Wyser-Pratte's proposal would have applied only when a company with a poison pill (in this case, Pennzoil) received an offer to purchase 100 percent of common stock at a 25 percent premium over the market price.[12]

This type of pill would allow a board of directors to continue using its poison pill to block an offer, but only for ninety days unless the shareholders approve the continued use of the pill to block the offer. More recently Lucian Bebchuk, a law school professor with 140 shares in CA, Inc. (formerly Computer Associates), sued CA to force it to adopt a bylaw provision that would have prevented the adoption of any poison pill that was valid for longer than one year unless approved by the shareholders.[13]

No Delaware court has addressed the legality of the shareholder rights bylaw. Management and anti-takeover lawyers argue that shareholder bylaws are illegal under Delaware law. The SEC has inexplicably endorsed this position, on the grounds that under various provisions of Delaware law, corporate directors have virtually plenary power to run the corporation and to invent new classes of stock and other securities. Specifically, under Delaware Code § 141(a), the business and affairs of every corporation shall be managed by or under the director of a board of directors. Also, under Delaware Code § 157, not only may corporations create and issue rights or options entitling shareholders to acquire shares in the corporation of any class or classes, but directors are also given the power to set the terms on which any securities are issued and decide what consideration, if any, the company may receive for the shares. Technically speaking, this is precisely what the directors are doing when they create the new class of preferred stock that constitutes the poison pill.

When adopting a poison pill, the target company's board of directors creates a new class of preferred stock with limited rights and distributes shares of that stock to the common shareholders. This new class of stock entitles corporate shareholders to buy the corporation's stock at a large discount whenever a third party "triggers the pill" by acquiring a certain percentage of the corporation's voting securities. Once a pill is triggered, the dilution of the voting value of a potential acquirer's stock significantly increases the cost to a bidder, usually making a takeover prohibitively expensive unless the pill is redeemed. The board retains the option to redeem the pill (the issued stock) for nominal consideration, thereby allowing the board to approve a bid without prohibitively increasing the cost of a takeover. Unless, however, the board agrees to redeem the pill, the existence of a pill deters acquisitions. There has never been a successful acquisition of a company with a poison pill except for those in which the target company voluntarily agreed to redeem their pill.

Poison pills should not be adopted unless shareholders are allowed to vote on them first.[14] Shareholder bylaw amendments protect shareholders and promote accountability in ways that corporate law should support.

(1) such bylaws do not require *expenditure* of corporate funds nor typically mandate the taking of any affirmative step (and may in fact economize on costly defensive tactics); (2) they also do not interfere with "ordinary business decisions," as that phrase is usually understood, because a poison pill represents a fundamental financial decision, and one having no impact on "ordinary" day-to-day operations; and (3) bylaw amendments serve to pro-

tect shareholder interests in an area where they have a vital interest—namely, the marketability of their shares—because poison pills and shareholder rights plans do necessarily restrict the field of eligible buyers and thus affect share marketability.[15]

A critical additional point is that the shareholder rights bylaw is a prime example of a voting device that is *generic* in nature. In a robust market for corporate control, shareholders in firms that are targets of hostile takeovers can amortize their investment in approving or disapproving a corporate governance device such as the shareholder rights bylaw over all of the companies in its portfolio, thereby dramatically reducing the rational apathy problem identified by Anthony Downs and others.

This "amortization solution" to the rational apathy problem may help explain certain mysteries in corporate law and perhaps in ordinary politics as well. Take, for example, the well-known fact that incumbents enjoy a huge advantage over challengers. Because the incumbents are a known entity, risk-neutral, and particularly risk-averse, shareholders will prefer the limited downside of the incumbent who is a known quantity rather than the unlimited downside (and upside) of outsiders. To put it cynically, voters know how much the incumbents typically steal; the insurgents might steal even more.

Of course, the "amortization solution" to the rational apathy problem does not imply that voting will be perfect, or even close to it. As a particular issue becomes more generic, the better this solution will work. But suppose, as is undoubtedly the case, that some companies would be better-off by adopting a poison pill, while others would be better-off without one. A company's shareholders would be better-off *with* a poison pill if the benefit from the higher price that bidders must pay when negotiating with target management of the company with a poison pill in place outweighs the costs associated with the reduction in the probability that a bid for the company ever will be made. On the other hand, another company's shareholders would be better-off *without* a poison pill if the value of the premium that the pill would add to a future bid is less than the value associated with increasing the probability of an outside bid will in fact be made.[16]

Thus, voting on implementing a poison pill in the first place may be a bad idea. On the other hand, once a company has adopted a poison pill, shareholders may be quite capable of deciding whether a particular bid is in their interests or not. They may decide, for example, that a premium of 10 percent is insufficient, while a premium of 15 percent is acceptable. In other words, amortizing information will not produce perfectly rational voting. If shareholders only amortize the information they receive about a particular corporate governance strategy or tactic across all the firms in which they have invested, voting will occur much more often and be more informed than traditional Downsian voting theory would predict, but it will not be perfect.

For example, imagine that both bidders and targets could vote on takeovers. Generally speaking, shares in bidding firms decline when they succeed in acquiring another company, while target shareholders benefit from the premium they get when they sell their shares. Under an unconstrained amortization rule, all "rationally non-apathetic" shareholders in target firms would vote in favor of being acquired. At the same time, the "rationally non-apathetic" or "rationally informed" shareholders in bidding firms would use the information they had built up about the wealth effects of takeovers on target firm shareholders to vote against acquisitions. This, of course, would result in a systematically suboptimal equilibrium in which no bids would ever be made because they would be voted down by the shareholders of putative acquirers.

One way out of this trap would be simply to deny shareholders the right to vote on takeovers and let management decide for the shareholders whether to permit companies to be acquired. This clearly would lead to managerial entrenchment in many cases. It would be impossible for even the most inept or corrupt managers to be displaced by the market for corporate control.

A second solution is to allow shareholders to vote on takeovers on the theory that shareholders can *supplement* the cheap generic information about the costs and benefits of mergers and acquisitions for both bidders and targets with more costly firm-specific information about a *particular* control contest. The idea is that the cost of acquiring the additional, firm-specific information necessary to make a particular decision will inevitably be lower than the combined cost of obtaining both the necessary the generic information as well as the necessary firm-specific information about a particular acquisition. Thus, the cost of obtaining the information necessary to make an adequate decision will be lower than previously thought.

The above argument suggests that the current policy consensus about shareholder voting, which is reflected in current law, is too restrictive. Following Downs's theory, Easterbrook and Fischel argue that shareholders should only be permitted to vote on issues of large magnitude because those are the only instances in which shareholders will be able to overcome the rational ignorance and voter apathy problems that plague the decision-making process and make voting uninformed and irrational.[17] Alternatively, the argument presented here suggests that voters also should be allowed to vote on generic issues, that is, on issues that come up again and again in the course of share ownership (or, in the political context, in the case of citizenship), and not just on the major issues. The costs of becoming informed on such generic issues can be amortized over every investment in the investor's portfolio in which these issues arise.

In analyzing the efficacy of shareholder democracy with respect to generic issues such as takeovers or accounting fraud, research by Hermang Desai, Chris Hogan, and Michael Wilkins found that 60 percent of a sample of public firms that restated earnings experienced a turnover of at least one senior manager (defined as the chairman, CEO, or president) within twenty-four months of being forced to restate their previously disclosed accounting results, compared to only 35 percent of comparable firms. Moreover, this research shows that 85 percent of these displaced managers were unable to secure comparable employment with rival firms later.[18]

From this perspective, voting on *issues*, like the shareholder rights bylaw discussed above, actually has broader amortization potential than voting on particular *people*, such as directors. Yet, voting on directors still makes more sense than rational ignorance theory would suggest to the extent that directors serve for several terms and/or as directors in several companies in a company's portfolio. An example of my rationally informed investor theory in operation can be seen in shareholder reaction to the scandals and collapse at Enron. All of the directors of Enron resigned from that company's board. Several Enron directors also served simultaneously as directors of other corporations. In total, Enron directors served as directors of twenty other companies at the time of Enron's collapse. The careers of these people as directors of these other companies virtually ended when their weak oversight of Enron was revealed. One director, Frank Savage, decided to fight the shareholder pressure for his resignation. He was forced to leave the Qualcomm board but hung on, at least for a while, at Lockheed Martin, where he was renominated to serve, but received "a near record low percentage of votes while remaining unopposed."[19] In other words, shareholders amortized the costly information they obtained about the directors on Enron over their entire investment portfolios, including other companies in which directors of Enron served as directors.[20]

Similarly, Suraj Srinivasan examined the turnover of outside directors who restate their earnings and found that directors of firms that experience financial reporting failures are more likely to lose their positions. He also reports that outside directors in general, especially outside directors who are members of the audit committee of the board of a company that is forced to restate its earnings, are more likely not only to leave the board of that company but also to lose directorships at other companies.[21]

Along these lines, it is worth observing that any shareholder who accumulates more than 50 percent of the shares in a corporation can ultimately obtain control of the board of directors, including complete control of the board, provided that the company does not have cumulative voting. Lucian Bebchuk and others argue convincingly that staggered boards of directors can delay changes in control.[22] But staggered boards are a matter of shareholder choice, and the incidence of staggered boards has been on the decline, indicating that shareholder preferences are reflected in corporate policy, at least with respect to generic issues like whether to support anti-takeover measures.

REMOVAL VERSUS REPLACEMENT

With regard to establishing a meaningful baseline to measure the efficacy of shareholder democracy, there are several questions worth asking. One that immediately comes to mind is whether dishonest or incompetent managers already are being replaced through market mechanisms that are cheaper and faster than corporate elections. It is far from clear that it matters *how* poor performers are replaced. Whether by internal governance mechanisms; pressure from private equity investors, venture capitalists, or other institutions; hostile takeover; or the mere threat of a contested election (whether or not such a threat ever materializes), the result of manager replacement is the same.

Another question that comes to mind is whether the worst-performing directors are more likely to be replaced than the worst-performing incumbents in Congress. During the period between 1990 and 2000, House incumbents were reelected at an average rate of 94.1 percent.[23] While reelection rates in congressional elections have actually been increasing, the reelection rates for directors in corporate elections have been decreasing.[24] This development is particularly interesting given the political context in which rival political parties actually generate rivals for incumbents. In corporate elections there is no similar institutional mechanism for automatically generating opposition candidates.

It is important to recognize that there are vast differences between the issues involved in removing directors and the issues involved in replacing politicians. Removing directors presents few practical problems, as long as there are enough remaining directors to constitute a quorum. In particular, removing directors avoids the very difficult issue of identifying and recruiting replacement directors. Perhaps Bebchuk and others are right to claim that directors should increasingly be removed by shareholder vote and that fixing the problem would not be difficult. A default rule requiring majority voting and the use of "withhold" votes, as was done in the Disney election in March 2004, should do the trick.[25]

Actually replacing rather than merely removing incumbent board members poses two intractable problems. First, we have no strategy or theory for how outside challengers to incumbent boards are to be identified and recruited. Second, even if we can figure out a way to identify and recruit outside directors, it is highly doubtful that outside challengers for board positions will be able to send a credible signal that they will be able to outperform the incumbent directors.

As for the recruitment problem, it is not easy to find able, experienced, and competent people who are eager to become directors of public companies. In the political context, democracies have highly developed systems in which two or more political parties recruit, screen, and legitimize potential nominees for political office. There is no analogous process for corporate elections, and it is not obvious how one could be created. Unlike rival politicians, potential board candidates compete along vectors such as competence, experience, and integrity, rather than along vectors such as ideology, interest-group identification, and loyalty. As such, it is far from clear how rival parties who nominate candidates in corporate elections might provide a signaling function.

A May 2007 proxy contest in which a CEO who was fired for fraudulently taking travel money from Atmel Corporation, the Silicon Valley, California, company for which he worked, chillingly illustrates the general problem. George Pergolas, a cofounder of Atmel, which makes microprocessors, was belatedly dismissed by the corporation's board of directors following the results of an investigation by the audit committee of the company's board. The audit committee investigation revealed that four top officials of the company had been involved in what newspaper reports described as "a travel scheme that allowed employees and friends to travel on company money, with some funds going into the pocket of the company employee who arranged the plan."[26]

Pergolas then went to court to force a special meeting of the shareholders to remove the five directors who voted to dismiss him from his post as CEO. He also is nominating his own, self-selected slate of five rival candidates for the firm's board of directors, which, if elected, will oust the current chief executive and choose a new one (presumably Pergolas himself). Institutional Shareholder Services (ISS), a firm that advises large shareholders about how to vote, actually put its support behind one of Pergolas's nominees, prompting Floyd Norris of the *New York Times* to observe that ISS may be right that board oversight was lacking in the past. But it is hard to see how a victory for Pergolas's candidates would lead to better corporate governance in the future.[27]

Adding to the general problem described here is the fact that the role of corporate director is both more time-consuming and riskier than ever before. Presumably, proponents of greater corporate democracy do not want directors to be held less accountable to regulators or shareholders than they are now. But in the current environment, a significant number, perhaps as many as half of all prospects, decline entreaties to serve on boards, even when such offers are initiated by the companies and not by insurgents.[28] Current proponents of shareholder voting simply assume away the acute problems of identifying, recruiting, and performing due diligence for potential challengers to incumbent directors.

In addition, even to the extent that we are able to locate challengers for board incumbents, it would be difficult to make such challengers credible candidates for office. Corporate elections are plagued by a variety of collective action and signaling. People launching proxy contests for control are unable to capture all of the gains that might be realized by shareholders in the event of a change in control because such gains inevitably will be shared among all of the equity claimants. Potential rivals for board seats will not fully internalize the potential benefits from launching such a contest.[29] To the extent that challengers bear the full costs of launching a proxy contest but do not reap the full rewards, some worthwhile challenges will not be launched. Moreover, challengers in proxy contests have a difficult time signaling credibly to shareholders that they are seeking to displace the incumbent directors because they are better managers, rather than for more nefarious reasons.

Bebchuk generally recognizes the existence of these sorts of problems when he writes that

> shareholders cannot infer from a rival's mounting a challenge that the rival directors would perform better. To begin with, even a rival team that believes it will perform better may be acting out of hubris. Furthermore, and very important, a rival's decision to mount a challenge does not even imply that the rival itself believes it will perform better. After all, a challenge could be motivated instead by a desire to obtain the private benefits associated with control.[30]

Bebchuk is absolutely correct in this analysis of signaling problems facing challengers to incumbents in corporate elections. The problem here is not with Bebchuk's analysis, but with his failure to see its implications in two key ways. First, the signaling and free-rider problems identified here go a long way toward explaining any perceived "deficiency" in the incidence of challenges to board incumbents. Challengers do not fully internalize the benefits of corporate control and thus cannot credibly signal their motivations for seeking such control. If challengers cannot persuade voters that they are not crooks out to loot the target company, it is extremely unlikely that they will be able to persuade voters that they will actually be able to run the company better than the incumbents.

Second, the free-rider problem cannot be addressed merely by making it easier for challengers to obtain reimbursement for the costs associated with mounting a proxy contest.[31] The problem with this proposed solution is that it fails to recognize that whatever the other merits of reimbursing rivals who attract significant support, such reimbursement will exacerbate, not mitigate, the credibility problems facing challengers. Rational shareholders will understand that if reimbursement is made easier, challengers will internalize even *fewer* of the costs of mounting a proxy contest for control, while still internalizing the same potential benefits. This, in turn, will provide less-qualified, lower-probability candidates with greater incentives to run, particularly since those candidates with the lowest opportunity costs to their time and effort will benefit most by the prospect of reimbursement for their election expenses.

Sources of Legitimacy for Corporate Directors

Shareholders' lack of meaningful democratic voice, particularly in replacing boards of directors, has been identified as a problem because it deprives directors of "legitimacy."[32] Similarly, I have observed here that the lack of any sort of electoral infrastructure like caucuses or parties for generating rival board candidates also deprives corporate elections of much robustness, at least on the surface.

The latter argument seems a bit stronger than the former. The legitimacy issue is a red herring because the current methods of electing directors are consistent with longstanding enabling statutes that have survived not only the test of jurisdictional competition for corporate charters but also the ability of entrepreneurs in search of capital to draft different, more democratic rules should investors prefer them. If one argues that acting pursuant to these statutes is not sufficient to confer legitimacy on corporate directors, one must confront the issue of what election procedures would be sufficient to convey legitimacy on corporate directors.

One also must confront the issue of whether *everything* done by U.S. directors is illegitimate, and if not, what particular aspects of directors' jobs are illegitimate because of the absence of a legitimate election process. For example, are the managers of U.S. corporations also illegitimate because they were appointed to their positions by directors who are not legitimate? Are mergers approved by such boards illegitimate? What about acquisitions or sales of assets?

It appears plausible that capital market performance rather than election results confers legitimacy on directors. The legitimacy of corporate managers and directors like Jack Welch and Warren Buffett is derived not from their ability to garner votes at election time from shareholders. Rather, their legitimacy comes from their ability to deliver strong returns to investors, after they have been elected in a manner consistent with applicable law. Being elected in a manner consistent with the minimum legal requirements would seem to be a necessary foundation for legitimacy of corporate directors, while competence and integrity are then also required to actually achieve legitimacy.

Thus, proven effectiveness over time and fulfillment of the necessary legal prerequisites are both necessary and sufficient to establish the legitimacy of an institution like the corporate board of directors. In contrast, applying the notion that elections are necessary to confer legitimacy on corporate directors suggests, counterfactually, that federal judges would lack legitimacy because they enjoy life tenure, are never elected, and cannot be removed from office by voters. In fact framework, federal judges in general and Supreme Court justices in particular have a great deal of legitimacy, yet voters have far less power to replace members of the Supreme Court than shareholders have to replace directors. The prestige and legitimacy of the judiciary in general and individual judges in particular depend on judges' ability to reason effectively and to present powerful and effective arguments for their opinions. As with judges, there is no reason to think that directors' legitimacy comes from the fact of their election rather than from the quality of their performance while in office.[33]

Further support for this point can be found by looking at the legitimacy of currencies like the dollar, the euro, and the yen. Complex factors, including economic strength, underlying political stability, and the perceived independence of the monetary authority, contribute to the strength and legitimacy of a particular currency. But there is little evidence to support the proposition that the legitimacy of an institution depends on whether the underlying institution is subject to democratic constraints. Indeed, the opposite appears to be true: the more independent monetary policy is from democratic institutions, the more stable the underlying currency is likely to be.[34]

Finally, in addition to the performance measures just described, the legitimacy of directors and other important figures in society derives initially from attaining their positions of power and authority through legitimate means. Thus, for example, when Ben S. Bernake became chairman of the Board of Governors of the Federal Reserve System, like his predecessor, Alan Greenspan, his initial legitimacy came not from his record of success in effectuating monetary policy but from the fact that he was properly nominated and confirmed in a process generally conceded to confer democratic legitimacy on nominees.

Interestingly, throughout much of U.S. history, and even in 1913 when the Federal Reserve Act was passed, the idea of a central bank was highly controversial. It was not clear to many whether Congress had the constitutional authority to create a central bank. Similarly, it was not initially clear to many whether centralized monetary policy was advisable in the move to a single European currency.[35] The legitimacy of the U.S. central

bank does not lie in the Constitution, or even in the democratic foundations of the institution, but rather in the strong historical record of performance and integrity generated over time by the institution. The same is
true for boards of directors. In other words, Bebchuk's claim that directors are illegitimate because they are not popularly elected by shareholders and because elections are not transparent or contested goes too far
because the same claims can be made with even more force against a host
of other plainly legitimate institutions, including central banks, cardinals
of the Catholic Church, and Supreme Court justices.

Under U.S. law in all fifty states, shareholders have the power to elect
directors and to govern the director nomination process. If desired, shareholders could cause a corporation's organizational documents to align
with voting arrangements different than those we actually observe. However, under extant state law, there is no statutory shareholder right of
subsidized access to a corporation's ballot box.

Rational shareholders have compelling reasons to doubt the motives of
outsiders who mount contests to remove incumbent directors. Subsidizing
losing contestants will not solve this problem, and would probably make
it worse. Moreover, the inability of shareholders to distinguish candidates
who will use their control to increase firm value from candidates who will
diminish firm value through ineptitude or looting may provide a complete
explanation for why we observe so few contested elections.

It has been suggested that flaws in the current system of electing directors mean that the election process does not give directors the legitimacy
it should. But the legitimacy of corporate directors comes, in the first
instance, from the fact that state law confers upon directors both the
power and the obligation to manage the business and the affairs of the
corporation.[36] Beyond that, legitimacy comes from demonstrating integrity and competence over extended periods of time. A glance at the prestige of national currencies, central banks, and elected and non-elected
judges raises serious questions about the assertion that a link exists between legitimacy and the extent to which incumbents are effectively contested by rivals in elections.

EMPTY VOTING: THE NEWEST PROBLEM
OR THE OLDEST PROBLEM?

Empty voting is another problem that has become quite salient in the
corporate context but does not appear to have gained much notice elsewhere, despite its general applicability. While empty voting has been loft-
ily characterized as involving "conflicts of interest created by exploiting

the separation of legal and beneficial ownership—aggravated by modern financial ownership,"[37] the problem is actually much simpler, not unique to corporations, and not much, if at all, aggravated by modern financial ownership. Rather, the age-old question of whether people with low or zero stake in an outcome should be permitted to vote is the central issue.

The problem has managed not only to preoccupy scholars in recent years but even to make front-page news. The problem is that institutional investors, such as hedge funds, can vote shares that they do not own by borrowing them, a process known as "morphable ownership." Critics say that this capability corrupts elections because "investors who don't have an economic stake can vote."[38] An even bigger issue is "empty voting," in which a fund hedges its position in a company so that while it still has the voting rights associated with the shares it owns, it no longer has any economic risk in the firm whose shares it is voting because of the hedge.

Imagine a close corporate election, such as the vote on Hewlett-Packard's (HP) merger with Compaq, which occurred in 2002. A successful merger of the two companies had the potential to richly reward shareholders in Compaq, the target firm, but would also reduce the value of the equity interests of the HP shareholders. The merger was strongly backed by HP management, though many HP shareholders opposed the deal. The resulting efforts by HP to consummate the merger led to most expensive proxy fight in history. There also have been rumors that Compaq shareholders may have used empty voting in HP shares to secure approval of the deal. The rumor is that Compaq's shareholders either borrowed HP shares and voted them, or bought HP outright and voted them, but hedged their financial risk by buying put options and selling short.

The case that brought into sharp focus the problem of empty and morphable ownership, as well as the extremely limited role that courts can play in assisting business regulation of these pervasive voting conflicts, is *High River Limited Partnership v. Mylan Laboratories, Inc.*[39] The case revolved around the attempt by Mylan Laboratories to acquire King Pharmaceuticals. Though Mylan made a bid for King Pharmaceuticals at a price of $16 per share, King shares traded after the bid at only around $12 per share. However, several major Mylan shareholders, including Carl Icahn, thought that the bidder, Mylan Labs, was offering too much for King's shares and wanted to prevent the transaction from occurring.

Against this background, a hedge fund, Perry Capital, entered the picture. Perry bought the shares in the target company, King Pharmaceuticals, for around $12 per share. If the transaction closed at the bid price of $16 per share, the hedge fund stood to make $26 million. In order to increase the probability that Mylan's bid for King would be successful, Perry went into the market and purchased 26.6 million shares, or 9.9 percent of the voting shares of Mylan, the bidding firm. Perry then entered into short sales and derivative trades that made the hedge fund perfectly hedged. By selling borrowed Mylan shares in an amount equal to the shares it had purchased, changes in the value of Mylan's shares had no effect on Perry. Perry, in other words, controlled almost 10 percent of the votes in Mylan without having any economic interest in the company whatsoever.

This transaction put Perry at a significant conflict of interest vis-à-vis the other Mylan shareholders. Other Mylan shareholders were skeptical about the desirability of Mylan's proposed acquisition of King Pharmaceuticals. Clearly, at a minimum, Mylan shareholders other than Perry, regardless of their general views about the desirability of an acquisition, wanted any purchases of King's shares by Mylan to take place on the best possible price and terms for Mylan. Perry, on the other hand, wanted Mylan to acquire King Pharmaceuticals, regardless of whether the acquisition was good for Mylan from a strategic or synergistic perspective. Further, Perry wanted such an acquisition to take place at the maximum possible price, since the higher the acquisition price, the greater the profit for Perry on its King Pharmaceutical shares.

Thus, Perry's interests not only conflicted with, but clearly were orthogonal to, that of its fellow shareholders.[40] Except for the fact that there was no actual vote-buying transaction, the arrangement was economically and functionally equivalent to vote buying. In fact, the costs to Perry of setting up the hedged structure can be thought of as the price for vote buying. Creating the hedged structure in Mylan was obviously not free and actually likely to be somewhat costly because there is a price to shorting shares. The actual price depends on whether Perry bought derivatives that could synthetically mirror the payoffs of a short, or actually took a short position, which typically has a higher risk profile. In any event, whatever Perry had to pay to create that position can be thought of as the "price" it paid to acquire the votes.

Interestingly, under current law related to corporate governance, fiduciary duties, and vote buying, it is not at all clear that this arrangement was illegal. With regard to corporate governance, there is no legal authority for boards of directors to unilaterally nullify the voting power of any shareholder or shareholder block. It would be inadvisable to give directors such power in light of the conflicts of interest that directors face in a wide variety of contexts. As for fiduciary duties, significantly, Perry was not an officer or a director or a majority shareholder in Mylan. Thus, Perry owed no fiduciary duties that would have constrained its ability to vote its shares in Mylan in precisely the way it wanted.

The vote-buying issue is somewhat more complicated, but it appears that under current law it is not readily apparent that what Perry did would be construed as vote buying. Even if Perry was deemed to have "bought votes" in Mylan, such vote buying probably was not illegal, at least under

Delaware law, for several reasons.[41] Not every separation of voting rights from the other emoluments of share ownership involves vote buying. Here, there were a series of independent transactions that resulted in a situation in which Perry had voting rights in Mylan, without being at any economic risk for the consequences of using bad or tainted judgment in the exercise of its franchise.

However, this is not unusual. Regarding the separation of shares from votes, companies can issue non-voting shares, and they also can issue shares with supermajority voting rights without running afoul of restrictions on vote buying. Voting trusts and related sorts of arrangements similarly result in the separation of the voting rights from the other property rights associated with share ownership. While what Perry did was admittedly extreme, the fact remains that shareholders frequently hedge their positions in the companies in which they invest. As will be seen in chapter 15, hedge funds trade not only in options, derivatives, and futures, but also simply by holding fully diversified portfolios of assets, which fully eliminate the firm-specific economic risk associated with an investment in a particular company.

Another obstacle to a finding that Perry had engaged in impermissible vote buying is dicta in the most recent Delaware case to deal with vote buying, *Hewlett v. Hewlett Packard Company*,[42] which arose out of disagreements over the shareholder vote on the HP merger with Compaq discussed above. In that case, the son of HP cofounder Bill Hewlett brought a shareholder derivative suit against Carly Fiorina, HP's CEO, for buying the votes associated with 17 million HP shares controlled by Deutsche Bank to induce the bank to vote these shares in favor of a proposed merger between HP and Compaq. Mr. Hewlett's allegation was that to foster and improve Deutsche Bank's investment banking business, Deutsche Bank changed its vote. In rejecting the vote-buying claim for lack of evidence,[43] Chancellor Chandler asserted that shareholders are free to do whatever they want with their shares. Applying this claim to my consideration of Perry Capital, it would seem beyond doubt that Perry, in its capacity as a Mylan shareholder, was certainly free to hedge those shares and then vote.

The shareholder voting controversy in *High River Limited Partnership v. Mylan Laboratories, Inc.*, presents an example of judicial incapacity to deal with, much less to resolve in any satisfactory manner, a clear conflict of interest within the firm with respect to voting. *Mylan Laboratories* involved a conflict within a single class of claimants, Mylan's common shareholders. Two additional sorts of conflicts among this group are worth noting. Besides the conflict between Perry and the other shareholders, there was also a conflict between Carl Icahn and the other shareholders, as well as conflicts among the diversified and non-diversified Mylan shareholders.

Carl Icahn, the maverick investor who complained most vociferously about Perry's actions, had apparently taken a large short position in King Pharmaceuticals, the target firm that Mylan had taken steps to acquire.[44] This clearly put Icahn in a conflict of interest situation vis-à-vis his fellow Mylan shareholders. Suppose, for example, that a Mylan acquisition of King would create important synergies that would result in benefits for Mylan shareholders as well as a substantial acquisition premium for shareholders in King Pharmaceuticals. While other shareholders might prefer that Mylan succeed in acquiring King, Icahn might not. Icahn could possibly lose more on his short position in King than he would gain on his long position in Mylan if Mylan succeeded in its acquisition attempt.

Thus, while Perry's hedge made it prefer that Mylan pay too much for King, Icahn's short position in King made him prefer that Mylan pay too little. Additionally, while Perry's hedge gave it an incentive to pursue a takeover of King, even where such a transaction was not in the interests of the other Mylan shareholders, Icahn's short position gave him an incentive to oppose Mylan's attempt to acquire King, even where such an acquisition was in the interests of the other Mylan shareholders.

In addition to the conflicts between Mylan shareholders and Perry Capital, and the conflicts between Mylan shareholders and Carl Icahn, there were also internal conflicts among the rest of the Mylan shareholders. Consider for a moment the Mylan shares owned and controlled by Mylan management. These management shareholders might have selfishly preferred an acquisition of King even if such an acquisition was not in the best interests of other Mylan shareholders, because such an acquisition would give managers more resources to control and potentially make them less susceptible to a hostile takeover by Mylan.[45] More subtly, fully diversified Mylan shareholders, like shareholders who owned Mylan stock through an investment in a mutual fund, were likely to hold shares in King Pharmaceuticals as well. Based on the size of each investment, these shareholders might have preferred that Mylan overpay for its King shares. Finally, as discussed above, certain Mylan shareholders might have a hedged investment and therefore might have been less concerned with a possible transaction involving King than would other Mylan shareholders. Similar conflicts existed among the King Pharmaceuticals shareholding population as well.[46]

The argument here is not that morphable ownership and empty voting are not problems. Rather, the point is that they are problems that are not unique to corporate elections. Indeed, all elections are plagued with this sort of problem.

At various points in U.S. history, there have been debates over voting rights for property owners, residents of brief duration regardless of their citizenship, convicted felons, non-citizen residents, and others. Recently, in both the United States and Europe, proposals have been heard to permit non-citizen immigrants vote in state and local elections.

U.S. law does not ban voting by non-citizens on the federal level.[47] For example, the U.S. Constitution does not require that voters be citizens. As is the case in corporate elections, decisions about who can vote in federal elections rest in the hands of the state legislatures. During the eighteenth and nineteenth centuries, at least twenty-two U.S. states and territories enfranchised immigrants in both state and federal elections; non-citizens voted in the United States as recently as 1928.[48] Similarly, in Europe, the Maastricht Treaty extended to all Europeans the right to vote in EU member countries other than their own.

Voting rights theorists convincingly assert that basic democratic principles require that a community should extend voting rights based "on an individual's stake in the community and her interest in the outcome" of the election.[49] The problem with this formulation is that it is far easier to articulate than to actualize. The idea of what it means to have a stake in a community such as a city or a corporation is remarkably hard to define.

Suppose the election is today, for example, and I plan to leave for another country tomorrow. Assume that I own shares in a corporation that I plan to sell tomorrow, or that are part of a fully diversified portfolio, so that I can be assured that if the shares in this particular company decline the shares of certain other of my holdings will go up. Perhaps I am voting on a municipal referendum to change the zoning laws to permit a manufacturing facility to operate in a particular area, but I own a competing facility in China. Or imagine I am to vote in a corporate election to expand operations to India, and I own shares in companies already doing business in India with whom this company will compete. These subtle conflicts suggest that proxies for having a stake in a community, such as property ownership, are not only crude but also both overinclusive and underinclusive. Of course, there are plenty of people who do not own property but have a stake in a community that should permit them to vote. Similarly, there are many individuals who do own property in a particular community but may have a vanishingly small stake because of other interests, including property interests elsewhere.

Oddly, these basic arguments about voting, which have plagued voting law for decades, are only now being raised in the context of corporate elections. Clearly, given the ability to hedge, to sell short, and to hold fully diversified portfolios, not all shareholders have interests or stakes in their corporations that are proportional to the percentage of shares that they own. Just as workers with huge interests and stakes in the firms in which they are employed cannot vote (except to the extent to which they own shares), so too it is the case that shareholders who have very little, if any, stakes in the firms in which they own shares can vote, unless otherwise prohibited from doing so.

Moreover, it is extremely rare (though not unheard of) for non-shareholder constituencies such as bondholders or employees to be permitted to vote in corporate elections. Complicating the issue still further is the fact that different classes of shares can be issued with different voting rights. In Europe, Asia, and, to a lesser extent, the United States, different classes of shares have different voting rights. For example, in Germany, 100 percent of the voting stock in the automobile company Porsche is owned by the Porsche family, which owns only 10 percent of the company's non-voting stock. Ferdinand Piech, grandson of the company's founder and chairman of the supervisory board, defends this voting pattern on the grounds that it allows the company to invest for the long term and take a stakeholder approach to their business. Piech once observed that while Porsche had "heard of shareholder value. . . . [W]e put customers first, then workers, business partners, suppliers and dealers, and then shareholders."[50]

The situation in which a company has two classes of shares, and one class of shares is voting and the other is non-voting, as at Porsche is common but not unique. Other companies have classes of shares with multiple voting rights that permit one class of shares to have more votes per share than another, as well as voting rights ceilings that provide a maximum number of votes that can be held by any single shareholder, irrespective of the number of type of shares held. An example of this latter voting configuration is Volkswagen, which places a ceiling on voting rights of 20 percent for any single shareholder in the company regardless of how many shares he owns.[51]

Among the most important statistical findings in corporate governance is that shares of stock with voting rights consistently trade at a premium compared to shares with no voting rights, and, all else equal, shares with higher voting rights trade at a premium to otherwise identical shares in the same companies that have lower voting rights. Moreover, the size of the price premium associated with the power to vote varies substantially across countries. R. C. Lease, J. J. McConnell, and W. H. Mikkelson find an average premium of only 5.4 percent in the United States.[52] B. F. Smith and B. Amoako-Adu find a median premium of 6.4 percent.[53] In Switzerland the premium is 18 percent.[54] In certain other countries, the premia are even higher. H. Levy finds a 45.5 percent premium in Israel.[55] In perhaps the most famous of these studies and certainly the one with the most intriguing result, Luigi Zingales found an 82 percent premium for voting shares over non-voting shares in Italy.[56]

At least four basic points emerge from this analysis. The first observation stems from the fact that shares of stock are "merely" financial assets. As such, there is no symbolic, dignitary, or other intrinsic value to voting in corporate, as opposed to political, elections. This, in turn, means that the value of the right to vote in corporate elections can be monetized.

Second, because shares of stock are financial assets, the mere fact that shares with votes are worth more than identical shares without votes is interesting from a corporate governance perspective. After all, if the shareholders in power (those with the votes) only received the benefits from such power available to all shareholders, such as the benefits from increased share prices and dividend payments and other indicia of improved corporate performance, voting shares would not be worth more than nonvoting shares. Thus, the relative advantage of owning voting shares as opposed to non-voting shares must be attributable to certain benefits from voting rights that the owners of voting shares receive that the non-voting shareholders do not since otherwise the voting and non-voting shares would sell for the same price. These sorts of benefits are known as "private benefits of control" and come in the form of above-market salaries, perquisites of office, and related advantages that those in control of corporate election contests enjoy while non-voting shareholders do not.

Third, the myriad problems of voting and incentives are so complex that only particularized rules formulated at the most local level make any sense whatsoever, at least in the corporate governance context. In corporate governance, unlike general electoral politics, there are no issues with discrimination on the basis of gender or race or other impermissible factors. Rather, the issue is purely economic, and each firm has strong incentives to solve these problems at least *ex ante* (at the time they go public) to maximize the value of their shares.

In the corporate context, this is an area in which the incentives of management are generally aligned with those of rational, value-maximizing investors, at least initially. Neither group wants an outsider or another shareholder to purchase the company on the cheap, or to cause the corporation to dilute its value by paying too much for a target firm. Thus, we can be confident that, to the extent that solutions to these problems can be found, we can count on management to find them. The same does not hold true for corporate law rules relating to shareholder voting. Indeed, there is a clear, palpable conflict between the interests of shareholders and the interests of management, with managers generally favoring voting rules that make takeovers more difficult to consummate, and shareholders generally favoring voting rules that make them less difficult to achieve.

Fourth, the incentives problems and conflicts that characterize shareholder voting strongly add to the other well-known evidence about rational ignorance and free-riding to suggest that Easterbrook and Fischel basically were correct in their view that however situations in which shareholder voting should be limited, shareholders clearly should be permitted to vote in contests for corporate control. The premium of voting over non-voting shares represents at least in part the "opportunity of those with votes to improve the performance of the corporation."[57] Suppose, for example, that a corporation has 100 shares of stock outstanding. The shares are worth $1 per share at present, but the value of the shares would double to $2 under a new management team. A shareholder with 40 shares for which she has paid a total of $40 would be willing to pay up to $62 (or $5.63 per share) to acquire the additional 11 shares necessary to obtain voting control of the corporation. Paying $5.63 per shares for 11 shares would bring the investors' total investment to $101.93 for 51 shares worth a total of $102 (or $2 per share).

In this example, after the acquisition of the control block, the remaining 49 minority block would double in value from $1 to $2 per share. Under these circumstances, the minority would be willing to grant the majority some private benefits of control to provide it with sufficient incentives to acquire control and to effectuate the necessary changes to the corporation's governance required to boost the value of the shares. Having shares with voting rights is the key, then, to the market for corporate control. Unless shares had voting rights attached to them, outsiders would have no incentive to pay a premium for control that would benefit all shareholders such as the one described above.

In light of the complexities and conflicts that mark shareholder voting, it makes sense that voting is used merely to supplement, rather than displace, board power. Just as republican forms of government characterized by divided power within a system of checks and balances are superior to direct democracy, so too are corporate governance systems in which the actions of shareholders are strictly limited and tempered by other corporate governance institutions, boards of directors, management, market forces, contract, fiduciary duties, and corporate charters.

The bottom line, then, is that shareholder voting is not a panacea for corporate governance problems any more than are boards of directors or the market for corporate control. At best, they are small parts of an extremely complex corporate governance system, whose success does not depend on any single factor.

CHAPTER 14

THE ROLE OF BANKS AND OTHER LENDERS IN CORPORATE GOVERNANCE

In 2002, the president of French bank Société Générale, Daniel Bouton, announced that European corporate giant Vivendi Universal would have to sell off assets to reduce some of its ballooning $18.5 billion debt. The bank declared that the media giant's "president will have to quickly change (the financial picture) and begin to sell assets."[1] When subsequently announcing the sale of a stake in one of its largest units to General Electric, the chairman and CEO of Vivendi touted the sale as "a very good agreement for Vivendi Universal's shareholders, both in terms of value creation and the reduction of our debt. This transaction will significantly lower Vivendi Universal's debt, which by the end of 2004, should be below [$6 billion]."[2]

Simultaneously, on the eastern side of the Atlantic at rival Time Warner, private equity investor Carl Icahn accused Chairman Richard Parsons of not acting to "enhance values for shareholders."[3] Icahn, who controls a 3.3 percent stake, thereby making him one of the largest shareholders in the giant, banded with other equity holders in 2005 to launch a bid to split up the Time Warner media empire, much like Société Générale did with Vivendi. While Icahn did win some cost-cutting concessions, he was unable to gather enough of the thousands of equity claimants to affect the election of the company's board of directors. So disparate were the shareholders that Icahn was forced to retreat.[4]

As these stories and others in this book suggest, the American mechanisms for monitoring and controlling corporate managers differ from those utilized in Europe. Germany, for example, is a country with a universal banking system that has "the position, information, and power to monitor the activity of management effectively and, when necessary, to discipline management,"[5] and commercial banks take an active management role to mitigate managerial shirking and misconduct.[6] In stark contrast to their German counterparts, American banks have been traditionally barred from taking an active role in corporate governance. Because American banks lack both the power and incentive to monitor their borrowers with the same intensity as German banks, the monitoring role in the American corporate governance system is occupied by those who provide only equity capital to the corporation—the shareholders. As a result, relative to, say, Germany and Japan, the American structure of corporate governance focuses power in management.[7] Too disaggregated to monitor management's activities and typically unable to galvanize into effective political coalitions, American shareholders are largely powerless to affect management decisions. Legal scholars have frequently criticized the lack of banks in the American system of corporate governance, routinely depicting the United States as having "sharply constrained the development of multidimensional governance relationships."[8] In particular, American mechanisms for monitoring and controlling corporate managers are said to be grossly inferior to those available in countries that allow universal banking. American firms are disparagingly described as "Berle-Means" corporations,[9] characterized by widespread share ownership, separation of management and risk-bearing, and significant agency conflicts between managers and shareholders.[10]

Households historically have owned over half of all shares in U.S. companies compared to fewer than 20 percent in Germany. On the other hand, banks and enterprises[11] have historically owned more than half of German shares, while less than 10 percent of shares in American companies.[12] While voting power in American corporations is dispersed, voting power in Germany is relatively much more aggregated. Is one system clearly better? The current paradigm of corporate governance theory suggests that the German universal bank system, on which this chapter will focus as the model for universal banking regimes, encourages the socially optimal corporate decision-making. The argument goes that commercial banks, if allowed to function free of regulation, are able to monitor and influence the corporate governance of public corporations in ways that are likely to improve corporate performance. U.S. law, however, limits banks' influence to a suboptimal level by restricting the size of banks and the scope and geographical range of their activities. Only able to rely on disparate shareholders, American governance institutions have been forced to follow a unique Berle-Means pattern of successive efforts, ranging from independent directors to hostile takeovers, to bridge the separation of ownership and management in the face of dispersed shareholdings.

This chapter discusses the role of banks in the corporate governance of publicly held companies. It is doubtful that it is even desirable, much less preferable, to have commercial banks actively involved in corporate governance. The proponents of bank involvement in corporate governance along what is sometimes known as the "universal bank" model, or the "main bank" model, fail to address the significant costs bank-dominated corporate governance and ignore important benefits of the American system of equity-dominated corporate governance.

Advocates of an active role for banks in corporate governance ignore the critical differences between the monitoring incentives of equity holders and the monitoring incentives of debt holders. Once the incentive issues facing commercial banks that purport to insert themselves in corporate governance are understood, it becomes clear that greater bank involvement in the governance of American corporations will not cure the problems created by the separation of ownership and control. Rather, bank incursion into corporate governance carries with it an entirely new set of conflicts between the risk-averse claimants who make loans and the residual claimants who invest risk capital. For this reason, the United States is better served by working to repair its own corporate governance system by freeing up the market for corporate control and loosening regulations of hedge funds and private equity rather than seeking to adopt an entirely new system, with all its attendant problems.

Part I of this chapter describes the conflict of interest between a firm's fixed claimants, including banks, on the one hand, and a firm's equity claimants on the other. Understanding this conflict is critical to an analysis of the supposed advantages bank-dominated systems have over the American system. This chapter shows that the current paradigm's core assumption about the role of banks in corporate governance—namely, that what is good for a nation's banks is also good for the nation's borrowers—is flawed. Utilizing basic principles of economies and corporate finance, this chapter shows that, to the extent that banks control corporate borrowers, they are likely to reduce corporate risk-taking below the socially optimal level.

Part II applies the theory articulated in part I. Focusing on the German governance system as the paradigm of universal banking system, this part evaluates the system against the background of the conflict described in part I. In Germany, banks exert more influence in corporate decision-making than do banks in the United States. The banks have used this influence to reduce risk-taking among borrowers and to retard the market for corporate control. Current wisdom holds that the German banking systems substitute for robust markets for corporate control because such systems reduce agency costs and improve managerial performance.[13] This chapter argues that the bank-dominated system of corporate governance actually prevents the development of robust markets for corporate control in those countries.

Part III turns to the implications of these observations for the ongoing debate about American corporate governance. This part argues that simply giving fixed claimants more power over borrowers will not solve any of the perceived problems in American corporate governance. Rather, firm performance can be more effectively enhanced by eliminating restrictions on the market for corporate control and on hedge funds and private equity firms, thereby improving the voice of American equity holders. Moreover, critical features of American law—including environmental law, partnership law, and lender liability rules—limit the ability of banks in the United States to monitor and control the moral hazard of borrowing firms to the same extent as European rules allow. For these reasons, universal banking offers fewer benefits than is commonly perceived, and other, more incremental changes in legal rules offer greater potential rewards.

I. The Conflict of Interest Between "Pure" Equity Claimants and Banks

Modern scholars have formalized the conflict between the interests of fixed claimants (such as banks) and the interests of shareholders who hold residual claims to the firm's earnings that exists within the modern publicly held corporation.[14] When choosing how to allocate assets, firms that increase risk will transfer wealth from the fixed claimants to the residual claimants.[15] Thus, to the extent that shareholders can influence corporate decisions through their voting power, they can enrich themselves at the expense of fixed claimants by shifting assets to risky investments. Similarly, to the extent that banks and other fixed claimants can influence corporate decisions through corporate governance structures (or, as in Germany, through their ability to vote shares owned by others), they can enrich themselves at the expense of shareholders. The following example illustrates this point.

Suppose that a borrower has assets of $1,000 and liabilities of $500. Assume the $500 represents the principal and interest due on money borrowed from banks. This leaves the firm with $500 in shareholders' equity. The firm must choose between investment strategy A, which has an expected payoff of $2,020 and investment strategy B, which has an expected payoff of $1,875.[16]

As strategy A indicates, there is a 5 percent chance that the bank will suffer a small loss because if the investment returns only $400, the firm will be unable to repay the full $500 loan. In contrast, strategy B poses absolutely no risk of loss to the bank because even under the worst possible scenario, strategy B returns enough to repay in full the principal and interest on the firm's bank debt.

There are, however, two other important differences between strategies A and B. First, strategy B is significantly inferior to strategy A from the shareholders' perspective. Strategy B has an expected return for shareholders of only $1,375, compared with an expected shareholder return

TABLE 14.1
Investment Strategies

A. Probability	Firm	Bank	Common	Firm	Bank	Common
.05	$400	$400	$0	$20	$20	$0
.20	$1,000	$500	$500	$200	$100	$100
.50	$2,000	$500	$1,500	$1,000	$250	$750
.20	$3,000	$500	$2,500	$600	$100	$500
.05	$4,000	$500	$3,500	$200	$25	$175
1.0				$2,020	$495	$1,525

B. Probability	Firm	Bank	Common	Firm	Bank	Common
.25	$1,000	$500	$500	$250	$125	$125
.50	$2,000	$500	$1,500	$1,000	$250	$750
.25	$2,500	$500	$2,000	$625	$125	$500
1.0				$1,875	$500	$1,375

C. Probability	Firm	Bank	Common	Firm	Bank	Common
.30	$0	$0	$0	$0	$0	$0
.50	$1,000	$500	$500	$500	$250	$250
.20	$7,000	$500	$6,500	$1,400	$100	$1,300
1.0				$1,900	$350	$1,550

of $1,525 for strategy A. The demonstrated disparity in expected returns may be explained by the simple fact that strategy A has both a greater potential upside and a greater potential downside than strategy B. Because the equity claimants capture all of the gains on the upside after the bank has been repaid, but share the losses on the downside with the bank, they obviously prefer the riskier investment.

Strategy B also is inferior from the perspective of society as a whole, since the expected value of strategy A is $2,020, compared with only $1,875 for strategy B. Thus, if an economy were to allocate plenary authority over investment decisions to fixed claimants such as banks, productivity and gross domestic product would decline to suboptimal levels as the banks steered investments away from the highest-valued projects and toward lower-valued projects. Thus, as Frank Easterbrook and Daniel Fischel have observed, as residual claimants under American corporate governance structures, shareholders retain plenary authority to guide investment decisions because, over a wide range of issues, it is the shareholders who have the greatest incentive to maximize the value of the firm.[17]

Of course, just as it would be suboptimal to give plenary authority to the firm's fixed claimants, so also would it be suboptimal to give plenary authority over all investment decisions to the equity claimants: equity claimants have an incentive to transfer wealth to themselves by increasing the riskiness of the firm in which they have invested. Left to their own devices, the shareholders might select strategy C.

Shifting to strategy C would increase the expected value of the shareholder's stake from $1,525 under strategy A to $1,550, but would reduce the expected value of the bank's investment from $495 to $350, and the total value of the firm from $2,020 to $1,900. As before, the risk of each strategy, as represented by the probability of particular outcomes, determines the expected value of each project. For strategy A, the standard deviation from its expected value, $2,020, is relatively small, just $853.[18] For strategy B, which from the bank's perspective is the best investment among the three, the standard deviation from its expected value of $1,875 is even less, just $545.[19] For strategy C, however, the standard deviation from the expected value of $1,900 is quite large, $2,784.[20] For this reason, strategy C is the worst investment among the three from the bank's perspective, but the best from the shareholder's perspective.[21] The shareholders capture the lion's share of the huge upside potential associated with strategy C but share the downside loss with the bank.

In a properly functioning capital market, an equilibrium emerges from the disparate interests of fixed claimants, equity claimants, and, indeed, all other claimants on the firm's cash flows, such as workers, managers, suppliers, and customers. Rational banks demand compensation in the form of higher interest payments for the danger that they will loan money to firms with investment portfolios resembling B, only to have the firm shift its resources toward A or C. Shareholders, on the other hand, will pay less for stock in firms whose investment patterns resemble strategy B rather than A or C.

Following Ronald Coase, through bargaining, the parties can improve on any equilibrium that does not maximize the overall value of the firm.[22] Shareholders, for example, could agree to pay a higher interest rate in exchange for allowing equity claimants to pursue riskier projects. Similarly, bondholders could accept a lower interest rate in exchange for a credible shareholder promise not to shift their investments toward riskier projects after credit has been extended. Thus, the equilibrium that emerges in a properly functioning capital market not only protects both banks and equity holders but also promotes allocational efficiency (the efficient allocation of resources within society) because it guarantees that investments that maximize the overall value of the firm will be pursued.

Two important insights emerge from the preceding discussion that are relevant to the ongoing debate about alternative corporate governance mechanisms. First, the clear conflict of interest between fixed claimants (including banks) and equity claimants strongly suggests that banks are not ideal institutions to monitor corporate performance on behalf of shareholders.[23] Second, legal and structural problems within capital markets raise transaction costs, thereby impeding the operation of capital markets and making it more difficult for market participants to resolve the inherent conflicts between fixed and residual claimants—as well as among other participants in the corporate enterprise. Managers, for example, tend to be more risk-averse than shareholders are because the amount of their compensation is predominantly fixed, aligning their incentives more closely with those of fixed claimants than with those of equity claimants. Managers' incentives for risk-taking are further reduced because of their investment of nondiversifiable human capital in their jobs.[24] The value of this human capital would depreciate significantly if their firms were to fail. Transaction costs, particularly the high costs of contracting and the impossibility of predicting the future with certainty, make it is impossible to design executive compensation contracts that perfectly align the interests of managers with the interests of shareholders.[25] The deviation of managerial risk preferences from shareholder preferences often results in a suboptimal level of risk-taking by firms.[26]

Legal rules and institutions can exacerbate these inefficiencies. Rules that artificially restrict the market for corporate control, or that artificially increase the bargaining power of one group of claimants (e.g., by guaranteeing them places on corporate boards of directors), can prevent investing parties from reaching a wealth-maximizing bargaining equilibrium and achieving allocational efficiency.

II. Germany's Universal Banking vs. U.S. Shareholder Control

The previous part outlined the theoretical workings of two disparate systems: one in which fixed claimants are in control and one in which equity claimants are. This part discusses this theory in action. Viewing Germany as the paradigm of a delegated monitoring regime, this part begins by discussing the real world functioning of the nation's universal banking system, and then contrasts this system with the equity claimant control present in the United States.

Theory in Action: Germany

"The universal bank sits at the epicenter of German corporate governance."[27] Scholars tend to romanticize the characteristics and benefits of this system.[28] Commentators argue that, in sharp contrast to American banks, German banks have "the position, information, and power to effectively monitor the activity of management and, when necessary, to discipline management."[29] As a result, bank involvement supposedly improves the profitability of firms.[30]

The German Aktiengesellschaft (AG) is the corporate organizational form most comparable to the American publicly held corporation.[31] Unlike the American corporation, however, the AG features a two-tier board structure, featuring both a management and executive committee (vorstand), as well as a supervisory board of directors (Aufsichtsrat).[32] The supervisory board appoints the vorstand, but its other powers are limited: "The supervisory board cannot, even by purported delegation, take any steps in the actual management" of the firm,[33] but it does screen management's investment plans, and it can veto plans of which it disapproves.[34] One commentator has analogized the role of the supervisory board to that of the U.S. Senate in advising and consenting to the president's appointments and to treaty agreements.[35]

The most striking aspect of the AGs is that fixed claimants, banks and employees, almost completely dominate the supervisory boards of these firms. Because German banks are heavily represented on the supervisory boards,[36] and the boards of companies with more than two thousand employees must have employee representation equal to that of the shareholders,[37] the combined power of the fixed claimants dominates the board.

German banks own only a modest share of firms to which they lend money, but they exercise a degree of control significantly greater than their proportionate holdings. Though banks account for only about 6 percent of large-share stakes in German firms,[38] they tend to exert effective control over a majority of the shares voted in annual meetings.[39] For example, Deutsche Bank owned 28 percent of the common stock of Daimler-Benz before it became partially Americanized via its merger with Chrysler; however, because German banks customarily hold shares owned by institutional and individual clients, the bank voted 42 percent of all shares. In addition, such owners of large blocks are able to review management's plans and decisions as insiders, while outsiders have less influence, with hostile takeover extremely rare.[40]

The disparity between the small equity positions and the large voting power of German banks is attributable to a combination of three factors. First, German banks vote bearer shares that they hold as custodians for small shareholder-clients of the banks' brokerage operations. These individual investors deposit their shares with banks, and the banks vote by proxy at shareholders' meetings.[41] Second, German companies frequently pass resolutions capping the voting rights of any single shareholder at 5 to 15 percent of total votes, regardless of the size of its shareholding.[42] Because such restrictions do not apply to banks voting shares by proxy, these rules further increase the voting power of the universal banks.[43] Finally, German banks augment their voting rights by voting the shares owned by mutual funds they operate.[44]

Although German banks have substantial political power that stems from their voting power, their stake in AGs is primarily the result of corporate lending. German firms obtain most of their external financing from bank borrowing rather than capital markets.[45] Bank borrowing, primarily in the form of long-term loans, makes up 20 percent of the external financing for German companies.[46] Historically, German firms have borrowed $4.20 from banks for every dollar they obtain from capital markets, whereas American firms have borrowed $0.85 for every dollar they raise in the capital markets.[47]

The German bank's dual role as creditor and shareholder also creates a significant conflict of interest. Banks have an economic incentive to vote against risk-taking at firms to which they have lent money. However, from the perspective of shareholders on whose behalf the banks vote, banks reduce aggregate risk-taking to a suboptimal level and thereby transfer wealth from shareholders to themselves. Furthermore, labor interests on the supervisory board are unlikely to oppose banks' efforts to reduce aggregate risk-taking because they, too, are fixed claimants; their interests are aligned with those of the bank.

The above description of German corporate governance illustrates that the United States is not the only country to separate corporate ownership and control. As with small U.S. shareholders, individual German shareholders lack "the information, skill, and incentive to monitor managers."[48] The difference appears to be that in the United States the managers wield the decisive power, while in Germany management shares this power with the banks and labor. German banks do protect incumbent management by effectively eliminating the market for corporate control. In fact, the total number of takeovers in Germany during the last boom during the 1980s was less than one-half of that in the United Kingdom, and there have only been four recorded cases of hostile takeovers in Germany since World War II.[49]

Theory in Action: The U.S. System

When President Clinton signed the Gramm-Leach-Bliley Act on November 12, 1999, many predicted it would herald a shift in corporate governance in the United States toward the German system of delegated monitoring.[50] With the repeal of the Glass-Steagall Act of 1933 that separated commercial and investment banking, and other accompanying reforms, critics of the U.S. corporate governance system saw a chance for universal banks to arise and eventually more effectively monitor American companies. Certainly, from the perspective of American banking organizations, greater involvement in the securities business has brought benefits in the form of lower risk through diversification and lower operating costs through increased economies of scale and scope. In fact, studies have shown that far from increasing the riskiness of banking institutions, securities activities actually make banks safer. It has not, however, led to a universal banking system in the likeness of that of Germany.

These reforms are important in the context of corporate governance because, in theory, they could support the argument that the financial industry in the United States is evolving in the direction of the German universal banks. The reforms to Glass-Steagall in the United States, however, have not had a great impact on American corporate governance because they do not permit American banks to control the corporations with which they have lending relationships. The well-developed capital markets for debt and equity in the United States provide outlets for American firms that need capital, thereby precluding dominance by commercial banks. In other words, even if American banks are allowed to make equity investments in firms to which they have loaned money, those banks will be unable to control the borrowers' corporate governance.

American banks will not have any expanded securities powers under the new legislative proposals; they will simply be allowed to form more extensive affiliations with securities firms. And American securities firms, unlike European banks, make a point of refraining from intrusion into the corporate governance of their clients. Rather, American investment banks limit their activities to underwriting, trading, and providing general investment banking advice about mergers and acquisitions and corporate finance.

American investment banks are further unlikely to disrupt internal corporate affairs because the U.S. financial services sector is uniquely characterized by both intense competition and heterogeneity. Investment banking firms that attempted to make unwelcome intrusions into the corporate governance of their clients would quickly find themselves without clients because, unlike German corporations, American firms can switch investment banking relationships with impunity. Moreover, in the United States, powerful, independent, non-bank institutional investors such as insurance companies, pension funds, and mutual funds, would strongly object to efforts by financial services holding companies to assert themselves in the corporate governance of publicly traded companies.

Path dependence provides a final reason why the current proposals to liberalize the scope of permissible bank affiliations does not pose any cognizable danger to the corporate governance of American firms. Simply put, American capital markets have replaced the languishing commercial lending industry as the principal supplier of capital to American industry.

Consequently, it is too late for American banking organizations to use their influence over corporate governance to retard the growth of American capital markets.

Thus, by permitting the new affiliations, reforms could strengthen the American banking industry, but the acts do not, in and of themselves, pose the danger that banking institutions will use their influence over corporate clients to advance their interests as lenders at the expense of other shareholders. Under current legislation, the United States remains within a system in which disaggregated shareholders have the theoretical control, thus providing management with the real power, while banks are relatively weak. Under this setup, it is the market for corporate control that reduces managerial inefficiency and restrains managerial self-interest. The United States' robust corporate control market spurs hostile takeovers; new owners replace inefficient management teams.[51] Strong evidence indicates that hostile takeovers and the threat of hostile takeovers discipline managers and improve corporate performance.[52] Despite the reforms of the 1990s and early 2000s, the American system remains intact.

The purpose of this chapter is not to argue for the superiority of the U.S. system of corporate governance over the German universal banking model. Instead, the purpose of contrasting the two systems is merely to show that the advantages of the German system have been exaggerated, while the costs have been underemphasized. These costs not only come in the form of excessive risk-aversion, which leads to a stifling of innovation, but also manifest themselves in the form of illiquid, undeveloped, and poorly functioning capital markets. For several reasons, in delegated monitoring regimes such as Germany's capital market participants have fewer incentives than do similarly situated Americans. First, German banks reduce the potential gain from investing in the stock market by limiting upside gains to residual claimants. Second, the highly concentrated patterns of share ownership in Germany have made hostile takeovers, a major source of potential gains for target company shareholders, practically impossible for most insurgent groups to mount successfully. Third, these concentrated patterns of share ownership also reduce order flow in the market, thereby depriving it of liquidity. Finally, and perhaps most important, the core purpose of the German corporate governance system has been to produce stability for systems that were characterized by massive uncertainty in the immediate postwar period.[53] But there is growing evidence that this kind of stability is not a virtue today, with global competition and rapid technological innovation placing a far higher premium on innovation and flexibility than on stability. The U.S. system, for all of its faults, does provide some unique advantages, as discussed in the following part.

III. Implications: What American Corporate Governance Can Learn from Universal Banking Regimes

For the purposes of comparing the American system of corporate governance with the German system described above, here I focus on three sets of problems existing within the American system. The first is the possibility of excessive risk-taking. Just as the German bank-dominated systems described above may cause firms to forsake potentially profitable projects that appear too risky to them, the American system may cause firms to undertake excessively risky projects because weak banks in the United States are unable to monitor and control excessive risk-taking as effectively as German banks do. The second consideration is the declining capacity of market forces to discipline managers and improve corporate performance in the American system. In recent years, politics increasingly has interfered with the functioning of the market. In particular, politics has reduced the efficacy of the market for corporate control, which is the central device for disciplining managers in market-oriented corporate governance systems such as those in the United States. Finally, a set of seemingly minor rules in the United States artificially impedes the ability of fixed claimants to monitor and control borrowers. Thus, while the level of control observed in the German bank-dominated system probably is too high, the level of bank control in the American system probably is artificially low.

The Problem of Excessive Risk-taking

Just as fixed claimants can transfer wealth to themselves from equity claimants by reducing a firm's riskiness *ex post* (i.e., after a firm's capital structure has been determined), so too may equity claimants increase their own wealth at the expense of the fixed claimants by increasing the firm's riskiness.[54] In a properly functioning corporate governance structure, the fixed claimants and the shareholders will reach the appropriate bargaining equilibrium between the risk-preferring proclivities of the shareholders and the risk-averse proclivities of the fixed claimants.

Several features of the American corporate governance system prevent shareholders from acting opportunistically through increased risk-taking. First, fixed claimants may protect themselves against this contingency contractually.[55] Second, American banks often make loans with relatively short maturities, thereby forcing borrowers to rely on revolving lines of credit. Because borrowers realize that they must obtain bank approval for additional credit when their loans reach maturity, banks gain leverage over borrowers through repeat dealings. Third, by buying convertible bonds (convertible into equity claims), fixed claimants may reduce borrowers' incentives to engage in excessive risk-taking because borrowers know that the bondholders are first in line for repayment in the event of default. If the shareholders' risky investments are successful, however, convertible bondholders convert their fixed claims into equity and share in the upside. Fourth, because American shareholders are generally widely dispersed—each owning only a tiny fraction of a company's outstanding shares—they have little incentive to monitor managers and are largely subject to managers' risk preferences. Because managers are averse to the high levels of risk-taking shareholders prefer, this agency cost helps other fixed claimants such as banks. For these reasons, the danger that American firms will engage in excessive risk-taking appears relatively small compared to the danger that German firms will avoid socially efficient risks.

The Market for Corporate Control

As discussed in chapter 8, the market for corporate control has traditionally been a central feature of the American system of corporate governance. Hostile bidders target poorly performing firms and replace their inadequate or shirking managers with rival management teams.[56] Moreover, innovations in corporate finance, such as bridge financing and junk bonds, created a competitive environment in which virtually every firm was a potential takeover target. Hostile takeovers are associated with increases in managerial efficiency, as high share price is considered the strongest hostile takeover defense.[57]

American corporations are not beleaguered by too many hostile takeovers; rather, regulatory restrictions and misguided legal policies stifle the market's demand for hostile takeovers, thereby limiting their number. The number of hostile takeovers in the United States declined precipitously in the early 1990s from a high of forty-six in 1988,[58] but it has been rising worldwide in conjunction with the increasing mergers and acquisitions activity during the second half of the decade and into the 2000s.[59] With thirty-one in 2002, the yearly numbers of hostile takeovers have struggled to eclipse the record during their heyday of the late 1980s.[60] State anti-takeover laws are ever more prevalent and prohibitive, a testament to management's political acumen in dealing with state legislatures at the expense of out-of-state shareholders.[61] Perhaps the worst consequence of America's widely dispersed share ownership is shareholders' inability to form effective political coalitions to block management's political mobilization against hostile takeovers. Political maneuvering, for example, culminated in the Pennsylvania's 1990 anti-takeover law, which represents a massive wealth transfer from shareholders to incumbent management.[62]

In addition to anti-takeover laws, incumbent management has successfully persuaded state legislatures to pass so-called other constituency statutes. These statutes empower corporate management to consider the interests of employees, local communities, suppliers, and customers when deciding whether and how to resist a hostile takeover.[63] These thinly disguised efforts to advance management interests at the expense of shareholders permit managers to defend themselves against shareholders' lawsuits after adopting defensive tactics to entrench themselves in office.[64] Pursuant to these statutes, managers may mount credible arguments that their resistance to takeovers furthers the interests of some non-shareholder constituency or other, thus giving courts a legal hook upon which to hang their decisions favoring incumbent management. State court judges have provided little, if any, comfort to shareholders. In particular, they have done little to curb the use of anti-takeover devices, such as the poison pill, which may be adopted by a target company's board of directors without a shareholder vote.[65]

One legitimate complaint against hostile takeovers as a corporate governance mechanism is that because they are so costly, "companies have to go further off course before attracting a hostile bid than they might if managers were monitored continuously."[66] Hostile bids are extremely capital intensive, not only because they require major financing commitments but also because bidders must invest a substantial amount of resources in research to identify undervalued targets before ever making a takeover bid. Unless a firm is substantially undervalued, bidders will be unable to recoup these capital and search costs.

For at least three reasons, however, this flaw in the corporate control market does not disadvantage the American system of corporate governance relative to the German and other universal banking systems. First, it does not really distinguish the American system of corporate governance from its German counterparts. Like American corporations, German firms must go substantially off course before attracting outside intervention. As fixed claimants, German banks are not concerned about small deviations from optimal performance levels that do not threaten their return on capital.

Second, the market for corporate control affects managerial performance even in the absence of a formally announced takeover bid. A robust market for corporate control improves management's performance because incumbents inevitably prefer to reduce the probability that an outside bid will be made. Incumbent management will be unsure how much better a particular rival management team is; consequently, management will be unsure how far the firm's share price must fall before attracting a hostile bid. This uncertainty creates an incentive for managers to improve the firm's performance, even if a hostile offer never materializes.[67]

Third, commentators who argue that takeovers are too expensive erroneously conceptualize takeovers as an all-or-nothing proposition. Investors need not launch a full-blown tender offer to put a target company effectively in play. Through a proxy contest, for example, investors may launch a takeover for as little as $5,000 (down from $1 million a few years ago).[68] Similarly, institutional investors often purchase large stakes in troubled firms, then use their votes to install directors on corporate boards to "agitate for better performance."[69] To exploit these strategies such that management improves, potential insurgents must present a credible threat.[70] In the German system, insufficient capital market liquidity—combined with the intense loyalty of the banks toward incumbent management—limits the ability of insurgent shareholders credibly to threaten a hostile takeover in the event that performance fails to improve.

This is not to suggest that the market for corporate control worked perfectly in the United States during the 1980s. Critics are correct to argue that share prices must decline too far before the market reacts. Rather, the point is that monitors in Germany also lack the incentive to intervene before firm values have declined significantly. Moreover, if the problem with the takeover market is that performance must decline too much before the market begins to operate, the solution is to design a regulatory system that decreases the costs of intervention. This is not occurring in Germany or the United States, largely because of the awesome power of incumbent management to resist change.[71]

Rules Limiting Monitoring and Control by U.S. Intermediaries

Perhaps the most valid criticism of the American system of corporate governance is that legal rules prevent American financial intermediaries from contractually protecting themselves against the moral hazard problem posed by shareholders. Although fixed claimants clearly have an incentive to monitor and control corporate borrowers, a variety of legal rules in the United States constrain fixed claimants' ability to control moral hazard.[72] As Mark Roe observes in his book on banks and corporate governance, "American legal restrictions have historically kept American banks small and weak, by banning them from operating nationally, entering commerce, affiliating with investment banks, equity mutual funds, or insurers, or from coordinating stockholdings with these other intermediaries."[73] This chapter's emphasis differs from Roe's, focusing on the legal restrictions that prevent American banks from even protecting their exposure as fixed claimants. These restrictions raise capital costs and reduce allocative efficiency by raising the costs of fixed claims in American firms.

In a nutshell, several American legal doctrines expose lenders to potential liability if they attempt to write contracts that protect themselves from borrowers' moral hazard.[74] Many of these liability rules derive from the reasonable doctrine that banks have a general obligation of good faith toward borrowers,[75] but courts often interpret them in a manner inconsistent with basic freedom of contract. As a result, expanded rules of lender liability have enabled borrowers to transfer wealth to themselves by opportunistically suing banks when banks threaten to enforce their contracts with borrowers.[76]

When banks have threatened, for example, to enforce a management change clause (a contractual provision ostensibly allowing lenders to declare a default if top officers are appointed who are not approved by lenders), borrowers have been successful in suing banks for interfering with contractual relations between borrowers and their employees.[77] Courts even have forced banks to loan more money or to give more advance notice of termination of a lending relationship than required by contract.[78] Furthermore, banks that become actively involved in the affairs of borrowers in order to protect the value of their security interests may face massive liability for environmental harm the firm causes.[79]

Bankruptcy rules further chill American banks' incentive to take an active role in the affairs of borrowers, thereby discouraging intervention when it would be most helpful—when borrowers are in financial distress. Specifically, U.S. bankruptcy law strips senior lenders of their claims to collateral or subordinates their claims to those of junior lenders, or both, if the lender exercises some degree of control over the borrower. This principle, which is known as equitable subordination, provides a strong disincentive for banks to play an active role in corporate governance. In the classic *American Lumber* case,[80] an American bank assisted in restructuring a troubled debtor after it had advanced the debtor extra funds. When the debtor began to fail despite these efforts, the bank tried to recover its funds. Other creditors complained of preferential treatment, and they persuaded the court to subordinate the bank's claims to theirs.

Although the bank argued that subordination would cause members of the financial community to feel that they could not give financial assistance to failing companies, but must instead foreclose on their security interests and collect debts swiftly, not leaving any chance for survival, the court was singularly unimpressed.[81] Thus, America's corporate governance problem may not stem from a lack of concentrated share blocks and powerful financial intermediaries, as Roe suggests.[82] Rather, the problem may arise from American courts' and legislatures' unwillingness to enforce the contractual provisions upon which financial intermediaries and borrowers agree. Enforcing such contractual provisions not only would protect the banks from moral hazard but also would help borrowers avoid excessive borrowing costs.

CONCLUSION

Vigorous competition in the product and labor markets is the most powerful corporate governance device of all. Competition in the marketplace forces firms to compete fervently for capital. For this reason, the rapid globalization of trade and investment should lead to improved corporate governance throughout the world. Naturally, the economies with the best corporate governance structures will outperform rival economies at the margin.

The purpose of this chapter has been to show that the "continuous and textured" monitoring that characterizes relational investing in Germany is not a panacea.[83] The problems posed by these systems result from straightforward conflicts of interest between risk-averse fixed claimants, who control investments, and residual claimants, who have the greatest stake in the firm's financial success. The highly leveraged capital structure of banks and their large exposure to demand deposits further enhance the banks' conservative tendencies. As fixed claimants, banks' risk preferences are more closely aligned with management's than with those of equity investors—or society; banks make poor monitors and cannot be expected to maximize the value of the firm.

The failure of existing theories of relational investing to recognize the conflict of interest between equity markets and fixed claimants exemplifies an unfortunate tendency to treat all financial intermediaries alike.[84] Moreover, commentators who extol the virtues of bank-dominated corporate governance systems fail to consider adequately the adverse effects such systems have had on the development of capital markets in the countries that have employed them. Put differently, the strong role played by financial intermediaries has retarded the growth of primary and secondary markets for equity, and has thereby stifled an important source of risk capital for firms.

The point here is not, of course, that the optimal amount of bank involvement in corporate governance is zero. Banks play a valuable and important role as "delegated monitor" that helps all investors. For example, in the case that started this chapter, Société Générale was far more successful in effectuating change at Vivendi than was Icahn's coalition of minority shareholders at Time Warner. This reflects the fact that in the United States, shareholders must rely more on the threat of a takeover to discipline managers. Outside bidders protect shareholder interests by monitoring management in publicly traded firms and by launching hostile bids when firms underperform. But in recent years, politics has interfered with the efficacy of the market for corporate control: state anti-takeover statutes have dramatically reduced the number of hostile takeovers in the

United States, diverting wealth from shareholders, who must endure firms' suboptimal performance, to managers, who no longer face the threat of displacement. In the absence of a healthy takeover market, the weakness of American financial intermediaries is disturbing. Unfortunately, several American legal doctrines have artificially limited the ability of banks to monitor corporate borrowers. As a result, while the degree of banks' influence in Germany is probably excessive, the level of banks' influence in the United States is likely too low.

The problem in Germany, and like nations, is that the interests of equity investors are insufficiently represented in corporate governance. The problem in the United States is that fixed claimants are unable to protect themselves contractually from the moral hazard posed by the equity-dominated corporate borrowers. Both of these deficiencies in corporate governance structures raise the cost of capital and reduce allocational efficiency. Rather than investing resources in copying each other's systems, each system would profit by focusing on, and repairing, its own problems.

CHAPTER 15

HEDGE FUNDS AND PRIVATE EQUITY

Hedge funds and private equity funds are the newest big thing in corporate governance and are likely to remain an important and controversial feature of the financial and legal landscape for some time to come. And they are for real. Indeed, a primary argument of this book is that traditional corporate governance mechanisms and devices, including boards of directors, shareholder voting, and derivative and securities class action lawsuits, are not the panaceas for corporate governance problems that they often are touted as being.

The market for corporate control, by contrast, as discussed in chapter 8, is a powerful tool, but it has shortcomings. It is over-regulated. Its effectiveness is diminished by poison pills, captured state legislatures, and the provisions of the Williams Act that wrongfully deprive bidders of their legitimate property rights in information by requiring that they share their strategic plans for the bidder with the entire marketplace. The point of this chapter is that hedge funds, which at least until now have been largely (though not entirely) unregulated, are an extremely important addition to the market for corporate control in any nation's arsenal of corporate governance devices.

Private equity refers to pooled investment funds that attempt to generate strong returns for their investors by providing capital and forming partnerships with the management of private companies for a relatively long period of time. Private equity firms invest large percentages of their investment capital (often as high as 10 percent of the total fund) in order to obtain a majority stake in a target company. In return, they generally receive significant management and governance rights (including board seats). The company is typically delisted and held privately for multiple years. During that period, the private equity firm works with management to reshape its strategy, restructure its organization, strengthen its corporate governance, and improve its overall performance. After this process is complete, the private equity firm then "unlocks the value" of the investment by selling the company in a public or private offering for a much higher price than its initial investment. It is in this way that private equity funds are said to "create value" for investors. Private equity firms will typically invest in ten to fifteen target companies over the life span of a fund, with no single investment amounting to more than 10 percent of the total commitment.

While generalizations are difficult and there is considerable evidence that the line between private equity and hedge funds is becoming blurred, hedge funds are generally said to pursue an investment strategy of finding value, rather than creating it. Hedge funds find value by identifying "pre-existing value inherent in market efficiencies and pricing anomalies."[1] For example, a hedge fund may buy the stock of a company that is the subject of a hostile takeover attempt while simultaneously selling the stock of the company making the hostile bid. In doing so, the hedge fund is pursuing a short-term investment strategy that exploits the law of averages: share prices in target companies generally go up, while share prices in bidders, particularly successful bidders, generally decline.

More generally, hedge funds often utilize sophisticated computer models to determine whether particular assets (like real estate, oil, individual stock, or currency) are over- or underpriced relative to other assets. The hedge fund will buy the underpriced asset and/or sell the overpriced asset until the traditional pricing relationship is restored. A famous example of the opportunistic nature of hedge funds is George Soros's speculative attack against the British pound in September 1992; Soros made $1 billion in a matter of days by betting that the British pound would fall against the dollar and other currencies.

Another generic difference between hedge funds and private equity funds is in the nature of their investors' capital contributions. Individuals and institutions who invest in private equity funds agree to commit their capital for a much longer length of time than do hedge fund investors. As a result, investors in a private equity fund expect the private equity firm to gradually commit the capital over time in longer-term bets. In contrast, investors in hedge funds expect that their money will be put to work almost immediately. Because hedge funds may need to accommodate investor withdrawal sooner than do private equity funds, hedge funds generally take shorter-term positions in more liquid assets.

Both hedge funds and private equity funds are usually organized as limited partnerships. The founder and manager of the fund is the general partner, and the investors are the limited partners or members. There is a steep minimum investment requirement—usually a minimum of anywhere from $1 million to $10 million. While the agreed-upon "lock up" period varies across funds, a first-time investor in a hedge fund should not expect to be able to withdraw money for at least one year, while the money put in private equity funds often cannot be withdrawn for ten or more years. The high investment minimums for both hedge funds and private equity funds mean that the small investor or "general investing public" is automatically excluded. Indeed, most funds are open exclusively to institutional investors and/or high net-worth individuals known as "accredited investors."

Hedge funds and private equity funds are subject to far less regulation than investments offered to the general public, such as mutual funds. For example, when most companies, including investment companies or mutual funds, sell securities to the public, they are required to register the securities being sold with the SEC and to make all sorts of disclosures about themselves and the securities. Hedge funds have avoided this regulation by not making public offerings of their securities and instead relying on private placements for their funds.

In addition, big public companies whose shares are publicly traded, widely held, or sold on organized stock markets or exchanges also are required to register under the Securities Exchange Act of 1934. Hedge funds have avoided this regulation by not issuing publicly traded shares and not listing their shares for trading anywhere.

Finally, hedge funds also have avoided regulation under the Investment Advisers Act of 1940. The SEC has long regulated "investment advisers," who are defined as those who are compensated for advising others about the value of securities or the advisability of investing. But investment advisors with fewer than fifteen clients who did not hold themselves out to the public as an investment advisor were exempt from such regulation. The SEC historically took the position that investment advisors such as hedge fund managers were advising the funds themselves. Under this interpretation of the rule, as long as a hedge fund manager had fewer than fifteen funds under his wing, he would be exempt from SEC regulation.

This lack of regulatory oversight is critical in allowing hedge funds to differentiate their strategy from mutual funds. Mutual funds must register with the SEC and are required by law to disclose their investment positions and financial condition. Hedge funds, by contrast, remain secretive about their positions and investment strategies, even to their own investors. While mutual funds cannot trade on margin or engage in short sales, hedge funds are subject to no such restrictions. In fact, trading on margin and engaging in short selling are both core elements in many hedge funds' investment strategies. Of course, the irony here is that lack of regulation of hedge funds and private equity funds has led to the creation of a two-tiered market. Wealthy investors are able to access promising investments through unregulated investment vehicles, leaving the public investors, whom the law is supposed to protect, with access only to less-promising investments.

In 2004, the SEC moved to regulate hedge funds for the first time by attempting to force them to register. To reach this end, the SEC created a new type of mutual fund, called a "private fund," which was defined as any investment company that (a) is exempt from registration under the Investment Company Act because it has fewer than one hundred investors or only qualified investors; (b) permits investors to redeem their interests within two years of investing; and (c) markets itself on the basis of the skills, ability or expertise of the investment advisor. These new private funds included virtually all hedge funds. Previously, hedge funds were thought to advise the funds themselves, not the actual investors in the fund. But the SEC ruled that these new private funds had to include in their count of fund clients all shareholders, limited partners, members, or beneficiaries of the fund. This meant that all of the investors in these private funds (hedge funds) counted toward the minimum number of fifteen that triggered registration under the Investment Advisers Act. The new rule reinterpreting the term "clients" moved the number of clients of most funds from one to some number greater than fifteen, which, in turn, gave the SEC authority to regulate.

In 2006, in *Goldstein v. Securities and Exchange Commission*,[2] the U.S. Court of Appeals for the District of Columbia Circuit struck down the SEC's attempt to regulate hedge funds. The court ruled that the SEC's new definition of "client" that counted investors in hedge funds as "clients" of the hedge fund's advisor was invalid. The court looked at the Investment Advisers Act and its legislative history and concluded that an advisor is somebody who provides advice directly, and that investors in hedge funds, who do not even know what the funds are investing in, may receive the benefits of advisors' expertise, but they are not clients because they do not receive investment advice from the advisors. Rather, the advisors give advice to the fund in which the investors have put their money. In other words, the fund manager does not tell or advise investors about anything, so those investors are not clients. Having bought into a fund, the investor "fades into the background; his role is completely passive."[3] Because the person controlling the fund (the investment advisor) is not an investment advisor to each individual investor but rather to the fund itself, then it must be the case, the court reasoned, that these investors cannot be clients of the person controlling the fund. Rather, the client is the fund itself.

HEDGE FUNDS, PRIVATE EQUITY FUNDS, AND CORPORATE GOVERNANCE

The big news in corporate governance over the past few years has been the convergence of the focus of hedge funds with that of private equity funds. These days, increasing numbers of hedge funds are coming to re-semble private equity funds in the extent to which they are focusing on corporate governance. Of particular interest is the fact that both hedge funds and private equity funds are becoming increasingly involved in the governance of publicly held corporations.

Indeed, hedge funds and private equity funds are serving precisely the same economic role as mergers and the market for corporate control did before regulations like the Williams Act along with the inexplicable judicial tolerance for the anti-takeover devices like the poison pill gradually reduced the role of the market for corporate control in the economy. Recently, however, the role of monitoring and disciplining management, originally identified as being played by the market for corporate control, has been played by hedge funds and private equity funds, in both small and large corporations.

In the middle of 2006, for example, Sebastian Holdings, a private equity firm that acquired 4 percent of Vivendi, opposed Vivendi's plan to acquire the French directory company PagesJaunes, arguing before the board of directors that "a project aimed at constructing a conglomeration of assets would be detrimental to the interests of all shareholders."[4] With Vivendi's market cap at half its peak, "the company has generated enough investor dissatisfaction to arouse the interest of private-equity investors who think they can turn the operation around."[5]

At about the same time, on the western side of the Atlantic, at rival Time Warner, hedge fund manager Carl Icahn accused Time Warner's chairman, Richard Parsons, of wasting corporate assets, failing to run the company in an entrepreneurially creative way, and not acting aggressively enough to "enhance values for shareholders."[6] After months of maneuvering, Icahn forced the media giant to agree to buy back $20 billion in stock, cut costs by an additional $500 million in 2007, and add two independent directors to the board.[7]

According to one commentator, "The hostile takeover has to some extent been replaced by substantial equity investments through hedge or other private equity funds."[8] Taking significant minority and majority positions in companies, private equity investors "use these positions to pressure managers to make changes, often involving sale of weak divisions and distribution of more cash to shareholders."[9] In doing so, "private equity has added a significant disciplinary force."[10] Hedge funds have also been declared the "new sheriffs of the boardroom," "offering shareholders the best hope for better returns."[11] Indeed, some view hedge funds as "the dominant economic and governance power" that "have the capacity to control issues of shareholder voting and corporate governance, and are exercising this power on an unprecedented scale."[12]

The importance of private equity and hedge funds in corporate governance forces one to question whether the intense focus on regulating these investment vehicles is a result of the fact that they are working so well in holding managers' noses to the grindstone. Just as many attribute over-regulation in the market for corporate control to a desire to protect incumbent management, so too does it seem plausible that the incumbent management will respond by seeking regulation to free themselves from the market discipline imposed upon them by activist hedge funds and private equity investors.

Hedge funds and private equity investors have become increasingly important to corporate governance now that it has become so difficult and costly for companies to go public. Hedge funds and private equity investors only benefit when the firms in which they invest prosper. Hedge funds and private equity investors are highly motivated to make sure that their "portfolio companies" (i.e., the companies in which they have invested) succeed. They do this by securing board seats, monitoring management, and, where appropriate, launching proxy fights to replace management. These are precisely the same sorts of disciplinary activities provided by a properly functioning market for corporate control.

In particular, if a company's share price is undervalued because of inefficient, corrupt, or lackadaisical management, hedge funds will view this as a classic arbitrage opportunity. They can take a long position in the company and use their share ownership to motivate managers, to retrain managers, and, where necessary, to replace managers. In other words, activist funds create a positive externality for all investors: the mere threat of intervention by activist investors creates strong incentives for managers of companies to act in the interest of shareholders in order to avoid losing autonomy and control, not to mention their jobs.

When the threat alone is insufficient to spur management to action, hedge funds will not hesitate to attempt to gain seats on their portfolio company's board in order to influence the company's decisions. A number of recent empirical studies suggest that hedge funds succeed in gaining board representation in approximately three out of every four attempts.[13] Moreover, these same studies suggest that "in nearly half of the instances when the hedge fund failed to gain a board seat, it still won some other concession from management."[14] For example, Appaloosa and Formation Capital failed to gain a board seat at Beverly Enterprises, but it got management to agree to reorient the company's strategy toward focusing on finding a buyer. Beverly Enterprises was sold months later for a 40 percent premium, generating a nice return for the hedge funds and general shareholders alike.[15]

Hedge funds and private equity firms also play a critical role in safeguarding shareholders' interests when it comes to mergers and acquisitions. It may seek to block a portfolio company's transaction outright if it feels that it is strategically inappropriate. One example, already mentioned earlier, is the efforts of Sebastian Holdings, a private equity firm, to block the acquisition by its portfolio company, Vivendi, of Pages Jaunes. In this case, Sebastian Holdings convinced shareholders that the acquisition was a bad strategy because it would reinforce perceptions of Vivendi as a holding company and therefore further accentuate the discount on Vivendi's shares.

Hedge funds and private equity firms also play a critical role in exposing when boards of directors and management irresponsibly sell a company or its assets at a discount relative to its fair market premium. Unlike many other ordinary investors, a hedge fund or private equity firm has more tools at its disposal to accurately calculate valuations. And it can use its own assets to issue a competing offer, if necessary, to demonstrate its resolve. Hedge funds led the charge in opposing Chiron's board's recommendation for a merger with Novartis. In the end, Novartis was forced to raise its bid to $49, nearly 25 percent more than its original offer and 10 percent more than the price to which management had agreed, before the deal was allowed to proceed. Institutional Shareholder Services has noted that "while detractors contend that hedge funds have short-term trading interests that diverge from the interests of companies and long-term investors, examples such as Chiron indicate that ordinary investors can benefit from the efforts of hedge funds."[16]

Moreover, hedge funds have a critical advantage over the market for corporate control in providing effective corporate governance because they can hold short positions. Thus, in cases like WorldCom or Enron, where share prices are overvalued as a result of faulty financial reporting and outright fraud, hedge funds can profit by bringing the situation to light after taking a short position. Hedge fund monitoring increases the probability that dishonest financial reporting will be detected, thereby reducing the chances that such dishonest reporting will occur.

Finally, hedge funds and private equity firms have played an important role in protecting shareholders' interests in deals in which the board seeks to disenfranchise shareholders. Relational Investors, a hedge fund, led a shareholders' revolt when the CEO of Sovereign Bancorp, one of its portfolio companies, tried to structure a deal in a way designed to circumvent the need for shareholder approval. Relational gained two seats on Sovereign Bancorp's board, and although this was only a minority position, within months, it managed to convince the board to oust the CEO.[17]

Mutual funds and other savvy investors generally will "vote with their feet" either by declining to invest in poorly performing companies in the first place, or by selling their shares in the poorly performing companies they already own. By contrast, rather than seeing bad performance as something to avoid, hedge funds and, to some extent, private equity funds, see investment opportunities.

A concrete example of a market opportunity pursued by both private equity and hedge funds is the market for distressed debt. Distressed debt is the debt of companies that have either already filed for bankruptcy or are likely to do so in the near future. Private equity firms and hedge funds sometimes pursue a strategy of buying the debt of distressed companies, particularly when they can purchase the debt at a fraction of the principal amount due upon maturity; this is often the case when the bond markets lose confidence in a company following a default or major downgrade in credit rating to below investment grade (such companies are colloquially known as "fallen angels").

Once a hedge fund or a private equity firm becomes the major creditor of the distressed company, if the company is forced into bankruptcy reorganization, it will be in control of the company's governance. If the company is liquidated, the firms holding the distressed debt will be in line for repayment of their investment ahead of most other investors, including the shareholders. During the course of the reorganization in bankruptcy of a distressed company, the hedge funds or private equity firms in charge frequently will forgive at least part of the debt that is owed them in exchange for equity in the emerging, reorganized company.

A critical difference between the sort of investment typically made by venture capitalists in start-up companies and the investments in distressed companies made by private equity firms and hedge funds is the investors' relationships with management. Hedge funds and private equity investors, unlike venture capitalists, are not giving management a "vote of confidence" by investing in them. Rather, the relationship between investors in distressed debt and the management of the issuer is tense and often hostile, particularly since the hedge fund managers and private equity investors taking positions in distressed debt often view incumbent management as being a major cause of the company's troubles. These investors will put pressure on management to shape up the company's performance, or otherwise seek to replace them.

In other words, private equity investors and hedge funds play a critical role in corporate governance. They fill the governance gap created by the passive credit-rating agencies, the moribund market for corporate control, the rational ignorance in shareholder voting, and the captured directors and self-interested management catalogued in the previous chapters. Because their compensation is inexorably tied to performance, private equity investors and hedge funds often use a very hands-on approach to ensuring that their portfolio companies perform as well as possible. Hedge funds and private equity investors are increasingly taking on the role of "active investors who contribute complementary skills to the management teams and companies they sponsor. The best private equity (and hedge fund) investors are *strategic partners* with management in the value-creation process."[18] Consistent with their increased role in corporate governance, both private equity investors and hedge funds are using longer-term time horizons when they plan their investments. In particular, the typical time frame for a private equity investor is five years, although hedge funds often will attempt to shake up the companies in which they invest even more quickly than that.

The reputation of private equity investors and hedge funds depends critically on their ability to evaluate the financial condition of potential portfolio companies before they invest in them and to spot weak or unscrupulous management. From the perspective of the manager of a hedge fund or a private equity fund, a corporate governance scandal will hurt not only the performance of the managers' portfolio but also the credibility of any fund that has invested in the company hit by scandal. This, in turn, will reduce the ability of that fund to attract investors in the future. The reputational effect of bad bets exacerbates the drag that such bad bets have on the performance of the fund and provides an even greater incentive for fund managers to play a strong role in monitoring the management of their investments.[19] A hedge fund or a private equity fund's failure to ensure strong corporate governance in a portfolio is, in other words, seen by the potential investors in the fund as an inability to manage their investments properly. This creates strong incentives for hedge funds and private equity funds to make sure that their portfolio companies are well governed.

The influence of hedge funds and private equity on U.S. corporate governance extends to larger publicly held companies as well as to smaller closely held companies. Small closely held companies need the management capabilities and the capital that hedge funds and private equity firms can supply. In contrast, large publicly held companies may not need (or think they need) either the management expertise or the capital that a hedge fund or a private equity investor can provide. Even management of these companies, however, is heavily influenced by private equity and hedge funds these days, particularly if they want to remain *independent*. Board rooms are buzzing with issues about how to deal with "activist" hedge funds and private equity firms, whose behavior is far different from that of traditional institutional investors such as insurance companies, mutual funds, pension funds, and individuals.

The activism of hedge funds can take several forms, including merely providing advice, putting private (or public) pressure on portfolio companies to change their strategy for growth and profitability, running a proxy contest to gain seats on the boards of directors of portfolio companies, and bringing lawsuits against managers and directors. A classic example of hedge fund corporate governance activism can be found in a famous letter from the hedge fund Third Point LLC to Irik Sevin, the CEO of one of its portfolio companies, the heating oil distributor Star Gas. The letter wondered, "How is it possible that you selected your elderly 78-year old mom to serve on the Company's Board of Directors, and as a full time employee?" Third Point advised Sevin that "[i]t is time for you to step down from your role as CEO and director so that you can do what you do best: retreat to your waterfront mansion in the Hamptons where you can play tennis and hobnob with your fellow socialites. . . . We wonder under what theory of corporate governance does one's mom sit on a Company board. Should you be found derelict in the performance of your executive's duties, as we believe is the case, we do not believe your mom is the right person to fire you from your job." Sevin resigned within a month of receiving this letter.[20]

The point here is that the key role being played by hedge funds and private equity funds in corporate governance affects *all* companies in a very profound way. Even companies that want to *avoid* being the target of an activist fund can only do this by improving corporate governance extensively so that there are no longer any arbitrage possibilities that allow fund managers to take a position in the target company and then start agitating for reform.

Of course, companies that either are, or are about to be, the target of an activist hedge fund investor will feel that they are under attack in much the same way as they would be if they were the subject of a hostile takeover. Martin Lipton, the lawyer who invented the poison pill anti-takeover device, recently advised his firm's clients, "The current high level of hedge fund activism warrants the same kind of preparation as for a hostile takeover bid. In fact, some of the attacks (by hedge funds) are designed to facilitate a takeover or to force a sale of the target. . . . Failure to prepare reduces a target's ability to control its own destiny."[21] Policy views of activist hedge fund investing generally track policy views on the value of a robust market for corporate control. Analysts and policymakers who favor a strong market for corporate control laud the salutary effects of hedge funds, private equity investors, and other activists. Those who question the value of the market for control also have doubts about the value of hedge fund investing.

As already noted, many activist private equity firms and hedge funds play a major role in selecting board members. Because the board members identified and selected by these outside directors are nominated by outside investors, they not only bring a fresh perspective to the board room, but, even more significant, they are not as prone to capture by management as directors who join the board via the traditional nominating process. They do not have their own reputations invested in the prior decisions of the board, and they have not endorsed the quality of management. Board members selected by hedge funds or private equity investors are chosen for their independence, for their expertise in corporate governance, and "for their industry or functional expertise . . . this means that they aren't captives to management's agenda."[22]

Because of the large stakes that hedge funds and private equity investors have in their portfolio companies, they typically engage in far more extensive monitoring than do either typical directors or typical institutional investors. Hedge funds and private equity investors are particularly effective in monitoring management because they do not restrict their interaction with management to regularly scheduled board meetings. Many become heavily involved in both strategic planning as well as in the tactical day-to-day operations of the company: "In monitoring investments, private equity investors work with CEOs, effectively serving various capacities that range from executive coach to consultant to investment banker, providing ongoing advice [and] analysis."[23] Perhaps the most salient difference between activist hedge funds and private equity investors on the one hand versus traditional investors on the other is that hedge funds and private equity firms are intensely interested in generating cash and in "cleaning up" their companies in order to reach the ultimate goal of selling the company or completing an initial public offering of securities. Private equity and hedge fund investors are less interested than management in empire building, making defensive acquisitions, or in adding an arsenal of defensive mechanisms against takeovers to a firm's corporate governance structure.

Distributing money to shareholders in the form of dividend payments or share repurchases often is resisted by managers, since it is seen as coming at a cost to managers' power. Paying shareholders reduces the amount of capital under management's control and triggers increased monitoring when they must obtain new outside capital.[24] Managers have incentive to expand the business—even when a smaller size may be of more benefit to shareholders—because it both increases the resources under their control and, since compensation is typically correlated with sales growth, is likely to line their own pockets.[25] Furthermore, a larger business increases the costs of a takeover, thereby better protecting the positions of incumbent managers and directors. Active participation by private equity investors and hedge funds can eliminate much of this self-interested behavior.

CASE STUDY: SHAMROCK HOLDINGS AND POLAROID CORPORATION

During the halcyon days of leveraged buyouts and hostile takeovers in the late 1980s, private equity fund Shamrock Holdings acquired around 5 percent of the outstanding shares of Polaroid Corporation. Polaroid had enjoyed rapid growth for twenty-five years following their introduction of the first instant camera in 1948. But by the 1980s, the company's growth and profitability had gone into a steep decline.[26] Much of the company's cash was being allocated to research and development (R&D), which cut into Polaroid's short-term profits and provided the foundation for long-term growth only to the extent that the capital markets think that such R&D investments can eventually be turned into commercially successful products. Polaroid also was carrying relatively little debt, and many equity investors thought that management was not capitalizing on the company's ability to borrow.

Polaroid's employees' ownership made the company's corporate governance situation even more problematic. Polaroid had been awarding employees large amounts of company stock since the early 1970s through an Employee Stock Ownership Plan (ESOP), which is a retirement plan designed to give employees "a stake in the company for which they work."[27] Polaroid's ESOP, which was friendly to incumbent management, used borrowed funds to acquire its own shares. These shares, which are called "unallocated" shares, are held separately and "allocated" to the ESOP, as payment for the shares is made by the corporation.

As is often the case with an ESOP, the employee-owned stock held in the Polaroid ESOP served as an important managerial entrenchment device. Employees are very risk-averse because they have undiversified human capital investments in the company in which they work. For this reason, employees generally vote with management, as they value the job security that comes from keeping the company independent far more than they value any potential premium that they might earn in a tender offer. And, of course, corporate strategies such as restructurings that lead to employee layoffs may be favored by shareholders generally but staunchly opposed by employees.[28] Polaroid management was well aware of this fact, and as it became clear that the company was a takeover candidate, Polaroid placed blocks of stock in the hands of employees and other "strategic" shareholders friendly to management.[29]

As Shamrock became increasingly concerned about its investment in Polaroid, and the apparently lackadaisical attitude of Polaroid management, rumors began to circulate that Shamrock would launch a hostile takeover for the Cambridge, Massachusetts, camera company. A key issue would be who would vote the unallocated shares in the Polaroid ESOP (it was clear that the allocated shares would be voted by the employees). Consistent with the theory that the ESOP was actually a defensive device rather than a mechanism for facilitating some vague notion of "worker participation," Polaroid and its anti-takeover lawyers argued that the unallocated shares should be subject to what is known as the rule of "mirror voting"—in which the unallocated shares would be voted in exactly the same way as the employees voted the shares already allocated to the ESOP. Shamrock sued to block the adoption of the Polaroid ESOP and its mirrored voting arrangement, but the Delaware courts sided with management and approved the ESOP. The ruling opened the door for the adoption of similar defensive devices by a large number of public companies.

The Delaware courts approved Polaroid's ESOP, despite the fact that management allowed the ESOP to buy shares on the cheap, with the price set at the average price before there was any indication that Shamrock was interested in a takeover. The court permitted this bargain price to be paid for the shares, despite the fact that Polaroid management knew that the company's shares were going to go up as a result of the impending takeover bid from Shamrock, and that the purchase was therefore dilutive.[30]

Shamrock was understandably concerned about its languishing investment in Polaroid, and believed that it could improve shareholder value by making some changes in the way the company operated. Toward this end, Shamrock attempted to negotiate with management to buy the company, but was unsuccessful at negotiating a friendly sale because management wanted to remain independent. Significantly, despite the negative court ruling, Shamrock continued to agitate for change.

Polaroid was only able to fend off its activist investor by improving shareholder value. The company made an $800 million self-tender offer and a $325 million post-tender buyback of shares on the market. The management also set about cutting costs and restructuring the company.[31] R&D was reorganized to focus its emphasis more toward specifically targeted areas of potential high profitability. The company also allocated resources toward entering the lucrative worldwide market for 35mm conventional film.[32]

This example is instructive for two reasons. First, it shows how effective defensive tactics by incumbent management can be in thwarting hostile takeover attempts. This, in turn, is because courts are overly receptive to pro-management arguments and are unwilling to facilitate the market for corporate control by enacting judicial rules that create a level playing field between bidders and targets.

Second, and more important, however, it shows that activist investors can lose the battle to remain independent, but still win the more important war of improving shareholder value and improving the work ethic of both management and the board of directors. Polaroid management responded to a disappointed activist investor by litigating to make a hostile takeover more difficult, and winning, but by then making decisive moves to improve shareholder value. The core question is why, having won the legal battle to block the operation of the market for corporate control, management did not just settle back into its old ways of doing business and ignore its activist shareholders. There are several reasons for this, and they are the keys to understanding how hedge funds and private equity investors are so important in corporate governance.

First, unlike typical outside bidders in a pure corporate control transaction, private equity investors and hedge funds have made a large investment in the target company, and they are not going to go away if they lose a takeover battle or a legal skirmish. They stay around, confront management, and continue to press their proposed solutions to the companies' problems. Management frequently will make changes in order to avoid deeper and more prolonged confrontations with investors, as well as the risk of a renewed hostile takeover bid.

Second, activist investors often are publicity seekers. Management and, even more important, boards of directors inevitably will want to avoid the negative publicity and concomitant reputational stigma that comes with being branded as a management stooge. Such a reputation can make it difficult to continue to serve on public company boards and make other companies that the directors are affiliated with subject to possible attack. Another related point is that when hedge funds or private equity funds take stakes in a private or public company (such investments in public companies are colloquially known as PIPES, for Private Investment in Public Equity Securities), they typically install themselves or independently minded people who share their investment philosophies on the board of directors of the company. These investors have close and frequent contact with management and, over time, they develop deep knowledge about the company and its problems, as well as about its customers, competitors, workforce, suppliers, and so forth. It appears that there is more conflict and give-and-take in companies with large strategic investors.[33] As one private equity investor cogently observed, "[T]he private equity model is premised on the idea that everyone needs a boss, including the CEOs of public companies." As such, when private equity firms make capital investments, the partners in the private equity firm "effectively become the bosses of the CEO. We have enough at stake, and are sufficiently involved in and knowledgeable about the business, to ask hard questions and to have awkward and difficult discussions when things aren't going well."[34]

CASE STUDY: CARL ICAHN V. TIME WARNER

While Shamrock Holdings was battling Polaroid in the 1980s, Carl Icahn was amassing a multibillion-dollar fortune during the junk bond era. Critics thought, unfairly, that Icahn was a shortsighted corporate raider who was harming his fellow investors by making "bear raids" on public companies; such raids allowed Icahn to make a quick profit from selling his own shares to management and forcing them to pay greenmail in order to be relieved of his negative influence on the companies in which he invested.

Carl Icahn now has his own hedge fund, and nobody can reasonably claim that he is not putting his own money at risk. Icahn invests significant amounts of his own private wealth into his endeavors. Icahn now operates as a one-man private equity fund. He takes significant long-term investments in companies with the purpose of adding value for shareholders by decreasing managerial slack, cutting costs, and forcing companies in his portfolio to focus their energies on their core strategies.

Icahn's most ambitious corporate governance initiative was his 2006 battle to improve corporate governance and shareholder performance at the media giant Time Warner. Already this battle has come to be viewed as a referendum on the efficacy of private equity investors and hedge funds in corporate governance.

Some scholars, most notably Stephen Bainbridge of UCLA, argue unpersuasively that Carl Icahn's failure to gain control of Time Warner shows that hedge fund activism and private equity investor activism "is (a) a bad idea and (b) unlikely to be the next silver bullet of corporate governance in agency costs."[35] Others, such as Larry Ribstein of the University of Illinois, take a different but equally traditional view, asserting that while "we still need the board to manage the big corporation, we also need board accountability, and private equity [and hedge funds are] one way to provide it."

Both of these perspectives are wrong. Bainbridge is wrong because his definition of success is too narrow. While Icahn did not succeed in gaining control of Time Warner, he did succeed in many important ways. He forced the company to make important changes in its business strategies. He got the company to cut costs. And, most important, he got management and the board of directors to focus on the task of maximizing wealth for shareholders and paying less attention to other, more congenial corporate constituencies, such as top management.

More broadly, hedge funds and private equity firms are not likely, as Bainbridge predicts, to "fizzle out the way hostile takeovers and, to a lesser extent, institutional investor activism have"[36] for several reasons. Primarily, as was noted in chapter 8, hostile takeovers were quite effective until the Williams Act and other statutes came along that made such takeovers far more expensive and therefore far less common. Because of the powerful pressure exerted by special interest groups such as the Business Roundtable (on behalf of management) and the organized labor unions (on behalf of local, unionized workers), the balance of power in the market for corporate control has shifted dramatically away from bidders and toward incumbent managers and entrenched boards.

Hedge funds and private equity firms differ dramatically from other equity investors such as mutual funds because their portfolios are far more concentrated and less diversified than mutual funds. This means that, unlike mutual funds, when private equity investors are unhappy with a particular investment in their portfolio, they do not have the luxury of selling their modest block and exiting. Their blocks are not modest, and therefore selling for hedge funds and private equity firms is far more costly than it is for other more traditional investors, such as mutual funds. Moreover, because hedge funds and private equity funds are often intensely involved with managers and board members in strategic planning and in evaluating performance, the insider trading laws prohibit them from trading actively the way traditional outside equity investors such as mutual funds can do. This, in turn, forces hedge funds to find some alternative to selling their shares as a means of dealing with disappointing investments and other examples of organizational decline. As Albert Hirschman famously observed, this alternative is voice, which hedge funds and private equity funds have proved can be very effective.

Moreover, as Hirschman pointed out, both exit (withdrawing from a situation in which one is involved by using an exit strategy such as selling shares) and voice (attempting to repair or improve a situation in which one is involved by constructive criticism and proposals for change) represent lack of confidence in a business. Mutual funds and other passive institutional investors use exit. Hedge funds and private equity firms use voice. Hirschman observed that voice is more informative than exit, because it requires the party using its voice to articulate the reasons for making criticisms and proposing change. In contrast, exit by itself provides only a warning sign of decline.

One of Hirschman's basic insights is that because it is cheaper to utilize the exit option than to utilize the voice option, all else equal, it is more likely that the exit option will be pursued as a strategy within an organization rather than the voice option. For hedge funds and private equity firms, exit is far more costly than for other types of investors.[37]

On the other hand, when the concept of loyalty is introduced into the exit and voice mix, it will affect the cost-benefit analysis of whether to use exit or voice. Where there is loyalty to the organization (as evidenced by strong personal affiliations between managers and the firm or between directors and management), the incidence of exit may be lower, particularly because exit options (i.e., the lack of alternative CEO or director positions) and the financial sacrifices involved are likely to be highly unappealing.

This, too, provides an explanation for the success of hedge funds as opposed to directors or to other classes of institutional investors. While directors and managers have investments in their firms, often they cannot exit because their relationship with the firm has clouded their judgment and subjected them to "capture" by the extant dominant corporate strategy and vision. In contrast, hedge funds and private equity funds, unlike, say, the members of a company's board of directors, are not subject to capture because they retain a healthy social distance from the firms in which they invest, despite their close involvement with them as investors.

Ribstein's conclusion that while "we still need the board to manage the big corporation, we also need board accountability, and private equity [and hedge funds are] one way to provide it" is wrong because it mischaracterizes the way that private equity firms and hedge funds function to improve corporate performance. It is wrong to suggest, as Ribstein does, that boards actually "manage the big corporation." In fact, it is management, not directors, who actually manage large corporations. Directors play a supporting role that can be extremely useful and important. At this point in the history of American corporate governance, however, we have a rather schizophrenic view of the role of directors. On the one hand, they are supposed to provide strategic direction and support for management, while on the other hand they are supposed to monitor management and make it responsive to the interests of shareholders, which is to maximize the value of the firm. This is too much rationally to hope for from any group. We expect hedge funds and private equity investors simply to safeguard their investments in companies they have selected for inclusion into their portfolios. This is not too much to expect, particularly in light of how richly success in this endeavor is rewarded by the markets.

For hedge funds and private equity firms, incumbent directors of public companies they view as poorly run (such as Time Warner), are as much, if not more, a part of the problem as incumbent management. This forces us to conceptualize the role of corporate boards of directors. We must *choose* whether we want directors to serve as monitors of management or as strategic counselors to management. As monitors, the directors are almost certain to fail. If they act as strategic counselors for management, a role in which they are likely to succeed, there will remain a big gap in the organization of corporate governance because the separation of managerial control and share ownership still exists. Somebody has to monitor both boards and management. It is this job that is done so well by outside private equity firms and hedge funds.

In 2000, the media giant Time Warner and the Internet mass marketer America Online (AOL) completed a merger that is generally acknowledged to have been a disaster. Most argue that the merger was simply a very bad idea from the beginning. Others contend that management did a terrible job of bringing the two companies together in an efficient, coherent way. Indeed, many observers contend that there really never was a true combination of the two companies at all. AOL was kept apart and viewed as simultaneously weak and threatening to the incumbent management team at Time Warner that was, ostensibly, the target of the acquisition. After the merger, corporate governance nightmare scenarios abounded. The stock languished. AOL and Time Warner continued to compete for cable television and broadband Internet subscribers.

In 2004, the company acknowledged its problems and vowed to try to achieve economies of scale and synergies by having the Time Warner units and the AOL unit work better with one another. Nevertheless, the word "disaster" is the term most used to describe this costly and ineffective merger (used over 500,000 times on Google to describe the transaction). Some estimate that the botched merger cost shareholders an astonishing $40 billion.

Sensing a classic arbitrage opportunity in which profits—and value for all Time Warner shareholders—could be created by buying stock and advocating for constructive change, Carl Icahn began buying shares in the company in 2005. Icahn calculated the breakup value of Time Warner to be in the range of $23.30 to $26.57 per share, significantly higher than the stock price at the time his acquisition program began. In Icahn's view, management of Time Warner had never operated the company in the shareholders' best interests. Management spent profligately and engaged in acquisitions for the sake of empire building rather than for the sake of creating shareholder value.[38]

As discussed above, as a result of the AOL and Time Warner merger in 2000, the combined companies had lost 70 percent of their value; and their combined market capitalization of the enterprise was down to a scant $84 billion. Icahn began aggressively accumulating shares, with his investment in Time Warner ultimately reaching a massive $2 billion. This translated into ownership of 120 million shares. But because of Time Warner's large market capitalization, Icahn's prodigious investment amounted to only a 2.6 percent stake of the business. Time Warner's sheer size essentially insulated it from the risk of a hostile takeover.

The company's share price traded in the $17 to $18 range prior to Icahn's investment in the company, down from a high of $94 per share in late 1999. Pointing to this dismal share price performance, particularly compared with market indices and comparable media companies, Icahn, along with other activist investors, commissioned a study of Time Warner by the investment banking firm Lazard Freres.

Icahn called on Time Warner to initiate immediate share repurchases totaling about $20 billion. He also suggested that Time Warner break itself up into four separate companies: Time Warner Cable; the AOL Internet business; the Time, Inc. publishing business; and the content business consisting of the Warner Bros. studios and cable channels such as HBO and CNN—with the ultimate goal of moving the value of the stock to $27 per share. He also actively campaigned to replace the incumbent CEO, Richard Parsons, under whose leadership the company had languished. In the meantime, Icahn urged Parsons to act in the best interest of the shareholders by also buying back more stock and cutting costs.

The nature of Icahn's efforts are well characterized by the letter that Icahn, along with a number of allied hedge funds and private equity firms, sent to shareholders seeking support for their various proposed reforms at Time Warner. The content of the letter provides a vivid illustration of precisely the sort of pressure that activist hedge funds and private equity investors can exert on the managers and directors of the firms they target.

Dear Time Warner Shareholder:

In life and in business, there are two cardinal sins. The first is to act precipitously without thought, and the second is to not act at all. Unfortunately, the Board of Directors and top management of Time Warner already committed the first sin by merging with AOL, and we believe they are currently in the process of committing the second; now is not a time to move slowly and suffer the paralysis of inaction, yet we fear based on their recent statements that the current leadership of Time Warner does not recognize the need to take bold action for shareholders. The Time Warner PR machine would like you to believe that Mr. Parsons and the Time Warner Board have been performing well and taking the necessary steps to deliver value for shareholders, and it appears that many in the press have accepted this storyline. But after taking a closer look at the years following the merger with AOL, it is clear that there have been a series of significant missteps by the Board and Time Warner's senior management which have resulted in the further destruction of value. Unless this legacy of poor decision-making is fully recognized and the Board is held accountable, the dismal record of mistakes and inaction will continue to the detriment of shareholders. Let us examine the record.

The AOL Disaster

Understandably, the Board and top management at Time Warner wish to put their role in the disastrous merger of AOL and Time Warner behind them. The AOL disaster resulted in an incredible over $87 billion of goodwill write-downs over a two year period (greater than the current equity market capitalization of today's Time Warner) and the loss of over 75% of the Company's market value in two years. However, when we match the fingerprints on the deal with those of the current directors, it becomes clear that the direction of the Company is still largely in the hands of those who played key roles in the merger. Of the eleven pre-merger Time Warner directors who approved the deal, seven still sit on the Board. Five other current directors came from the pre-merger AOL and also voted for the merger, bringing the *total number of supporters of the merger to twelve out of fifteen on the current Board. Richard Parsons, the President of Time Warner at the time and a key negotiator of the merger, was afterwards promoted to CEO and later Chairman as well.*

The lingering presence of these individuals forces us to ask, why are a majority of the same directors who signed off on the disastrous AOL merger still steering the corporate ship? We also note that we are not the first to raise questions about the qualifications of the current members of the Board. In 2003, Institutional Shareholder Services recommended that shareholders withhold support for two current directors (Miles Gilburne and James Barksdale) saying they were too closely tied to the Company. Also in 2003, CalPERS (the nation's largest pension fund) withheld its votes for two of the current directors citing questions about their independence.

Describing the corporate culture at Time Warner in 2003 following the resignation of Ted Turner (who founded CNN) and Warren Lieberfarb (who has been credited with helping to invent the DVD market) from the Company's management, Sanford C. Bernstein's Tom Wolzien said, "These twin departures signify a fundamental shift to the bland by a company that now has no place for genius or contrary points of view." We believe that in the time following the merger the Board compounded their already colossal mistake by failing to hold management accountable to more quickly address the subscriber deterioration at AOL. Company management clearly had an early belief in broadband evidenced by the billions spent on Time Warner Cable, yet failed to effectively address the migration of AOL dial-up subscribers to broadband access providers (punctuating the question of why they merged with an approximately $150 billion narrowband business). While AOL was losing dial-up subscribers (approximately 9 million since 2001), Time Warner Cable promoted its own broadband service, Road Runner, yet never effectively promoted AOL on or integrated AOL with this platform. Additionally, during this time the Company allowed AOL to be marginalized on the internet while portals such as Yahoo! and search pioneers like Google captured larger online market share and currently have equity market values of greater than $45 and $85 billion, respectively. We believe that had the Board forced management to move more quickly, they could have not only demonstrated a commitment to the driving principle behind the merger (synergies between AOL and the Time Warner businesses), but perhaps could have preserved at least some of the shareholder value destroyed by the merger. Recently top management has begun highlighting AOL as a valuable asset and growth opportunity—where have they been since 2000? To the extent that opportunities are now available to enhance value at AOL, which we believe there are, we implore management and the Board to move more decisively than they have in the past.

*Fire Sale Prices Have Stripped Value from the Shareholders
and Created Windfalls for Others*
   Time Warner management and the Board have sold valuable assets at prices
that were at a substantial discount to their underlying value, thereby giving a
windfall to buyers to the detriment of their own shareholders.

- *Sale of Warner Music*—We believe that the sale of the Warner Music
  Group ("Warner Music") last year to a consortium of private equity buyers for $2.6 billion demonstrated both a lack of business judgment by the
  Board and Mr. Parsons and an inability to operate businesses efficiently.
  First, we believe the Company received a trough valuation and could not
  have chosen a worse time to sell this business given the state of the music
  industry at the time. In the ultimate embarrassment to Time Warner, Warner Music's current post-IPO enterprise value of over $4.7 billion, is an
  81% increase over the sale price (before even taking into account that the
  buyer group had already recouped the equity portion of their investment
  through pre-IPO dividends). Second, the fact that Warner Music had
  greater value to a group of financial investors than to the world's largest
  media company is difficult to conceive, yet the private equity group was
  able to find $250 million in cost savings in just one year of ownership,
  more than the trailing twelve month EBITDA of the business when Time
  Warner owned the company.

Rather than unloading this valuable asset, we believe that the Board should
have challenged management regarding potential cost savings and forced
management to turn this asset around. We believe Time Warner clearly
would have created far more value and lessened the debt burden on the Company had it focused more on the operations of Warner Music than on unloading it for what proved to be a cut-rate price.

- *Sale of Comedy Central*—The Board supported management's decision
  to sell the Company's 50% interest in Comedy Central to Viacom in 2003
  for $1.225 billion. Less than two years later, Morgan Stanley estimates
  the value of Comedy Central at greater than $4.5 billion(1), implying a
  valuation of $2.25 billion for Time Warner's stake, 83% more than it
  was sold for. Similar to the Warner Music sale, we believe the Company's
  management sold Comedy Central in an effort to appear proactive but
  achieved only a loss of value for shareholders. These asset sales were con-
  summated to achieve the goal of debt reduction. This goal, which in hindsight proved unnecessary (since Time Warner is currently underleveraged
  and has sufficient cash flow to support a much higher debt load), caused
  Time Warner management to sell valuable assets at distressed prices and
  thereby destroy shareholder value. We believe that if the Board had provided the appropriate level of oversight, Time Warner management might
  have focused more on delivering value through the operations of the businesses or on receiving full value for the assets.

Failure to Acquire MGM

The Company cited "fiscal discipline" when it publicly withdrew from the bidding for MGM last year. However, we believe that Time Warner management's habitual excess deliberation and inability to act decisively on behalf of shareholders were actually behind the Company's failure to win this important strategic acquisition. According to the MGM proxy statement and news reports, Time Warner had the opportunity to complete the deal in early August without competition from the Sony group and was the favored bidder of Kirk Kerkorian, MGM's controlling shareholder at the time. Yet Time Warner let three weeks slip away which ultimately paved the way for a group led by Sony Corporation to win the deal. Then ten days later it made a last ditch effort to increase its bid only 90 minutes prior to the MGM Board vote, an attempt which was ultimately unsuccessful because Time Warner could not negotiate a deal in time. As a result of the mismanagement of this process, MGM's extensive content library is today controlled by a major studio competitor (Sony) and a major cable competitor (Comcast). As a writer for the New York Times put it afterwards, "Time Warner's last-minute effort raises some awkward questions about the earlier comments of Mr. Parsons about withdrawing from the deal. If buying MGM was too expensive, as he had said, how would he justify making an even higher offer later?"

Bloated Cost Structure

We believe Time Warner has allowed costs to become bloated due to a lack of oversight by the Board and senior management. Nowhere is this more evident than by looking at the Company's landmark headquarters in New York, which cost the Company $800 million to construct and offers such lavish features as a grand employee cafeteria with two story windows overlooking Central Park. We question how such an extravagant building, which houses only a small fraction of Time Warner's employees, enhances shareholder value (and cannot help but wonder where the shareholders get to eat lunch). Given this extravagance and the failure to cut costs at businesses like Warner Music described above, we intend to hire, in the next few weeks, an industry consultant to analyze and compare Time Warner's costs to its peers on a number of different levels to determine what other excess fat may lie in the Company's cost structure, including, but not limited to, perquisites afforded to the Board and top management.

Conclusion

We have previously made certain proposals in an eleven page position paper which we believe, if followed, will meaningfully enhance shareholder value. First and foremost, we believe that the greatest investment the Board can make at this time is to initiate a $20 billion share buyback. The

Board should not lose this opportunity to benefit all shareholders by taking decisive action. We also believe that all of Time Warner Cable should be spun out to give shareholders a choice of owning the world's best collection of content assets, a well run and growing cable franchise or some combination of both. Furthermore, although we are generally supportive of the recent acquisition of the assets of Adelphia, we are baffled by the logic of taking Time Warner Cable public through the issuance of 16% of the shares to former Adelphia distressed debt investors, an example we believe of poor execution by management and a lack of adequate oversight by the Board. To follow the current course of a $5 billion buyback and the public distribution of only 16% of Time Warner Cable would be akin to inaction, which is inexcusable at this juncture, and would be yet another example of the Board's inability to perform.

But whether or not you agree with our proposals, we believe the simple truth is that Time Warner is a company sorely in need of new shareholder representation on the Board. We believe that Time Warner owns the most valuable collection of media properties in the industry and in fact the plan we have proposed is predicated upon the ultimate recognition of this value by the market. However, we think that there is a clear distinction to be made between the value of these assets and the creative skill of the day-to-day operators on the one hand and the demonstrable failure of top management and the Board to translate this value into returns for shareholders on the other.

Mr. Parsons has admitted that Time Warner's shares are undervalued and has made statements asserting that he intends to do something about it, but we believe that without the necessary conviction at the Board level no meaningful action will be taken. As we have described above, we believe the current Board has demonstrated to date an inability to preserve or create shareholder value. At the very least, bringing a new voice for shareholders to the Board will serve to remind the Board and management of their promises and priorities. It will also make the Board aware that it is accountable to the shareholders and will send a clear message that shareholders' patience is running out.

The incumbent members of the Board and top management may argue that the presence of new directors would be disruptive or is unnecessary. We believe however, the presence of new independent directors who will aggressively question excessive costs and management and director perquisites and work with management to deliver value for shareholders is exactly the type of disruption that Time Warner needs. With respect to whether a new voice for shareholders on the Board is necessary, we believe a review of the Company's stock price performance and the record described above should effectively end any argument that the Board is doing an adequate job and should be left to its own continued devices. Given the fact that, despite its exceptional assets and a generally favorable operating environment, the Company's stock price has underperformed significantly since 2002, we believe the time for steps to make the Board and management more accountable are long overdue. Mr. Parsons and the Board have made promises to address the stagnating stock price, but without new shareholder representation on the Board, we believe these promises, like so many others, will not be kept.

Shareholder expectations for the boards and senior managements of publicly held companies have changed dramatically in recent years. Shareholders across the globe have increasingly begun to realize that many of our managements and boards have failed to aggressively pursue value for shareholders and are holding them accountable. Additionally they have become outraged at the perquisites and inflated pay that "rubber stamp" boards award themselves and top management in situations where share prices have languished. We believe this is a healthy and necessary phenomenon and that there should be no sacred cows in the pursuit of shareholder value. In the coming months we will be continuing to speak out about our belief in the need for a new voice for shareholders on the Board of Time Warner. We already know that many of you agree and look forward to communicating with you in the future.[39]

Although Time Warner did not accede to all of Icahn's demands, the board ultimately acceded to the pressure Icahn exerted, resulting in considerable changes in Time Warner's business and strategic focus. Gone was the sense of complacency and lack of focus that had characterized the company for decades. Management finally began acting as though it is accountable to its shareholders. The company increased its planned share repurchase from $12.5 billion to $20 billion. It agreed to cut costs by $500 million in 2006 and another $500 million in 2007. While the company did not split into four, it did sell its book publishing division for $537.5 million and consented that a "different capital and corporate structure may be appropriate for Time Warner Cable."[40] And although Parsons remained the CEO, Icahn succeeded in getting Time Warner to increase the board's independence by naming two new independent directors.[41] Time Warner shares also increased in value by $2 per share, or 12 percent on the basis of his efforts, benefiting Icahn as well as all other Time Warner shareholders.

Although this was not a total victory, Icahn used his significant minority position to add value for all shareholders by altering the corporate governance of one of the world's largest companies, achieving his "long-stated goal of creating value for all shareholders" and proving once again that "hedge fund and private equity shareholder activism can be extremely effective."[42]

HEDGE FUNDS AND PRIVATE EQUITY: THE DOWNSIDE

The above discussion has focused on the important positive things that hedge funds can offer to investors. My basic points are that hedge funds and private equity are extremely powerful forces for better corporate governance. Hedge funds and private equity investors can literally solve the basic corporate governance problems associated with the separation of share ownership and management control in corporations, particularly public corporations.

Yet despite their seemingly obvious virtues, hardly a week goes by without some new argument being circulated among regulators about the supposed public policy problems associated with hedge funds and, to a lesser extent, their close counterparts, private equity firms. Generally speaking, the arguments for regulation fall into two categories. The first argument has already been dealt with—namely that hedge funds somehow harm the companies in which they invest. The overwhelming evidence is that hedge funds help investors by forcing managers to worry more about producing positive results for shareholders. But there is an argument on the other side, and it will be explored in the following subsection of this chapter.

The second, and more recent, argument leveled against hedge funds is that they present what are known as "systemic risk" to the economy as a whole. Systemic risk is risk that affects the entire financial system, causing shock waves and chain reactions such as contraction of the money supply or multiple bank failures. Worse, it is not possible to avoid systemic risk through holding a diversified portfolio of investments because it affects all, or virtually all, segments of the market. This argument will be explored as well.

Hedge Funds and Harm to Investors and Companies: Conflicting Time Horizons?

Some individuals in favor of greater regulation argue that hedge funds harm their portfolio companies and the companies' investors because they exert pressure on the companies' managers to produce short-term results at the expense of long-term gains. This allegation has been described as "the most severe attack leveled against hedge funds." It is the specific manifestation of the general problem that "[h]edge funds are set up to make money for their investors without regard to whether the strategies they follow benefit shareholders generally." Hedge funds, among all institutional investors, "come close to being the archetypical short-term investor,"[43] which, at least according to management lawyer Martin Lipton, means that hedge fund managers may refrain from making long-term investments because they are too focused on the short-term.[44]

The basic theory of present value posits that one can determine the current (present) value of an asset that will be received in the future by using the market discount rate to calculate the value today of whatever will be received in the future. The principal adjustments effected by the discount rate reflect the expected inflation rate and the business and financial risks associated with the investment, including the expected returns on rival investments and general macroeconomic conditions.

The basic financial concept of present value means that hedge fund managers are not confronted with any dilemma about whether to maximize a firm's current or short-term share price or its future share price. Rather, when making decisions, hedge fund managers will attempt to maximize the net present value of a firm's shares. As such, basic financial theory indicates that rational, portfolio-value-maximizing hedge fund managers will fully support any and all long-term investment decisions by companies even if those decisions will not result in a payoff for the portfolio company for many years because the *expected future cash flows* will have an immediate impact on a firm's share price, which is simply the value of those cash flows discounted to present value. The expected future cash flows simply will be discounted back to present value by the market and incorporated into a firm's current share price.

The argument that hedge funds sacrifice long-term management perspectives in order to serve the interests of short-term investors, and at the expense of long-term investors who adopt a "buy and hold" investment strategy, is precisely the complaint that one heard during the halcyon days of the market for corporate control. Then the argument was that hostile takeovers are bad for American business because they force U.S. managers to focus disproportionately on the short term and neglect long-term concerns that are important to the firm's financial well-being.

What these managers really were saying to outside raiders then, and to hedge fund managers today, is that, in their opinion, the capital markets are placing an unduly high discount rate on the expected earnings stream associated with their prized long-run investments. The high market discount rate is what causes the present value of the future cash flows associated with long-term investments to be too low. This argument has several flaws. It should be met with skepticism by independent policy analysts and economists because it cannot be disproved and because it is self-serving.

The statement that the market has assigned an excessive discount rate to a particular product is impossible to prove because it is not falsifiable in any empirical or even anecdotal way. As such, it is not something that a self-respecting social scientist should take seriously. Even indirect evidence does not support the assertion that hedge fund investors or private equity investors attempt to make profits by urging their portfolio companies to engage in strategies—such as slashing expenditures on research and development—that emphasize a short-term focus.

On the other hand, there is a wealth of evidence that capital markets are highly efficient, especially over time. Moreover, it is also clear that significant profits can be made by locating companies with great future prospects and buying up their shares in anticipation of the point in time when these prospects are actually realized or when market participants acknowledge these future prospects by bidding up the price of the shares. Thus, it is not entirely plausible that markets systematically undervalue long-term projects. Indeed, the dot-com bubble and other similar periods of extremely high valuations of companies with no earnings (and sometimes no products) suggest that it is at least as likely that the opposite is true: sometimes markets may overvalue long-term projects at the expense of short-term projects.

Moreover, in examining the claim that managers feel pressured by hedge funds and private equity investors to focus excessively on the short term at the expense of longer-term investments, it is important to keep in mind the source of this dubious assertion. Incumbent corporate managers and their hired guns are the primary sources of this complaint, which serves their private interests. To the extent that people believe that focusing on the short term is bad, managers can rationalize the poor share price performance of their companies with the old excuse that they are "focusing on long-term goals rather than on short-term share prices."

Of course, it is undeniably true that share prices provide a very public, objective measure of management performance. To the extent that managers do not wish to be evaluated by this metric, they must try to refute its credibility. They do this by claiming that the prices established in the capital markets are inaccurate because they do not sufficiently reward long-term corporate strategies. Actually, basic human nature often provides a more realistic explanation of the disparity: corporate managers who make investment decisions are more optimistic about their company's future success than is the rest of the market.

Combining the insights of present value theory with the insights of efficient capital markets theory leads us to the significant realization that stock price returns are the best measure of firm performance, even if they are not perfect. Other sorts of data, particularly accounting data on earnings or, worse, management's self-serving protests that their long-term brilliance is being unappreciated by the capital markets, are much less reliable since they cannot be tested. Moreover, to the extent that capital markets *are not* efficient, no one has offered a good explanation for why they are not biased *in favor of* rather than against long-term investment strategies. The more plausible theory is that while markets may not be perfectly efficient, they are certainly *unbiased* because market participants can profit just as much from finding overvalued investments as from finding undervalued investments.

Systemic Risk: Real or Imagined?

Systemic risk is policy-speak for the risk that some event, such as the collapse of a large number of hedge funds, could spark a financial system collapse that includes waves of bank failures, the collapse of the stock market, and general panic and chaos in the financial system. The allegation that hedge fund investing poses a threat of systemic risk is, perhaps not coincidentally, identical to the claim that such investing harms the economy by reducing managerial attention to long-term investments in one important way: it is a very scary prospect that is impossible to disprove.

Indeed, the vague notion that our resilient financial system will mysteriously experience some sort of systemic collapse due to hedge fund investing is so frightening that corporate managers can ask for, and compliant regulators can justify, massive regulatory intervention even with only a slight chance that such a catastrophe will actually occur. Generally speaking, we cannot know for sure whether a particular economic activity poses systemic risk until an event occurs that provides a natural experiment. In the case of hedge funds, however, it is easy to show that the very structure of the industry itself proves that hedge funds do not pose any systemic risk to the economy.

Unlike the accounting and investment banking industries, the hedge fund industry is disaggregated and highly diverse. There are more than ten thousand hedge funds and no two are identical. Many, but not all, specialize in equity investments, others in debt, and some in foreign exchange. Some hedge funds are entirely independent, while others are linked with various sorts of financial institutions, including investment banks and mutual funds. Some, but by no means all, hedge funds are highly leveraged. Many invest in companies whose stock is heavily traded. Moreover, unlike private equity funds and commercial banks, hedge funds tend toward investments with short-term time horizons, which allows for access to liquidity.

Arguments in favor of increased hedge fund regulation in order to lower systemic risk are flat wrong. Such arguments fail to consider that hedge funds pose no systemic risk because of the incredible diversity in their investment strategies, an assertion bolstered by evidence from decades of experience with hedge funds. In 1998, a massive hedge fund, Long-Term Capital Management, suffered substantial losses when Russia threatened to default on its debt. In September 2006, it was reported that Amaranth Advisors had lost almost $5 billion on risky investments in natural gas. In both cases, the financial markets continued to operate seamlessly, without a hint that any sort of systemic risk would manifest itself.

Moreover, the secrecy in which hedge funds operate ensures that such funds will not present systemic risk. Unlike investments by corporate insiders or mutual funds, because hedge funds are lightly regulated, they need not disclose their investment choices to other investors. Some decry this lack of "transparency." In fact, the current unregulated market environment protects the valuable intellectual property interests that hedge funds have in the investment strategies that generate their portfolio selections. More important, the secrecy prevents systemic risk by preventing copycat investments and other forms of "herding" behavior that might actually generate systemic risk.

In other words, from an economic perspective, the absence of hedge fund regulation both increases wealth by protecting hedge funds' property rights in information and eliminates systemic risk by preventing other investors from rushing like lemmings to copy the investment strategies developed by hedge fund managers.

Moreover, hedge funds differ from other institutional investors and insiders in two important ways, already discussed. First, they take active roles in corporate governance. They agitate to remove underperforming CEOs. They lobby directors and management to streamline their businesses and to return cash to shareholders. Second, because they are unregulated, hedge funds can sell stock short. They thereby profit not only when they predict increases in share prices, but also when they are able to predict that shares will drop in value. As a result, hedge funds actually reduce risk by contributing to the efficiency of the capital markets: the more efficient the markets are, the more information we have about which firms are doing well and which ones, like Enron, are on the verge of imploding.

The people who push for greater hedge fund regulation do so because of ulterior motives. Regulators are seeking to expand their own turf. Corporate executives dislike the increased pressure from hedge funds to perform and believe that greater regulation will decrease the power of hedge fund oversight. To couch their argument for increased regulation in the notion of minimizing systemic risk, however, is without merit.

THE REGULATION OF HEDGE FUNDS

While hedge funds are not subject to very much regulation, the regulation to which they are subject is misguided and burdensome because it undermines the extent to which they can effectively participate in the corporate governance of large public corporations. Hedge funds are regulated by the Williams Act, part of the Securities Exchange Act of 1934, which forces investors with even the slightest prospects of gaining control over a public company to make all sorts of disclosures about themselves.

For example, under Section 13D of the Securities Exchange Act of 1934, any investor (or group of investors) who acquires in any way more than 5 percent of the beneficial ownership of a public company must disclose its identity and background, the sources of the funds used to make the acquisition, and any plans or proposals to make major changes in the business or corporate structure of the company whose shares are being acquired. Investors also must provide a reason why they are buying their shares, and explain whether they are doing so in order to acquire control or simply as a passive investment. In addition, these sorts of disclosures must be made immediately when an investor launches a public bid or "tender offer" for the shares of a company. The problem with these requirements is that it forces inefficient wealth transfers from hedge fund managers and other investors to the shareholders of target firms.

Worse, Section 13F of the Williams Act requires all institutional managers, including pension funds and hedge funds, as well as certain private equity investors who own shares or listed options in public companies (defined as those companies whose shares are registered with the SEC), to make disclosures about their holdings on a quarterly basis if they own more than $100 million worth of securities in public companies. There is significant anecdotal evidence that these disclosure requirements are harmful to reasonable activist hedge fund investors.

The most prominent example of an activist investor whose investment efforts are thwarted by the disclosure rules is billionaire Warren Buffett, who runs the insurance and investment firm Berkshire Hathaway, Inc. In the second quarter of 2006, Berkshire Hathaway purchased 22.6 million shares of Johnson & Johnson and 1.97 million shares of Target Corp., the second-largest U.S. discount chain. Berkshire Hathaway sought to keep these and similar acquisitions confidential, but the SEC denied its repeated requests. As a result, Berkshire Hathaway, which had not previously disclosed any stake at all in Target, was forced to disclose its status in its 13F filings. The same filings also revealed Berkshire Hathaway to be one of Johnson & Johnson's largest shareholders, having increased its stake from slightly under 2 million shares to 24.6 million.

The problem with these disclosure requirements is that hedge funds, like other investors, must be compensated for the costs of investigating and identifying investment opportunities. As Sanford Grossman and Oliver Hart have indicated with respect to outside bidders early in the intellectual debate about takeovers, value-maximizing shareholders will use the disclosure made by hedge funds and other activist investors to revise upward the price at which they are willing to sell their shares.[45] Grossman and Hart have shown that once selling shareholders are aware that an outsider such as a hedge fund may add value by making strategic changes in the business of the target, they will raise the price at which they are willing to sell to a price at least equal to the value of the firm to the hedge fund.[46] Grossman and Hart based their conclusion on the reasonable assumption that each shareholder in the typical large U.S. publicly held corporation is small enough that his tendering decision will not affect the outcome of the tender offer. This places target firm shareholders in a collective action problem akin to prisoner's dilemma.

Suppose, for example, that a shareholder owns shares in a publicly traded company whose shares are currently trading at a price of $15 per share. A hedge fund announces it is making a tender offer for $20 per share (or has acquired, over time, 5 percent of the shares in the target company at an average price of, say, $16 per share). After the hedge fund makes the disclosures required by the Williams Act, the target firm's shareholders conclude, quite logically, that the target is worth even more than the hedge fund is willing to pay; otherwise the acquisition would not make sense. After all, the hedge fund only profits to the extent that it can make the target firm's shares worth more than it is paying. Thus, since each shareholder can refuse to sell his shares to the hedge fund without affecting the probability that the hedge fund will succeed in acquiring the number of shares it needs to make its investment profitable, it is rational for him to decline to sell. By holding onto his shares, the non-selling shareholder can obtain even greater profits from the investment than the hedge fund can, both because the non-selling shareholders did not have to pay any premium over market price for their shares and because they do not have to incur the same research costs in investigating the target firm's potential that the hedge fund had to incur before making its investment. In other words, target firm shareholders can "free ride" on the research about the potential of the target company made by the hedge fund investors.

Moreover, the best possible outcome for the target firm shareholders is to hold onto their shares when competent activist hedge fund investors come along. This was a point recognized early on by Harvard's Louis Loss, the father of American securities markets regulation, when he observed that "one result of full disclosure may well be: the better the reputation and attainment of the offeror, the higher the price he will have to pay."[47] And ironically, the opposite is also true; the worse the reputation and attainment of the offeror, the lower the price he will have to pay, at least if target firm shareholders think that the poorly performing acquirer is likely to succeed in gaining a position of influence on the corporate governance of the target company. So the best possible outcome for target firm shareholders is to sell to incompetent, corrupt, or dishonest bidders and to decline to sell to able, incorruptible, and honest bidders. The worst possible outcome for the target firm shareholders is to sell out too quickly and too cheaply. So holding onto their shares by declining to sell to a hedge fund or some other honest and competent activist investor is the most rational strategy for individual target firm shareholders, although not for the target shareholders as a group.

All of this is another way of pointing out that requiring an activist hedge fund to disclose its investment in an undervalued company before it chooses to do so dilutes the property rights in information of the hedge fund.[48] This, in turn, will reduce the likelihood that hedge funds will engage in an activist investment because it is less profitable for hedge funds to do so than it would be in the absence of the Williams Act. This, in turn, means that all investors suffer because hedge funds also will not invest in monitoring management's performance to the same extent as they would if they could lower their acquisition costs by avoiding disclosure.

As one highly successful activist hedge fund manager cogently (and confidentially) observed to me, the law has the effect of "requiring every money manager with over $100 million in assets to disclose his entire portfolio 45 days after the close of a quarter. For a long-term investor, this requires us to give away our intellectual property. It is [l]ike requiring Microsoft to disclose its code . . . and for what reason?"

CONCLUSION

Private equity and hedge fund investors appear to be the great, shining beacon of hope on an otherwise bleak landscape. Where other corporate governance devices appear to promise much and deliver little, hedge funds and private equity firms actually deliver on their promise to provide more disciplined monitoring of management, to reduce the incidence of fraud on investors, and to improve actual operational performance. Hedge fund and private equity fund managers have the resources, the expertise, and the incentives to improve the way their portfolio companies are run.

In evaluating the efficacy of private equity and hedge fund investors, it is worth noting that as a purely descriptive matter, the corporate governance mechanism that works the best is the one that is the least regulated. Other, more heavily regulated corporate governance devices, including the market for corporate control, corporate boards of directors, and shareholder voting, have proven far less effective. This, in turn, raises the question whether these other corporate governance devices are less successful because they are so heavily regulated, or whether they are so heavily regulated because they proved so successful. In the case of the market for corporate control, it is clear that political pressure for regulation emerged because the success of this corporate governance device threatened managers. In the case of corporate boards of directors and shareholder voting, a less cynical though ultimately no more encouraging explanation is in order. The participants in these corporate governance mechanisms—directors and shareholders—have been transformed by popular mythology into the heroes of the historic effort to guard the watchers of the corporation. Valiant and honest independent directors, vigilant and well-informed shareholders do, of course, exist, and they provide tremendous benefits to corporate governance. But, like heroes generally, brilliant and vigilant shareholders and forcefully independent and competent directors are not particularly common. Dependable, quotidian, reliable, though less romantic institutions such as hedge funds and private equity investors are what is required to ensure the proper functioning of public corporations.

CONCLUSION

This book develops the idea that corporate governance is about keeping promises to investors. Such promises are made to induce investment and participation in business ventures. These promises, in turn, create expectations on the part of investors. Unless investors have confidence that their reasonable expectations, which stem from these promises, will be met, they will decline to invest. This, in turn, will have the predicable, dire economic consequences: stunted economic growth, high unemployment, and, of course, capital flight.

There are a wide variety of mechanisms and institutions, most notably contract, law, and norms, by which shareholders and other outside investors attempt to assure themselves that management will perform in a manner that is consistent with their promises. These mechanisms and institutions are at least as important for entrepreneurs and managers in search of capital as they are for potential investors. Investors who lack confidence that the promises made to them will be kept simply will walk away from the investment. Entrepreneurs and managers operating under a corporate governance system in which they cannot credibly persuade investors that they will keep their promises inevitably will fail to obtain the capital they require to start, maintain, or expand their businesses. In other words, they will fail to realize their dreams.

The modest premise here is that investors have certain discrete, comprehensible, and reasonable expectations about what corporate managers should and should not do with their power over the corporations in which they have invested. These expectations are based on promises. If investors doubt that the promises made to them will be kept, they will decline to invest.

One implication of this analysis is that the way to evaluate and compare systems of corporate governance is to gauge how well the corporations that operate subject to that system perform in meeting the corporate promises that form investors' expectations. In other words, the core issue in corporate governance is the extent to which corporations keep their promises to investors. Investors' relationships with their companies are contractual, so investors and companies are free to agree to whatever sort of arrangements they want. Profit maximization for shareholders is generally thought to be the goal of virtually every corporation. This is not because of some law or immutable rule: it is because that's the deal that corporations offer shareholders when they sell their shares to them. In other words, corporate governance attempts to cause corporations to maximize profits for shareholders because this is the promise that corporations make to their shareholders.

In my view, the purpose of corporate governance is to control corporate deviance, where deviance is defined as any action by management that is inconsistent with the promises made by corporations that form the basis of the legitimate, investment-backed expectations of investors. In the preceding chapters, I have evaluated the role of a diverse variety of corporate governance devices, institutions, and mechanisms. Each of these devices, institutions, and mechanisms influences decision-making and promise-keeping within a corporation and therefore is part of the system of corporate governance for that firm.

Like other sorts of promises, some of the promises that construct our system of corporate governance work better than others. Just as some promises are kept and others are not as a general matter, it is not surprising that some corporate governance mechanisms and institutions simply work better than others. What is striking about the analysis is the confusion about which corporate governance institutions work well and which do not.

The governance institutions on which we appear to rely most—such as shareholder voting, corporate boards of directors, whistle-blowers, credit-rating agencies, and banks—perform worse than perceived or hoped. In light of this fact, it seems more than passing strange that academics and government policymakers rely far more on these failed mechanisms of corporate governance than they do on alternative, highly effective mechanisms. These alternatives, which include dissident directors, the market for corporate control, and activist market participants such as hedge funds and private equity investors, are, at the moment, on the fringe of discussions about corporate governance. The purpose of this book is to identify what works in corporate governance and what does not, and to bring the governance mechanisms that do work onto center stage, both by describing their virtues and by pointing out the flaws in the alternative institutional arrangements.

In performing this analysis, it is impossible to avoid thinking about the close ties between the world of corporate governance and the world of politics. The corporate governance rules that agencies and lawmakers promulgate have profound effects on the job security, compensation levels, and autonomy of very powerful corporate actors. It is not surprising that such actors have galvanized into effective political coalitions to channel public demand for corporate governance rules that will reduce managerial power. These power-reduction "solutions," however, are not quite as effective as they appear to be, particularly with regard to the rules about shareholder voting, whistle-blowing, and the rules regulating credit-rating agencies. The focus in recent years on these corporate governance mechanisms is unlikely to affect managers' conduct.

Whistle-blowers often cannot be believed, and in any case it is difficult to distinguish the whistle-blowers who are telling the truth from hostile or disgruntled employees who are not. Rating agencies as described above not only are unreliable, they are typically so slow to change their ratings that shareholders have already lost most or all of their investments by the time the rating agencies get around to acting.

Most significantly, lawmakers keep piling responsibilities on corporate boards of directors in general and audit committees in particular. The public is told that they should rely on boards of directors not only to evaluate management and to provide strategic direction to managers, but also to monitor the corporation. Unfortunately, there is no evidence that boards of directors are competent to do all of these things, and certainly there is strong doubt that they are competent to do all of these simultaneously. One of the major themes of this book has been to identify board capture as a major obstacle to the notion that boards of directors can be relied on to protect shareholders from self-serving managers. The argument is not that all boards are captured. Many, perhaps most, corporate boards of directors are dominated by honest, faithful, conscientious agents of management. The problem is that it is not possible for investors to distinguish, until it is way too late, the good boards from the bad boards. This means that rational shareholders should not rely exclusively on boards of directors to protect them from avaricious management. At best, corporate boards of directors are but one small part of a multifaceted corporate governance system. Shareholders should certainly not be required to rely exclusively on boards of directors to scrutinize and control managerial shirking and other problems.

Investors are left to rely on corporate governance mechanisms that do not work because inefficient regulations increasingly hamper the corporate governance mechanisms that do work. This is particularly true in the case of the regulation of the market for corporate control where narrow political self-interest has triumphed over policy. As a result, tight regulation restricts this important market, thereby depriving investors of an important and truly effective corporate governance mechanism.

Similarly, in recent years hedge funds have become the subject of intense attention by regulators, ostensibly because they present public policy concerns, but more probably because hedge funds have become important players in boardrooms, putting pressure on poorly performing corporations. Hedge funds have become increasingly interested in corporate governance, and activist hedge fund managers have made their opinions known in boardrooms throughout the United States. This, it seems, provides a more plausible explanation for the demand for hedge fund regulation than do alternative explanations such as the danger of "systemic risk" or the problems posed by the opacity of hedge funds' balance sheets.

Two observations made by James Madison at different points in the Federalist Papers apply with as much force to the study of corporate governance as they do to the study of constitutional formation. By analogy from the world of government to the world of corporations, the first of these insights, which is contained in Federalist 62, observes that good corporate governance requires two things. The first of these is fidelity to the objects of the corporation, namely to maximize value for shareholders. The second is the knowledge by which these things can be best attained. The core dilemma of corporate governance is that shareholders have the first of these qualities, but not the second. While managers and directors, who often (though of course not always) have the knowledge (skill) to run the business, they often lack sufficient commitment to the objectives of the shareholders of the corporation.

The famous insight from Federalist 10 that "enlightened statesmen will not always be at the helm" reinforces the agency problem identified in Federalist 62. The various institutions and mechanisms of corporate governance must address both of these problems. Shareholder voting, of course, powerfully addresses the agency issue, but it provides no help with regard to the knowledge and skill issue. And, as society has become more complex and markets ever more specialized, the problem has gotten worse over time, not better. Placing highly knowledgeable insiders on boards of directors directly confronts the knowledge and expertise problem but confounds the agency problem.

Not surprisingly, it turns out that the institutions and mechanisms of corporate governance that are the most successful are those that manage simultaneously to deal with the incentives problem and the knowledge problem. The market for corporate control, hedge funds, and dissident director slates all fit into this category. It is these institutions and mechanisms of corporate governance that we should seek to reinforce and strengthen through public policy initiatives. But, for the same reason, it is these corporate governance mechanisms that are the most vulnerable to attack by special interest groups in the political realm.

Investors in corporations, however, have a couple of significant advantages over citizen-voters. First, government performance is extremely hard to evaluate, especially for citizens far removed both geographically and by inclination from the locus of government power. The evaluation of governmental performance is not made any easier by the fact that politicians, of course, like corporate managers virtually always claim to be performing well, regardless of the facts. Worse, the evaluation of the performance of government is made exponentially more difficult because governmental performance must be evaluated across so many different dimensions and from so many different perspectives. As we all know, reasonable people can have vastly divergent views on what constitutes good foreign policy toward various countries as well as what is good domestic policy in a wide range of policies from education to health care to transportation and communications.

In contrast, shareholders evaluate corporate performance along only one particular vector: share price performance. This makes it possible to evaluate objectively the performance of managers. The ability of investors to make such an objective evaluation stands in sharp contrast to the inability of citizens to evaluate the performance of politicians. The efficacy of share prices as a corporate governance device is enhanced immeasurably by the existence of a public market for firms' shares. The markets that price the equity of public corporations are objective and unbiased because participants can profit by identifying undervalued shares and bidding up their prices by buying as well as by identifying overvalued shares and driving down their prices by selling. These markets exert a powerful disciplinary effect on managers. The information and discipline on management imposed by the capital markets make such markets the most effective corporate governance device there is. Critical corporate governance mechanisms such as hedge funds and the market for corporate control could not function without the pricing and information provided by capital markets. For this reason, the pricing capabilities of the capital markets emerge as the greatest corporate governance mechanism we have: every one of the corporate governance mechanisms discussed in this book relies to at least some extent on these share-pricing capabilities.

NOTES

INTRODUCTION
CORPORATE GOVERNANCE AS PROMISE

1. The term "corporate governance" is surely the most overused and poorly defined in the lexicon of business. Widely used definitions of the term—with my commentary on each—include the following:

- "Corporate governance refers to corporate decision-making and control, particularly the structure of the board and its working procedures. However, the term corporate governance is sometimes used very widely, embracing a company's relations with a wide range of stakeholders or very narrowly referring to a company's compliance with the provisions of best practices codes" (Colin Melvin and Hans Hirt, *Corporate Governance and Performance,* Hermes Pensions Management Ltd., December 2004, available at http://www.hermes.co.uk/corporate_governance/corporate_ governance_and_performance_feature.htm#definingcorporategovernance). This definition is both too broad and too narrow. It is too narrow because it wrongly limits the focus of corporate governance to internal institutions like boards of directors. Moreover, to the extent that corporate governance is thought to include toothless devices such as codes of best practices that do not actually constrain deviant corporate behavior, the definition is too broad because it suggests that the purpose of corporate governance is to serve some vague general purpose rather than govern deviant corporate behavior.
- According to the Organisation for Economic Co-operation and Development (OECD), "Corporate governance is the system by which business corporations are directed and controlled. The corporate governance structure specifies the distribution of rights and responsibilities among different participants in the company, such as, the board, managers, shareholders and other stakeholders, and spells out the rules and procedures for making decisions on corporate affairs. By doing this, it also provides the structure through which the company objectives and strategy are set, and the means of attaining those objectives and monitoring performance." This definition is consistent with the one presented by Adrian Cadbury in "Report of the Committee on the Financial Aspects of Corporate Governance," December 1992, available at http://www.ecgi.org/codes/documents/cadbury.pdf. Although this is a pretty good definition, it is a bit confusing because it is not clear whether the term "corporate governance" is being

used to discuss a set of internal rules within firms or more broadly to include legal rules and societal norms, as I think it should.

- "Corporate governance is about promoting corporate fairness, transparency and accountability" (J. Wolfensohn, former president of the World Bank, as quoted in the *Financial Times,* June 21, 1999). Corporate governance is about governance. It is really not about "promoting" anything. However, to the extent the corporations are well governed, they are likely to exhibit characteristics like fairness, transparency, and accountability.
- "Some commentators take too narrow a view, and say it (corporate governance) is the fancy term for the way in which directors and auditors handle their responsibilities towards shareholders. Others use the expression as if it were synonymous with shareholder democracy. Corporate governance is a topic recently conceived, as yet ill-defined, and consequently blurred at the edges" (Nigel Maw and Michael Craig-Cooper, *Maw on Corporate Governance* [Brookfield, VT: Dartmouth Publishing, 1994], 1). This last definition is at least frank about the lack of a generally recognized definition of the term "corporate governance." As broad as it is, however, this definition, like many of the others, provides no concrete sense of whether corporate governance is a descriptive term that tells us what directors actually do, or a normative term that describes what directors ought to be doing.

2. Stephanie Strom, "Businesses Try to Make Money and Save the World," *New York Times,* May 6, 2007, *http://www.nytimes.com/2007/05/06/business/yourmoney/06fourth.html?_r=1andoref=sloginandemc=eta1andpagewanted=print* (accessed October 8, 2007).

3. Ibid.

4. Frank H. Easterbrook and Daniel R. Fischel, "Voting in Corporate Law," *Journal of Law and Economics* 26 (1983): 395–433 at 403.

CHAPTER 1
THE GOALS OF CORPORATE GOVERNANCE

1. The IBM corporate charter is available at http://www.ibm.com/investor/corpgovernance/cgcoi.phtml (accessed February 25, 2007).

2. Frank Easterbrook and Daniel R. Fischel, *The Economic Structure of Corporate Law* (Cambridge, MA: Harvard University Press, 1991).

3. R. H. Coase, "The Nature of the Firm," *Economica* 4 (1937): 1, reprinted in R. H. Coase, *The Firm, The Market and the Law* (Chicago: University of Chicago Press, 1988), 33.

4. 6 Del. Code, § 18–1101(c) (2008).

5. Tim Annett, "Gap Reflects Failures in Corporate Governance; Slow Wage Growth Is Blamed on Global Competition," *Wall Street Journal,* May 12, 2006, *http://online.wsj.com/article/SB114719841354447998.html?mod=home_whats_news_us* (accessed February 25, 2007).

6. Andrew P. Campbell and Caroline Smith Gidiere, "Shareholder Rights, the Tort of Oppression and Derivative Actions Revisited: A Time for Mature Development?" *Alabama Law Review* 63 (2002): 316–17.

7. See "Buy-Sell Agreement-FAQ: Don't Neglect to Write a Business Prenup before Putting Money into a Venture," *http://www.nolo.com/article.cfm/ObjectID/ 02DF02FD-4CE0–46D0–9B7990F281AEF4B7/catID/C1DBB6FC-F9C3–40CA- 8A4D77366ED0D4D5/111/254/FAQ*; CCH Business Owner's Toolkit, "The Buy- Sell Agreement," http://www.toolkit.cch.com/Text/P12_6940.asp.

8. CCH Business Owner's Toolkit, "The Buy-Sell Agreement."

9. Practitioners often consider buy-sell agreements to be important in bankruptcy to avoid the risks associated with the declaration of personal bankruptcy by one of the shareholders of a closely held corporation. In particular, investors will want to avoid the risk that a bankruptcy trustee in such a personal bankruptcy will bring a successful action to liquidate the business in order to obtain cash for payment of the owner's personal debts. To guard against this contingency, and to prevent the company from getting immersed in litigation in bankruptcy court in case of a shareholder contemplating bankruptcy, the owners can enter into a buy-sell or buyout agreement. Such agreements typically require shareholders to notify other shareholders before filing a petition in bankruptcy court. Under the terms of such agreements, the filing of a bankruptcy petition constitutes an automatic offer to sell the bankrupt owner's shares back to the other owners or to the corporation at a price determined by formula. Where such an agreement exists the funds used to effectuate the buyout are paid to the bankruptcy trustee, who can use it to satisfy the bankrupt shareholder's debts, and the business can continue uninterrupted.

10. Buy-sell agreements are popular in jurisdictions in which divorce law gives the spouses of shareholders rights to their proportionate interests in their spouse's stock. In community property states like Arizona, California, and Texas, among others, both spouses have a right to the "community property" generated during the marriage, including all of the money earned during the marriage and all of the property acquired with those earnings. In non-community property states the law requires that the property of the divorcing parties be divided equitably, leaving open the possibility for divorcing spouses to claim an equitable ownership interest in the stock owned by the spouse involved in the closely held business. Buy-sell agreements address this problem by requiring the former spouses of divorced owners to sell shares or other ownership interests received in a divorce settlement back to the company or the other owners or shareholders, according to the valuation formula provided in the agreement.

11. Often, buy-sell agreements stipulate that purchases triggered by the retirement of a shareholder cannot be made before the retiring partner reaches a certain age, or else stipulate for graduated purchase prices that increase annually in order to provide disincentives for shareholders to retire prematurely when a buy-sell agreement is in place.

12. Eric Hilt, "Corporate Ownership and Governance in the Early Nineteenth Century" (manuscript on file with author, February 2006), 23.

CHAPTER 2
CORPORATE LAW AND CORPORATE GOVERNANCE

1. Bernard S. Black, "Is Corporate Law Trivial?: A Political and Economic Analysis," *Northwestern University Law Review* 84 (1990): 542.
2. Easterbrook and Fischel, *The Economic Structure of Corporate Law.*
3. Mark J. Roe, "Corporate Law's Limits," *Journal of Legal Studies* 31 (2002): 233–71.
4. Jonathan Macey, "The Nature of Conflicts of Interest within the Firm," *Journal of Corporation Law* 31 (2006): 615.
5. Joseph W. Bishop Jr., "Sitting Ducks and Decoy Ducks: New Trends in the Indemnification of Corporate Directors and Officers," *Yale Law Journal* 77 (1968): 1099 (stating that the search for cases in which directors have been held liable for "negligence uncomplicated by self-dealing" is "a search for a very small number of needles in a very large haystack"). See also Mark J. Roe, "The Shareholder Wealth Maximization Norm and Industrial Organizations," *University of Pennsylvania Law Review* 149 (2001): 2063.
6. E. Norman Veasey and Christine T. DiGuglielmo, "What Happened in Delaware Corporate Law and Corporate Governance from 1992 to 2004?" *University of Pennsylvania Law Review* 153 (2005): 1399.
7. *Smith v. Van Gorkom*, 488 A.2d 858 (Del. Supreme Court 1985).
8. Lynn Stout, "In Praise of Procedure: An Economic and Behavioral Defense of *Smith v. Van Gorkom* and the Business Judgment Rule," *Northwestern University Law Review* 96 (2002): 579, 586; Dennis R. Honabach, "*Smith v. Van Gorkom*: Managerial Liability and Exculpatory Clauses—A Proposal to Fill the Gap of the Missing Officer Protection," *Washburn Law Review* 45 (2006): 307.
9. Charles M. Elson and Robert B. Thompson, "*Van Gorkom*'s Legacy: The Limits of Judicially Enforced Constraints and the Promise of Proprietary Incentives," *Northwestern University Law Review* 96 (2002): 579; Daniel R. Fischel, "The Business Judgment Rule and the *TransUnion* Case," *Business Lawyer* 40 (1985): 1437.
10. Honabach, "*Smith v. Van Gorkom*," 322.
11. Richard A. Posner, "Social Norms and the Law: An Economic Approach," *American Economic Review* 87 (1997): 365–69 (Papers and Proceedings of the Hundred and Ninth Annual Meeting of the American Economic Association).
12. American Law Institute, *Principles of Corporate Governance: Analysis and Recommendations*, 2 vols. (Philadelphia: American Law Institute, 1994).
13. A. A. Sommer, "A Guide to the American Law Institute Corporate Governance Project," *Business Lawyer* 51 (1996): 1331.
14. Roe, "The Shareholder Wealth Maximization Norm and Industrial Organization," 2063.
15. Ibid., 2073.
16. Franklin Allen and Douglas Gale, *Comparing Financial Systems* (Cambridge, MA: MIT Press, 2000).
17. David A. Skeel Jr., "Shaming in Corporate Law," *University of Pennsylvania Law Review* 149 (2001): 1812 (quoting from an October 25, 2000, interview

with Nell Minow, editor, The Corporate Library, http://www.thecorporatelibrary .com).

18. Jonathan Macey and Geoffrey Miller, "An Interest Group Theory of Delaware Corporate Law," *Texas Law Review* 65 (1987): 469.

19. Francis Fukuyama, *Trust: The Social Virtues and the Creation of Prosperity* (New York: Free Press, 1995).

20. James S. Coleman, "Social Capital in the Creation of Human Capital," *American Journal of Sociology* 94, supplement (1988): 95–120.

21. Robert D. Putnam, *Making Democracy Work: Civic Traditions in Modern Italy* (Princeton: Princeton University Press, 1993).

22. Francis Fukuyama, "Social Capital and Civil Society" (paper presented at the International Monetary Fund Conference on Second Generation Reforms, October 1, 1999), http://www.imf.org/external/pubs/ft/seminar/1999/reforms/ fukuyama.htm (accessed February 25, 2007).

23. Dan M. Kahan, "Signalling or Reciprocating? A Response to Eric Posner's Law and Social Norms," *University of Richmond Law Review* 36 (2002): 367–85.

24. Fukuyama, "Social Capital and Civil Society," 1.

25. Marcel Kahan, "The Limited Significance of Norms for Corporate Governance," *University of Pennsylvania Law Review* 149 (2001): 1881.

26. Lawrence Harrison, *Underdevelopment Is a State of Mind: The Latin American Case* (New York: Madison Books, 1985), 7–8.

27. Fukuyama, "Social Capital and Civil Society," 3.

28. Ibid.

29. Richard H. McAdams, "The Origin, Development, and Regulation of Norms," *Michigan Law Review* 96 (1997): 338.

30. Xavier Gabaix and Augustin Landier, "Why Has CEO Pay Increased So Much?" *http://ssrn.com/abstract=901826* (accessed February 25, 2007).

CHAPTER 4
BOARDS OF DIRECTORS

1. American Law Institute, *Principles of Corporate Governance,* section 3.02.

2. *In re The Walt Disney Company Derivative Litigation,* 825 A.2d 275 (Del. Ch. 2005).

3. *Id.*

4. See, e.g., Delaware General Corporate Law, sec. 102(b)(7) or Model Business Corporation Act, sec. 2.02(b)(4), both of which shield directors from personal liability for breach of the fiduciary duty of care.

5. Permanent Subcommittee on Investigations of the Committee on Governmental Affairs, U.S. Senate, *The Role of the Board of Directors in Enron's Collapse,* July 8, 2002, http://fl1.findlaw.com/news.findlaw.com/cnn/docs/enron/ senpsi70802rpt.pdf.

6. "The Role of Non-Executive Directors," *The Economist,* February 10, 2001, p. 68 (reporting on a survey of corporate boards performed by PriceWaterhouseCoopers).

7. Renee Adams and Daniel Ferreira, "A Theory of Friendly Boards," *Journal of Finance* 62 (2007): 217.

8. Ibid.

9. Ibid.

10. Ibid.

11. Jonathan Macey and Arnoud Boot, "Monitoring Corporate Performance: The Role of Objectivity, Proximity and Adaptability in Corporate Governance," *Cornell Law Review* 89 (2004): 356.

12. See David G. Myers, *Social Psychology* (New York: McGraw-Hill, 1983), 46–47.

13. See Ralph K. White, "Selective Inattention," *Psychology Today,* November 1971, p. 82 (observing that "there was a tendency, when actions were out of line with ideas, for decision-makers to align their actions").

14. Thomas Gilovich, *How We Know What Isn't So: The Fallibility of Human Reason in Everyday Life* (New York: The Free Press, 1991), 86; Robert P. Abelson, "Beliefs Are Like Possessions," *Journal for the Theory of Social Behavior* 16 (1989): 222.

15. Jerald G. Bachman and Patrick O'Malley, "Self-Esteem in Young Men: A Longitudinal Analysis of the Impact of Educational and Occupational Attainment," *Journal of Political Economy* 85 (1977): 370–76.

16. Of course in the case of leveraged buyouts by management, where the participants in the market for corporate control are managers, cognitive bias may be an issue.

17. See Daniel Kahnman and Dan Lovallo, "Timid Choices and Bold Forecasts: Perspectives on Risk Taking," *Management Science* 39 (1993): 24–27.

18. In this interpretation, the board monitors management. In a two-tier system (e.g., the Netherlands and Germany), this is clearly the supervisory board's task. Under a one-tier system (e.g., the United States and United Kingdom), nonexecutive directors act as monitors.

19. Bainbridge argues for group decision-making. He emphasizes, however, not the effectiveness of monitoring the CEO but rather the potential benefits of team decision-making versus individual decision-making. See Stephen M. Bainbridge, "Why a Board? Group Decision Making in Corporate Governance," *Vanderbilt Law Review* 55 (2002): 19–38. Holmström defends the opposite view, however, and argues that group decision-making may undermine each individual's incentive to engage in monitoring. See Bengt Holmström, "Moral Hazard in Teams," *Bell Journal of Economics* 13 (1982): 326–28, 334–40.

20. Lucian Bebchuk, Jesse Fried, and David Walker, "Executive Compensation in America: Optimal Contracting or Extraction of Rents," 2001, p. 31, available at http://www.bepress.com/cgi/viewpdf.cgi?article=1052&context=blewp& preview_mode (accessed February 15, 2008).

21. Ibid.

22. Donald Langevoort, "The Human Nature of Corporate Boards: Law, Norms, and the Unintended Consequences of Independence and Accountability," *Georgetown Law Journal* 89 (2001): 810–11.

23. Renee Jones, "Policing Corporate Boards: Behavior Analysis Suggests Enforcement Mechanism Needed," http://www.bc.edu/schools/law/alumni/magazine/2005/winter/currents.html.

24. http://www.berkshirehathaway.com/letters/2002pdf.pdf.

25. Business Roundtable, "Principles of Corporate Governance," May 2002, http://www.businessroundtable.org/.

26. Cynthia A. Glassman, U.S. Securities and Exchange Commission, "Remarks on Governance Reforms and the Role of Directors," speech before the National Association of Corporate Directors, October 20, 2003, http://www.sec.gov/news/speech/spch102003cag.htm.

27. http://www.nyse.com/pdfs/finalcorpgovrules.pdf.

28. Ibid.

29. NASDAQ Rule 4200(a)(15), available at http://nasdaq.complinet.com/nasdaq/display/display.html?rbid=1705&element_id=1479.

30. Mike O'Sullivan, "Can Any Special Litigation Committee Satisfy Strine?" July 30, 2003, http://www.corplawblog.com/archives/000161.html.

CHAPTER 5
CASE STUDIES ON BOARDS OF DIRECTORS IN CORPORATE GOVERNANCE

1. *Van Gorkom* 488 A.2d at 894.

2. Bayless Manning, "Reflections and Practical Tips on Life in the Boardroom after *Van Gorkom*," *Business Lawyer* 41 (1985): 1.

3. Fischel, "The Business Judgment Rule and the *TransUnion* Case," 1455.

4. See generally, Jonathan R. Macey, "*Smith v. Van Gorkom* Insights about C.E.O.s, Corporate Law Rules, and the Jurisdictional Competition for Corporate Charters," *Northwestern University Law Review* 96 (2002): 607 (arguing that while the *Van Gorkom* decision "may have dramatically improved the quality of deliberations in corporate boardrooms[,] imposing liability on the defendants was, nonetheless, unjust").

5. See ibid., 609–10.

6. William M. Owen, "A Shareholder Named Smith," *Directors and Boards* (Spring 2000): 39.

7. *Van Gorkom,* 488 A.2d at 880n21.

8. *Id.* at 891.

9. Macey, "*Smith v. Van Gorkom* Insights," 607.

10. Ibid.

11. Ibid., 609.

12. Ibid., 610.

13. *Van Gorkom,* 488 A.2d at 889.

14. Richard Leisner, "Boardroom Jitters: A Landmark Court Decision Upsets Corporate Directors," *Barron's,* April 22, 1985, p. 34.

15. *Van Gorkom,* 488 A.2d 858.

16. *In re The Walt Disney Company Derivative Litigation,* 907 A.2d 693, 702 (2005).

17. See *id.*

18. *Id.* at 712n105.

19. *Id.*

20. *Id.* at 712.

21. Stephen Bainbridge, September 28, 2004, http://www.professorbainbridge.com/2004/09/disney_ovitzs_c.html.

22. *In re The Walt Disney Company Derivative Litigation,* 907 A.2d at 763.

23. *Id.* at 743n386.

24. *Id.* at 741n373.

25. *Id.*

26. The business judgment rule provides generally that courts will not second-guess actions of corporate boards of directors that reflect the exercise of reasonable business judgment, even if the actions turn out to have been mistaken in hindsight. Jonathan R. Macey and Geoffrey P. Miller, "Trans Union Reconsidered," *Yale Law Journal* 98 (1988): 127n3.

27. Troy Paredes, "Enron: The Board, Corporate Governance and Some Thoughts on the Role of Congress," in *Enron: Corporate Fiascos and Their Implications,* ed. Nancy B. Rapoport and Bala G. Dharan (New York: Foundation Press, 2004), 495.

28. Ibid., 535.

29. Ibid., 504–5.

30. Ibid., 505.

31. U.S. Senate, *The Role of the Board of Directors in Enron's Collapse,* 9.

32. Paredes, "Enron," 504.

33. Benjamin Neuhausen was a member of the Professional Standards Group for Enron's accounting firm, Arthur Andersen, and David Duncan ran the Andersen audit engagement team that was assigned to Enron. U.S. Senate, *The Role of the Board of Directors in Enron's Collapse,* 25.

34. Ibid., 35.

35. Robert E. McCormick and Robert D. Tollison, *Politicians, Legislation, and the Economy* (Boston: Martinus Nihhoff, 1981), 7–12.

36. U.S. Senate, *The Role of the Board of Directors in Enron's Collapse,* 12.

37. Brooke A. Masters, "Enron's Quiet Outages: Uncharged in the Fraud, Directors Settled, Resigned, Lay Low," *Washington Post,* June 2, 2006, D1.

38. U.S. Senate, *The Role of the Board of Directors in Enron's Collapse,* 4.

39. Quoted in Gretchen Morgenson, "Sticky Scandals, Teflon Directors," *New York Times,* January 29, 2006.

40. Ibid.

41. Masters, "Enron's Quiet Outages."

42. David Hancox, "Could the Equity Funding Scandal Happen Again? Auditors Need to Guard against the Scenario That Led to One of Auditing's Darkest Hours," *Internal Auditor,* October 1997, http://www.allbusiness.com/accounting-reporting/auditing/641903–1.html.

43. Ibid.

44. Raymond Dirks and Leonard Gross, *The Great Wall Street Scandal* (New York: McGraw-Hill, 1974), 202.

45. *In re Equity Funding Corporation,* 603 F.2d 1353 (1979).

CHAPTER 6
DISSIDENT DIRECTORS

1. "Fighting Words for Time Warner: Carl Icahn on Gambits to Goose the Stock—Including a Possible Breakup," Business Week Online, November 28, 2005, http://www.businessweek.com/magazine/content/05_48/b3961119.htm (accessed January 21, 2008).

2. Michael C. Jensen and Joe Fuller, "What's a Director to Do?" The Monitor Group, 2002, http://www.monitor.com/binary-data/MONITOR_ARTICLES/object/163.PDF (accessed January 21, 2008).

3. Spencer Stuart, "A Closer Look at Lead and Presiding Directors," *Cornerstone of the Board* 1, no. 4 (2006): 1.

4. Council of Institutional Investors, Council Policies, http://www.cii.org/policies/boardofdirectors.htm.

5. Spencer Stuart, "A Closer Look," 4.

6. Ibid., 9.

7. Jonathan Macey, "Promoting Public-Regarding Legislation through Statutory Interpretation: An Interest Group Model," *Columbia Law Review* 86 (1986): 223.

8. C. Rossiter, ed., The Federalist No. 10 (J. Madison) (1961): 77.

9. C. Rossiter, ed., The Federalist No. 78 (A. Hamilton) (1961): 468.

10. James M. Buchanan and Gordon Tullock, *The Calculus of Consent: Logical Foundations of Constitutional Democracy* (Ann Arbor: University of Michigan Press, 1962).

11. Sanjai Bhagat and Bernard Black, "The Uncertain Relationship between Board Composition and Firm Performance," *Business Lawyer* 54 (1999): 921.

12. Roberta Romano, "The Sarbanes-Oxley Act and the Making of Quack Corporate Governance," *Yale Law Journal* 114 (2005): 1530.

13. Bhagat and Black, "Uncertain Relationship," 3.

14. Dennis C. Carey and Nayla Rizk, "Seismic Shift in Board Composition," Spencer Stuart Governance Letter, Third Quarter, 2005, p. 37.

15. Ibid.

16. Ibid.

17. Adrian Cadbury and Ira Millstein, "The New Agenda for ICGN," *International Corporate Governance Network 2005 Yearbook,* pp. 5, 7.

CHAPTER 7
FORMAL EXTERNAL INSTITUTIONS OF CORPORATE GOVERNANCE

1. Thompson is a former governor of Illinois and a partner with the law firm of Winston and Strawn; Burt is a former U.S. ambassador to Germany; and Kravis is the spouse of the financier Henry R. Kravis and a member of the boards of the Ford Motor Company and IAC/InterActive Corp.

2. Richard Siklos, "S.E.C. Puts Three Hollinger Directors on Notice," *New York Times,* December 15, 2005, C1.

3. Ibid., C2.

4. See *Business Roundtable v. SEC*, 905 F.2d 406 (D.C. Cir. 1990) (litigation related to the SEC's attempt to bar securities exchanges from listing corporations that reduced the per share voting rights of already existing common share holders).

5. See Stephen Taub, "GAO Criticizes SEC Internal Controls," November 23, 2005, http://www.cfo.com/article.cfm/5213245?f=search (accessed January 13, 2008).

6. Susan Dudley and Melinda Warren, "Regulatory Spending Soars: An Analysis of the U.S. Budget for Fiscal Years 2003 and 2004," 2004 Annual Report (July 2003): 14–19, http://wc.wustl.edu/Reg_Budget_final.pdf (accessed August 9, 2004).

7. U.S. Senate Committee on Appropriations, Subcommittee News, April 8, 2003, http://appropriations.senate.gov/text/subcommittees/record.cfm?id=203432 (accessed February 22, 2005).

8. Ibid.

9. Actually, the SEC's 2005 budget request totaled $913 million, and was 12.5 percent above the amount authorized in 2004. The amount consisted of $893 million in new budget authority and $20 million in anticipated balances from the prior year. This budget request—the first crafted by Chairman Donaldson since his arrival in February 2003—permitted the commission to hire 106 new employees. Press Release, Securities and Exchange Commission, "SEC Releases FY 2005 Budget Information," http://www.sec.gov/news/press/2004-11.htm (accessed August 9, 2004).

10. Press Release, Office of the Press Secretary, "Fact Sheet: Restoring Economic Confidence and Tackling Corporate Fraud," January 11, 2003, http://www.whitehouse.gov/news/releases/2003/01/20030111-1.html (accessed July 24, 2004).

11. Investor and Capital Markets Fee Relief Act, Public Law 107–23, § 8, 115 Stat. 2390, 2398 (2002). See also Securities and Exchange Commission, "Pay Parity Implementation Plan and Report," March 6, 2002, http://www.sec.gov/news/studies/payparity.htm.

12. John C. Coffee Jr., "A Course of Inaction: Where Was the SEC When the Mutual Fund Scandal Happened?" 2004-APR Legal Aff. 46, 49 (2004) (discussing the SEC's passivity with regard to the mutual fund crisis); Jonathan R. Macey, "Administrative Agency Obsolescence and Interest Group Formation: A Case Study of the SEC at Sixty," *Cardozo Law Review* 15 (1994): 948–49.

13. "Senators Slam SEC in Funds Scandal," November 3, 2003, http://www.cbsnews.com/stories/2003/11/04/national/main581683.shtml; see also "Senators Blast SEC over Mutual Fund Trading Scandal," November 3, 2003, http://www.usatoday.com/money/perfi/funds/2003–11–03-fund-hearing_x.htm.

14. Jonathan R. Macey, "Wall Street in Turmoil: State-Federal Relations Post–Eliot Spitzer," *Brooklyn Law Review* 70 (2004): 120–21.

15. "Exemption from Shareholder Approval for Certain Subadvisory Contracts," Federal Register No. 61720, vol. 68 (October 29, 2003).

16. Only shareholders who meet the following four criteria will have access to the company's proxy materials: (a) beneficial ownership of more than 5 percent of the company's voting stock, held continuously for at least two years; (b) decla-

ration of intent to continue owning the requisite number of securities through the date of the relevant shareholders' meeting; (c) eligibility to report their holdings on Schedule 13G rather than 13D; and (d) they have filed a Schedule 13G before their nomination is submitted to the corporation.

17. "Exemption from Shareholder Approval for Certain Subadvisory Contracts."

18. Securities and Exchange Commission, Security Holder Director Nominations, Exchange Act Release No. 34–48626 (proposed October 14, 2003), http://www.sec.gov/rules/proposed34–48626.htm.

19. Jonathan R. Macey, "Securities and Exchange Nanny," *Wall Street Journal*, December 30, 2003, A10.

20. See Jonathan R. Macey, "The Legality and Utility of the Shareholder Rights Bylaw," *Hofstra Law Review* 26 (1998): 837.

21. "Exemption from Shareholder Approval for Certain Subadvisory Contracts," 60797–98.

22. Ibid., 60799.

23. Macey, "Wall Street in Turmoil," 136.

24. "Disclosure Regarding Approval of Investment Advisory Contracts by Directors of Investment Companies," 17 C.F.R. §§ 239, 240, and 274, Federal Register No. 39798, vol. 69.

25. Cynthia A. Glassman, "Statement by SEC Commissioner Regarding Investment Company Governance Proposal," address at U.S. Securities and Exchange Commission Open Meeting, June 23, 2004, http://www.sec.gov/news/speech/spch062304cag.htm.

26. Ibid.

27. Macey, "Wall Street in Turmoil," 137.

28. Coffee, "A Course of Inaction," 46, 49.

29. Jonathan Macey and Maureen O'Hara, "From Markets to Venues: Securities Regulation in an Evolving World," *Stanford Law Review* 59 (2005): 569.

30. The available evidence here consists largely of series of episodes in which the exchanges fail to self-regulate, often followed by a coordinated regulation led by the SEC. Self-regulation by the exchanges is in general dysfunctional in significant part because securities are often traded simultaneously in multiple venues, thus inhibiting the ability of exchanges to unilaterally enforce regulations. See Macey and O'Hara, "From Markets to Venues," 577–79: "As a purely descriptive matter, the available evidence is inconsistent with the assertion that rival trading venues compete to produce corporate law rules. Rather, the accurate depiction of the competitive situation is that the SEC coordinates the regulatory standards of the exchanges and the Nasdaq to prevent competition among these trading venues from occurring at all."

31. Macey and O'Hara, "From Markets to Venues," 571, 577. See also Robert Todd Lang et al., American Bar Association, "Special Study on Market Structure, Listing Standards and Corporate Governance," *Business Lawyer* 57 (2002): 1503.

32. See Securities and Exchange Commission Office of Chief Economist, "Update: The Effects of Dual-Class Recapitalizations on Shareholder Wealth: Including Evidence from 1986 and 1987," July 16, 1987, table 1. See also Jeffrey N.

Gordon, "Ties That Bond: Dual Class Common Stock and the Problem of Share-holder Choice," *California Law Review* 76 (1988): 4 (counting over eighty public firms that have "adopted, or proposed to adopt, capital structures with two classes of common stock"). In footnote 2, Gordon adds, "One recent estimate is that since 1985 the number of companies with dual classes of stock has risen from 119 to 306."

33. *Business Roundtable v. SEC,* 905 F.2d 406, 407 (D.C. Cir. 1990), declared the SEC's rule invalid. However, by the time of this ruling, the NASDAQ, the AMEX, and the NYSE had adopted the SEC's proposed rule, and none was will-ing to risk its ongoing relationship with the SEC by returning to its previous rule. Barbara Franklin, "New Stock Issue Rules; Technical Changes Seen Resulting in Tougher Enforcement," *New York Law Journal,* September 7, 1989, p. 5. It should be added that the holding in *Business Roundtable v. SEC* that the SEC lacked authority to promulgate rules of corporate governance has been weakened considerably, if not eviscerated entirely, by the Sarbanes-Oxley Act of 2002, which gave a significant amount of new power to the SEC in the realm of corporate governance. Sarbanes-Oxley Act of 2002, 15 U.S.C.A. §§ 7211–19.

34. Securities and Exchange Commission, "Written Statement of Raymond W. McDaniel, President, Moody's Investors Service," November 21, 2002, http://www.sec.gov/news/extra/credrate/moodys.htm.

35. House Committee on Financial Services, "Credit Rating Agency Duopoly Relief Act of 2005: Hearing on H.R. 2990 before the Subcommittee on Capital Markets, Insurance and Government Sponsored Enterprises," 109th Cong., 1st sess., 2005 (statement of Frank Partnoy, professor of law, University of San Diego School of Law).

36. Ibid. ("Numerous academic studies have shown that ratings changes lag the market.") See also "Rating Agencies and the Use of Credit Ratings under the Securities Laws, Concept Release No. 33–8236," Federal Register No. 35258, vol. 68 (June 4, 2003).

37. Jonathan R. Macey, "Efficient Capital Markets, Corporate Disclosure, and Enron," *Cornell Law Review* 89 (2004): 406.

38. On the effects of cartelization in the credit-rating industry, see generally, Claire A. Hill, "Regulating the Rating Agencies," *Washington University Law Quarterly* 82 (2004): 43 (calling particular attention to reforming the industry by encouraging a less concentrated market structure). For empirical evidence on the perceived poor quality of credit-rating agencies, see House Subcommittee on Capi-tal Markets of the House Financial Services Committee, "Rating the Rating Agen-cies: The State of Transparency and Competition," 108th Cong., 1st sess., 2003, http://financialservices.house.gov/media/pdf/108–18.pdf.

39. See note 35.

40. Securities and Exchange Commission, Hearings on Issues Relating to Credit Rating Agencies, "Statement of Amy Lancellotta, Senior Counsel, Invest-ment Company Institute," November 21, 2002, http://www.ici.org/statements/tmny/02_sec_2a-7_stmt.html.

41. Daniel M. Covitz and Paul Harrison, "Testing Conflicts of Interest at Bond Ratings Agencies with Market Anticipation: Evidence That Reputation Incentives

Dominate," December 2003 draft, http://www.federalreserve.gov/Pubs/feds/
2003/200368/200368pap.pdf.

42. Nigel Jaquiss, "The Producer: How PGE Manipulated the Record to Try
to Raise Our Electricity Rates," *Willamette Week,* December 6, 2006, p. 1, http://
www.wweek.com/editorial/3304/8297/.

43. Ibid.

44. Ibid.

45. See "Standard and Poor's Rating Services, Code of Conduct," Sections
1.18, 2.1, October 2005, http://www2.standardandpoors.com/spf/pdf/media/
sp_code.pdf.

46. Ibid.

CHAPTER 8
THE MARKET FOR CORPORATE CONTROL

1. The U.S. system has historically confronted agency problems through takeovers. A wealth of theoretical arguments and empirical evidence supports the
proposition that takeovers address corporate governance problems, particularly
by controlling managerial discretion. Shleifer and Vishny observe that "[t]ake-
overs are widely interpreted as the critical corporate governance mechanism in
the United States, without which managerial discretion cannot be effectively controlled." Andrei Shleifer and Robert W. Vishny, "A Survey of Corporate Governance," *Journal of Finance* 52 (1997): 756.

2. Henry G. Manne, "Mergers and the Market for Corporate Control," *Jour-
nal of Political Economy* 73 (1965): 113; Frank H. Easterbrook and Daniel R.
Fischel, "The Proper Role of a Target's Management in Responding to a Tender
Offer," *Harvard Law Review* 94 (1981): 1169.

3. See Michael C. Jensen and Richard S. Ruback, "The Market for Corporate
Control: The Scientific Evidence," *Journal of Financial Economics* 11 (1983): 5.
While the vast majority of scholars seem to agree with Jensen and Ruback that
corporate takeovers generate positive value, there are a few notable dissents: see,
e.g., Robert B. Reich, *The Next American Frontier* (New York: Penguin, 1983):
140–72; Robert H. Hayes and William J. Abernathy, "Managing Our Way to
Economic Decline," *Harvard Business Review* (July–August 1980): 67, 73–74,
also available in *Managerial Excellence: McKinsey Award Winners from the
Harvard Business Review, 1980–1994* (Boston: Harvard Business School
Press, 1996).

4. My colleague Roberta Romano has similarly observed in her article, "A
Guide to Takeovers: Theory, Evidence, and Regulation," *Yale Journal on Regulation* 9 (1992): 120–21, that "[t]he empirical evidence is most consistent with
value-maximizing, efficiency-based explanations of takeovers. Yet the thrust of
regulation is to thwart and burden takeovers, as if they were non-value-maximiz-
ing wealth transfers." Romano goes on to catalogue the variety of regulations that
serve to restrict the market for corporate control.

5. The Business Roundtable is made up of the CEOs of about 200 of the leading
U.S. corporations, representing about 50 percent of the U.S. GDP. It was founded

in 1972 in order to do the following: (1) enable chief executives from different corporations to work together to analyze specific issues affecting the economy and business; and (2) present government and the public with knowledgeable, timely information, and with practical, positive proposals for action. See "Business Roundtable History," http://www.businessroundtable.org/aboutUs/history.html; Amitai Etzioni, "Special Interest Groups Versus Constituency Representation," *Research in Social Movements, Conflicts and Change* 8 (1985): 184.

    6. Roberta Romano, ed., *Foundations of Corporate Law* (New York: Oxford University Press, 1993), 230.

    7. Theodor Baums and Kenneth E. Scott, "Taking Shareholder Protection Seriously? Corporate Governance in the U.S. and Germany," *Journal of Applied Corporate Finance* 17 (2005): 59, 59n55; Gregg A. Jarrell, James A. Brickley, and Jeffry M. Netter, "The Market for Corporate Control: The Empirical Evidence since 1980," *Journal of Economic Perspectives* 2 (1988): 52.

    8. See Easterbrook and Fischel, "The Proper Role of a Target's Management in Responding to a Tender Offer," 1174 ("Managers will attempt to reduce agency costs to reduce the chance of takeover, and the process of reducing agency costs leads to higher prices for shares"). See also Daniel R. Fischel, "The Corporate Governance Movement," *Vanderbilt Law Review* 35 (1982): 1264 (arguing that the market for corporate control "simultaneously gives managers of all firms who wish to avoid a takeover an incentive to operate efficiently and to keep share prices high").

    9. In this context, the term "contestable" means susceptible to the market for corporate control. A firm's shares are contestable in the market for corporate control if a majority of the shares are in the hands of independent (non-management-affiliated), value-maximizing shareholders. Where, for example, a majority of the voting shares of a company are in the hands of small-stake shareholders or institutional investors focused on share price performance, the company's shares are contestable. By contrast, where shares are parked with friendly institutional investors or incumbent management and their allies have shares with supermajority voting rights that prevent an outside acquirer from obtaining a majority of the voting shares, the company's shares are not contestable.

    10. As important as the market for corporate control clearly is, it nonetheless is possible to overstate the role played by this device in corporate governance. In particular, the market for corporate control has not been capable of dealing with recent corporate governance problems at firms like Enron and WorldCom, which involve artificially inflated earnings, profits, and other measures of corporate performance. See E. S. Browning, "Abreast of the Market: Investor Confidence Remains Fickle," *Wall Street Journal*, September 9, 2002, C1 ("Scandals at Enron, WorldCom, Global Crossing, Tyco International, Adelphia Communications, ImClone Systems and a host of other companies have raised questions about whether corporate earnings reports and corporate executives can be trusted"). The problem is that the market for corporate control only disciplines bad management when the target firm's share prices are depressed. Because accounting fraud causes share prices to be artificially inflated rather than depressed, the takeover entrepreneurs who drive the market for corporate control have no incentive to launch hostile takeovers.

11. Baums and Scott, "Taking Shareholder Protection Seriously," 58–59.

12. Ibid.

13. Ibid.

14. Williams Act of 1968, Pub. L. No. 90–439, § 3, 82 Stat. 454, 456 (1968).

15. Baums and Scott, "Taking Shareholder Protection Seriously," 58.

16. Henry G. Manne, "Bring Back the Hostile Takeover," *Wall Street Journal,* June 26, 2002, A18.

17. Baums and Scott, "Taking Shareholder Protection Seriously," 58–59.

18. See, e.g., Ronald Gilson, "A Structural Approach to Corporations: The Case against Defensive Tactics in Tender Offers," *Stanford Law Review* 33 (1981): 837–38.

19. *Moran v. Household International,* 500 A.2d 1346 (Del. 1985).

20. Easterbrook and Fischel, *The Economic Structure of Corporate Law,* 204.

21. Baums and Scott, "Taking Shareholder Protection Seriously," 59.

22. *Moran,* 500 A.2d at 1354.

23. See Baums and Scott, "Taking Shareholder Protection Seriously," 59 (observing that the requirement that use of the pill must pass muster with the Delaware Supreme Court "proved hollow").

24. Baums and Scott, "Taking Shareholder Protection Seriously," 59.

25. *Paramount Communications v. Time, Inc.,* 571 A.2d 1140, 1154 (Del. 1989).

26. See also *Unitrin v. American General Corp.,* 651 A.2d 1361, 1385 (Del. 1995).

27. *Paramount,* 571 A.2d at 1142.

28. William J. Carney, "Shareholder Coordination Costs, Shark Repellents, and Takeout Mergers: The Case against Fiduciary Duties," *American Bar Foundation Research Journal* 8 (1983): 350–53.

29. *Moran,* 500 A.2d at 1356.

30. See also *Ivanhoe Partners v. Newmont Mining Corp.,* 535 A.2d 1334, 1342 (Del. 1987) ("[t]his Court has recognized the coercive nature of two-tier partial tender offers"); *Unocal Corp. v. Mesa Petroleum Co.,* 493 A.2d 946, 956 (Del. 1985) (the court found a "grossly inadequate" two-tier offer to be coercive).

31. *Paramount,* 571 A.2d at 1140.

32. *Moran,* 500 A.2d at 1354.

33. There are at least two ways that bidders can obtain the approval of the target firm's board. The first is by making the tender offer contingent on the decision by the target company's board to redeem the pill. This contingency is now a routine part of the tender offers bidding process. Bidders can also obtain the approval of the target firm's board by launching a proxy contest for control of the target board simultaneously with the announcement of a tender offer. By acquiring control of the board, the bidder can use such control to redeem the pill. Staggered boards of directors, of course, make the latter tactic more difficult for bidders. See Lucian Arye Bebchuk, John C. Coates IV, and Guhan Subramaniam, "The Powerful Antitakeover Force of Staggered Boards: Theory, Evidence, and Policy," *Stanford Law Review* 54 (2002): 887.

34. Baums and Scott, "Taking Shareholder Protection Seriously," 59.

CHAPTER 9
INITIAL PUBLIC OFFERINGS AND PRIVATE PLACEMENTS

1. Frank H. Easterbrook, "Two Agency-Cost Explanations of Dividends," *American Economic Review* 74 (1984): 654.

2. The seminal article on the economic effect of underwriters' civil liability on the new issues market is Michael Dooley, "The Effects of Liability on Investment Banking and the New Issues Market," *Virginia Law Review* 58 (1972): 776. When prices go up, supply goes down. Since increased risk of liability is, from the issuer's point of view, a cost of going public, when the risk of liability goes up, the supply of public offerings will decline. Overimposing of civil liability on securities underwriters creates other inefficiencies in the public offerings market. See, e.g., Seha M. Tahic, "Anatomy of Initial Public Offerings of Common Stock," *Journal of Finance* 43 (1988): 790 (discusses empirical evidence demonstrating that "gross underpricing [of IPOs] serves as an efficient form of protection against legal liabilities . . . it is a form of implicit insurance against potential liabilities that may arise from the 'due diligence' and disclosure requirements of the federal securities regulations").

3. Easterbrook, "Two Agency-Cost Explanations of Dividends," 650–51.

4. Historically, dividends were taxed as ordinary income, at rates as high as 38.6 percent. The Jobs and Growth Tax Relief Reconciliation Act (JGTRRA) of 2003 reduced the taxes on dividends received from U.S. companies, certain mutual funds, and so-called qualified foreign corporations (generally those incorporated in a U.S. possession, eligible for benefits under a U.S. tax treaty that meets certain criteria, or readily traded on an established U.S. exchange as stock or an ADR (American Depository Receipt) to 15 percent for most taxpayers. For lower-income individuals, the tax rate on dividends drops to 5 percent, decreasing to zero percent in 2008. These lower rates of 15 percent and 5 percent became effective for dividends received beginning January 2003 and are scheduled to expire beginning in 2009. Jobs and Growth Tax Relief Reconciliation Act, Pub. L. No. *108–27, § 303, 117 Stat. 752, 764 (2003).*

CHAPTER 10
GOVERNANCE BY LITIGATION

1. Reinier Kraakman et al., "When Are Shareholder Suits in Shareholder Interests?" *Georgetown Law Journal* 82 (1994): 1733.

2. "Litigation Reform Proposals," hearing before the House Subcommittee on Telecommunications and Finance, Committee on Commerce, 104th Cong., 1st sess. (1995) (statement of Arthur Levitt, chairman of the U.S. Securities and Exchange Commission), http://www.sec.gov/news/testimony/testarchive/1995/spch025.txt.

3. See, e.g., *Basic v. Levinson,* 485 U.S. 224, 245 (1988) (noting that shareholder class actions are necessary to implement the policy embodied in the Securities and Exchange Act of 1934).

4. Fed. R. Civ. P. 23(a).

5. Elliott J. Weiss and John S. Beckerman, "Let the Money Do the Monitoring: How Institutional Investors Can Reduce Agency Costs in Securities Class Actions," *Yale Law Journal* 104 (1995): 2056–57.

6. Ibid., 2060. See also *Koening v. Benson,* 117 F.R.D. 330, 337 (E.D.N.Y. 1987) (plaintiff did not speak, read, or write English and was unfamiliar with the facts of his case).

7. Jonathan R. Macey and Geoffrey P. Miller, "The Plaintiffs' Attorney's Role in Class Action and Derivative Litigation: Economic Analysis and Recommendations for Reform," *University of Chicago Law Review* 58 (1991): 20.

8. Ibid.

9. Ibid.

10. See *In re Cendant Corp. Litigation,* 264 F.3d 201, 255 (2001).

11. *Id.* See also Weiss and Beckerman, "Let the Money Do the Monitoring," 2065 (noting that conflicts of interest cause plaintiffs' attorneys to try to maximize their fee income when considering settlement); Andrew Rosenfeld, "An Empirical Test of Class-Action Settlements," *Journal of Legal Studies* 5 (1976): 116–17 (observing that plaintiffs' attorneys earn a "settlement premium" in cases that settle compared to fees earned in cases that are adjudicated on the merits).

12. *In re Cendant Corp. Litig.,* 264 F.3d at 255.

13. See, e.g., Del. Ch. Ct. R. 23.1; Fed. R. Civ. P. 23.1; see also "Principles of Corporate Governance: Analysis and Recommendations," § 7.03(b) (1994) (recommending a universal demand requirement).

14. See *Zapata Corp. v. Maldonado,* 430 A.2d 779, 784 (Del. 1981).

15. See Macey and Miller, "The Plaintiffs' Attorney's Role in Class Action and Derivative Litigation," 35.

16. Ibid.

17. Ibid.

18. Ibid., 37.

19. See *Aronson v. Lewis,* 473 A.2d 805 (Del. 1984); *Marx v. Akers,* 666 N.E.2d 1034 (N.Y. 1996).

20. Joel Seligman, "The New Corporate Law," *Brooklyn Law Review* 59 (1993): 29n119 (noting that the vast majority of special litigation committee recommendations conclude that litigation is not in the company's best interest), citing James D. Cox, "Searching for the Corporation's Voice in Derivative Suit Litigation: A Critique of *Zapata* and the ALI Project," *Duke Law Journal* (1982): 963.

21. *Zapata,* 430 A.2d 779.

22. See Macey and Miller, "The Plaintiffs' Attorney's Role in Class Action and Derivative Litigation," 38.

23. Ibid.

24. Ibid., 39.

25. Ibid.

26. See Robert B. Thompson and Randall S. Thomas, "The Public and Private Faces of Derivative Lawsuits," *Vanderbilt Law Review* 57 (2004): 1747.

27. Ibid., 1759, citing Randall S. Thomas and Kenneth J. Martin, "Litigating Challenges to Executive Pay: An Exercise in Futility," *Washington University Law Quarterly* 79 (2001): 576–80.

28. Thompson and Thomas, "The Public and Private Faces of Derivative Lawsuits," 1772.

29. Ibid., 1773.

30. See, e.g., Roberta Romano, "The Shareholder Suit: Litigation without Foundation?" *Journal of Law, Economics and Organization* 7 (1995): 65; Stephen M. Bainbridge, *Corporation Law and Economics* (New York: Foundation Press, 2002), 404 ("Derivative litigation appears to have little, if any, beneficial accountability effects").

31. See Thompson and Thomas, "The Public and Private Faces of Derivative Lawsuits," 1790.

32. Ibid.

33. See Macey and Miller, "The Plaintiffs' Attorney's Role in Class Action and Derivative Litigation," 40.

34. Ibid., 41.

35. Ibid.

36. Ibid., 47.

37. Micah Morrison, "High-Profile Trial Looms Large for Controversial Class-Action Leader," *The Examiner,* January 2, 2007, http://www.examiner .com/a-485585~High_profile_trial_looms_large_for_controversial_class_action _leader.html.

38. Before the Private Securities Litigation Reform Act of 1995, the class action rules awarded a huge benefit to lawyers representing the first lead plaintiff to file a class action lawsuit on a particular claim in response to evidence of corporate wrongdoing: the lawyers of the representative plaintiff who "won the race to the courthouse" received control the litigation and, as a result, the lion's share of the fees.

39. First Superseding Indictment, *United States v. Milberg Weiss Bershad and Shulman LLP,* CR 05–587(A)-DDP (C.D. Cal. October 2004), http://www.law .com/pdf/ca/milberg_indictment.pdf.

40. Peter Elkind, "The Fall of America's Meanest Law Firm," *Fortune,* November 3, 2006, pp. 155, 157, http://money.cnn.com/magazines/fortune/fortune _archive/2006/11/13/8393127/index.htm.

41. Morrison, "High-Profile Trial Looms Large for Controversial Class-Action Leader."

42. Ibid.

43. Ibid.

44. See Macey and Miller, "The Plaintiffs' Attorney's Role in Class Action and Derivative Litigation," 45.

45. See ibid.

46. *In re QVC, Inc. Shareholders Litigation,* No. 13590-NC, 1997 Del. Ch. LEXIS 14 (February 5, 1997).

47. Jill E. Fisch, "Class Action Reform, *Qui Tam,* and the Role of the Plaintiff," *Law and Contemporary Problems* 60 (1997): 167.

48. *In re QVC, Inc. Shareholders Litig.,* 1997 Del. Ch. LEXIS at *6.

49. *Id.* at *11–12, quoted in Fisch, "Class Action Reform," 167.

50. *In re QVC, Inc. Shareholders Litig.,* 1997 Del. Ch. LEXIS at *12.

51. Jonathan R. Macey and Geoffrey P. Miller, "Toward an Interest-Group Theory of Delaware Corporate Law," *Texas Law Review* 65 (1987): 469.

52. *In re Caremark Int'l Inc. Derivative Litigation,* 698 A.2d 959 (Del. Ch. 1996).

53. *Id.* at 961.

54. *Id.*

55. Robert W. Hamilton and Jonathan R. Macey, *Cases and Materials on Corporations, Including Partnerships and Limited Liability Companies,* 9th ed. (St. Paul, MN: Thomson/West, 2005), 702–3.

56. See Romano, "The Shareholder Suit," 60.

57. Lawrence W. Schonbrun, "The Class Action Con Game," *Regulation* 20 (Fall 1997): 54–55 at 50, also available at http://www.cato.org/pubs/regulation/reg20n4j.html.

58. See Romano, "The Shareholder Suit," 57.

59. See ibid.

60. See ibid., 57n1.

61. See, e.g., Macey and Miller, "Trans Union Reconsidered," 105–16.

62. Ibid.

63. See *In re Cendant Corporation Litig.,* 264 F.3d at 259.

64. *Id.* at 259–60.

65. See Macey and Miller, "Trans Union Reconsidered," 116; Andrew K. Niebler, "In Search of Bargained-For Fees for Class Action Plaintiffs' Lawyers: The Promise and Pitfalls of Auctioning the Position of Lead Counsel," *Business Lawyer* 54 (1999): 831–34.

66. Richard M. Phillips and Gilbert C. Miller, "The Private Securities Litigation Reform Act of 1995: Rebalancing Litigation Risks and Rewards for Class Action Plaintiffs, Defendants and Lawyers," *Business Lawyer* 51 (1996): 1009. See also Edward R. Becker et al., "The Private Securities Law Reform Act: Is It Working?" *Fordham Law Review* 71 (2003): 2382 (noting that in passing the PSLRA, "a dominant concern among Members of Congress . . . was frivolous litigation").

67. U.S. Senate, *A Bill to Amend the Securities Exchange Act of 1934 to Establish a Filing Deadline and to Provide Certain Safeguards to Ensure That the Interests of Investors Are Well Protected under the Implied Private Action Provisions of the Act,* 104th Cong., 1st sess., 1995, S. Rep. 104–98, 240, 276.

68. Phillips and Miller, "The Private Securities Litigation Reform Act of 1995," 1011.

69. Ibid., 1013.

70. Ibid., 1014.

71. See ibid., 1015.

72. Romano, "The Shareholder Suit," 60.

73. Ibid., 61.

74. U.S. Senate, *A Bill to Amend the Securities Exchange Act of 1934.*

75. 15 U.S.C., § 78u-4(a)(3)(B)(vi).

76. 15 U.S.C., § 78u-4(f).

77. *In re Cendant Corp. Litig.,* 264 F.3d 201.

78. *Id.* at 281.

79. *Id.* at 221–22.

80. 15 U.S.C., § 78u-4(a)(3)(B)(v).

81. *In re Cendant Corp. Litig.*, 264 F.3d at 224–25.

82. *Id.* at 220.

83. *Id.* at 277–86.

84. See, e.g., *In re Razorfish Corp. Litigation*, 143 F. Supp. 2d 304, 311 (S.D.N.Y. 2001) (stating that "such modest intervention by the Court is fully consistent with the mandate of the Reform Act that the lead plaintiff's selection and retention of counsel be subject to a court approval that is meaningful and not simply perfunctory").

85. See, e.g., *In re Bank One Shareholders Class Actions*, 96 F. Supp. 2d 780 (N.D. Ill. 2000); *In re Lucent Techs., Inc. Sec. Litig.*, 194 F.R.D. 137 (D.N.J. 2000); *Sherleigh Assocs. v. Windmere-Durable Holdings, Inc.*, 184 F.R.D. 688 (S.D. Fla. 1999); *Wenderhold v. Cylink Corp.*, 188 F.R.D. 577 (N.D. Cal. 1999).

86. *In re Lucent Techs., Inc. Sec. Litig.*, 194 F.R.D. at 156.

87. *Id.* (quoting *In re Baan Co. Sec. Litig.*, 186 F.R.D. 214 [D.D.C. 1999]).

88. See Fed. R. Civ. P. 23 (e) (for class actions); Fed. R. Civ. P. 23.1 (for derivative actions).

89. Macey and Miller, "The Plaintiffs' Attorney's Role in Class Action and Derivative Litigation," 46.

90. Ibid.

91. Ibid., 47.

92. Federal Deposit Insurance Corporation Improvement Act of 1991, title IV, sec. 476, 105 Stat. 2387 (codified at 15 U.S.C., § 78aa-1).

93. Julie Pitta and James Flanigan, "Companies Cheer State Voters' New Attitude," *Los Angeles Times*, November 7, 1996, D1.

CHAPTER 11
ACCOUNTING, ACCOUNTING RULES, AND THE ACCOUNTING INDUSTRY

1. Michael Greenstone, Paul Oyer, and Annette Vissing-Jørgensen, "Mandatory Disclosure, Stock Returns and the 1964 Securities Acts Amendments," *Quarterly Journal of Economics* 121 (May 2006): 399–460.

2. Theodore Eisenberg and Jonathan R. Macey, "Was Arthur Andersen Different? An Empirical Examination of Major Accounting Firm Audits of Large Clients," *Journal of Empirical Legal Studies* 1 (2004): 266.

3. Thus, external auditing firms do not perform services that the companies do not already perform for themselves. The auditing firm's role is not to prepare financial reports for clients—that is the accountant's role. Rather, the auditing firm's role is to provide a reliable verification of a company's financial reports. See generally Rick Antle, "Auditor Independence," *Journal of Accounting Research* 22 (1984): 1; George J. Benston, "The Value of the SEC's Accounting Disclosure Requirements," *Accounting Review* 44 (1969): 515; Ronald R. King, "Reputation Formation for Reliable Reporting: An Experimental Investigation," *Accounting Review* 71 (1996): 375; Brian W. Mahew, "Auditor Reputation Building," *Journal of Accounting Research* 39 (2001): 599; Brian W. Mahew et al.,

"The Effect of Accounting Uncertainty and Auditor Reputation on Auditor Objectivity," *Auditing: A Journal of Practice and Theory,* September 2001, p. 31; Norman Macintosh et al., "Accounting as Simulacrum and Hyper-reality: Perspectives on Income and Capital," *Accounting, Organizations, and Society* 25 (2000): 13; Ross L. Watts and Jerold L. Zimmerman, "Agency Problems, Auditing, and the Theory of the Firm: Some Evidence," *Journal of Law and Economics* 26 (1983): 613.

4. Eisenberg and Macey, "Was Arthur Anderson Different," 266.

5. Ibid.

6. Jonathan R. Macey and Hillary Sale, "Observations on the Role of Commodification, Independence, and Governance in the Accounting Industry," *Villanova Law Review* 48 (2003): 1168.

7. Independence is measured by the percentage of an audit firm's billings derived from a particular client. For example, Arthur Andersen was considered independent of Enron because it had 2,300 other auditing clients, and Enron accounted for about 1 percent of its total revenue from auditing. Arthur Andersen's revenues from Enron were $100 million in 2001, compared with total revenues of $9.34 billion. Of course, its independence as an auditing firm did not extend to the individual partners responsible for Enron's auditing work. Macey and Sale, "Observations," 1168.

8. *DiLeo v. Ernst & Young,* 901 F.2d 624, 629 (7th Cir. 1990).

9. Eisenberg and Macey, "Was Arthur Andersen Different," 267.

10. An auditing firm's resignation sends a very powerful negative signal to investors and can entail dire consequences—not only for the company from which the auditing firm resigns but for the company's managers as well. See, e.g., Martin Fackler, "Drawing a Line: Unlikely Team Sets Japanese Banking on Road to Reform," *Wall Street Journal,* August 6, 2003, A1 (describing how an auditing firm's failure to certify a large Japanese bank's financial projections caused a crisis, forcing the bank to seek a $17 billion government bailout and thereby putting it under government control).

11. Daniel B. Thornton, "Financial Reporting Quality: Implications of Accounting Research, Submission to the Senate (Canada) Standing Committee on Banking, Trade and Commerce, Study on the State of Domestic and International Financial System," May 29, 2002, http://www.icfaipress.org/1004/ijar.asp?mag= http://www.icfaipress.org/1004/ijar_sub.asp.

12. See U.S. Gen. Accounting Office, Pub. No. GAO-03–864, "Public Accounting Firms: Mandated Study on Consolidation and Competition," July 2003, pp. 20–22, http://www.gao.gov/new.items/d03864.pdf.

13. See U.S. Department of Justice, *Horizontal Merger Guidelines* (Washington, DC: Federal Trade Commission, 1992), 15 (explaining HHI).

14. See Thornton, "Financial Reporting Quality," 18–20.

15. "The Future of Auditing: Called to Account," *The Economist,* November 20, 2004, pp. 71–73.

16. Lawrence A. Cunningham, "Too Big to Fail: Moral Hazard in Auditing and the Need to Restructure the Industry before It Unravels," *Columbia Law Review* 106 (2006): 1698.

17. See Thornton, "Financial Reporting Quality," 18–20.

18. Ibid.

19. Report to the Senate Committee on Housing and Urban Affairs and the House Committee on Financial Services, *Public Accounting Firms: Mandated Study on Consolidation and Competition*, July 2003, p. 4, GAO 03–864, available at http://www.gao.gov/new.items/d03864.pdf.

20. "Sarbanes-Oxley: A Price Worth Paying?" *The Economist*, May 19, 2005, pp. 71–73.

21. Sarbanes-Oxley Act of 2002, § 404, 15 U.S.C. § 7262 (Supp. 2002).

22. Cunningham, "Too Big to Fail," 1698.

23. According to a 2002 Gallup poll, 70 percent of U.S. investors stated that business accounting issues were hurting the investment climate "a lot." Paul S. Atkins, "Remarks at the Federalist Society 20th Annual Convention," November 14, 2002, http://www.sec.gov/news/speech/spch111402psa.htm.

24. Eisenberg and Macey, "Was Arthur Anderson Different?"

25. The shift of organizational form from the general partnership to the limited liability partnership reduced the threat of liability faced by auditing firm partners not directly involved in auditing a particular client. This, in turn, may have reduced accounting firm partners' incentives to monitor their colleagues' performance. The removal of aider and abettor liability risk also reduced auditors' incentives to monitor one another. *Central Bank of Denver v. First Interstate Bank of Denver*, 511 U.S. 164 (1994) (holding that Section 10[b] and SEC Rule 10b-5 prohibit only "the making of a material misstatement [or omission] or the commission of a manipulative act" and do not prohibit the aiding and abetting of such acts). This decision was thought to have substantially alleviated the legal risks to outside advisors such as auditors and lawyers. This reduction in incentives was exacerbated by passage of the Private Securities Litigation Reform Act (PSLRA) in 1995, Pub. L. No. 104–67 (codified at 15 U.S.C., § 78 [1998]). The PSLRA established new rules of pleading that require plaintiffs' complaints to "state with particularity all facts giving rise to a strong inference that the defendant acted with the required state of mind" when making a misstatement or omission in financial reporting. The PSLRA also delayed the beginning of discovery until after a court decides whether to allow the case to go forward on the basis of the heightened pleading standards. Prior to passage of the PSLRA, plaintiffs' attorneys could begin gathering documents and interviewing witnesses as soon as their complaints were filed. The PSLRA also sharply limited the doctrine of "joint and several liability," which ensures that victims can recover full damages even if some of the parties to the fraud cannot pay. Under the PSLRA, those whose reckless misconduct contributes to the fraud can be held responsible for only their proportionate share of victims' losses. As a result, when the primary perpetrator of the fraud is bankrupt, investors cannot fully recover their losses from other entities, such as auditing firms.

26. Auditing became more complex as new and more sophisticated methods of financing proliferated and as auditing rules themselves became more technical and complex. As a consequence, auditing firms found that "audit engagement teams" assigned to large public companies spent increasingly large amounts of time on those clients.

27. Where auditing firms also provide consulting services, they might be tempted to use auditing work either as a loss leader or "as a mechanism for 'opening the door' with a client for the purpose of pitching their (higher margin) consulting services." Macey and Sale, "Observations," 1178. Providing consulting services further erodes auditing firm independence by shifting the balance of power away from auditors in the direction of clients when discussing auditing work and retention issues. Worse, consulting services allow clients to reward auditing firms for succumbing to client wishes about what accounting treatment should be used to report novel or complex transactions and business practices. Where auditing firms only offer auditing services, unsatisfied clients may only fire them if they are found to be insufficiently aggressive or compliant. But when auditing firms also peddle consulting services, the client can employ a "carrot and stick" strategy, rewarding the auditing firm for being compliant and punishing it for being inflexible. This pressure is particularly acute in environments in which a company is an engagement partner's sole client, since a partner's inability to procure lucrative consulting work would be reflected in salary, promotion, and bonus. As John Coffee has observed, it is difficult for auditing clients to fire auditing firms because such dismissals invite "potential public embarrassment, public disclosure of the reason for the auditor's dismissal or resignation, and potential SEC intervention." John C. Coffee Jr., "Understanding Enron: It's about the Gatekeepers, Stupid," *Business Lawyer* 57 (2002): 1411–12. Where a company is both an auditing and consulting client of a particular auditing firm, "the client can easily terminate the auditor as a consultant or reduce its use of the firm's consulting services, in retaliation for the auditor's intransigence." Macey and Sale, "Observations," 1178. When a client terminates high-margin consulting services provided by an accounting firm and retains only low-margin auditing services, there is no need to make any public disclosure. This means that there is no risk that firing an auditing firm from consulting engagements will provoke heightened scrutiny from investors, the SEC, or plaintiffs' class action law firms.

28. "Sarbanes-Oxley: A Price Worth Paying?"

29. Ibid.

30. Ibid.

31. See Susan W. Eldridge and Burch T. Kealey, "SOX Costs: Auditor Attestation under Section 404," June 13, 2005 (unpublished manuscript, on file with the *Columbia Law Review*), 2.

32. See note 27.

33. See note 27.

34. "London as a Financial Centre: The Capital City," *The Economist,* October 21, 2006, pp. 34–36.

35. Ibid.

36. See note 27.

37. See note 27.

38. Macey and Sale, "Observations," 1169.

39. Harry S. Davis and Megan Elizabeth Murray, "Corporate Responsibility and Accounting Reform," *Banking and Financial Services Policy Report,* November 2002, p. 1, http://www.aspenpublishers.com/product.asp?catalog_name=

Aspen&product_id=SS0730689X&cookie%5Ftest=1#Description (accessed February 22, 2008).

40. Ivy Xiying Zhang, "Economic Consequences of the Sarbanes-Oxley Act of 2002," p. 20, http://w4.stern.nyu.edu/accounting/docs/speaker_papers/spring2005/Zhang_Ivy_Economic_Consequences_of_S_O.pdf (accessed February 22, 2005).

41. G. J. Stigler, "Theory of Economic Regulation," *Bell Journal of Economics and Management Science* 2 (1971): 3.

CHAPTER 12
QUIRKY GOVERNANCE

1. In the past, whistle-blowing was viewed as radical and vaguely subversive, if not downright disloyal and unpatriotic. See, e.g., Gerald Vinten, ed., *Whistleblowing: Subversion or Corporate Citizenship?* (London: Paul Chapman, 1994); Joyce Rothschild and Terance D. Miethe, "Whistleblowing as Resistance in Modern Work Organizations: The Politics of Revealing Organizational Deception and Abuse," in John M. Jermier, David Knights, and Walter R. Nord, eds., *Resistance and Power in Organizations* (London: Routledge, 1994), 252–73; Frederick A. Elliston, John Keenan, Paula Lockhart, and Jane van Schaick, *Whistleblowing: Managing Dissent in the Workplace* (New York: Praeger, 1985); Frederick A. Elliston, "Civil Disobedience and Whistleblowing: A Comparative Appraisal of Two Forms of Dissent," *Journal of Business Ethics* 1 (1982): 23–28; David W. Ewing, *Freedom Inside the Organization: Bringing Civil Liberties to the Workplace* (New York: Dutton, 1977); Brian Martin, "Whistleblowing and Nonviolence," *Peace and Change* 24 (1999): 15–28.

2. Eric Boehlert, "The Betrayal of the Whistle-blowers," *Salon*, October 21, 2003, http://dir.salon.com/story/news/feature/2003/10/21/whistleblower (accessed February 22, 2008).

3. Ibid.

4. http://www.whistleblowers.org.

5. Brian Martin and Will Rifkin, "The Dynamics of Employee Dissent: Whistleblowers and Organizational Jiu-Jitsu," *Public Organization Review* 4 (2004): 221–38.

6. The centerpiece of the new corporate governance regime is the Sarbanes-Oxley Act of 2002, Pub. L. No. 107–204, 2002 U.S.C.C.A.N. (116 Stat.) 745, to be codified in scattered sections 15 and 18 U.S.C. This bill contains significant protections for private sector whistle-blowers, discussed in part VIII of this chapter. Upon signing the bill into law, President George W. Bush observed that "today I sign the most far reaching reforms of American business practices since the time of Franklin Roosevelt. The law says to every dishonest corporate leader: You will be exposed and punished; the era of low standards and false profits is over; no boardroom in America is above the law." "Remarks on Signing the Sarbanes-Oxley Act of 2002," *Weekly Compilation of Presidential Documents* 38 (July 30, 2002): 1284.

7. "Sarbanes-Oxley: A Price Worth Paying?"

8. Selling short involves selling shares that one does not own with the intention of profiting by "covering the short position," which entails buying shares more cheaply in the future when the price declines.

9. For example, whistle-blowing has been defined in one regulation as conduct that involves disclosure of information by an employee or applicant for employment that the employee or applicant reasonably believes evidences a violation of law, rule, or regulation, gross mismanagement, a gross waste of funds, an abuse of authority, or a substantial and specific danger to public health or safety, unless such disclosure is specifically prohibited by law, and if such information is not specifically required by executive order to be kept secret in the interest of national defense or the conduct of foreign affairs. U.S. Department of Transportation, Transportation Security Administration, "Interim Policy on Whistleblower Protections for TSA Security Screeners," November 20, 2002, http://www.osc.gov/documents/tsa/tsa_dir.pdf; see also C. Fred Alford, *Whistleblowers: Broken Lives and Organizational Power* (Ithaca: Cornell University Press, 2001).

10. 31 U.S.C., § 3730(h).

11. "Qui tam" is an abbreviation of the Latin "qui tam pro domino rege quam pro se ipso in hac parte sequitur," which means "who brings action for the king as well as himself." *Qui tam* actions date back to at least the fourteenth century.

12. Harassment and dismissal of whistle-blowers and the revelation of widespread waste and fraud in defense contracting led Congress to strengthen the position of whistle-blowers in 1989.

13. John Figg, "Whistleblowing," *Internal Auditor,* April 2000, http://www.findarticles.com/p/articles/mi_m4153/is_2_57/ai_63170650/pg_4 (accessed December 12, 2005).

14. U.S. Newswire, "Justice Department Recovers $1.4 Billion in Fraud and False Claims in Fiscal Year 2005; More Than $15 Billion since 1986," November 7, 2005, http://releases.usnewswire.com/GetRelease.asp?id=56318 (accessed December 13, 2005); U.S. Department of Justice Whistleblower Statistics, October 1, 1986–September 30, 2004, http://www.phillipsandcohen.com/CM/Whistleblowerrewardsstories/DOJ%20stats%20fy2004.pdf.

15. The United States alleged that HealthSouth, the nation's largest provider of rehabilitative medicine services, engaged in various schemes to defraud the government. Multiple civil lawsuits by private plaintiffs and government agencies resulted in three multimillion-dollar settlements. The first, for $170 million, resolved HealthSouth's alleged false claims for outpatient physical therapy services that were not properly supported by certified plans of care, administered by licensed physical therapists, or for one-on-one therapy as represented. The second, for $65 million, resolved claims that HealthSouth engaged in accounting fraud that resulted in overbilling Medicare on hospital cost reports and home office cost statements. The third, a $92 million settlement, resolved allegations of billing Medicare for a range of unallowable costs, such as lavish entertainment and travel expenses incurred for HealthSouth's annual administrators' meeting at Disney World, and other claims.

16. In *qui tam* cases, brought under the False Claims Act (FCA), private parties, called "relators," are permitted to bring lawsuits against government contractors and other parties in the name of both the relator and the government. Under the

FCA, the government has the right to intervene in the relator's case. But if the government declines, the relator can still pursue the case. If the relator wins money from the defendant, he is entitled to keep a portion of the recovery, plus his attorneys' fees and other costs.

17. Although there is a potential financial benefit to whistle-blowing, it is generally difficult to demonstrate that such benefit is the primary motivating factor rather than just a contributing one. By contrast, in the case of insider trading, the primary motivation often is to profit from the information. Highlighting wrongdoing may merely be a secondary or fringe benefit. It does appear, however, to be naïve to assume that whistle-blowers are altruistic or that they as a group have a "moral edge" on inside traders.

18. Dan Ackman, "Sherron Watkins Had Whistle, But Blew It," *Forbes*, February 14, 2002, http://www.forbes.com/2002/02/14/0214watkins.html.

19. Besides being hailed as one of *Time* magazine's People of the Year in 2002, Watkins "has been hailed as a whistleblower so often it's starting to sound like part of her name." Ackman, "Sherron Watkins."

20. "Federal Energy Regulatory Commission Release of E-mails," http://www.itmweb.com/f012002.htm.

21. Ibid.

22. Ibid.

23. Ibid.

24. Ibid.

25. Ibid.

26. Ibid.

27. Ibid.

28. Despite the recent surge in popularity, whistle-blowers and whistle-blowing still face image problems not demonstrably different from the image problems faced by people accused of insider trading. For example, one whistle-blower, Jesselyn Radack, a former legal advisor to the Justice Department's Professional Responsibility Advisory Office, observes being called "traitor," "turncoat," and "terrorist sympathizer." She was so described after advising the criminal division of the FBI that any interrogation of "American Taliban" John Walker Lindh outside the presence of his lawyer would be unethical. The FBI ignored Radack's advice and interrogated Lindh when he did not have the benefit of legal counsel. Later Radack claimed a number of e-mails she had written explaining her legal position had been destroyed after the judge in the Lindh case ordered that all the these documents be turned over to the court. Radack then turned whistle-blower, disclosing the existence of the missing e-mails to *Newsweek*. Radack claims that she believed this was permitted by the Whistleblower Protection Act. Writing about the incident, Radack observes that "[w]histleblowers are stereotyped as disgruntled employees, troublemakers and snitches. The conscientious employee is often portrayed as vengeful, unstable or out for attention." Jesselyn Radack, "Whistleblowing: My Story," *The Nation*, July 4, 2005, posted June 16, 2005, http://www.thenation.com/docprem.mhtml?i=20050704&s=radack (accessed December 12, 2005).

29. See Daniel P. Westman and Nancy M. Modesitt, *Whistleblowing: The Law of Retaliatory Discharge*, 2nd ed. (New York: BNA Books, 2004).

30. It also is possible to trade shares in rival firms on the basis of material inside information. For example, when an employee in a company obtains good (bad) news about her company's prospects, she may sell (buy) shares in rivals, particularly in markets with high levels of concentrations and barriers to entry. See Ian Ayres and Joseph Bankman, "Substitutes for Insider Trading," *Stanford Law Review* 54 (2001): 235–94.

31. For a broad defense of insider trading as an efficient mechanism for compensating management, see Henry G. Manne, *Insider Trading and the Stock Market* (New York: The Free Press, 1966).

32. Daniel R. Fischel and David J. Ross, "Should the Law Prohibit 'Manipulation' in Financial Markets," *Harvard Law Review* 105 (1991): 503.

33. The proposition that stock markets are efficient has been formalized in the well-known Efficient Capital Markets Hypothesis (ECMH). For a discussion of the ECMH, which posits that a market is efficient if the prices of the assets traded in that market fully reflect all available information relevant to the pricing decision, see Jonathan Macey, *An Introduction to Modern Financial Theory* (Los Angeles: American College of Trust and Estate Counsel Foundation, 1998). See also Burton Gordon Malkiel, *A Random Walk down Wall Street: The Time-Tested Strategy for Successful Investing,* 8th ed. (New York: Norton, 2004); Burton Malkiel, "The Efficient Markets Hypothesis and Its Critics," *Journal of Economic Perspectives* 17 (2003): 59–82.

34. Mere trading does not affect share prices. Rather, trading only affects share prices to the extent that it reveals new information about the returns to investors in the underlying asset.

35. Short selling is so costly that very few shares are actually sold short. See Robert Shiller, "From Efficient Markets to Behavioral Finance," *Journal of Economic Perspectives* 17 (2003): 83–104 at 101.

36. See *Chiarella v. United States,* 445 U.S. 222 (1980); *Dirks v. SEC,* 463 U.S. 646 (1983); and *United States v. O'Hagen,* 521 U.S. 642 (1997).

37. See table 12.1.

38. *Dirks,* 463 U.S. 646.

39. *Id.,* Transcript of Oral Argument 27 at 661n21.

40. *Id.,* Brief for Respondent 43–44.

41. *Dirks,* 463 U.S. at 680.

42. Under the False Claims Act, the whistle-blower first files a lawsuit against the individual or business association charged with defrauding the government. Copies of the complaint must be served on the Department of Justice, along with a written disclosure of all material evidence and information in the whistle-blower's possession so that the federal government may investigate the claim prior to deciding whether to intervene. While the statute provides for sixty days for the Department of Justice to make up its mind whether to intervene, this period can be and often is extended at the request of the government in the court in which the complaint was filed. If the government declines to intervene, the whistle-blower may continue to pursue the litigation on her own. If the government decides to intervene, the whistle-blower receives a slightly smaller percentage of any recovery. (If the government intervenes, the whistle-blower is entitled to 15 to 25 percent of the proceeds of the action or settlement, plus expenses and attorneys' fees. If the

government does not intervene, the whistle-blower is entitled to 25 to 30 percent of the settlement plus expenses and attorneys' fees.)

43. Sharron Watkins testified at Ken Lay's criminal trial that she sold $47,000 worth of Enron stock in August and October 2001 on what may have been, by her own admission, nonpublic information. As one commentator observed, "Watkins' testimony was downright bizarre regarding her $47,000 in insider trades of Enron stock that she made after delivering her memo to Lay and prior to the company's announcement of the charge to earnings. Despite having certified in a 2002 Enron employment agreement and sworn in Congressional testimony that she had not engaged in any illegal insider trading while at Enron, Watkins yesterday conceded on direct examination that the trades were not 'proper' because 'I had more information than the marketplace did.' " Tom Kirkendall, "The Insufferable Sherron Watkins," March 16, 2006, http://blog.kir.com/archives/002963.asp (accessed February 22, 2008).

44. Jathon Sapsford and Paul Beckett, "Whistleblower Reels from Actions' Fallout," *Wall Street Journal*, http://www.careerjournal.com/myc/survive/20021217-sapsford.html (accessed February 15, 2007).

45. Brian Trumbore, "Ray Dirks and the Equity Funding Scandal," available at http://www.buyandhold.com/bh/en/education/history/2004/ray_dirks.html (accessed February 22, 2008).

46. Ibid.

47. Ibid.

48. Ibid.

49. *Dirks,* 463 U.S. 646.

50. *Id.*

51. *Id.*

52. Trumbore, "Ray Dirks and the Equity Funding Scandal."

53. *Dirks,* 463 U.S. 646.

54. Trumbore, "Ray Dirks and the Equity Funding Scandal."

55. Sapsford and Beckett, "Whistleblower Reels from Actions' Fallout."

56. Jonathan Macey, "Efficient Capital Markets, Corporate Disclosure and Enron," *Cornell Law Review* 89 (2003): 356.

57. Sapsford and Beckett, "Whistleblower Reels from Actions' Fallout."

58. "Statement of the Honorable Ray Garrett Jr., Chairman, SEC, before the Subcommittee on HUD—Space—Science—Veterans, Committee on Appropriations, United States Senate," October 11, 1973, http://www.sechistorical.org/collection/papers/1970/1973_1011_Garrett_HUDSSV.pdf.

59. *Chiarella,* 445 U.S. at 231.

60. Chiarella clearly breached a fiduciary duty to his employer, Pandick Press, when he traded on information that he had promised, as a condition of his employment, to keep confidential. However, because the government had not presented this theory of liability to the jury, the Court held that Chiarella could not be convicted for trading in breach of a fiduciary relationship of trust and confidence to Pandick.

61. John Locke, *Two Treatises of Government,* ed. Mark Goldie (London: Everyman, 1993).

62. Alan Strudler, "Moral Complexity in the Law of Nondisclosure," *UCLA Law Review* 45 (1997): 337, 375.

63. Hernando de Soto, *The Mystery of Capital: Why Capitalism Triumphs in the West and Fails Everywhere Else* (New York: Basic Books, 2000); see also Richard Pipes, *Property and Freedom* (New York: Vintage, 1999). For an extremely useful comparison of the work of Locke and de Soto, on which this paragraph draws, see Donald Krueckeberg, "The Lessons of John Locke or Hernando de Soto: What If Your Dreams Come True?" *Housing Policy Debate* 15 (2004), http://content.knowledgeplex.org/kp2/cache/documents/38182.pdf (accessed January 5, 2006).

64. 18 U.S.C., § 1514A(a) (2002).

65. Stephen M. Kohn, Michael D. Kohn, and David K. Colapinto, *Whistleblower Law: A Guide to Legal Protections for Corporate Employees* (New York: Praeger, 2004).

66. See *Gutierrez v. Regents of the University of California,* 98-ERA-19, DandO of ARB, p. 6, November 13, 2002 (finding that, in addition to contacting members of Congress, communicating with reporters and a public interest organization, leading to the whistle-blower being quoted in three "prominent" newspapers, were protected activities designed to "publicly reveal information" about misconduct).

67. The standard was articulated in *Halloun v. Intel Corp.,* 2003-SOX-7, DandO of ALJ, p. 10 (March 4, 2004).

68. Section 1107(a) of Sarbanes-Oxley amends 18 U.S.C., § 1513 to provide that "[w]however knowingly, with the intent to retaliate, takes any action harmful to any person, including interference with the lawful employment or livelihood of any person, for providing to a law enforcement officer any truthful information relating to the commission or possible commission of any Federal offense, shall be fined under this title or imprisoned not more than 10 years, or both."

69. *Whistleblower Protection Act of 1989,* 101st Cong., 1st sess., *Congressional Record* 135 (March 16, 1989), S2779.

70. Ibid.

71. Locke, *Treatise I,* ¶ 42, p. 31.

72. In an interview, Dean Henry Manne, when asked about the corporate scandals at Enron and Global Crossing, indicated that insider trading, if permissible, would have prevented these and other frauds: "I don't think the scandals would ever have erupted if we had allowed insider trading . . . because there would be plenty of people in those companies who would know exactly what was going on, and who couldn't resist the temptation to get rich by trading on the information, and the stock market would have reflected those problems months and months earlier than they did under this cockamamie regulatory system we have." See Larry Elder, "Legalize Insider Trading?" *Washington Times,* June 15, 2003, http://www.washtimes.com/commentary/20030615–112306–2790r.htm (accessed December 18, 2005).

73. See Ayres and Bankman, "Substitutes for Insider Trading."

74. Heather Tookes, "Information, Trading and Product Market Interactions: Cross-Sectional Implications of Insider Trading" (working paper on file with author, 2004).

75. Clearly it should be illegal for a government official involved in the investigation or prosecution of activity, either in the public sector or the private sector, to engage in any sort of trading on the basis of that information. The ability to engage in such trading would present a profound moral hazard, as the government official would have incentives to bring cases against innocent companies to benefit from stock price movements around the time of the announcement of contemplated regulatory action.

76. Henry Manne has suggested that there is no problem here because insider trading enables investors to receive "virtual" full disclosure in the form of immediate and correct price adjustments. See Henry Manne, "The Case for Insider Trading," AEI-Brookings Joint Center Policy Matters 03–05, April 2003, http://aei-brookings.org/policy/page.php?id=129 (accessed February 22, 2008).

77. Kristen Hays, "Midlevel Enron Corp. Executive Pleads Guilty to Filing False Fax Return," *Abilene Reporter-News*, Wednesday, November 27, 2002, http://www.texnews.com/1998/2002/texas/texas_Midlevel_1127.html (accessed February 15, 2007).

78. Alexei Barrionuevo, "10 Enron Players: Where They Landed after the Fall," *New York Times*, January 29, 2006, http://select.nytimes.com/search/restricted/article?res=F0061FF83A5B0C7A8EDDA80894DE404482.

79. Simon Romero, "Hard Times Haunt Enron's Ex-Workers: Few Find Jobs of Equal Stature Years after Company's Collapse," *New York Times*, January 25, 2006, http://select.nytimes.com/search/restricted/article?res=F60C17FC3B5B0C768EDDA80894DE404482.

80. Ibid.

81. Ari Weinberg, "The Post-Enron 401(k)," *Forbes*, October 20, 2003, http://www.forbes.com/2003/10/20/cx_aw_1020retirement.html; Michael W. Lynch, "Enron's 401(k) Calamity," *Reason*, December 27, 2001, http://www.reason.com/ml/ml122701.shtml. In early 2001, Enron decided to contract its 401(k) administration to an outside company. This transfer required that Enron's 401(k) accounts be frozen. Thus, for a certain period of time in October and November 2001, employees could not move their retirement funds out of Enron stock. There is a dispute about whether the accounts were frozen for twelve trading days (from October 26, 2001, through November 12, 2001), as the company claims, or for a longer period. The period when the accounts were frozen, whatever the precise dates actually were, was a time of extreme upheaval at Enron. On October 16, 2001, the company announced that it had to take a $1.1 billion charge for bad investments. On October 22, the SEC announced an informal investigation into Enron's accounting practices. On October 29, Moody's downgraded their ratings of Enron's debt. On October 31, the SEC announced that its investigation was formal. On November 8, Enron restated its financial results for every year since 1997. On October 26, 1991, the day Enron claims it froze its 401(k) accounts, its stock was trading at $13.81 per share. By the time 401(k) investors could sell again, the stock was at $9.98.

82. Corey Rosen, "Questions and Answers about Enron, 401(k)s, and ESOPs," http://www.nceo.org/library/enron.html.

83. Testimony of Douglas Kruse before the House Subcommittee on Employer-Employee Relations of the Committee on Education and the Workforce, February

12, 2002 (reporting that "about 70–75% of participants in plans that are heavily invested in employer stock [ESOPs, 401(k) plans, and profit sharing plans] are in companies that also maintain diversified pension [or other retirement] plans").

84. Weinberg, "The Post-Enron 401(k)."

85. John Rawls, *A Theory of Justice* (Cambridge, MA: Harvard University Press, 1971), 83, 302; see also Daniel Markovits, "How Much Redistribution Should There Be?" *Yale Law Journal* 112 (2003): 2291, 2326–29.

86. Easterbrook and Fischel, *The Economic Structure of Corporate Law*, 110.

87. Ibid.

88. Ibid., 111.

89. Ibid., 124.

90. J. J. Thomson, "A Defence of Abortion," *Philosophy and Public Affairs* 1 (1971): 47–66 (defining a Good Samaritan as "someone who goes out of his way, at some cost to himself, to help").

91. *Goodwin v. Agassiz*, 283 Mass. 358, 186 N.E. 659 (1933); Comment, "Insider Trading at Common Law," *University of Chicago Law Review* 51 (1984): 838.

92. See Dennis W. Carlton and Daniel Fischel, "The Regulation of Insider Trading," *Stanford Law Review* 35 (1983): 857 (noting that corporate charters do not prevent insider trading).

93. Compare *FMC Corp. v. Boesky*, 573 F. Supp. 242 (N.D. Ill. 1987), reversed in part, 852 F.2d. 981 (7th Cir. 1988) on remand, 1989 U.S. Dist. LEXIS 13353 (N.D. Ill.) (corporation suing arbitrageur for insider trading on information about a corporate recapitalization that would distribute cash to shareholders in exchange for reducing their equity stakes in the company to give managers a larger share of the corporation's equity, on the theory that the corporation had to pay more to acquire the shareholders' equity because insider trading drove up the price of the company's shares).

94. The problem of distinguishing among whistle-blower complaints is likely exacerbated by the fact that whistle-blowers often are mavericks who may have personality conflicts with supervisors to begin with.

95. Thus it is not surprising that whistle-blowers are viewed with some moral ambiguity: "To some, whistle blowing is considered to be an ultimate expression of accountability. To others, whistle blowing is the spiteful behavior of disgruntled employees and an act of organizational disloyalty." American Society for Public Administration, "Position Statement on Whistleblowing," http://www.iit.edu/departments/csep/codes/coe/aspa-a.html (accessed December 12, 2005).

96. Henry E. Smith, "The Harm in Blackmail," *Northwestern Law Review* 92 (1998): 861; James Lindgren, "Unraveling the Paradox of Blackmail," *Columbia Law Review* 84 (1984): 670; Jennifer Gerarda Brown, "Blackmail as Private Justice," *University of Pennsylvania Law Review* 241 (1993): 1935.

97. This is not to say that blackmail involves no benefits. To the extent that the possibility of blackmail deters undesirable conduct, there are benefits. The social costs of blackmail, however, clearly outweigh the private benefits to the blackmail contract.

CHAPTER 13
SHAREHOLDER VOTING

1. Lucian A. Bebchuk, "The Myth of the Shareholder Franchise," *Virginia Law Review* 93 (2007): 105.
2. Stephen Bainbridge, "The Case for Limited Shareholder Voting Rights," *UCLA Law Review* 53 (2006): 616.
3. Easterbrook and Fischel, "Voting in Corporate Law," 402.
4. See Bainbridge, "The Case for Limited Shareholder Voting Rights."
5. Easterbrook and Fischel, *The Economic Structure of Corporate Law*, 70.
6. Ibid.
7. Easterbrook and Fischel, "Voting in Corporate Law," 402.
8. Ibid.
9. Ibid.
10. See Anthony Downs, *An Economic Theory of Democracy* (New York: Harper, 1957); Mancur Olson, *The Logic of Collective Action: Public Action and the Theory of Groups* (Cambridge, MA: Harvard University Press, 1971); Joseph A. Schumpeter, *Capitalism, Socialism, and Democracy*, 5th ed. (London: Allen and Unwin, 1976).
11. Mark Roe, *Strong Managers, Weak Owners: The Political Roots of American Corporate Finance* (Princeton: Princeton University Press, 1996), 162.
12. Jonathan R. Macey, "Manager's Journal: A Poison Pill That Shareholders Can Swallow," *Wall Street Journal*, May 4, 1998, A22.
13. *See Bebchuk v. CA, Inc.*, 902 A.2d 737 (Del. Ch. 2006).
14. Jonathan R. Macey, "The Legality and Utility of the Shareholder Rights Bylaw," *Hofstra Law Review* 26 (1988): 835.
15. John C. Coffee Jr., "The Bylaw Battlefield: Can Institutions Change the Outcome of Corporate Control Contests?" *University Miami Law Review* 51 (1997): 613 (analyzing shareholder power to constrain management from resisting corporate control contests through bylaw amendments).
16. David D. Haddock, Jonathan R. Macey, and Fred S. McChesney, "Property Rights in Assets and Resistance to Tender Offers," *Virginia Law Review* 73 (1987): 701.
17. See Easterbrook and Fischel, "Voting in Corporate Law."
18. Hermang Desai, Chris E. Hogan, and Michael S. Wilkins, "The Reputational Penalty for Aggressive Accounting: Earnings Restatements and Management Turnover," August 2004, *http://www.fma.org/NewOrleans/Papers/1401148.pdf*.
19. See John Chevedden, "Proxy Statement and Notice of 2003 Annual Meeting of Stockholders, Lockheed Martin," *Stockholder Proposal B*, April 4, 2003, p. 52.
20. See Reed Abelson, "Enron's Many Strands: The Directors; Endgame? Some Enron Board Members Quit or Face Ouster at Other Companies," *New York Times*, February 9, 2002, C5; Dan O'Shea, "Ex-Enron Director Leaves Qualcomm Post," *Insight*, May 18, 2004.

21. Suraj Srinivasan, "Consequences of Financial Reporting Failure for Outside Directors: Evidence from Accounting Restatements and Audit Committee Members," *Journal of Accounting Research* 43 (2005): 293–94.

22. Lucian Arye Bebchuk et al., "The Powerful Antitakeover Force of Staggered Boards: Theory, Evidence, and Policy," *Stanford Law Review* 54 (2002): 887; Lucian A. Bebchuk and Alma Cohen, "The Costs of Entrenched Boards," *Journal of Financial Economics* 78 (2005): 409.

23. See Norman J. Ornstein, Thomas E. Mann, and Michael E. Malbin, *Vital Statistics on Congress: 2001–2002* (Washington, DC: American Enterprise Institute for Public Policy, 2002), 69, tables 2–7; see also "Reelection Rates over the Years," www.opensecrets.org/bigpicture/reelect.asp?cycle-2004; http://www.laits.utexas.edu/gov310/VCE/conreelection/index.html (showing, for example, that reelection rates for the U.S. House of Representatives between 1990 and 2006 were as follows: 1992: 88%; 1994: 90%; 1998: 98%; 2000: 98%; 2002: 96%; 2004: 98%).

24. See Bebchuk, "The Myth of the Shareholder Franchise."

25. Corporate voting rules require that public corporations give shareholders three alternatives: to vote for all of the board's nominees for directors, to withhold support for all such candidates, or to withhold support from certain specified nominees. See 17 C.F.R. § 240.14a-4(b)(2) (2006). In March 2004, Michael Eisner was stripped of his post as chairman of Disney Corporation when 43 percent of Disney shareholders withheld their votes from the embattled Disney chair, resulting in a decision by the Disney board to split the posts of board chair and CEO. See Michael McCarthy, "Disney Strips Chairmanship from Eisner," *USA Today,* March 4, 2004, B1.

26. Floyd Norris, "High and Low Finance: A Fired Boss Seeks His Revenge," *New York Times,* May 18, 2007, D1.

27. Ibid.

28. See "Key Considerations for Serving on a Board of Directors," in *Advantage* (RSM McGladrey, Minneapolis), January 2006, p. 2, http://www.rsmmcgladrey.com/RSM-Resources/Articles/Advantage/Governance-Board-Room/Key-considerations-for-serving-on-a-board-of-directors/ (accessed February 22, 2008).

29. See Bebchuk, "The Myth of the Shareholder Franchise."

30. Ibid.

31. Ibid. (suggesting that free-rider problems make it "worthwhile to consider providing reimbursement of costs to rivals who attract significant support but fall short of winning").

32. Ibid., 3–4.

33. Of course it is undeniable that a benevolent dictator who stages a violent coup d'état but thereafter abides by the rule of law and promotes equality and prosperity is, nevertheless, an illegitimate ruler. No matter how skillfully a person performs her self-appointed role, the issue of whether she obtained her office via legitimate means, both substantively and procedurally, is always relevant. Bebchuk, however, cannot seriously claim that U.S. directors cannot make legitimate claims on their offices because of the insufficiencies that he asserts plague the electoral system. The ineluctable reality is that shareholders support directors in

elections that are, as a positive matter, entirely legal and therefore legitimate from the perspective most closely associated with H.L.A. Hart, which is that "law and morality are best kept separate; that rules are the heart and soul of the legal process." Allan C. Hutchinson, "A Postmodern's Hart: Taking Rules Sceptically," *Modern Law Review* 58 (1995): 788. In other words, because there is an appropriate legal infrastructure that establishes procedures for electing directors, and those procedures generally are followed, the necessary conditions for the legal validity of the election of U.S. directors clearly have been met. Thus, while Bebchuk is free to contest the desirability of the current process for electing directors, his claims about legitimacy are unconvincing.

34. See Geoffrey P. Miller, "An Interest-Group Theory of Central Bank Independence," *Journal of Legal Studies* 27 (1998): 434.

35. See Federal Reserve Bank of Chicago, "Money Matters: The American Experience with Money," http://www.chicagofed.org/consumer_information/money_matters.cfm.

36. See Model Bus. Corp. Act § 8.01(b) (2005). This set of model statutes is available from the American Bar Association, http://www.abanet.org/abastore/index.cfm?section=main&fm=Product.AddToCart&pid=5070548.

37. Marcel Kahan and Edward Rock, "Hedge Funds in Corporate Governance and Corporate Control," *University of Pennsylvania Law Review* 155 (2007): 1021.

38. Kara Scannell, "How Borrowed Shares Swing Company Votes," *Wall Street Journal,* January 26, 2007, A1.

39. *High River Ltd. P'ship v. Mylan Labs., Inc.,* 353 F. Supp. 2d 487 (M.D. Pa. 2005).

40. See also Peter Safirstein and Ralph Sianni, "Is the Fix In?—Are Hedge Funds Secretly Disenfranchising Shareholders?" *Bloomberg Law Reports: Corporate Governance* 2 (January 2005): 1–7 (explaining that "Perry Corp. was essentially buying votes so that it could cause Mylan to enter into a deal with King which would benefit Perry Corp. arguably to the detriment of other Mylan shareholders").

41. *See Schreiber v. Carney,* 447 A.2d 17 (Del. Ch. 1982) (holding that although a corporation's loan to the holder of its stock in return for voting as the corporation desired constituted vote buying, it was not illegal per se, as it did not defraud or disenfranchise other shareholders); see also note 43.

42. *See Hewlett v. Hewlett-Packard Co.,* Civ. A. No. 19513-NC, 2002 Del. Ch. LEXIS 35 (Del. Ch. April 30, 2002); *Hewlett v. Hewlett-Packard Co.,* Civ. A. No. 19523-NC, 2002 Del. Ch. LEXIS 44 (Del. Ch. April 8, 2002).

43. The court held that the "plaintiffs . . . failed to prove that HP management improperly enticed or coerced Deutsche Bank into voting in favor of the merger." *Hewlett,* 2002 Del. Ch. LEXIS 35 at *63–64. With regard to the vote-buying claim, Chancellor Chandler added, "The plaintiffs can point to nothing in those exchanges [between Deutsche Bank and HP] that indicates a threat from management that future business would be withheld by HP." *Id.* at *63.

44. Business Law Prof Blog, "Hedge Fund Paranoia: Fretting over the Mylan/King Deal Hedge," October 27, 2005, http://lawprofessors.typepad.com/business_law/2005/10/hedge_fund_para.html (noting that "in the Mylan deal, Icahn, the complainer, was shorting the shares of King while he was trying to block the Mylan deal").

45. George W. Dent, "Unprofitable Mergers: Toward a Market-Based Legal Response," *Northwestern University Law Review* 80 (1986): 781 (suggesting that "empire-building" by corporate managers motivates many acquisitions, thereby explaining the disparity between large gains to target firm shareholders and small gains to acquiring firm shareholders).

46. For example, King Pharmaceutical managers might have preferred to resist a takeover, even where such a transaction was in the best interests of King's outside shareholders, because of the significant risk that they would lose their jobs if King were merged into Mylan-King. Even if they didn't lose their jobs, they likely would have preferred to remain as top officers and directors in King to being mere underlings and functionaries in a larger corporate enterprise.

47. Jennifer Gordon, "Let Them Vote: A Response to 'The Immigrant as Pariah' by Owen Fiss," *Boston Review,* October/November 1998, available at http://bostonreview.net/BR23.5/Gordon.html (accessed February 22, 2008).

48. Ibid. See also *Minor v. Happersett*, 88 U.S. 162 (1874), in which the U.S. Supreme Court observed that "citizenship has not in all cases been made a condition precedent to the enjoyment of the right of suffrage," and pointed out that in several states, including Missouri, Texas, Indiana, Georgia, Alabama, Arkansas, Florida, Kansas, and Minnesota, non-naturalized immigrants were allowed to vote. *Id.* at 177. As Jennifer Gordon has observed in "Let Them Vote," "offering the franchise to new arrivals was a way of attracting new settlers to a vast and under-populated country."

49. See *Minor v. Happersett*, 88 U.S. 162.

50. Colin Mayer and Julian Franks, "Different Votes for Different Folks," October 16, 2006, *http://www.ft.com/cms/s/ceb8f2b6–5f79–11db-a011–0000779 e2340.html* (accessed March 26, 2007).

51. Ibid.

52. R. C. Lease, J. J. McConnell, and W. H. Mikkelson, "The Market Value of Control in Publicly Traded Corporations," *Journal of Financial Economics* 11 (April 1983): 439–72.

53. B. F. Smith and B. Amoako-Adu, "Relative Prices of Dual Class Shares," *Journal of Financial and Quantitative Analysis* 30 (June 1995): 223–39.

54. James J. Angel and Roger M. Kunz, "Factors Affecting the Value of the Voting Right: Evidence from the Swiss Equity Market," *Financial Management Magazine* 25 (Autumn 1996): 19.

55. H. Levy, "Economic Evaluation of Voting Power of Common Stock," *Journal of Finance* 38 (March 1983): 79–93.

56. Luigi Zingales, "The Value of the Voting Right: A Study of the Milan Stock Exchange Experience," *Review of Financial Studies* 7 (Spring 1994): 125–48.

57. Ibid.

CHAPTER 14
THE ROLE OF BANKS AND OTHER LENDERS IN CORPORATE GOVERNANCE

1. "Vivendi Will Have to Sell Assets," *The Times of India,* July 8, 2002, http://timesofindia.indiatimes.com/articleshow/15297327.cms.

2. "General Electric and Vivendi Universal Sign Agreement to Merge NBC and Vivendi Universal Entertainment," Business Wire, October 8, 2003, http://www.findarticles.com/p/articles/mi_m0EIN/is_2003_Oct_8/ai_108625382.

3. "Icahn Prods Time Warner to Take Action," CNNMoney.com, August 15, 2005, http://money.cnn.com/2005/08/15/news/fortune500/icahn_timewarner/.

4. Steven Levingston, "Icahn, Time Warner End Fight; Dissident Investor Won't Seek Control," Washington Post, February 18, 2006, http://www.washingtonpost.com/wp-dyn/content/article/2006/02/17/AR2006021702017.html.

5. Ronald T. Gilson and Reinier Kraakman, "Investment Companies as Guardian Shareholders: The Place of the MSIC in the Corporate Governance Debate," Stanford Law Review 45 (1993): 988; see also Mark J. Roe, "A Political Theory of American Corporate Finance," Columbia Law Review 91 (1991): 13–16 (discussing recent criticisms of the U.S. corporate governance system).

6. See Mark J. Roe, "Some Differences in Corporate Structure in Germany, Japan and the United States," Yale Law Journal 102 (1993): 1927–48 (describing the influence of large block shareholders in German corporations).

7. Ibid., 1928–30. Historically, this concentration of power in American management occurred because the rise of large-scale production capabilities in the late nineteenth century demanded huge inputs of capital, which could only be supplied by large numbers of disaggregated investors. Ibid., 1933.

8. Gilson and Kraakman, "Investment Companies as Guardian Shareholders," 989; see also Roe, "A Political Theory of American Corporate Finance," 13–16.

9. The term "Berle-Means" corporation is derived from the classic text describing the separation of ownership and control in the large public corporation. Adolph A. Berle Jr. and Gardiner C. Means, The Modern Corporation and Private Property (1932; reprint, Buffalo, NY: W. S. Hein and Company, 1982).

10. Indeed, some commentators have concluded that shareholder passivity, combined with disaggregated share ownership, allows management to dominate corporate governance at almost every turn. See, e.g., Carol Goforth, "Proxy Reform as a Means of Increasing Shareholder Participation in Corporate Governance: Too Little, But Not Too Late," American University Law Review 43 (1994): 413–14 (stating that the American corporate governance system, with its structural emphasis on dominant management and widespread share ownership, has led to self-interested and inefficient decision-making by management).

11. This includes open-end investment companies and broker dealers but excludes insurance companies and pension funds.

12. Gary Gorton and Frank A. Schmid, "Universal Banking and the Performance of German Firms" (working paper no. 5453, National Bureau of Economic Research, February 1996), http://www.nber.org/papers/w5453.pdf.

13. Steven N. Kaplan and Bernadette A. Minton, "Appointments of Outsiders to Japanese Boards: Determinants and Implications for Managers," Journal of Financial Economics 36 (1994): 257. See also Randall Morck and Masao Nakamura, "Banks and Corporate Control in Japan" (working paper no. 6–92, Institute for Financial Research, Faculty of Business, University of Alberta, revised July 26, 1993), 3–5.

14. See, e.g., William A. Klein and John C. Coffee Jr., Business Organization and Finance: Legal and Economic Principles, 10th ed. (New York: Foundation

Press, 2007), 225–26; Barry E. Adler, "Finance's Theoretical Divide and the Proper Role of Insolvency Rules," *Southern California Law Review* 67 (1994): 1107; Frank H. Easterbrook and Daniel R. Fischel, "The Corporate Contract," *Columbia Law Review* 89 (1989): 1416; David Millon, "Theories of the Corporation," *Duke Law Journal* (1990): 201. This discussion and the example that follows have been adapted from Jonathan R. Macey and Geoffrey P. Miller, "Bank Failures, Risk Monitoring, and the Market for Bank Control," *Columbia Law Review* 88 (1988): 1153.

15. Klein and Coffee, *Business Organization and Finance,* 257 ("From any starting point, holding the total market value of the firm and of all securities constant, a decision that shifts investments in such a way as to increase such risk will result in an increase in the value of the common and a decrease in the value of the bonds"); Roberta Romano, "Financing the Corporation," in *Foundations of Corporate Law,* ed. Romano, 123.

16. For investment strategy A, assume that there are five possible outcomes, represented by the firm's monetary returns in the second column of the table for strategy A. The probability of each of these outcomes occurring is shown in the first column. Regardless of the outcome, the firm pays the bank first and any residual accrues to the common shareholders. The expected value of each outcome to the firm, the bank, and the common shareholders is simply the monetary return multiplied by the probability that it will occur. The sums of the expected values represent the overall expected values of investment strategy A to the firm, the bank, and the equity holders. All of the investment strategies discussed in this example follow the same basic outline.

17. Easterbrook and Fischel, "Voting in Corporate Law," 403–6. But see Eugene F. Fama, "Agency Problems and the Theory of the Firm," *Journal of Political Economy* 88 (1980): 290–92 (describing the market for managerial labor as producing the dominant incentive for maximizing the value of the firm).

18. The standard deviation, which provides a convenient index of portfolio risk, summarizes the spread of possible expected outcomes for a portfolio. Richard A. Brealey, Stewart C. Myers, and Franklin Allen, *Principles of Corporate Finance,* 8th ed. (New York: McGraw-Hill, 2006), 134. The standard deviation, represented by s, is the square root of the variance. The variance is calculated by: $s[su'2'] = (x-m)[su'2']p(x)$; where x is the dollar outcome, p(x) is the probability that the outcome will occur, and m is the expected value of the investment strategy. Here, $s[su'2'] = (400–2020)[su'2'](.05) + (1000–2020)[su'2'](.20) + (2000–2020)[su'2'](.50) + (3000–2020)[su'2'](.20) + (4000–2020)[su'2'](.05) = 727,600$. The square root of 727,600 is $853, which is the standard deviation of strategy A.

19. For strategy B, the variance is calculated by: $s[su'2'] = (1000–1875)[su'2'](.25) + (2000–1875)[su'2'](.50) + (2500–1875)[su'2'](.25) = 296,875$. The standard deviation of strategy B is $545.

20. For strategy C, the variance is calculated by: $s[su'2'] = (0–2000)[su'2'](.30) + (1000–2000)[su'2'](.50) + (7500–2000)[su'2'](.20) = 7,750,000$. The standard deviation of strategy C is $2,784.

21. The degree of outcome variance is not, strictly, the basis for a fixed claimant's aversion to a particular investment scheme. While outcome variance may

indicate the likelihood of the borrower's ability to meet fixed claims, it is not necessarily determinative. A fixed claimant is less concerned about upside potential than with downside risk—the probability of an outcome that prevents the borrower from meeting fixed claims. A large outcome variance may result from a substantial disparity between upside and downside potential, or simply from a substantial downside risk.

22. Coase, "The Nature of the Firm."

23. See Easterbrook and Fischel, "The Corporate Contract," 1444–47 (suggesting that corporate law exists because it minimizes transaction costs to competing interest groups within the corporation).

24. Klein and Coffee, *Business Organization and Finance,* 266–67.

25. Ibid.

26. See Irwin Friend and Larry H. P. Lang, "An Empirical Test of the Impact of Managerial Self-Interest on Corporate Capital Structure," *Journal of Finance* 43 (1988): 271. Friend and Lang find that high levels of debt (and hence greater risk) in corporate capital structures correspond to low levels of managerial stock ownership. Firms where principal stockholders were not managers tend to assume higher risk levels (280).

27. Gilson and Kraakman, "Investment Companies as Guardian Shareholders," 988.

28. See, e.g., John Cable, "Capital Market Information and Industrial Performance: The Role of West German Banks," *Economic Journal* 95 (1985): 118–30 (finding a "significant, positive relationship between the degree of bank involvement" in a firm and its financial performance). But see Roberta Romano, "A Cautionary Note on Drawing Lessons from Comparative Corporate Law," *Yale Law Journal* 102 (1993): 2021 (noting that legal and institutional differences among countries make it difficult to conclude that one country's corporate governance system is superior to another's).

29. Gilson and Kraakman, "Investment Companies as Guardian Shareholders," 988.

30. Cable, "Capital Market Information and Industrial Performance," 121.

31. See Norbert Horn, Hein Kötz, and Hans G. Leser, *German Private and Commercial Law: An Introduction,* trans. Tony Weir (Oxford: Clarendon, 1982), 257–71 (describing the legal structure of AGs in Germany).

32. Ibid., 258–59.

33. Ibid., 260.

34. See Julian Franks and Colin Mayer, "Corporate Control: A Synthesis of the International Evidence," p. 11 (unpublished manuscript, on file with the *Stanford Law Review,* November 19, 1992).

35. See Roe, "Some Differences in Corporate Structure in Germany, Japan and the United States," 1942.

36. In 1988, German bank representatives sat on the supervisory boards of 96 of the 100 largest German firms. Roe, "Some Differences in Corporate Structure in Germany, Japan and the United States," 1939. Bank representatives chaired fourteen of those boards.

37. M. C. Oliver, *The Private Company in Germany: A Translation and Commentary,* 2nd ed. (New York: Kluwer Law and Taxation Publishers, 1986), 12;

Friedrich Kubler, "Institutional Owners and Corporate Managers: A German Dilemma," *Brooklyn Law Review* 57 (1991): 98.

38. "Those German Banks and Their Industrial Treasuries," *The Economist*, January 21, 1995, p. 71 (stating that 85 percent of Germany's 171 largest nonfinancial firms have single shareholders who own more than 25 percent of the voting stock; only 6 percent of these large blocks are owned by banks). Ten percent of the total market capitalization is owned directly by banks. Michael Hauck, "The Equity Market in Germany and Its Dependency on the System of Old Age Provisions," in *Institutional Investors and Corporate Governance,* ed. Theodor Baums, Richard Buxbaum, and Klaus Hopt (New York: Walter de Gruyter, 1993), 561n34.

39. Three banks (Deutsche Bank, Dresdner Bank, Commerzbank) controlled an average of 45 percent of the voting stock in 32 of the 100 largest AGs in 1986. A combination of eight banks control over 80 percent of the voting stock. Jonathan Macey and Geoffrey P. Miller, "Corporate Governance and Commercial Banking: A Comparative Examination of Germany, Japan, and the United States," *Stanford Law Review* 48 (1995): 88n80.

40. "An Overview of Corporate Financing," Brealey/Myers Presentation (McGraw-Hill 1996), fisher.osu.edu/~makhija_1/mba811/PowerPoint/CH14.PPT.

41. When German investors deposit their stock certificates, the custodian bank obtains a revocable proxy authorization from the owner, allowing the bank to vote the stock by "depositary voting right" (Depotstimmrecht). The proxy authorization has a duration of fifteen months. Aktengesetz [AktG] 135 (1995) (German Corporate Code). Although depository shareholders do have the right to direct their vote, only about 2–3 percent do so. Michael Purrucker, *Banken in der kartellrechtlichen Fusionskontrolle* (Berlin: Duncker and Humblit, 1983), 96.

42. Franks and Mayer, "Corporate Control," 8. The corporate charter (Satzung) can be modified by a vote of three-quarters of the shares to limit the voting power of large-block shareholders. AktG 179 (1995). See Judgment of December 19, 1977, Bundesgerichtshof [BGH], 70 Entscheidungen des Bundesgerichtshofes in Zivilsachen [BGHZ] 117, 121 (German Supreme Court).

43. Macey and Miller, "Corporate Governance and Commercial Banking," 88n80.

44. Gilson and Kraakman, "Investment Companies as Guardian Shareholders," 987–88 (noting that German banks' voting control derives from their direct holdings, the proxies they exercise, and their control of mutual funds).

45. The German stock market capitalization is about 25 percent of the German GDP, while U.S. stock market capitalization is close to 65 percent of the U.S. GDP. See Matthew Bishop, "Watching the Boss: A Survey of Corporate Governance," *The Economist*, January 29, 1994, 6.

46. Cable, "Capital Market Information and Industrial Performance," 119.

47. William A. Klein and J. Mark Ramseyer, *Cases and Materials on Business Associations: Agency, Partnerships, and Corporations,* 2nd ed. (New York: Foundation Press, 2000), 3.

48. Roe, "Some Differences in Corporate Structure in Germany, Japan and the United States," 1939.

318   NOTES TO CHAPTER 14

49. Franks and Mayer, "Corporate Control," 8; see also Bishop, "Watching the Boss," 13 ("There is little prospect of hostile bids coming to . . . Germany").

50. Timothy W. Guinnane, "Delegated Monitors, Large and Small: The Development of Germany's Banking System, 1800–1914," Center Discussion Paper No. 835, http://www.econ.yale.edu/growth_pdf/cdp835.pdf.

51. Henry G. Manne, "Mergers and the Market for Corporate Control," *Journal of Political Economy* 73 (1965): 112–13 (describing the process of replacing inefficient management).

52. See Michael C. Jensen and Richard S. Ruback, "The Market for Corporate Control: The Scientific Evidence," *Journal of Financial Economics* 11 (1983): 29–30 (stating that hostile takeovers limit managerial inefficiency); Randall Morck, Andrei Shleifer, and Robert W. Vishny, "Alternative Mechanisms for Corporate Control," *American Economic Review* 79 (1989): 851–52 (studying 454 of the 1980 Fortune 500 firms and finding that hostile takeovers constitute the main force behind the removal of unresponsive firm managers in poorly performing industries).

53. This is especially true in postwar Japan. See Morck and Nakamura, "Banks and Corporate Control in Japan," 6, despite the postwar efforts of the occupation forces. Roe, "Some Differences in Corporate Structure in Germany, Japan and the United States," 1972. Germany, which has relied heavily on central banks since Bismarck, naturally looked to central banks as sources of economic stability after World War II. See ibid., 1971.

54. Michael E. Porter, "Capital Disadvantage: America's Failing Capital Investment System," *Harvard Business Review* (September–October 1992): 67 ("The U.S. system first and foremost advances the goals of shareholders interested in near-term appreciation of their shares—even at the expense of the long-term performance of American companies").

55. Clifford W. Smith Jr. and Jerold B. Warner, "On Financial Contracting: An Analysis of Bond Covenants," *Journal of Financial Economy* 7 (1979): 124–26 (describing various contractual mechanisms used by fixed claimants to control shareholders).

56. See Roberta Romano, "A Guide to Takeovers: Theory, Evidence, and Regulation," *Yale Journal on Regulation* 9 (1992): 129–31 (describing takeovers as a backstop mechanism for monitoring performance when other corporate governance devices fail).

57. High share prices make takeovers prohibitively expensive. See Frank H. Easterbrook and Daniel R. Fischel, "The Proper Role of a Target's Management in Responding to a Tender Offer," *Harvard Law Review* 94 (1981): 1174 ("Managers will attempt to reduce agency costs in order to reduce the chance of takeover, and the process of reducing agency costs leads to higher prices for shares"); and Fischel, "The Corporate Governance Movement," 1264 (arguing that the market for corporate control "simultaneously gives managers of all firms who wish to avoid a takeover an incentive to operate efficiently and to keep share prices high").

58. Marcel Kahan and Michael Klausner, "Antitakeover Provisions in Bonds: Bondholder Protection or Management Entrenchment?" *UCLA Law Review* 40 (1993): 979. In the first quarter of 1995, however, mergers and acquisitions in the United States reached $73.2 billion, the highest first-quarter level since 1989. Ste-

ven Lipin, "Mergers and Acquisitions in 1st Quarter Increased 35% from the Year Before," *Wall Street Journal,* April 4, 1995, A3. Recent mergers and acquisitions in the United States do not appear to be directed at ousting inefficient management but at achieving synergistic gains through economies of scale or scope in operations. Some acquisitions may be designed to increase the acquirer's market share rather than to benefit from improving the target's performance. See Greg Steinmetz, "Mergers and Acquisitions Set Records, But Activity Lacked That 80s Pizazz," *Wall Street Journal,* January 3, 1995, R8.

59. Henri Servaes and Ane Tamayo, "The Response of Industry Rivals to Control Threats" (working paper, 2006), http://faculty.london.edu/hservaes/paper%20 servaes%20tamayo.pdf.

60. "ICM Crisis Report: News Coverage of Business Crises during 2002," May 2003, http://209.85.165.104/search?q=cache:-DDggm9ZLGoJ:www.crisisexperts .com/02creport.htm+%22hostile+takeovers+were%22+in+the+United+States+ 2006andhl=enandct=clnkandcd=10andgl=us.

61. Jonathan R. Macey, "State Anti-Takeover Legislation and the National Economy," *Wisconsin Law Review* (1988): 468–70.

62. See act of April 27, 1990, P.L. 129, 1990 Pa. Laws 36 (codified in scattered sections of 15 Pa. Cons. Stat.). Pennsylvania's anti-takeover rules are "more extreme than those of any other state." Klein and Ramseyer, *Cases and Materials on Business Associations,* 819.

63. Macey, "State Anti-Takeover Legislation and the National Economy," 469.

64. The statutes also advance management interests at the expense of employees. See Romano, "A Guide to Takeovers," 171–73.

65. See Dennis J. Block, Nancy E. Barton, and Stephen A. Radin, *The Business Judgment Rule: Fiduciary Duties of Corporate Directors,* 5th ed. (New York: Aspen Law and Business, 2001), 233–37.

66. Bishop, "Watching the Boss," 13.

67. See Macey, "State Anti-Takeover Legislation and the National Economy," 472–73. Naturally, some managers will divert their efforts to the legislative arena and work for legal protection rather than aim for protection through robust performance in the market.

68. Bishop, "Watching the Boss," 16.

69. Ibid.

70. The paradigmatic American example of this threat is Warren Buffett of Berkshire Hathaway. Buffett does not threaten the continued existence of nonperforming companies but rather the management of such companies; that is, he replaces the management of such companies with managers who are more likely to improve the company's performance. See Bishop, "Watching the Boss."

71. Japanese main bank intervention, for example, is consistently unlikely regardless of the firm's performance according to various indicia. See Morck and Nakamura, "Banks and Corporate Control in Japan," 25–26, 55; Morck, Shleifer, and Vishny, "Alternative Mechanisms for Corporate Control," 850 (analyzing low turnover among Fortune 500 companies).

72. Mark Roe has chronicled a number of these rules. See Roe, "A Political Theory of American Corporate Finance," 16–31 (analyzing these rules in the context of financial institutions); Mark J. Roe, "Political and Legal Restraints on

Ownership and Control of Public Companies," *Journal of Financial Economics* 27 (1990): 9–21 (describing how law constrains financial institutions' role in the corporate structure).

73. Roe, "Some Differences in Corporate Structure in Germany, Japan and the United States," 1948.

74. See, e.g., *United States v. Fleet Factors Corp.*, 901 F.2d 1550, 1557 (11th Cir. 1990) (holding that "a secured creditor may incur . . . liability . . . by participating in the financial management of a facility to a degree indicating a capacity to influence the corporation's treatment of hazardous waste"), cert. denied, 498 U.S. 1046 (1991); *K.M.C. Co. v. Irving Trust Co.*, 757 F.2d 752, 759–60 (6th Cir. 1985) (finding an implied good faith contractual obligation requiring a lender to give notice to a borrower before refusing to advance funds under their agreement); *Brown v. Avemco Investment Corp.*, 603 F.2d 1367, 1375–76 (9th Cir. 1979) (stating that a good faith belief of security impairment is needed to enforce an acceleration provision; technical breach is insufficient); *Connor v. Great Western Savings and Loan Ass'n*, 447 P.2d 609, 617–20 (Cal. 1968) (stating that a financier of home builders has a duty to exercise reasonable care in ascertaining that houses are not defective, and other parties' negligence does not insulate the financier from liability); *State Nat'l Bank v. Farah Mfg. Co.*, 678 S.W.2d 661, 686 (Tex. Ct. App. 1984) (stating that a lender's attempts to enforce a management change clause constituted duress).

75. Macey and Miller, "Bank Failures, Risk Monitoring, and the Market for Bank Control," 1153.

76. See Daniel R. Fischel, "The Economics of Lender Liability," *Yale Law Journal* 99 (1989): 140–42 (discussing various interpretations of the duty of good faith and relevance of this duty in deterring opportunistic behavior by both lenders and borrowers).

77. See, e.g., *Farah Mfg. Co.*, 678 S.W.2d at 690.

78. See, e.g., *K.M.C. Co.*, 757 F.2d at 759–63.

79. See *Fleet Factors Corp.*, 901 F.2d at 1557–68 (noting that a creditor may incur liability for a borrower's affairs if its participation in management indicates ability to intervene in the corporation's affairs). But see *In re Bergsoe Metal Corp.*, 910 F.2d 668, 672 (9th Cir. 1990) (stating that "some actual management of the facility" is required to establish the liability of a secured creditor for a borrower's affairs).

80. *In re American Lumber Co.*, 5 B.R. 470 (Bankr. D. Minn. 1980).

81. *Id.* at 478.

82. See text accompanying note 74.

83. Jonathan R. Macey and Geoffrey P. Miller, "Universal Banks Are Not the Answer to America's Corporate Governance 'Problem': A Look at Germany, Japan, and the U.S.," *Journal of Applied Corporate Finance* 9 (1997): 57.

84. See, e.g., Helen Garten, "Institutional Investors and the New Financial Order," *Rutgers Law Review* 44 (1992): 590–91 (describing two models of institutional influence—the "stability" model and the "profitability" model). Challenges to this trend are increasing. See Richard M. Buxbaum, "Comparative Aspects of Institutional Investment and Corporate Governance," in *Institutional Investors and Corporate Governance*, ed. Baums, Buxbaum, and Hopt 3, 13

(challenging the common wisdom that pension-fund-backed investors necessarily behave as typical equitable share owners, and suggesting that they have more in common with fixed claimants).

CHAPTER 15
HEDGE FUNDS AND PRIVATE EQUITY

1. Franci Blassberg, ed., *The Private Equity Primer: The Best of the Debevoise & Plimpton Private Equity Report* (New York: Debevoise and Plimpton, 2006), 3.

2. *Goldstein v. Securities and Exchange Commission,* 451 F.3d 873 (D.C. Cir. 2006).

3. *Id.* at 880.

4. http://www.finanznachrichten.de/nachrichten-2006–06/artikel-6573799.asp.

5. Steve Rosenbush, "Fresh Barbarians at the Gates?" *Business Week,* June 13, 2006, http://businessweek.com/investor/content/jun2006/pi20060613_736996.htm.

6. "Icahn Prods Time Warner to Take Action."

7. "Why Icahn Backed Down," *Time,* February 27, 2006.

8. Larry E. Ribstein, "Accountability and Responsibility in Corporate Governance," *Notre Dame Law Review* 81 (2006): 1476.

9. Ibid.

10. Ibid.

11. Allan Murray, "Hedge Funds Are the New Sheriffs of the Boardroom," *Wall Street Journal,* December 14, 2005, A2.

12. Andrew M. Kulpa, "The Wolf in Shareholder's Clothing: Hedge Fund Use of Corporate Governance Game Theory and Voting Structures to Exploit Corporate Control and Governance," *U.C. Davis Business Law Journal* 6 (2005): 4.

13. Jonathan R. Laing, "Insiders, Look Out!" *Barron's,* February 19, 2007, p. 1; April Klein and Emanuel Zur, "Entrepreneurial Shareholder Activism: Hedge Funds and Other Private Investors," table 5, American Accounting Association, 2007, Financial Accounting and Reporting Section (FARS) Meeting, available at http://papers.ssrn.com/sol3/papers.cfm?abstract_id=913362#PaperDownload.

14. Laing, "Insiders, Look Out!"

15. "Beverly Enterprises Sold to North American Senior Care," *Memphis Business Journal,* August 17, 2005, http://www.bizjournals.com/memphis/stories/2005/08/15/daily19.html.

16. Institutional Shareholder Services, "2006 Postseason Report: Spotlight on Executive Pay and Board Accountability," 25 (2006), http://www.issproxy.com/pdf/2006PostSeasonReportFINAL.pdf.

17. "Sovereign Shareholders to Confront Board," Townhall.com, September 17, 2006, http://www.townhall.com/News/NewsArticle.aspx?ContentGuid=f96e8265-c3af-488f-b211-fefe36ba232d; Council of Institutional Investors, "2006 Spring Meeting Wrap-Up: Whitworth Anticipates Next Steps at Sovereign," http://www.cii.org/meetings/index.html.

18. John J. Moon, "Public vs. Private Equity," *Journal of Applied Corporate Finance* 18, no. 3 (2006): 76, http://www.ingentaconnect.com/content/bsc/jacf/2006/00000018/00000003/art00007;jsessionid=766sct71fqe7m.alice.

19. See ibid., 78.

20. Kahan and Rock, "Hedge Funds in Corporate Governance and Corporate Control."

21. Martin Lipton, "Attacks by Activist Hedge Funds," March 7, 2006, client memo, Wachtell, Lipton, Rosen and Katz, http://interactive.wsj.com/documents/wsj-law_act-Hfunds.pdf.

22. Boston Consulting Group, "What Public Companies Can Learn from Private Equity," http://www.bcg.com/publications/files/What_Public_Companies_Can_Learn_from_Private_Equity06.pdf.

23. Moon, "Public vs. Private Equity," 76, 80.

24. Frank Easterbrook, "Two Agency Costs of Dividends," *American Economic Review* 74 (1984): 650–59.

25. Michael C. Jensen, "Agency Costs of Free Cash Flow, Corporate Finances, and Takeovers," *American Economic Review* 76 (1986): 323.

26. *Shamrock Holdings, Inc. v. Polaroid Corp.*, 559 A.2d 257, 260 (Del. Ch. 1989).

27. Eric Grannis, "A Problem of Mixed Motives: Applying 'Unocal' to Defensive ESOPs," *Columbia Law Review* 92 (1992): 851–86 at 861.

28. Ibid.

29. 15 Del. J. Corp. L. 377, 481.

30. Grannis, "A Problem of Mixed Motives," 868.

31. 15 Del. J. Corp. L. 377, 397.

32. Ibid.

33. See "Morgan Stanley Roundtable on Private Equity and Its Import for Public Companies," *Journal of Applied Corporate Finance* 18 (2006): 8–37, especially the comments of Michael Jensen at page 13.

34. See ibid., 25 (comments of Cary Davis).

35. Victor Fleischer, "The Future of Hedge Fund Regulation," November 11, 2005, Conglomerate Blog of the Business Law Economics Society, http://www.theconglomerate.org/2005/11/hedge_funds_loc.html (accessed February 28, 2008) (arguing that hedge fund investors "rely primarily on something extremely squishy—reputation—to ensure that managers will act in [their] best interests").

36. Ibid.

37. Albert O. Hirschman, *Exit, Voice, and Loyalty: Responses to Decline in Firms, Organizations, and States* (Cambridge, MA: Harvard University Press, 1970).

38. Paul R. La Monica, "Icahn Calls for Time Warner Breakup, Buyback," CNNMoney.com, February 8, 2006, http://money.cnn.com/2006/02/07/news/companies/timewarner_icahn/index.htm.

39. The letter is available at http://money.cnn.com/2005/10/11/news/fortune500/icahn_letter/index.htm.

40. "Time Warner Statement on Agreement with Icahn Partners,"*Business Wire*, February 17, 2006, http://www.findarticles.com/p/articles/mi_m0EIN/is_2006_Feb_17/ai_n16070367.

41. Johnnie L. Roberts, "Crunch Time," *Newsweek*, August 22, 2005, http://www.newsweek.com/id/56499.

42. Levingston, "Icahn, Time Warner End Fight."

43. Kahan and Rock, "Hedge Funds in Corporate Governance and Corporate Control."

44. Lipton, "Attack by Activist Hedge Funds."

45. Sanford Grossman and Oliver Hart, "The Allocational Role of Takeover Bids in Situations of Asymmetric Information," *Journal of Finance* 36 (1981): 253.

46. Sanford Grossman and Oliver Hart, "Disclosure Law and Takeover Bids," *Journal of Finance* 35 (1980): 323.

47. Louis Loss and Joel Seligman, *Fundamentals of Securities Regulation*, 4th ed. (New York: Aspen, 2004), 580.

48. For a similar argument as applied to takeover regulation, see G. Jarrell and M. Bradley, "The Economic Effects of Federal and State Regulation of Cash Tender Offers," *Journal of Law and Economics* 23 (1980): 371.

INDEX

governance, 19–20; "shadow of the
state," written under, 31–32; as source
of corporate governance, 9; sufficiency
of for corporate governance, 20–21
corporate charters: changes in to impede
market for corporate control, 122; as
contract of corporation with shareholders, 18–20; insider trading and whistle-
blowing, silence on, 194–97
corporate governance: contract theory, primacy and sufficiency of, 19–21 (*see also*
contracts); definitions of, 2, 5, 16, 279–
80n.1; Enron and a new approach to,
82; executive compensation and, 9–10;
"generic" and "firm specific" issues, distinguishing between, 200–1; good and
bad, 1, 9; institutions and mechanisms
for enforcing, 8–16, 46–50; international
embrace of U.S. "shareholder-centric"
model of, 5; Madison's insights extended
to, 277; the managerial and regulatory
threat to, 275–77 (*see also* regulation);
measuring the quality of mechanisms of,
47–48; objectivity and proximity in,
trade-off between, 57–59; politicization
of, 44–45; "process culture" in, 31–32;
purpose of, 1–3, 8, 16–17 (*see also* corporate-governance-as-promise approach); reform of, political conditions
and, 16; regulation of effective and promotion of ineffective devices for, 10–11,
15–16, 45–49, 111–12; shareholders'
role in, 4, 7, 12–13, 199–202 (*see also*
shareholder voting); share prices and,
277–78; social capital and, 40–44; social
norms in, 32–44 (*see also* social
norms); sources of, 8–9
corporate-governance-as-promise approach: analysis of corporate governance, as basis for, 274–75; less rather
than more governance, value of, 11–12;
mandatory disclosure, 158; normative
and descriptive potential of, 11; promises, content of, 2–3, 5–6; promises as
premise of, 1–2, 17, 274; shareholders
and the law, tension between, 12–13;
shareholder voting rights and, 11–12;
universal applicability of, 11
corporate law: contract law and, 19–20;
contractual freedom, trend toward more,
23; deviance, role in constraining managerial, 1; non-contractual, contracting

paradigm guiding, 28–29; process,
courts' emphasis on, 30–32; shareholders, minimal protection of, 29–30; on
shareholder voting, 203; social norms
and (*see* social norms); as source of corporate governance, 9; transaction costs
and, 28, 316n.23
corporate raiding, 254–55
corporations: charitable/not-for-profit, 3,
6; as contracts, 18–20 (*see also* contracts); governance of, 2 (*see also* corporate governance); hybrid model of for-
profit and not-for-profit, 6; legislatures
and, differing goals of, 100–1; managers'
views on ownership, dividends, and purpose of, 4, 35; as "nexus of contracts,"
5, 7, 22, 26, 32; ownership structure of
U.S., 3–5; as political entities, 19; promissory theory of, 7, 17 (*see also* corporate-
governance-as-promise approach); shareholder wealth maximization as goal of,
2–3, 5–8, 34–37, 100–1
Council of Independent Directors, 98
courts: deference to corporate decisions,
board composition as factor in, 53; Delaware (*see* Delaware courts); poison pills,
failure to protect shareholders from use
of, 125–26
Cowen & Co., 178
Craig-Cooper, Michael, 280n.1
credit-rating agencies, 113–17
Credit Rating Duopoly Relief Act of 2006,
115–17
Cuomo, Andrew, 108

Daimler-Benz, 230
Delaware, attracting corporate litigation,
142–43
Delaware courts: director independence, attempt to confront, 65–67; personal liability of directors, 52; poison pills, decisions regarding, 123–26, 204; Polaroid's
ESOP, approval of, 253; process, emphasis placed on, 30–31; shareholder rights
bylaw not addressed by, 205; *Smith v.
Van Gorkom*, 30–31, 52, 70, 72–75;
Walt Disney Litigation, In re, 70, 77–79;
the *Zapata* test, 134–35
Deloitte Touche Tohmatsu, 160, 162
democracy, shareholder. *See* shareholder
voting
Democratic Party, 139

Fukuyama, Francis, 40–41
Fuller, Joe, 95

Gabaix, Xavier, 43
Gale, Douglas, 35
Garcia-Molina, Hector, 66
General Electric (GE), 9–10, 223
General Motors Corporation, 113
Germany: banks and corporations in, 229–31; central banks, tradition of, 318n.53; ownership of corporations, managers' view of, 4, 35; premise behind the corporation in, 11; proxy authorization and shareholder voting in, 317n.41; shareholder control in the U.S. vs. universal banking in, 231–37, 240; stock market capitalization in, 317n.45; universal banking system in, 223–24, 317n.39
Gilburne, Miles, 260
Gilovich, Thomas, 58
Glaser, Herbert, 88
Glassman, Cynthia, 64, 110
Glass-Steagall Act, reforms to, 231–33
Goldberg, Arthur, 96
Goldblum, Stanley, 86, 88–89
Goldstein v. Securities and Exchange Commission, 244
Google, 112
Gordon, Jennifer, 313n.48
government: contracts, role of the state regarding, 22; the Securities and Exchange Commission (*see* Securities and Exchange Commission)
Gramm, Wendy, 80, 85
Greenspan, Alan, 214
Greenstone, Michael, 157–58
Gross, Leonard, 88
Grossman, Sanford, 270–71
Grundfest, Joseph, 66
Gutierrez v. Regents of the University of California, 307n.66

Halliburton, 141
Hamilton, Alexander, 100
Hart, H. L. A., 312n.33
Hart, Oliver, 270–71
Hawkins Delafield, 177
Hayden, Stone, Inc., 178
HealthSouth Corporation, 169–70, 303n.15
hedge funds: case study: Icahn vs. Time Warner, 254–64; corporate governance,

role in, 200, 241, 244–51, 254, 265, 272–73; distressed debt, activity in the market for, 248; morphable ownership and empty voting by, 215–18; mutual funds and, contrast between, 243; private equity funds and, similarities and differences between, 242–43; regulation of, 243–44, 268–73, 276–77; short-term time horizons, concerns regarding, 265–68; systemic risk and, 268–69
Henley, Jeffrey, 65–66
Hewlett, Bill, 217
Hewlett-Packard, 112, 215, 217, 312n.43
Hewlett v. Hewlett Packard Company, 217, 312n.43
High River Limited Partnership v. Mylan Laboratories, Inc., 215–18
hindsight bias, 47–48
Hirschman, Albert, 256
Hirt, Hans, 279n.1
Hogan, Chris, 208
Hollinger Corporation, 105–6
Holmström, Bengt, 284n.19
Household International, 124
hypothetical bargaining approach, 20

Icahn, Carl: as corporate raider, 254–55; the Mylan/King deal, actions regarding, 215, 217–18, 312n.44; Time Warner, corporate governance initiative against, 90–91, 223, 239, 245, 255, 258–64
implied covenants of good faith, 21–22
information: available to directors, management control of, 83–84, 96–97; uncovering negative, 165–67, 173–74 (*see also* insider trading; short selling; whistleblowing/whistle-blowers)
initial public offerings (IPOs), 127–28, 294n.2
insider trading: blackmail, distinguished from, 197–98; in corporate charters, lack of provisions regarding, 194–95; as corporate governance device, problems with, 187–88; Dirks' prosecution for, 181 (see also *Dirks v. SEC*); distributional effects of, 192–93; fairness of, 189–91; law of and property rights, 181–84; legalizing, arguments for, 184–87, 307n.72; negative information, as a source of, 165, 173; by Watkins, 176–77, 306n.43; as whistle-blowing, 172–74 (*see also* whistle-blowing and insider